Blavatsky and her teachers

JEAN OVERTON FULLER

Blavatsky
and her teachers

AN INVESTIGATIVE BIOGRAPHY

EAST–WEST PUBLICATIONS
LONDON AND THE HAGUE
in association with
The Theosophical Publishing House Ltd, London

This publication has been made possible by the assistance of
The Blavatsky Trust

Typeset by Clifford Design-Associates, Farnham, Surrey
Printed by Whitstable Litho Printers Ltd, Whitstable, Kent

ISBN 0 85692 171 8

To Timothy d'Arch Smith

Contents

List of Illustrations

Acknowledgements

My first acknowledgement must be to Miss Lilian Storey, Librarian of the Theosophical Society in England, for the willingness with which she has hunted references out for me, and to the General Secretary, Dr Hugh Gray, for a print of the most famous of Madame Blavatsky's photographs. At Adyar, I am indebted to Miss R. Padmini, Officer in Charge of the Archives, for photostats of letters in the Coulombs' handwritings and of the medical certificate, and to Mr C.R.N. Swamy, Editor of Publications, for further photographs. At Wheaton, USA, I have to thank Mrs Caroline Ross for photostats of some pages of *The Path*.

By far my biggest debt, however, is to Mr Leslie Price, who is in the unusual position of being a member of the Library committee of the Society for Psychical Research who had joined the Theosophical Society. He most generously allowed me to see a then unpublished paper which he read to the Society, and turned over to me some fruits of his own delvings, chiefly into the SPR angle. It was he who put me into touch with researchers in America devoted to the defence of Madame Blavatsky's name: Mr Ted Davy, Editor of *The Canadian Theosophist*, Mr Michael Gomes, Mr Nicholas Weeks and Ms Anita Atkins, who sent me Olcott's divorce papers.

At the Society for Psychical Research, I have to thank the Librarian, Mr D.N. Clark-Lowes, for opening up their Blavatsky boxes for me and letting me have photostats of Hodgson's copy of the Coulomb pamphlet with handwritten comments by Madame Blavatsky in the margins, of their copies of parts of letters from Madame Blavatsky to Hurrychund Chintamon and C.C. Massey, and other papers; and also Dr John Beloff, Editor of the SPR *Journal*, for permission to reproduce passages from the same, and also from the cancelled passages in the 1884 Report sent me by Mr Leslie Price.

I am grateful to Dr Timothy Hobbs, Sub-Librarian of Trinity College, Cambridge, for finding for me the passage in Professor Sidgwick's unpublished, manuscript journal, which I reproduce.

Mr John Cooper of Australia has kindly sent me a complimentary copy of his reprint of Beatrice Hastings' critique of Solovioff's book. Mr Tony Finchett-Maddock sent me photostats of his copy of the original Pekin edition of *The Voice of the Silence*; he put me in touch with Mr Michael Freeman, of Canada, a copy of whose reprint of the Pekin edition I was able to buy, and who gave me permission to reproduce from it the photograph of the Panchèn Lama.

In the Manuscripts Department of the British Museum, I have to thank Dr C.J. Wright for his comments on the Mahatma Papers and for examining them through a video spectral comparator for me.

Dr Philip Denwood, Lecturer in Tibetan at the School of Oriental and African Studies of the University of London, has told me about the pronunciation of the Tibetan names and devised for me a phonetic transcription.

Scientists who have been helpful are Dr Hugh Murdoch, Senior Lecturer in Physics at the University of Sydney, Australia, and Dr Victor Clube, of the Royal Observatory, Edinburgh.

Dr Margaret Little has considered with me Dr Oppenheimer's medical certificate for Madame Blavatsky and drawn for me three diagrams showing what she thinks he means. On the physics side, she also called in for me her husband, John, a physicist at the University of Glasgow.

Ms June Leech-Guiness has been diligent in digging things out of the India Office Library for me.

Mr Douglas Matthews, of the London Library, has looked out numerous things for me and put me in touch with Miss Sybilla Jane Flower; he has, as usual, made my index.

My friend, Mr Timothy d'Arch Smith, came with me on one of my visits to the Mahatma Papers to give me of his bibliographical expertise, and he has, as always, read my proofs.

Wymington, 1988

CHAPTER 1

Childhood

Helena Petrovna Blavatsky was born in 1831; by the old Julian calendar (referred to hereafter as Old Style) during the night of 30/31 July, which is, by the Gregorian calendar used in the West, 11/12 August. Though she believed hers was an a.m. birth, the various horoscopes that have been put up for her are strictly speaking speculative, the times stated to the minute and second being those for which the charts have been calculated, not those at which she is known to have been born.[1] In England, William IV was briefly on the throne before the accession of Queen Victoria; in Russia, Nicholas I was reigning, and it was the year of the great cholera epidemic.

Her father was Peter Alexeyevich von Hahn, Captain, later Colonel, in the Royal Horse Artillery (*Corps des Pages Impériaux*). He was the son of General Gustavovich von Hahn, descended from a branch of the Mecklenburg Counts Hahn von Rottenstern-Hahn who had settled in Russia during the brief reign of the pro-Prussian Peter III. Russia has no 'h', only a 'kh', so in Russia the name was written and pronounced 'Gan'. Helena's paternal grandmother was Elizabetha Maximovna Hahn or Gan, formerly Countess von Proben. Helena's younger sister, Vera, will tell us that to see this grandmother's white curly hair was to perceive where Helena got her fair curly mop from. Vera adds (I translate from her Russian): 'She took after her grandmother, in face and in vivacity'.[2]

Helena's mother was Helena Andreyevna, née Fadeyef. A distinguished novelist, she wrote under the pseudonym of Zenaida B-va. She was the daughter of Privy Councillor Andrei Mihkhailovich Fadeyef and Helena Paulovna, née Princess Dolgorouky, painter of butterflies, moths and flowers.

In Russia, everyone has not only a surname but a patronymic, coined out of the Christian name of the father, ending in 'ovich' or 'evich' for boys, 'ovna' or 'evna' for girls; hence Helena Petrovna.

Helena was born prematurely in Ekaterinoslav (modern Dniepropetrovsk) on the Dnieper, in southern Russia, her mother being abed with cholera. She had not been expected to survive, or to have her child born alive, and a priest was called to the house to perform the baptism quickly. In the Greek Orthodox Church, all stand through any service. Behind the priest, with his two assistants, in golden robes, stood not only the two pairs of godparents but the whole household of vassals and serfs. The ceremony was long, and Nadyezhda Andreyevna Fadeyef, a child aunt of Helena, born in 1829 and therefore only two or three years older than her niece, became drowsy and allowed her lighted taper to set fire to the robe of the priest.[3]

Hahn was on the Russo–Polish front, but he returned in the following year to join his wife and their first-born at Romankovo, in the province of Ekaterinoslav. At the turn of 1833–34, they moved with his battery to Oposhya in the province of Kiev, and then back to Romankovo. In 1834 Helena's grandfather Fadeyef was posted to Odessa, where she and her mother joined him and his family. There on 17 April (Old Style), her sister Vera was born (she is our source for material concerning their early days).

In 1835 the children travelled with their parents through the provinces of Tula and Kursk, in the Ukraine. In the spring of 1836 they went to St Petersburg, where Hahn's battery had been posted. Then, grandfather Fadeyef was appointed trustee for the nomadic Kalmuk tribes of Astrakan, and the two little girls and their mother joined him and his family there in May 1837, to stay for about a year. The Kalmuks, Helena would later point out, being Mongolian Buddhists, provided her first contact with Buddhism and the Mongolian lamaic system, with its affinities to the Tibetan system. Her interest in this thus went back to the age of 6 years. In the same year, Miss Antonya Christianovna Kühlwein was engaged as governess to the children. In the spring of 1838 they moved to Odessa, and a Miss Augusta Jeffries, Jeffers or Geffers from Yorkshire was engaged to teach Helena English.

In December 1838, grandfather Fadeyef was appointed Governor of Saratov, on the Volga, and Helena's mother took the children to join him there. The French version of Vera's children's book, *Kak Ya Bila Malen'koi* (*When I was Little*) is illustrated with a vignette showing Helena sitting up beside her mother, holding the younger child on her lap, in a coach drawn by three black horses. Its swaying, she adds, was so rhythmic that they passed most of their snowy journey in sleep. Colonel Hahn visited them when he could, and in June 1840 Leonid Petrovich was born.[4]

In the spring of 1841, their mother took them to rejoin their father in the Ukraine, and it was here that Helena learned to ride astride his Cossack horse, which was much too big for her.

In the spring of 1842, they returned to Odessa, taking the two governesses. Their mother was now sinking from tuberculosis, yet she would sit writing most of the day, relaxing to play the piano and sing to them.[5] A music teacher was engaged who came three times a week to give piano lessons to Helena.[6] A German teacher also came three times a week,[7] but Helena did not progress well in German. She was always out to play, running everywhere, crawling through a hedge from their garden into another, which was forbidden, or climbing their tall pear tree, calling 'Cuckoo!' and raining down pears around Vera.[8]

On 6 June 1842, their mother died. They had not been taught to expect this, which made the shock the greater. Vera felt it was at this moment that they ceased to be children. Helena was 10 years and 10 months old. She would always treasure her mother in her heart. Later in life, when people were slinging mud at her, she forbade Sinnett, in the book he was writing about her, even to mention her mother as she would not have her name desecrated.

The three children were now taken to live with their grandparents at Saratov. Here they shared with Nadyezhda a French governess, Mademoiselle Henriette Peigneur, inherited from the previous Governor's service.

The popular notion that Helena's education was neglected is false. So much concentration upon modern foreign languages, with no classics and no mathematics, may seem to us unbalanced. She had not, however, to pass examinations or qualify to enter any profession since it was not conceived that she would need one. Neither was she taught anything domestic; waited upon by serfs, she would not need to cook or darn. It was, essentially, an education to take her place in the drawing-room. This included, primarily, speaking and writing good French, essential in the Russian aristocracy. She was expected to be able to read poems and stories in French, and to begin to do the same in English. Then came the graceful arts of the piano, water-colour painting (taught by her grandmother, Princess Dolgorouky) and embroidery.

Helena had, however, preceptors she preferred to those who had been engaged, particularly an elderly serf, Baranig Bouyak, who kept bees and was reputed to know their language. To Vera he once said, 'This little lady is quite different from all the rest of you'.

She loved to ride out from the old mansion. On one side of the Volga was forest, with narrow riders' paths; on the other was the Kirkiz Steppe. Apart from the Central Asian Desert, there was nothing between there and Tibet. That space was crossed by Tartar nomads who would come from Tibet. She learned sufficient of their language to talk with them.

Once she fell from her horse, one foot still caught in the stirrup. Her brains would have been dashed out, but she felt somebody raise her head so that it did not touch the ground; her horse, which had started to bolt,[9] stopped as if reined by a tall Indian in white linen, whom hitherto she had seen only in dreams but who now interfered in her waking life to save it. Though he was gone again as quickly and mysteriously as he came, she knew now that she had a protector.

In 1844 or 1845, her father took her from Saratov to the Pimlico district of London and thence to Bath, where she received piano lessons from the great pianist, Moscheles.[10] There are puzzles here. A pianist of the fame of Moscheles would hardly give lessons to an unknown child except upon recommendation, and Colonel Hahn would hardly have taken her upon such a long journey without prior assurance that Moscheles would teach her. Madame Blavatsky would later write to Sinnett it took them two or three months to travel across Russia and Europe to the Channel, and of course the same back again ('Puffing Billy' had been built in 1813, but there were as yet no passenger trains, so it was coach all the way). Olcott adds to the mystery when he writes, after her death, from memory of what he had gathered from her,[11] 'She was the pupil of Moscheles and when in London as a young girl with her father played at a charity concert with

Madame Clara Schumann and Madame Arabella Goddard in a piece of Schumann's for three pianos'.

This reads circumstantially, but is obviously reconstituted from memory in an incorrect manner. Robert and Clara Schumann spent the first five months of 1844 on a tour of Russia. Arabella Goddard was at that time only 10 years old, and it does not appear that Miss Goddard and Madame Schumann were ever in the same country at the same time. I am therefore tempted to reconstruct the story as follows. While the Schumanns were in Russia, Colonel Hahn persuaded Madame Schumann to hear his small daughter play and tell him if she had talent. He was told Helena had so much talent that Madame Schumann would be prepared to recommend her to Moscheles, who had been her own teacher. Moscheles spent much of his 'London period' in Bath. As Helena and Arabella were much of an age, it may have struck the aging virtuoso that the two little girls would look pretty playing a duet.

The late Boris de Zirkoff dismisses Helena's trip to England with her father on the ground that it is not mentioned in her sister Vera's book *Moyo Ortrochestvo* (*My Adolescence*), wherein it is stated that in the summer of Vera's eleventh year they 'had a visit from father', whom they had not seen for three years, and that he stayed a month with them at Saratov. This book, the sequel to *Kak Ya Bila Malen'koi*, is not possessed by the British Library. However, I wrote to Wheaton, and Mrs Caroline Ross sent me prints from the negatives of the pages cited by de Zirkoff which she found amongst his papers. They are very grey and as some of the characters have not come out some words are illegible, yet the passage on which de Zirkoff based his remarks is identifiable and clear enough. I translate from the Russian:[12]

> . . . he had come back from being very far away and was reunited with us.
>
> We had not seen Papa for three years, and hardly recognised him. I was to the last degree astonished. I remember that I felt very sorry for him, because he lived so far away, quite alone, but when he asked me if I would not like to go with him, I took fright. How could I leave all my relatives, dear Grandmother, the aunts Antonia and little Lucy [sic]? No! I could not think of it without trembling and crying. I do not know how I answered him.

Now, this does not make on me the same impression as it did on de Zirkoff. Apart from the fact that the sex of the youngest child has been changed, her elder sister is not mentioned amongst those Vera would not wish to leave. Could this be because Helena had just come back with him on the long journey from England? Vera is very much the heroine of her own memoir, Helena being reduced to a merely supporting role, and my impression is that in this semi-fictionalised reconstruction, it is Vera herself whom her father offered to take on a trip to faraway lands, which she gets out of having to describe by saying that she refused to go. Vera's following pages describe the way in which the family passed the summer. They put on a play and there were visits from a troupe of gymnasts and some Kalmuks; Helena is not mentioned in connection with those events. We come to riding (I translate from the Russian):[13] 'The aunts rode with distinction, Lolya from time to time took her place in the cavalcade but I had not yet mounted a horse'. Lolya was in the early book her name for her elder sister, but its introduction here does not prove to me that Helena was with them that summer. We go on to Vera's first adventure on her aunt's white horse. At the end of the summer a friend who had been staying with them had to go back to her parents. She and Vera exchanged inscriptions in each other's autograph albums (I translate):[14] 'We and Lolya lamented her departure'. Is not Lolya here brought in as an afterthought? My feeling is that Vera used her artistic licence to cut Helena's visit to England out as it would distract attention from the main subject. It would not be the only thing to do with Helena edited out. One misses any reference to Helena's early interest in occult and fairy lore, so prominent in the article written by Vera for the Russian magazine *Rebus*, which Sinnett used (presumably in a translation given to him by Vera or Helena) for his *Incidents in the Life of Madame Blavatsky*. But then, Vera was trying to hide from the children who would read her childhood memoir that 'Lolya' grew up to become Helena Petrovna Blavatsky.

CHAPTER 2

Marriage

Later in 1845, when she was 14 years old, Helena was taken by one of her uncles, probably Rotislav, through the Urals and across central Asia to the mining town of Semipalatinsk, where he had property in the forest, close to the borders of both Siberia and Mongolia.[1] She loved to ride into the country of the Harrachin Lama, where she heard also of the lamas of Tibet. In Semipalatinsk she heard a story of a murder in a cave, by an underground lake, which she would later work into a story, 'The cave of echoes'.[2]

In January 1846, her grandfather Fadeyef was appointed Director of State Lands in Trans-Caucasia. Until their grandparents were settled, Helena, Vera and Leonid were taken to live with their mother's sister, Catherine Andreyevna Witte, wife of Yuliy Feodorevich Witte, with whom they spent a year in a small place on the other side of the Volga. In May 1846, they were taken by boat down the Volga to Astrakan, where they stayed for a couple of days before going on to join their grandparents at Tiflis.

In May 1848, Helena and Nadyezhda were taken by the Wittes to the spas of Pyatigorsk and Kislovodsk and thence to Elizabethpol, before joining the rest of the family at Ekaterinenfeld.

Helena would later write to an acquaintance of the pen[3] that when she was 16 she ran away from her Aunt Catherine. This was because she had refused to kiss the hand of the Metropolitan Archbishop, and her aunt wanted to put her into a convent for a year and then marry her to an old man.

The running away more likely comes in when she was 17, before they all went back to Tiflis for the winter of 1848–9 and she found herself engaged to Nikifor Vassilyevich Blavatsky. She represents him as an elderly man, but he was born in 1809 so he cannot have been more than 39 or 40. Yet she was only 17, and if he was staid and dull it may have made him seem older. Her Aunt Nadyezhda averred that she became engaged to spite her governess (Peigneur?), who had taunted her with making herself so unattractive that she would never get any man to propose;[4] and indeed she herself confirms that, but says that she found herself trapped, unable to extricate herself from the preparations for the wedding that had been set in motion. She observes that her father was 4,000 miles away, having married Countess von Lange. The remarriage of a father can seem like desertion to a favourite daughter, but when she speaks of the ruthlessness with which all the preparations were being pushed ahead, it is only her Aunt Catherine whom she blames.

On the eve of the wedding, she was instructed in the duties of a wife by her Aunt Catherine, and on 7 July 1849 she was married at Dzhelal-Ogli, near Yerivan in Georgia. The honeymoon was to be at Darechegan, a resort for Tiflis. On the way, she dashed off on horseback, hoping to be able to ride across the border into Persia and so to freedom, but a Cossack she had trusted to guide her brought her back to her husband.

The wedding night was calamitous. The reason for this will become apparent only much later in the story. After a wretched honeymoon they moved into Yerivan, where her husband was to take up on 27 November his appointment as Vice-Governor of the newly formed province of Yerivan. As the Governor was away, he would become also acting Governor, and Helena Petrovna Blavatskaya would have been known in their new position as *Son Excellence* Madame de Blavatsky; but in October she took to horse and rode back to her grandparents at Tiflis.

CHAPTER 3

Constantinople to Cairo

Her grandparents wrote to Helena's father, who was in St Petersburg, and he replied saying she should be escorted to Poti, on the Black Sea, whence she should take a steamer to Odessa, where he would meet her. She was nervous in case his intention was to send her back to her husband, and contrived to miss the steamer, taking instead an English sailing vessel, *Commodore*. It was bound first for Kertch, in the Crimea, on the Straits connecting the Black Sea with the Sea of Azov; then for Taganrog, in the Sea of Azov; and finally, after returning through the Straits, for Constantinople.

Helena landed at Kertch, whence she was supposed to proceed overland to Odessa, told the two servants to book lodgings for the night, then, leaving them, slipped back to the ship and went on with it to Taganrog. When they stopped at Kertch again, on their way back through the Straits, she persuaded a cabin-boy to lend her his clothes, in case a search-party should come aboard to look for a girl. There was no interception, and the ship carried her across the Black Sea to Constantinople.

Here she found a Countess K. (probably the Countess Kisselev she mentions elsewhere), whom she had known previously. She gives us no description of her time there, but something may be glimpsed through the lines of a story she later wrote under the pseudonym of Hadji Mora, 'The luminous circle'.[1] It is set in Constantinople, written in the first person, and, though details are doubtless altered, the 'Miss H.' is probably Countess Kisselev. It was in a hotel on the heights of Pera that she and the latter shared a suite of rooms. One of them lost a spaniel, Ralph. The offer of a reward for his return brought a succession of vagrant Maltese with many dogs, but not Ralph, and the head waiter said he had probably been eaten by cannibal curs. A Greek woman suggested they enquire of the dervishes. 'The monotonous cry of the muezzin from the top of a minaret had just proclaimed the noon of the day as we, descending from the heights of Pera to the port of Galata, with difficulty elbowed our way through the unsavoury crowded streets of the commercial quarter . . .'.[2] A Greek urchin, for a coin, led them to a vacated stable where the dervishes were resting. They approached the chief, who received alms and ordered a weird rite, after which he took Madame Blavatsky's hand, apparently causing her to see first the bridge spanning the Golden Horn from Galata to Stamboul; then quarter after quarter of the city; and at last, near the Palace of the Minister of Finance, behind a mosque, poor Ralph, in a pool of mud, his silken coat all bedraggled. There and in that state they found him.

Into this setting entered a person destined to play an intermittent role in her life, the Hungarian or Serbian singer, Agardi Metrovitch (or Mitrovitch):[3]

> . . . whose apparently dead corpse I stumbled over in Pera, at Constantinople, as I was returning one night from Bougadira to Messire's hotel. He had received three good stabs in the back, from one, two or more Maltese ruffians who were paid for it by the Jesuits. The only Turkish policeman meanwhile who chanced to come up asking for a *baksheesh* and offering to roll the supposed corpse into a neighbouring ditch, then showing a decided attraction to my own rings and bolting only when he saw my revolver pointing at him. Remember it was in 1850 and Turkey. Then I had the man carried to a Greek hotel over the way, where he was recognised and taken sufficient care of, to come back to life. On the next day he asked me to write to his wife and Sophie Cruvelli (the Duchess's dear friend now Vicomtesse de Vigier at Nice and Paris, and at the time his mistress. No. 1 scandal). I wrote to his wife and not to the Cruvelli. The former arrived from Smyrna, where she was, and we became friends.

From Constantinople, Madame Blavatsky and the Countess went to Greece, where they saw the usual sights, then to Egypt. Madame Blavatsky does not tell us what she saw on that first visit, but an artist, A.L. Rawson, ran into them in Cairo, where, he tells us, they were both staying at Shepherd's Hotel.[4] (Madame Blavatsky was probably receiving by this time the allowance from her father which kept her in decency on her travels.) He tells us also that they went to visit a Copt, Paulos Metanon, reputedly a magician – both of them went in Muslim dress, which undoubtedly saved them from being pestered when passing through parts of the city where it was unusual to see European women.

Unfortunately, Rawson did not write his article on Madame Blavatsky until after her death, when her name was already a legend, and spoils what would have been the value of this early reminiscence by feeding into it matter from the legend. He makes her take hashish and attribute to it her memory of 'my previous existences, my past incarnations'. Nobody ever saw Madame Blavatsky take hashish, and it is in the highest degree improbable she ever did so. She could not have attributed to it her recollection of previous incarnations, for she did not at that time believe in reincarnation. It would be thirty years before she accepted the doctrine, and then not as the result of spontaneous recall.

We do not know how long she stayed in Cairo, but when she left she was alone. She crossed Europe, using the train this time, passing through Germany, dodging a mesmerist who sought to detain her in Paris, and heading for a Channel port.

CHAPTER 4

Morya: London and Ramsgate

Madame Blavatsky seems to have arrived in London early in 1851. First she took furnished rooms in Cecil Street, off the Strand. Then she moved to join a friend of her family, her godmother, Princess Bagration-Murransky, at Mivarts Hotel, which is today Claridge's. The allowance she was receiving from her father must have been very substantial to allow her to stay at a hotel of such distinction – especially in that year.

London was unusually full in 1851. It was the year of the Great Exhibition. An immense Crystal Palace, of glass, upon iron girders and pillars, with towers, had been erected in Hyde Park; it was opened on 1 May by Queen Victoria. Thereafter people from all over the world flocked to it throughout the summer. Indeed, one of the ideas behind it was that this marriage of art with commerce would contribute to peace by bringing together people from far-flung foreign countries to view one another's produce, manufactures and objects of art in friendly concourse.

Curiously, it was through this that Madame Blavatsky met her Master. There are several accounts of how it happened, not exactly alike. Leadbeater writes:[1]

> Madame Blavatsky used to tell us how she met the Master Morya in Hyde Park, London, in the year 1851, when he came over with a number of other Indian Princes to attend the first great International Exhibition.

When Sinnett was writing his book on her she wrote to him:[2]

> I saw Master in my visions ever since my childhood. In the year of the first Nepaul Embassy I saw and recognised him. Saw him twice. Once he came out of the crowd. He ordered me to meet him in Hyde Park. I *cannot*, I *must not* speak of this.

To her Aunt Nadyezhda, in answer to questions from her, she would write from New York in July 1877 that she had known her Sahib (Master) for;[3] '. . . about 25 years. He had come to London with the Premier of Nepal . . .'.

The Times for 22 March 1850 announced the embassy bearing a letter from the Raja of Nepal to Her Majesty, about to depart from Katmandu, consisting of the following persons: General Jung Bahadur Koonwur Ranajee, Prime Minister; his two brothers, Colonel Juggut Shumshere Koonwur Ranajee and Colonel Dheer Shumshere Koonwur Ranajee; followed by 'Captain Runmihr Singh Adhikaree; Kajee Kurbeer Khutree; Kajee Hemdal Singh Khutree; Lieutenant Kurbeer Khutree; Lieutenant Lall Singh Khutree; Lieutenant Bheem Sen Rana; a Nepalese doctor, two Soobas; one Subadar'. It will be noticed that they are listed in order of rank; military ranks correspond roughly to age. After a stop in Calcutta, where the Governor-General, Lord Dalhousie, and his entire staff gave them an imposing reception and a nineteen-gun salute was fired in Jung's honour, they landed at Southampton on 25 May.[4]

The Times for 3 June gives the composition of the party substantially as before, but with the names differently spelt, and in the case of the man most important after the three royal brothers, an alteration to his rank; for Captain Runmihr Singh Adhikaree is surely Colonel Ranmahur Odhekary. The suite now appears as 'Kajee Kurbeer Khattry; Kajee Himdulsing; Kajee Dhilleesing; Col. Ranmahur Odhekary; Lieut. Carbeer Khattry; Lieut. Laulsing; Lieut. Rhemshen Rana; Soobha Leedmansing; Soobha Leednursing'.

In their progress through the London streets, they must have made a spectacular party, and the *Illustrated London News* of 8 June carried an enormous drawing of Jung, resplendent in his uniform, with sword and the sash of some order, capped with a turban richly set with jewels and a rising plume. Unfortunately, the artist has not extended his impressions to include the suite.

On 20 June, Queen Victoria received Jung and his two brothers in the throne room, and the Raja's letter conveying his compliments was ceremoniously presented to her. Madame

Blavatsky tells her aunt that the Master was not amongst those presented to the Queen.

It is in the suite that the civic identity of the Master Morya lies concealed, and, as we can rule out the two soobhas, that leaves us with a short list of only eight names, headed by Adhikaree.

There is a minor difficulty. The embassy stayed for six months, visiting factories, arsenals and other places of interest,[5] but the Great Exhibition was not until the following year. Madame Blavatsky may, in retrospect, have thought of them as both being in the same year. If Morya – to use what was obviously his mystic name – left with the rest of the party, he must have come back or he may simply have stayed on for the Great Exhibition.

Countess Wachtmeister, a friend of Madame Blavatsky in her later years, writes:[6]

> she saw a tall Hindu in the street with some Indian princes. She immediately recognised him as the same person she had seen in the Astral. Her first impulse was to rush forward to speak to him, but he made her a sign not to move, and she stood as if spellbound while he passed on. The next day she went again into Hyde Park for a stroll, that she might be alone and free to think . . . Looking up, she saw the same form approaching her, and then her Master told her that he had come to London with the Indian princes on an important mission, as he was desirous of meeting her personally . . . I was in England at the time of the visit of the Indians, and remember hearing that they and their suite were a fine set of men and one of them immensely tall.

Countess Wachtmeister, confusing two periods, represents Madame Blavatsky's father as being with her at the time, and says it was after 'three days' serious consideration and consultation with her father' that she decided to accept Morya's offer to train her in Tibet to become the founder of the Theosophical Society. Madame Blavatsky herself warns Sinnett not to confuse her 1845 visit to London, with her father, with her visit, alone, to London in 1851. Colonel Hahn was by his scepticism precluded from understanding anything esoteric. Never would Madame Blavatsky have consulted with him – or anybody – as to whether she should do what Morya told her. Morya's least word was for her an order, taking precedence over everything. It must have been Countess Wachtmeister's Victorian respectability that caused her to weave the distortion.

Countess Wachtmeister says that shortly after Madame Blavatsky had told her of her first meeting with her Master, a trunk was sent by her Aunt Nadyezhda; in it she found an old diary, with the entry:

> Nuit mémorable. Certain nuit par clair de lune qui se couchait à – Ramsgate. 12 Août, 1851 – lorsque je rencontrai le maître de mes rêves.
> 12 Août – c'est 31 juillet style russe, jour de ma naissance. Vingt ans!

I translate from her French:

> Memorable night. A certain night by light of the moon which set at – Ramsgate. 12 August, 1851 – when I met the Master of my dreams.
> 12 August – that is 31 July Russian style, my birthday. Twenty!

It reads as though what is important has been left out – this is a private note, meaningful for herself alone. Yet one detail strikes, and struck Countess Wachtmeister, who adds:

> On seeing this manuscript, I asked why she had written 'Ramsgate' instead of 'London', and H.P.B. told me it was a blind, so that any one casually picking up her book would not know where she had met her Master, and that her first interview with him had been in London as she had previously told me.

This reads oddly, because London is so vast that to say one had met someone in London could hardly compromise anyone or anything, whereas Ramsgate is so small a seaside resort that mention of it immediately prompts a question about what Morya could have been doing there.

The diary glimpsed by the countess has now come to light, and proves to be more of a sketch-book. The entry concerning the *'nuit mémorable'* is underneath Madame Blavatsky's sketch of a little port, with sailing boats, a jetty with lamp and round towers with conical roofs, reminiscent of the oast-houses or hop-drying kilns that are so special a feature of Kent. One of them is probably the little lighthouse that can be seen on the jetty in an engraving of Ramsgate dated 1868. She is looking up at it from beneath, and as there is only water in the foreground one might think from the sketch that she must have been in a small boat. However, she was probably seated on the lower, opposing arm of the harbour that one can see in an engraving of 1854. An engraving of 1851 shows other features in her sketch.[7] She was, then, at Ramsgate on 12 August 1851; it was 'London' that was the blind.

Probably when she rummaged through the old notebook she had forgotten that she had written in it a place-name she had not the right to reveal, and she covered the slip as best she could.

Yet Hyde Park enters, one way and another, into all the accounts, and her hotel was very near the Crystal Palace. I am therefore inclined to reconstruct the story as follows: She was strolling in the park, idly watching the people going in and out of the Great Exhibition, when she recognised in the flesh the tall Indian she had seen from childhood in dreams and visions. She rushed forward. It was not a good place to talk of their profound relationship. Hyde Park would have been overflowing with people who had come for the exhibition; those who could not afford the refreshments served within the Crystal Palace spreading out their hampers on the grass. So he gave her an appointment at Ramsgate.

Why Ramsgate? Kent is the 'orchard of England' – acres upon acres of cherry trees, apple trees, strawberry fields and hop gardens. Artists favour it because the oast-houses always make a focal point to any picture. Yet foreigners fail to explore it. I mentioned the problem to my friend Mr Timothy d'Arch Smith, and he suggested that perhaps in those days there was a shipping-line from Ramsgate to France and that one or other of them was leaving England from there.

I wrote to the archivist at Ramsgate Public Library, and received a reply from Miss Charlotte A. Hodkin of the North-East Kent County Archives Office, saying she thought that at that time most of the continental traffic went through Folkestone. She found a line advertised in 1849, from Boulogne-sur-Mer and run by a Frenchman, but it did not appear to have endured, probably because Folkestone had the monopoly. There was a railway from Folkestone to London, but no railway to Ramsgate until 1853. (Its image as a popular resort would date from the coming of the railway; it was still the Ramsgate of Jane Austen.)

This added a new element to the problem. Ramsgate was difficult to get to. To meet there, they would have had to travel seventy miles from London by horse-drawn cab. A good horse hardly does more than forty miles in a day, at an average of seven miles to the hour; with a cab with two people in it trailing behind it would do rather less. It would have taken them two days.

I had first thought what had to be kept secret was an address. For ordinary conversation, a restaurant or hotel lounge may be sufficiently quiet, but there is a kind of conversation for which public places are not suitable. I thought of this because of my experience in researching mysteries of the Resistance in the last war. When secret agents have to confer what they need is a 'safe house', a place belonging to some trusted person, where they can talk without being overheard. It had occurred to me that if it would have been too unconventional for her to invite Morya into her room at the hotel, and if where he was staying he had no private sitting-room in which he could receive her, he might have given her an appointment at the house of a friend whose identity she did not feel she should mention – but which in a seaside place it would not be difficult to discover.

Was there at Ramsgate anything he could have wanted to take her to? There is one thing in that vicinity which I hardly know whether to mention or not. That is the Grotto. Also called the Shell Temple, it is at Margate, only five miles from Ramsgate. It was discovered accidentally in 1835; a souterrain of about 80 ft in the chalk under Dane Hill, comprising a serpentine, pointed arch, rotunda and rectangular end chamber, above which is a dome pierced by a small aperture to the sky. It was through this that the discoverer fell to find himself in a labyrinth, every inch of which is covered with mosaic in shells. Prominent in the design are many suns, also hearts within hearts, tree-like forms, flowers, what looks like a turtle and what might be an elephant's head. When I went with my mother as a child, the people who took our sixpences to show us round were quite unpretentious about it, saying it could be some relatively modern folly. Yet to quarry out 80 ft of labyrinth would exceed one man's capacity; and even supposing the shells, largely winkles of the local type, to have been gathered from the beach, to have collected and carried up so many thousands or millions of them could hardly have been done without attracting notice and curiosity, whilst to place them so finely would surely have been the work of a lifetime.

The tendency now is to regard it as genuinely archaic.[8] Howard Bridgewater supposes that the aperture in the dome was to admit a gleam of light to fall from the moon at certain times – perhaps when it was full – into the initiation chamber, as he takes the end chamber to be. Two such shell temples have been found at Erich, in Chaldea, near Babylon; and while some have taken the Margate one to be Mithraic, Bridgewater thinks it far older, and suggests Phoenician.

Unfortunately, no old records remain of visitors to the Grotto. Nevertheless, in *Isis Unveiled*,[9] one reads the following, after a paragraph concerning the Eleusinian Mysteries and their passage into other mysteries:

> At this time Grecian, Asiatic and Egyptian ideas had undergone a remarkable transformation. The Mysteries of Dionysus-Sabacius had been replaced by Mithras, whose 'caves' superseded the crypts of the former god, from Babylon to Britain.

Now, where in Britain had Madame Blavatsky been to get the idea of anything like that?

In one of the zaniest monographs ever to issue from an academic press, *Bulwer-Lytton's Novels and Isis Unveiled*, (Harvard, 1957), S.B. Liljgren theorises that the Master Morya whom Madame Blavatsky met in Ramsgate was Bulwer-Lytton transmogrified. I consulted Ms Sybilla Jane Flower, who is researching into Bulwer-Lytton, as to whether he could have been in Ramsgate on the night of 11/12 August 1851. She replied that she did not think so. He dated letters from Knebworth, Hertfordshire, on 7, 10 and 14 August 1851. Given that there were then no trains to Ramsgate, that makes a visit to Ramsgate impossible.

Liljgren's theme, that in Bulwer-Lytton's *Last Days of Pompeii* Madame Blavatsky found the teaching that went into *Isis Unveiled*, is absurd. In the novel, the priest of Isis is a false priest, of false mysteries, and the hero and heroine end by becoming Christian – not a theme to commend itself to Madame Blavatsky, as we shall see when we come to *Isis Unveiled*. Liljgren makes many mistakes. For instance, he says (p.48), 'with *Isis Unveiled* her interest in the Augoeides was exhausted. We do not find it in her later works . . .'. Yes, we do; in *The Secret Doctrine*, the *Instructions* to the Esoteric School and her *Theosophical Glossary* – but with a caution it is too holy for too much to be said about it.

Then, he writes (p.22), 'The appearance of Count Witte's Memoirs caused much fear and annoyance to her. She wrote to Sinnett . . .'. Count Witte's *Memoirs* first appeared in 1921. She died in 1891. What she referred to in the letter to Sinnett which Liljgren quotes was the book Sinnett was writing about her, which he first proposed to call *Memoirs of H.P. Blavatsky*. She did not wish him to use that title as it would cause people to think it was by her, and although she helped by giving him some information because she appreciated that his aim was to sustain her reputation, she apprehended that it would spark off new annoyances.

CHAPTER 5

Round the world

In the autumn of 1851, Madame Blavatsky left for Canada, thinking to meet North American Indians. In Quebec, they stole from her. This made them less romantic than in novels of Fenimore Cooper she had read, and she left for the USA.

Whilst in the United States, at uncertain date, she received a legacy from her godmother, Princess Bagration. Sinnett says it was 80,000 roubles, but this, at the then rate of exchange multiplied by the difference in purchasing power up to 1984, would give such an enormous figure that I think Sinnett must have put a zero too many by mistake. The equivalent of £50,000 would be a more realistic figure, still high enough to account for his thinking of it as 'considerable'. In any case, she used a large part of it to buy property for which she lost the papers, and she still had the wherewithal to travel.

She had thought to investigate voodoo in New Orleans, but being warned off it by Morya, she made her way down through Texas into Mexico, where she looked at Mayan remains; Copau, Honduras, where unexpectedly she met a Hindu pupil of Morya; and thence into Peru. Here a descendant of the ancient Incas told her an Inca queen had offered a fabulous ransom to Pizzaro for the life of her husband. Then she learned he was tricking her, for her husband had been murdered already, so she sealed up her treasure – gold, filling a spacious hall hollowed out within the body of a mountain. The entrance depended only on the turning of a slab – but that slab would never be turned so long as there remained a trace of Spanish influence in their continent. At Arica, on the border of Peru with Chile, she saw through opera glasses what she believed to be ancient inscriptions comprising the needed key to the location of that slab, perhaps in Bolivia, on an Andean peak; but if she was understanding it correctly, it would be extraordinarily difficult of access and, bearing in mind the negative prophecy, she did not think it worthwhile to go further.[1]

We come to a period over which there has been confusion. Sinnett has her leaving from the West Indies for Ceylon in 1852, but then he goes on to have her make a journey to the north of India that occurred three years later, and my feeling is there were not two separate journeys to India within two years. It would seem more likely that she remained longer in America, and that the journey which he records across the United States, through Chicago to San Francisco, partly by covered wagon, in fact fills this gap. Chicago was one of the earliest railway centres, but the line westward from Chicago did not link up until later in Utah with the Union Pacific, so there would have been a gap which she would have to cross by some other means. De Zirkoff asserts that in Salt Lake City she stayed overnight with a Mrs Emmeline Blanche Wells (née Woodward), editor and publisher of *The Woman's Exponent*, who told her granddaughter, Mrs Daisy Woods Allen, that Madame Blavatsky was wearing heavy shoes as she expected to cross rough country.[2]

I would not be too certain, upon the basis of Madame Blavatsky's *Caves and Jungles in Hindostan*,[3] that she was necessarily in London at the time when Morya came again, and that she met him 'in the house of a stranger in England, where he had come in the company of a dethroned native prince'. *From the Caves and Jungles of Hindostan*, like her short stories, draws upon real facts but combines them in a semi-fictionalised manner. She was always frank about that. But it could have been in 1851 that one of her meetings with Morya was in the house of a stranger.

Nevertheless, the dethroned Prince Duleep Singh, sailed with his suite in April 1854, aboard SS *Colombo*, and landed at Southampton, on 18 June.[3] Morya may have come with him. (The Prince was presented to Queen Victoria on 1 July.)

If she did come over to meet him in London, the build-up to the outbreak of the Crimean War, which began in September, would have engendered a climate embarrassing to a Russian, accounting for her return to America.

When Sinnett says she sailed from the West Indies, in company with an Englishman and a Hindu, for Colombo, I think it was after this. She herself wrote, from her memory,[4] 'Went to India in 1856 – just because I was longing for Master'. That is the first reference to going to India that she makes. Once arrived, she said goodbye to her two companions and went north alone, heading for Darjeeling.

CHAPTER 6

First attempts to enter Tibet

Corroboration of Madame Blavatsky's assertion that her first attempt to enter Tibet was foiled by the British Resident in Nepal[1] comes from an unexpected quarter. Two years after her death, Colonel Olcott and S.V. Edge were, on 3 March 1893, in a train between Nalhati and Calcutta when they fell into conversation with Major-General Charles Murray, of the 70th Bengal Infantry, retired, Chairman of the Moghyr Municipality. He told them that while a junior officer, in command at Darjeeling, he had been informed that there was a white woman at Punkabaree, at the foot of the Darjeeling Hills, trying to cross the Runjit or Ranjit River because she wanted to pass through Nepal into Tibet 'to write a book'.[2] The British Resident had told Murray not to let any Europeans cross the border, as they might be murdered by savage tribes. Tibet was infested with tribes of brigands who even set upon the Tibetans, and two French missionaries had been murdered in the previous year.[3] Murray therefore had Madame Blavatsky brought to him. She was very angry at having been intercepted, but he detained her as a guest in his house for about a month, mainly in the company of his wife, Eliza, daughter of Charles Coventry of the 70th Bengal Native Infantry.

Realising the importance of his witness, Olcott wrote out what he had understood from him and invited him to sign it, which he did, as follows:[4]

The above memo is correct.

> (Signed) C. Murray
> Major-General

In the presence of H.S.O. Olcott and S.V. Edge

This memo (now at Adyar) was made and signed in the railway carriage, and Major-General Murray was therefore without access to papers from which to verify the date, but according to his memory the incident was in 1854 or 1855.

I have had a research made at the India Office, whence it emerges that on 11 July 1854, Lieutenant Charles Murray was appointed Commandant of the Sebundy Sappers and Miners in Darjeeling. On 30 October 1855, the Superintendent, Dr Campbell, wrote a letter asking if he might take a period of leave in the endeavour to recover his health, passing over to Lieutenant Murray the remainder of the duties with which the latter was already helping him. Murray was, therefore, acting as Superintendent after this date; on 17 March he handed over to Captain H.C. James, who had been appointed as the official replacement to Campbell.

We have, then, terminal dates earlier and later than which his interception of Madame Blavatsky cannot be. She herself put the episode into 1856 (Sinnett, notwithstanding, puts it back into 1852 or 1853 but is plainly wrong). McGovern, who entered Tibet that way some seventy years later, observes that in winter all paths through the passes are blocked with snow, and in summer they are washed out by rain, the only sensible seasons to essay them being spring or autumn.[5] It is hardly likely that Madame Blavatsky would have thought to make the attempt in mid-winter (when the snow can be breast-high and a slip into a gulley means total immersion), but she might have arrived in February, thinking to try as soon as the snow disappeared, and that is the most likely month for her stay with the Murrays.

During that month, Murray strenuously represented to her the folly of proceeding. In the end, she reconciled herself to the fact that he would not permit her to do so, and turned back. The last he heard of her she was at Dinajpore. That is almost straight south from Darjeeling, yet a little west, on the route one would take if making for Benares. She passed through Bareilly. (Olcott tells us she was recognised by an Indian in whose house she had spent some days, when many years later they passed through it together on his first visit to northern India.)[6] Bareilly is on the route from Benares to Lahore.

At Lahore she encountered Kühlwein, probably a relative of her governess of that name, for he told her that, as he and two friends were planning an expedition to Tibet, her father had asked him to look out for her as he supposed her to be trying to do the same thing. They joined forces and set out, happy to have amongst their guides a Tartar shaman, who wanted to regain his home in Siberia, whence he had come via Kiachta and the Gobi Desert. He should know the way.

Madame Blavatsky's enemies have asserted she could not have made this expedition. Thus, an American journalist, Marion Meade, writes:[7]

Any explorer setting out for Tibet would need to equip herself with baggage ponies, tents, stoves, an escort of native bearers, an interpreter, and – most crucial – food, water and fuel for the entire trip.

Is it possible she found this idea in an earlier book by a Gertrude Marvin Williams?[8]

As no reprovisioning would be possible a traveller would require elaborate and expensive equipment: pack team, coolies, interpreter, tents, bedding, stoves, enough consumable supplies for a return trip – food, water and fuel.

I wonder why these two American women writers think that to travel in Tibet one would need to pack as if to cross the North Pole. There are markets in Tibet.

Did Miss Meade follow Miss Williams, or can they both have drawn upon the Spiritualist, Arthur Lillie, one of Madame Blavatsky's oldest enemies? Recounting a paper read to the Royal Geographical Society on 20 February 1893 by Captain Bower, Lillie says:[9]

He started on the 17th April and took six weeks to get to Leh, a distance of some 130 miles from Shri Nager, as the crow flies . . . Captain Bower had baggage ponies, but so steep is the Zoji La Pass that an army of coolies had to carry his baggage as far as Leh, and the ponies had to be led without burdens . . . Thus when we read that Madame Blavatsky was smuggled into Tibet . . . we must ask if this means that she succeeded in traversing the formidable *ghats* without baggage ponies, without tents, without an army of baggage ponies and a store of food.

The crucial phrase, which should be italicised, is 'as the crow flies'. If one lays a ruler across the map from Srinagar to Leh, it goes through appalling mountains. There are things which should be understood. During the latter part of the nineteenth century, Britain and Russia were competing for dominance in Asia; and Tibet, being between the two spheres of influence, was watched by both, to see if the other was moving into it. British concern was lest, if a Russian army occupied Tibet, it should filter down through the passes to invade India. Hence, in 1891 Captain Hamilton Bower was sent,[10] as earlier (in 1887) Younghusband had been sent, to investigate that seemingly impassible block of mountains and find every cranny in it through which the British might be surprised by foes. Madame Blavatsky had no interest in looking for passes in a seemingly passless land. All she wanted was to get into Tibet by the easiest route. I think she and her friends would have started, at least, by the route taken by my mother and her father, Colonel Frederick Smith, in 1911. They went comfortably by houseboat, towed from the bank, up the Jhelum and Indus rivers, riding their horses only from Pindi to the Jhelum, between the Jhelum and Indus, and from the Indus to Gilgit and Lake Gangabal, at the foot of the Mount Haramouk glacier, their goal. She always supposed that if one went on the same way for long enough, one must eventually arrive in Tibet, and I feel sure that is what Madame Blavatsky and her friends thought, themselves. That would explain why they passed through Islamabad, which puzzles de Zirkoff;[11] he, like Lillie, apparently would have expected them to have gone 'as the crow flies' across the mountains instead of making the obvious detour. As they do not mention a boat, probably they rode, and, unless there is some point at which the banks of the Indus become so steep and gorge-like as to force them from the river's course, they should have ended up in Tibet near Gartok. Indeed, this was exactly the route taken in 1944 by Mr Heinrich Harrer[12].

At Leh, Kühlwein went down with a fever, and the others had to leave him, presumably dividing the equipage. When the other two men gave up, sixteen miles beyond the frontier, she probably thought the worst was over and that there would be little risk in going on alone with the Tartar shaman. He could do their shopping in the villages through which they passed, so that her slight disguise would not be penetrated through too close encounters, and he knew the way.

But now there comes a complication. The Tartar shaman wanted to reach Siberia, and if he thought to retrace the route by which he had come, Tibet was not on his way. Leaving Leh for Kiachta, he should have gone north, through the Kuen Luns, and skirted the Tarim basin (Sinkiang); that is, taking in reverse Younghusband's 1887 route. Did he, after the others left him just inside Tibet, strike north and try to recover what should have been his own route? Is that how they came to be lost?

Fortunately, they came upon a Tartar encampment under an enormous tent, and the Tartar shaman obtained from the occupants permission for them both to come in to share their living space and their food. The tribe were unable to give them their bearings, so they stayed on, not knowing what to do.

She asked her companion why, like all shamans, he carried a stone beneath his left armpit. At first he would not tell her, but one evening when all the others had left the tent, in which they had lived now for about two months, he propped up outside the flap, upon a wooden peg, a goat's head, with prominent horns. This, he explained, was a sign that he was about his magical work as a shaman, and that no one must re-enter until it was removed. Then he re-entered and pulled down the flap. Suddenly, she felt the silence:[13]

> The sun was setting, and were it not that the dying embers flickered in the centre of the tent, complete darkness would have been added to the oppressive silence which reigned. We have lived in the Prairies of the West, and in the boundless steppes of Southern Russia, but nothing can be compared with the silence at sunset on the sandy deserts of Mongolia . . .

If they were really in Mongolia, the shaman must have dragged her with him not only into the Tarim basin but to the fringes of the Gobi, of which Younghusband would write, thirty-one years later, 'So marked, indeed, was this silence of the desert that when we arrived at . . . the end of our journey, the ordinary hum of insects and singing of birds seemed almost deafening'.[14]

In silence, the shaman took the stone from beneath his armpit, unravelled it carefully, revealing it to be the size of a walnut, and put it in his mouth. His limbs stiffened and he fell stiff as a corpse. A voice that seemed to come up out of the earth pronounced peace and asked them what they wanted. She asked that a Kutchi of Lhasa, with whom she had earlier made friends and who often travelled to British India, be apprised of their situation.[15] (The Abbé Huc mentions the Kutchi or Katchi of Lhasa as a group of Kashmiri Muslim merchants settled there for centuries, who travel regularly to India for the purpose of trade.[16] They have their own mosque at Lhasa.)

A few hours after this, a party of horsemen rode up to them. The leader was a chaberon who was a friend of the Kutchi.[17] Under this escort, she was taken to the frontier and put back into India.

For the next few months she wandered about India, until instructed by Morya to go to Java for him. She left on a Dutch vessel, just before the Indian Mutiny broke,[18] in May 1857.

From Java she went to south-east Asia; succumbed to 'a fearful fever' near Rangoon 'after a flood of the Irawadi river'; was cured by a mendicant with a herb, 'kukushan';[19] and, after crossing the Pacific, America and Atlantic, landed in France, to make her way through Germany and so home.

CHAPTER 7

Return to Russia

The entire family was assembled at Pskoff on Christmas night (Old Style) 1858 (that is 6 January 1859), for a wedding.[1] Vera was now the widow of Nikolai Nikolayevich Yarmontoff, and a sister of her late husband was being married. Colonel Hahn, for the second time a widower, was there with Leonid and Lisa, his child by his second marriage. The health of the bride and bridegroom was being proposed when there was a ring at the door. Vera forestalled the footman and opened the door herself. On the step was Helena.

How had she known they were at Pskoff? The house, near the Esthonian border, belonged to Vera's father-in-law, General Nikolai A. Yarmontoff. Helena was brought in with joy, for it was more than nine years since she had left Russia.

Colonel Hahn and his reunited children stayed on for some time at the Yarmontoffs'. The family now noticed raps, occurring on furniture, walls, floors, windows and clocks; and also furniture moving around.[2] At first, Helena tried to conceal or deny that these phenomena were connected with her, then she admitted that they occurred without her wishing for it. She could, by an exercise of her will, direct them to occur in one place rather than another, or even, though this was more difficult, diminish or stop them. Asked what caused them, she said, 'Kikimore'[3] (goblins). Had she unintentionally picked these up from the Tartar shaman? They were not malignant, yet a nuisance. In the drawing-room, she would sit at her embroidery, affecting indifference to the hubbub.

The greatest sceptics were her father and Leonid. The latter, now a university student believing in nothing, stood one evening behind her chair in the drawing-room. Some were at the piano, others playing cards. She was saying some people could make light things heavy and the reverse. He challenged her to do it.

In front of her was a chess table about three feet high, the board supported on a single leg. She bade him lift it. He did. She looked at it with intense concentration, then bade him lift it again. He could not, nor could another young man who got down and put his shoulder underneath it. She warned Leonid she would release it, and because of the way he was straining it came up with such violence that his arm was nearly dislocated.[4]

Vera had to see a lawyer in St Petersburg, and Colonel Hahn went with her with the rest of his children. They all stayed in the Hôtel de Paris. There they ran into an old companion of his from the Corps des Pages, who suggested he should write down a word and see whether Helena Petrovna's raps could spell it out (one for A, two for B and so on). Colonel Hahn left the room, and Vera kept the score of the raps. They spelled 'ZAITCHIK'. When Colonel Hahn came in again and was told this the colour left his face. He showed them a piece of paper on which he had written, while out of the room, 'What was the name of my favourite war-horse during my first Turkish campaign?', and beneath it, in brackets, 'ZAITCHIK'.[5] The word means 'little hare', white sea-foam or what is called 'white horses' in the sea.

Then they all set out for a property lately purchased by Vera's husband, which had now come to her, at Rougodevo in the province of Novgorod; near Lake Ilmen, it stood in grounds surrounded by forest. Vera (with her two baby sons) and Helena settled themselves into the nine or ten rooms along the first-floor front. The servants were at the back and Colonel Hahn in the ground-floor front rooms to the right of the central front door. This left the ground floor rooms to the left for guests.

On the second or third day after their arrival Helena and Vera were walking in the front garden when the windows of the empty rooms caught the golden light of the setting sun. Helena looked at them fixedly and exclaimed that the people in them were not of this world. Vera, who could see no people, was alarmed. Helena said they looked alive, but were not. Their dress was like that in old portraits. Strangest of them was a tall, gaunt, elderly man in black headgear, with a look of suffering in his face, who wore his nails over an inch long so that they looked like claws. Vera was so frightened that she ran back into the house.

The village of Rougodevo was on Vera's land; the villagers being serfs who had become hers with the property. In the morning, she sent for the eldest of them to come to the house and asked him if the description her sister had given her meant anything to him. Yes, he said. That was the late master, Nikolai Nikolaivich Shousherin, whose granddaughter was the wife of the person from whom Vera's late husband had bought the property. Whilst in Lithuania, he caught a terrible skin disease, koltoun. Anybody with it must never cut his hair or his finger- or toe-nails, or he would bleed to death. The ground-floor left rooms had been used for laying out deceased members of the family before they were taken to the chapel.[6]

At Rougodevo Helena discovered that she could cause the piano to play, without opening it.[7] If the lid had been raised, would the keys have been seen going up and down, on their own?

At Rougodevo, a wound beneath her heart, sustained on her travels, reopened. A doctor was called, but as he was about to anoint it, he saw a brown hand pass between his own and the wound and retreated, appalled. Vera could not persuade him to come back.[8]

In the spring of 1860, Helena and Vera set out to visit their grandparents. It took them three weeks on the road. At Zadonsk, they learned that at the church, which is a place of pilgrimage, the service was being taken by Archbishop Isidore. They knew him, for before becoming Metropolitan (as the Russian Church calls its archbishops) of Kiev, he had been Exarch (senior Bishop) of Georgia and often a visitor to their grandparents' home at Tiflis. So, they went to hear him. He recognised them, and afterwards sent word they were invited to call on him.

They did, but as they entered the room where he was seated at a heavy table, the furniture began moving about, cracking and thumping, while each single pendant in the crystal chandelier seemed to have become endowed with independent life and motion. He did not appear unduly perturbed, even when he saw an armchair gliding towards him and felt the table move beneath his elbows, but asked which of the sisters had this power. He was told the phenomena were connected with Helena, and questioned them both for about three hours. Finally, he asked Helena if her 'invisible' would answer a question he would put mentally. Presumably, it was Morya, not the goblins, who replied, for he was satisfied by the answer. (Unfortunately, Vera does not tell us what this was.) He said she was not blameworthy, and if she acted with discretion and judgement, might be able to use her power for good.[9]

They arrived in Tiflis only just in time to see their grandmother Fadeyef again, for she died on 24 August.

Since Helena left, their grandfather, liberal for his day, had freed his serfs. They remained on the estate and continued in the family's service, but were now paid wages.

Helena experienced a moment of softening towards the Russian Church, and made a general confession. Some years later, she would reflect upon this as the source of a danger, in that the general remission of sins could take away one's sense of duty to make reparation for each individual thing one might have done amiss;[10] further, at the moment of giving the absolution, ideas from the priest's head became planted in that of the recipient.

However, it was in this year that she made a new friend, to whom she would later refer as 'A Greek gentleman whom I have known since 1860'.[11] The reference is to Illarion or Hilarion Smerdis, now usually known as the Master Hilarion. Greek has no character for H, but uses a small, inconspicuous mark to show when a vowel has an aspirate before it. The I would be a capital, and Madame Blavatsky, writing with her hand, probably does not bother with the little mark. Where did they meet? From an article he would later write, we see that he was at one time in Armenia.[12] Tiflis is only thirty miles from the Armenian border.

Metrovitch and his wife arrived, having been engaged to sing at the Tiflis Opera House. Helena brought out her old sketch-book, which must have been unused for years since the drawing of Ramsgate is separated by only a few undatable poetic fragments from portraits of her family, done in Tiflis, and a scene in which a woman with dark, sleek hair parted in the middle prays before a crucifix. Beneath, Madame Blavatsky has written:[13]

Teresina
Signora Metrovich (Faust) Tiflis, 7 Avril, 1862.

Behind Teresina, as Marguerite, more lightly sketched, is a Mephistopheles with upturned moustachios, pointed beard, arched eyebrows and a few wisps of fluffy hair on a balding pate. This must be Metrovitch. (Gounod's *Faust* had had its première in Paris in 1859, so it could now be performed abroad.)

The year 1862 saw, also, something mystifying. Madame Blavatsky was reconciled with her husband, lived in one house with him, though not as his wife, and joined with him in the adoption of a child. This we know from a passport issued to her at Tiflis on 23 August 1862, pursuant to an application by her husband that she be allowed to proceed to Pskoff and other places, for one year, taking their 'infant ward Yury'.[14]

Why did she wish to return to Pskoff? One can imagine that Vera wanted for company in her isolated property at Rougodevo, and had rejoined her father-in-law at Pskoff – where she still needed Helena. In Pskoff in 1862, Helena went down with a bladder infection, which necessitated a first gynaecological examination by two physicians, Bodkin and Pirgoff.[15] This is mentioned only in passing here, but will be taken up later when it assumes significance within a pattern.

The immediately pressing question is why Nikifor and Helena should have gone through the external motions of a reconciliation by sharing an address for a few weeks, in order jointly to adopt a baby. The motive must have been to provide a semblance of parentage for a child born out of wedlock to a member of the family. We shall gather from Madame Blavatsky's letters to Sinnett that the father, regarded by her with contempt, was a Baron Nikolai Meyendorff, of Esthonia. Olcott will later write that for years he had in his possession letters proving Madame Blavatsky accepted the child to cover another woman's indiscretion,[16] and Madame Blavatsky, writing to Sinnett, tells him Olcott has letters written by Meyendorff to his 'darling Nathalie', extolling her raven black hair, '*Long comme un beau manteau de roi*'[17] (Long as a king's beautiful mantle). Madame Blavatsky was fair, with blue eyes and her hair was a crinkled mop of very light brown. Further, her sister Vera, in the material she supplied to Sinnett, mentions that there was a Nathalia Blavatsky, with whom Helena was sometimes confused.[18] She says this in passing, yet Blavatsky, Russianised from Ukranian 'Blavatko', was probably a unique name. Have we not here the clue to the mystery? Nathalie Blavatsky must have been a close blood relative, perhaps an unmarried sister, of Nikifor Blavatsky. Would he, otherwise, have adopted the child and persuaded his estranged wife to assume the appearance of motherhood? How did the letters from Meyendorff come into Olcott's hands, save that Nathalie gave them to Nikifor, who gave them to Helena, who gave them to Olcott for safe-keeping? Madame Blavatsky mentions also that the child's mother was known both to her sister and aunt.

Madame Blavatsky spent the following year, 1863, with her grandfather at Tiflis. Some time in 1864, she made a tour of the neighbourhood of the River Riom (classical Pharsis), the ancient Colchis, where Jason found the Golden Fleece. In the woods, she bought herself a house and set up a factory for the making of spunk. That is, wood converted by the action of a certain type of fungus, particularly *Polyporus squamosus*, to a soft, white substance, highly inflammable and able to remain burning for a long time. It is used as touchwood to start a fire. *Polyporus squamosus* grows on oak, beech, birch and lime. Probably she noticed its profuse growth upon the trees in that district and that gave her the idea of harvesting it and putting it with some of the felled timber to make the spunk. She floated the product down the river to be shipped and exported.

Then she was thrown from her horse, fractured her spine and fell into a coma for months. She was not delirious; if addressed by name she would answer rationally but then relapse into what had become a dream of being somebody else, somewhere else. Her weight went down so far that it was feared she would die, and she was transported, mainly by boat, up the Riom, back to Tiflis and her grandfather's home.

When she emerged from the coma, spontaneously, a signal benefit was noticed. She was no longer subjected to embarrassment by unwanted raps and movements of furniture.

CHAPTER 8

Transylvania and Serbia

Later in 1865 Madame Blavatsky visited Venice, but how long she stayed in Italy we do not know. In 1866 she was again resident with her relatives in Tiflis.[1] Either at the end of that year or at the beginning of 1867, she made a tour of Transylvania and Serbia. This we know from a diary which she kept of the tour, but it does not tell us what she was doing there. Olcott would later say that she toured France and Italy giving piano recitals, as Madame Clara. There seems to be no trace of her having toured France and Italy in this way; one must be prepared for inaccuracies in hearsay reporting, and I believe this Transylvanian–Serbian tour to have been that of her piano recitals. Her cousin, Count Witte, asserts that she became manager of the Royal Choir of King Milan of Serbia. That is impossible, because Milan's reign had not begun at the time of Madame Blavatsky's visit to Serbia; nevertheless, Witte's slip testifies to his impression that her period of professional musical activity related to this part of the world.

Did Metrovitch accompany her? Some have imagined it, yet I think not. His wife died just after Madame Blavatsky left, and was buried at Tiflis, so that he would have been morally free. As a member of the Tiflis Opera House repertory company, however, he would not have lost his position because he was widowed. Opera is something very special, and it is impossible for me to believe that he would have given up his steady job in order to sing here and there. Nowhere in Madame Blavatsky's diary of the tour does she mention him, nor does she allude to any companion.

Hers is the sketchiest of diaries, giving brief impressions of towns and hotels, often with the name of the proprietor, and names of some persons encountered and some comments on the theatre or hall. There is occasional mention of a bass, baritone or soprano, or, at Kolozsvar, the one-word comment '*Orchestre*'. (The diary is in French.) This last could mean that the hotel which had engaged her for the evening had provided an orchestra to accompany her solo performance. In Arad, there was a '*Petit théatre infect*' (small, nasty theatre or concert hall). Nothing is said about any performance she attended in it as a member of the audience. Does the jotting perhaps mean that she found she had to give her piano recital in a small nasty theatre?

Arriving from Bucharest, she made her stops at Brassó, Szeben, Gyulafehérvár, Kolozsvár, Nagyvárad, Debreczen, Arad (where they were 'fêting the Constitution'), Temesvár and Belgrade where:

> The Turks were just vacating the fort, Rezi Pacha leaving, by order of the Sultan, and the Serbs fêting their liberty. Michael Obrenovitz left for Constantinople to thank the Sultan. 101 canon-shots. Serbian song to the Prince.

This needs explaining. It was a time when small nations were, everywhere, trying to throw off the yoke of foreign domination. It was seven years since Garibaldi had landed in Sicily with his 'Thousand' in their red shirts, and an initially victorious campaign against the Austrians had ejected them from about half of Italy but slowed up just south of Rome. Hungary and Transylvania (including the part now in Romania) had long striven to throw off Austrian domination, as witness the uprising of 1703–11 under the national hero Prince Francis Rákóczy. On 1 July 1866, at Königgratz, Austria had lost a battle to the Prussia of King William IV and Bismarck, and now her empire was virtually divided in two, Transylvania and the south Slav states forming the unquiet southern or Hungarian half of the dual monarchy of Austria–Hungary. On 17 February 1867, the office of Governor–General was abolished and a responsible Hungarian ministry came into being. That is why Madame Blavatsky found the people in Arad fêting the constitution; it must have been on 17 February that she was there.

In Serbia, it was Turkish domination that the people had long been trying to throw off. They had suffered it ever since the defeat of the Serbian national hero, King Marco 'Kralievitch' on the field of Kossovo in 1389. On 13 April 1867, the Turks at last left, the keys being handed over to Prince Michael Obrenovich, who went to Constantinople to thank the Sultan. This pin-points the moment at which Madame Blavatsky arrived, and, though she gives no dates, shows that two months must have elapsed between her Arad and Belgrade entries. She had, on an earlier occasion, met Prince Michael, and now came to know his aunt, Princess Catherine.

Then she resumed her tour, passing into Austria; and then back into Hungary and Transylvania, stopping at Pancsova, Semlin, Neusatz, Betchkerek, Eczek, Verchetz, Horowitz, Temesvár, Kikinda, Herzfeld, Mehadia, Körös-Makos and Lugos.

The diary ends with the note of some train fares: Vienna to Graz, Vienna to Trieste, Trieste to Venice and Graz to Leibach.

CHAPTER 9

Metrovitch

Agardi Metrovitch was an illegitimate son of the Duke of Lucca, and was, therefore, Italian on his father's side, but he had taken his name from the town of Mitrovitch or Metrovitch, in Serbia, where he was born. He had, however, become mixed up with the politics of his father's country. When Madame Blavatsky says, 'He was a Carbonaro, a revolutionist of the worst kind', she probably means 'worst' only in the sense of imprudent, liable to get himself into trouble and so to be a nuisance to his friends, for elsewhere she writes:[1]

> Agardi Metrovitch was my most faithful, devoted friend, ever since 1850. With the help of C. Kisseleff I had saved him from the gallows in Austria. He was a Mazzinist, had insulted the Pope, was exiled from Rome in 1864.

Was it by any chance to intercede for him and, with the help of Count Kisselev's influence, to save him from the gallows, that she had made the visit to Vienna witnessed by the note of the train fares? The unrest may have drawn him back from Tiflis, to assist in the pushing back of the Holy Roman Empire. At any rate, he seems now to have re-involved himself in Garibaldi's campaign to eject its armies from Italy. There she found him again, when she took Yuri to consult a specialist:[2]

> Then, when I took the poor child to Bologna, to see if I could save him I met him [Metrovitch] again in Italy and he did all he could for me, more than a brother. Then the child died, as it had no papers, nor documents and I did not care to give my name in food for the kind of gossips, it was he, Metrovitch, who undertook all the job, who buried the *aristocratic Baron's* child – under his, Metrovitch's name, saying, 'He did not care', in a small town of southern Russia in 1867. After this, without notifying my relatives of having returned to Russia to bring back the unfortunate little boy whom I did not succeed to bring back alive to the governess chosen for him by the Baron. I simply wrote to the child's father to notify him of this pleasant occurrence for him and returned to Italy with the same passport . . . Now shall I, in the illusive hope of justifying myself, begin by exhuming these several corpses – the child's mother, Metrovitch, his wife, the poor child himself, and all the rest? NEVER. It would be as mean and sacrilegious as it would be useless.

Metrovitch comes out of it nobly. Under no obligation whatever to have any part in the events, he helped bury and gave his name to a child deserted by both his parents, and even, it would seem, by his legally adoptive father – the child of Baron Meyendorff and Nikifor's relative, Nathalie Blavatsky.

CHAPTER 10

Mentana

Madame Blavatsky was wounded at the battle of Mentana. This has always seemed one of the strangest episodes in the life of Madame Blavatsky, implying an extraordinary degree of masculinity. Is it so? Let us look at Garibaldi's army.[1] It was always a volunteer force, and very informal. During Garibaldi's years of exile in South America, when he was fighting in local causes that seemed to him just, to keep in practice, his beloved Anita, when not actually pregnant or nursing, put on man's clothing and rode into battle at his side. At the same time, continually washing the resistant blood out of his clothes fatigued her; it was to lighten her burden that he acquired one of the red shirts worn by the local butchers, on which blood would show less. This was worn outside the trousers, belted, and covering the whole trunk. His followers thought this effective, and having till then worn a variety of clothes, they all obtained for themselves butchers' shirts, and so was born the famous Garibaldi shirt. Back in Italy, Anita had died on a campaign. With Sicily and Naples in the hands of the patriots and Victor Emmanuel crowned, Italy was half-liberated. At Mentana, on 3 November 1867, Garibaldi was trying to enter Rome, unaware that the Papal forces had been reinforced by a French contingent sent by Napoleon III. The French were carrying the new *chassepot* rifles, which had longer range than the muskets of the Garibaldini, of whom a terrible number fell. In England, Garibaldi's crusade had enjoyed immense popularity. Swinburne had written his *Song of Italy* about it. A respectable English woman, Jessie White Mario, was with Garibaldi on this campaign (she was taken prisoner just before Mentana). If Madame Blavatsky had, like Anita Garibaldi and Jessie White Mario, put on a red shirt with the intention of actively helping in any way she could, it would not have been extraordinary. Nevertheless, in later years, repudiating an article in an American paper which said she had been on Garibaldi's staff, she wrote, 'Never was on Garibaldi's staff. Went with friends to Mentana to help shooting the Papists and got shot myself'.[2] This may be about the measure of it. For this participation in the fun, she got two bullet wounds, one in the right shoulder and one in her leg, while her arm was broken by a sabre in two places.[3]

The battle of Mentana, on 3 November 1867, was the heaviest defeat suffered by Garibaldi. He was taken prisoner. Casualties were heavy. Madame Blavatsky was left for dead in a ditch in the Pontine marshes.

Yet if this account may make her involvement sound purely fortuitous and irresponsible, there must have been something more to it, for she wrote to Sinnett,[4] 'The Garibaldis (the sons) are alone to know the whole truth, and a few more Garibaldians with them'. Not Garibaldi himself, that strange wild man with the leonine face and yellow beard? What 'whole truth' was there to know? She had been in Venice. Had she brought intelligence from there or something like that? Garibaldi and Metrovitch were both Freemasons, and the Carbonari were perhaps a partly occult society. Was it through Metrovitch she came to be involved significantly?

Whatever the answers to these questions, Christmas 1867 found her in Florence.

CHAPTER 11

The Summons

She was still in Florence when, in the early summer of 1868, she received a message from Morya, telling her she was to come to Tibet. When she had gone to the borders on her own, trying to find him, she had failed. There is an occult saying that it is useless for the pupil to look for the Master; when the pupil is ready the Master is at hand. Since she had first met him in the flesh in Hyde Park and in Ramsgate, seventeen years had passed. Perhaps he had been waiting for her to mature. If she had been on a long probation, now she was summoned. She was to proceed, he said, to Serbia, where she would be met and given further instructions.[1]

It was just before she left Florence, that, on 10 June 1869, Prince Michael Obrenovich, his aunt, Princess Catherine, and the latter's daughter, were all butchered in the garden of their house in Belgrade. As Madame Blavatsky had met them all, it was a shock to her. She proceeded to Serbia, according to instructions. Prince Milan, nephew of the deceased, had been proclaimed. She met an elderly Serbian woman who had been devoted to the murdered family, who had with her a Rumanian gipsy girl, but it was not until much later she learned the role they had played in avenging the crime.

We can only glimpse her movements through her later notes for Sinnett:[2]

> I went from Florence to Antevari and towards Belgrade, where in the mountains I had to wait (as ordered by Master) – to Constantinople passing through Serbia and the Karpat mountains waiting for a certain [sic] he sent after me . . .

She says[3] she learned of the murder when she 'was in Florence after Mentana and on my way to India with Master'. When she says simply 'Master', she always means Morya. He must, therefore, have come to Constantinople to fetch her. Had she been going round the Cape of Good Hope, she would have had to go west, to sail from Marseilles. Morya must have been taking her by the short, direct, but terrible overland route. From Constantinople to Shigatsè, whither they were bound, is about 400 miles, across Turkey, Persia, Afghanistan, a bit of India and Kashmir. As she says Tartars ride between Tibet and eastern Europe, there may have been tracks, yet over such country they would hardly have made more than twenty miles a day.[4] Bumping up and down for several hours a day over so long a period would have made her exhaustingly saddle-sore.

She mentions the Kuen Luns. In English atlases, the Kuen Lun Mountains border Tibet to the north, but there is a point at which they merge with the Karakorums, and it seems that Tibetans use the same name for both ranges. They may, indeed, have taken the way into Tibet she had attempted in 1856, only this time she had a sure guide to conduct her up on to the roof of the world.

CHAPTER 12

Tibet

Morya lived near the Grand Monastery of Trashi Lhünpo, seat of the Panchèn Lama or (as the British tend to call him, after his residence) the Trashi or Tashi Lama. As McGovern puts it:[1]

> Politically . . . the Dalai Lama is greater than the Trashi Lama . . . but religiously the two great abbots rank as equal. Owing to the greater spiritual character of the Trashi Lama, many Tibetans regard the Dalai Lama as merely the secular and the Trashi Lama as the spiritual ruler of Tibet.

Trashi Lhünpo, and the little town of Shigatsè beneath its walls, are on the River Nyang, about four miles above its confluence with the Tsang-po (Brahmaputra); that is, about 150 miles west-south-west of Lhasa.

Morya's house was in a ravine, where a stream was flanked by higher mountains than those at Shigatsè. He had arranged that Madame Blavatsky should stay at the house of his friend and colleague Koot Hoomi (Koothumi or Kuthumi),[2] who had a widowed sister living with him. Koot Hoomi, like Morya, was Indian, or more exactly Kashmiri, of at least part Punjabi extraction. That will be why he, like Morya, was able to live in Tibet. As McGovern, half a century later, observed, Kashmiris and Nepalese, are by long–established custom allowed to settle in Tibet,[3] which is closed to other Indians, as to Europeans, except in exceptional circumstances. Morya, though of Rajput blood, had come over with the Nepalese embassy. Koot Hoomi, like Morya, had travelled. He had been in London and in Leipzig, and perhaps in Paris, for in addition to speaking English better than Morya, he spoke French.

Koot Hoomi received at his house young Tibetan chelas (pupils) wearing the yellow hats of the Gelukpa. Presumably, they had been sent from Trashi Lhünpo as suitable for special training. His house was near enough for them to have ridden there daily from the monastery. They would sit around him in a semi-circle, cross-legged – outside, if the weather was good. The most advanced of them, aged 15, was Djwal Khool (his name gets spelled all ways, Djual, Jwal, Jual, even Dguala Kul or Khul). Later, he made for Madame Blavatsky a picture of the ravine in which they had all lived together. On silk, in misty blue, green and silver tones, it shows the Master Morya in the angle between the bent tree and the left-hand edge of the picture. He is wearing a white pugri or pagri (turban of fine muslin, tied so that the ends fan out and descend to cover the neck, shoulders and part of the breast). He is riding a richly caparisoned horse, covered with an extended saddle-cloth. He is relaxed, seated well down in the saddle, his hands properly low. The angle at which his thighs decline shows that he is using long stirrups, as one sees in paintings of Akbar. He is approaching the steps of his house. Whereas Tibetans make only rectangular doors and windows and, for domestic dwellings, flat roofs, we see here the arched doors and windows, with lattices, and the sloping, tiled roof of Nepalese architecture. Morya came, after all, from Nepal. In Tibet the ground floor is usually devoted to stabling the horses and so on. The steps here would make that difficult, but there may be a ramp further along. One discerns, at the side, the external staircase to the human habitation usual in Tibet. As there was then no glass in Tibet, windows were usually kept small or not made at all, illumination being by yak-butter lamps. Tibetans like to have one floor or room which is light though cold, and one which is warm though dark. The master always sleeps at the top. I think the one shown is a three-storey house. The height from the 'human' row of windows to the roof is too great unless one assumes the presence of a windowless attic chamber. If the architecture represents a compromise between Nepalese and Tibetan styles, there is one feature purely Tibetan. From the roof rises a prayer-flag mast, with prayer-flag fluttering. Every flutter is a prayer. This was deference to the popular religion. The Master did not need such means of communication with higher powers, but the locals would have been pained to see a house without a prayer-flag.

The strange ovoid door cut in the rock, at bottom left, leads into an excavated chamber housing the Masters' library and museum. Again, the mosque-style arch is not Tibetan, and it was either executed under the Master's direction or survived from some earlier and more sophisticated civilisation such as Harrer felt there must have been in Tibet. A library in a cave may sound strange, but since then Sir Aurel Stein has stumbled on a deserted Buddhist library in a cave in the Gobi Desert.[4] Djwal Khool stands in the stream, holding a pole. At bottom right is a tiny temple, typically Tibetan, with two prayer-flags. Out of the picture, we are told, is a bridge leading to Koot Hoomi's house, off right round a bend. Madame Blavatsky used to tell people to whom she showed the picture that she used to follow the stream further to the right, to where it opened into a lake in which she used to bathe. It was bitterly cold, and as she was not a swimmer one can suppose the purpose of those freezing dips was just to wash.

She tells us little of the Masters' interiors, save that they sat on the floor, on rugs and cushions stuffed with bushy yak-tails. Probably they slept on the floor also. Indian ascetics abhor chairs and beds. There is a yogi's saying, 'Decadence began with furniture'. Cross-legged, one sits with the back straight and keeps the brain clear. Morya, however, at least in his own house, smoked a hookah pipe.[5] Enemies of Madame Blavatsky, who try to make out that she did not know Tibet, think to catch her out in making Morya smoke, for in Tibet smoking was against the law. It is true there was a law against smoking in Tibet, but it was not enforced with rigour. In any case, Morya was an ascetic, and to an ascetic in Tibet anything is forgiven. He is supposed to know best.

Madame Blavatsky tells us the usual salt tea with melted butter was served. It is practically Tibet's national dish, the poor consuming forty to eighty or more cups daily.

Morya and Koot Hoomi ate no flesh. In this, they were true to the teachings of the Buddha and of Tsongkapa, the founder of the Yellow Hatted Gelukpa order to which the Dalai and Trashi Lamas belong. Buddhists from other countries have been shocked to find that in Tibet (though everyone is careful not to kill insects) even the Dalai Lama eats meat. The present one and his brother say that the climate makes it too difficult to go without it. The necessity for the presence of a slaughterhouse in Lhasa is deplored, and the slaughterers have to live in isolation,[6] shunned because they live by sin; and everybody eating meat prays for a happier incarnation in which circumstances may not oblige him to partake of it.[7] Evans-Wentz, however, believes the excuses cover a liking for eating meat.[8] The staple diet is mutton, yak, barley and butter. Vegetables and fresh fruits are unknown.[9] Bogle, when he was received by the Trashi Lami in 1774, was smilingly offered mutton from his plate.[10]

The school for ascetics was, says Madame Blavatsky, 'attached to the private retreat' of the Panchèn Lama.[11] The British government spy, Pundit Sarat Chandra Das, who visited Shigatsè some fourteen years later (in 1882) reported that the Panchèn Lama, though he had both a summer palace and a winter palace within Trashi Lhünpo, had also a private palace, three miles from the monastery, to which he often withdrew. It was called Tobgyal.[12] This place is probably where Madame Blavatsky lived with her Master and Koot Hoomi.

Tibet is on the same latitude as North Africa; it is the altitude, combined with the wind, which makes it so cold. McGovern noted that as one went down a ravine it became warmer, and that especially just above the confluence of rivers, where the soil was washed down, it was fertile. The ravine in which the Master Morya lived had doubtless been chosen for its amenity; and with the chelas to help cultivate it and importation of rice from India or China, it was probably not too difficult to supply a vegetarian table. Koot Hoomi's sister probably cooked.

Although the Gelukpa are celibate, it is not unusual for them to own property outside their monastery and to have some female relative living with them.[13] Madame Blavatsky, however, distinguished Morya and Koot Hoomi, with their long and flowing hair, from the monks, with their shaven heads – and later she makes the point that as the hair stores vitality, the tonsured monks or lamas tend to live less long than the independent ascetics, who wear their hair uncut. Morya and Koot Hoomi were not subject to the monastery, yet they were in communion with it and protected by the Panchèn.

Sarat Chandra Das was not too favourably impressed by his glimpse of the Panchèn, whose countenance struck him as highly intelligent but cold and unsympathetic.[14] However it was entirely due to his grace that the secret school could exist adjacent to his grounds, and that

Madame Blavatsky could be invited to come and stay. We are wholly in his debt – or in his tutor's, for in the autumn of 1868, when Madame Blavatsky arrived, His Holiness the Panchèn Lama Jè Pèden Chökyi Trakpa Tènpé Wangchuk, was only 13 or 14.

Because a grand lama has to be found as a child, his responsibilities have to be exercised by a senior until he attains his majority at 17. Panchèn (cognate with Pundit) means 'learned', and as the little boy would have had to prepare for a long series of examinations into his understanding of the sacred scriptures, his tutor was important.

Madame Blavatsky was taken to visit the monastery. It is said that as the traveller crossing the arid desert nears Shigatsè, the first thing to catch his eye is a glint of gold.[15] It is the gilded roofs, up-turned, Chinese style, within the Grand Monastery of Trashi Lhünpo. Four of them cover tombs of Panchèn Lamas.

She must have been taken within the walls to look at the temple from the outside, for she describes a stone path to steps leading up to it; it stands, she tells us, on a slight, artificial elevation. She says the roof is surmounted with a triangular dagoba, marked with a gold globe, dragon and swastika, the dagoba standing on three small pillars.[16] This triangular dagoba can, with a magnifying glass, be discerned on the pictorial plan of the monastery made by Sarat Chandra Das and published with his story in 1902. Enemies of Madame Blavatsky, who aver she acquired her information about Tibet from the pages of the Abbé Huc, ignore the fact that Huc never visited Trashi Lhünpo or Shigatsè and so did not describe it; neither did Bogle, who was there in 1774, refer to the triangular dagoba. Madame Blavatsky's is the first and only description of it in words, though one sees it in the plan by Das published after her death. From the same plan, one sees it is right in the centre of the monastery, and that, as it is less tall than the Panchèns' tombs, two on either side of it, the details she describes could not have been seen by her except from close up.

On the other hand, she was not allowed to enter. This was probably in order to avoid scandalising the monks, who did not need to be told exactly why she was there. She was told what she would have seen if it had been possible for her to go inside. In particular, she was told that on the altar lay (with other holy objects) a pile of cubiform tablets, inscribed with verses in an ancient and sacred language called Senzar. These were recited for her until she knew many of them by ear and the meanings by heart. She would give them to the world, as we shall find later.

It is unlikely she was able to enter, either, the Great Congregation Hall, in which the contests in debate were held. On the other hand, it will emerge later that Morya and Koot Hoomi had special relations with the librarian, whom Madame Blavatsky came to know well. This suggests she may have been allowed into the library and shown round by him, though she would not have been able to read the works. It would have been largely a scroll library, and furnished with at least one scroll table – long and narrow, the ends bending over in the shapes of scrolls so as to facilitate the unrolling of a scroll over it, and rather high, so that one might conveniently stand to read at it. When not in use, the scrolls would be stored in cylinders.

Outside the walls of Trashi Lhünpo is a jong or fort at the beginning of Shigatsè town. When Sarat Chandra Das was there, there was a market which opened in the mornings at 11.00 a.m. to sell food (mainly mutton) and firewood. If Madame Blavatsky needed any addition to the clothing she had brought with her, she could perhaps have found it there. There would have been no proper shops, everything being laid out on stalls or the ground.

She made excursions to other parts of Tibet, though the only place she mentions by name is Lake Palti (otherwise Yambok or Yandro Tso),[17] the Turquoise Lake. Whether from Shigatsè or from India, it is on the route to Lhasa. More than thirty years later, Colonel Younghusband would describe it:[18]

> In shape it was like a rough ring, surrounding what is practically an island; and in colour it varied to every shade of violet and turquoise blue and green. At times it would be like the blue of heaven, reflecting the intense Tibetan sky. Then, as some cloud passed over . . . it would flash back rays of the deep greeny-blue of a turquoise. Anon, it would show out in various shades of violet.

On the 'road' or rather track they encountered a party of nuns coming from Lhasa. Her companion took her up to them, and she was able through his intermediacy (so he must have been Morya or Koot Hoomi) to exchange a few words with them. They said that normally they never left their convent, but they had been given a dispensation to make a pilgrimage to Kandi, in Ceylon, to pay their homage to the sacred relic of the Buddha.

She does not say that she went to Lhasa, and it may be that the Dalai Lama's permission had not been obtained for her visit. Yet, perhaps bypassing it, she went beyond it. In the early twentieth century a Major Cross, manager of the tea and other estates of the Dalai Lama, in which capacity he made travels in north-eastern Tibet, traced the progress of a white woman 'to a lamasery far north . . . ten years after the Mutiny'.[19] (The mutiny ended in 1858.) Some of the oldest people assured him they had seen her. He identified her with Madame Blavatsky. The monastery in the far north east will have been Kum Bum, built over the birthplace of Tsongkapa, of whom much more later.

The most important thing for Madame Blavatsky, however, was simply that she was with her Master Morya and his colleague, and was being given the teaching for which she had always longed. This will not have been in the company of the chelas. Being so unlike them, by her greater age as well as by being a woman, of totally different cultural formation, more advanced than they in some respects if less so in others and not knowing Tibetan, she would have had to be taught separately. It was intended that she should be their missionary to the western world.

How long was she there? She will have arrived in the autumn of 1868 and stayed throughout 1869 and until practically the end of 1870. In Russia, her family, now moved to Odessa, was without news and becoming desperate. Was she dead? On 11 November 1870, her aunt, Nadyezhda Fadeyef, was called upon by a man of Asian appearance who delivered a letter to her and then, before her eyes, vanished. The letter remained solid, and was in French. I translate:[20]

> To the Honourable,
>   Very honourable Lady,
>   Nadyezhda Andreevna Fadeev,
>   Odessa.
> The noble relatives of Mad. H. Blavatsky have no reason to give up hope of ever seeing her again. Their daughter and niece has not departed this world. She is alive and desires to make known to those she loves that she is well and very happy in the retreat she has chosen. She has been very ill, but is so no longer; for thanks to the protection of the Lord Sangyas [Buddha] she has found devoted friends, who take care of her physically and spiritually. May the ladies of her house set their minds at rest. Before 18 new moons have risen – she will have returned to her family.

The letter is unsigned, but it is in the hand of the later Mahatma Letters, now in the British Museum, which are signed K.H. or Koot Hoomi.

About a month after this, Madame Blavatsky said goodbye to Morya, Koot Hoomi, the latter's sister, the chelas and Tibet.

CHAPTER 13

Greek waters,
Egypt and the Lebanon

In December 1870, Madame Blavatsky returned through the newly opened Suez Canal, and heard how the previous year the Empress Eugénie had come out from France to perform the opening ceremony. Presumably she heard also that (while she had been in Tibet) there had been the Franco–Prussian War, Napoleon III had ceased to be Emperor and France had become a republic again. The victorious King Wilhelm IV of Prussia had become Kaiser of Germany.

She now 'went to Greece and saw Illarion, in *what place* I cannot and must not say'.[1] Greece may be a blind, as in another letter in which the name of Illarion is not mentioned, she writes, 'I cross . . . in December. Went to Cyprus . . .'[2] There is a Greek population in Cyprus, then under Turkish rule, and we shall find later allusion to Illarion's being Greek but coming from the Asian end of the Mediterranean. The need for discretion with regard to the home of a Master living in a place so accessible is obvious. Too close an indication could lead to an invasion of his privacy by the merely curious.

If she stayed for some time with Illarion (for tutoring in some subject not on the Tibetan curriculum?), she must eventually have gone to mainland Greece, if only to take ship at Piraeus, the port of Athens, aboard the SS *Eumonia*. Her first port of call was to have been Nauplia, in the Gulf of Argolis, but, on 4 July 1871, between the islands of Dokos and Hydra and in sight of the island of Spetsai (she spells it Spezza), the ship blew up. This was from powder she had been carrying in case of attack by pirates. There was no time to take to the boats; without warning, the passengers were simply blown from the ship, and Madame Blavatsky was one of the very few picked up, alive and floundering in the water, and taken back to Greek land. The Greek government accepted responsibility, but some time was probably occupied in sorting out damage or insurance claims before she accepted passage in another vessel, for Alexandria.

Here she spent the late summer and early autumn. Any funds she had been carrying in cash would have gone down in the *Eumonia*, but the Greek government would probably have given her immediate spending money in advance of such settlement as their lawyers would agree. There must have been a casino in Alexandria, for she wrote to Sinnett (though recommending him not to put it in his book) that she won a sum on the number 27.[3] This sounds like roulette, in which money staked is placed on a number. Flush with this windfall, she went on to Cairo, in October or November, and took rooms at the Hotel d'Orient.

In the hotel was a Miss Emma Cutting, an expatriate Englishwoman. Serving in some capacity as an employee, she was friendly with a Monsieur Alexis Coulomb, son of the woman who owned the hotel. Miss Cutting (Madame Alexis Coulomb, as she would eventually become) would later claim she lent Madame Blavatsky money. That seems unlikely, seeing that Madame Blavatsky had arrived in the hotel flush from a gambling win. Nevertheless, she was in some way good and helpful.

Madame Blavatsky now thought to found a *societé spirite*. She did not approve of attempts to get in touch with the dead, but her idea was that the mediums would perform in their usual way and she would then explain the phenomena in the light of the teaching she had received. However, she found the supposed mediums she had engaged were merely cheats and dismissed them, the society not having lasted a fortnight.

She met Maspero, the Egyptologist, at the Boulak Museum, went out to the Pyramids, and, if she had not done so before this, met the Coptic Adept, Serapis Bey. She will later make the point that it is not amongst the Arabs, who have entered the country from elsewhere, but amongst the Copts, though they have Greek names, that the blood of the ancient Egyptians still flows. Bey is a title of Turkish administrative authority. Egypt was at that time under the rule of the Turks, so he must have accepted some kind of civic office, probably as the means of protecting his people. He had under him a number of other Adepts, amongst whom was Tuitit Bey. The headquarters of their school was Luxor, and presumably Madame Blavatsky went there to meet them all, and to walk in Karnak, beneath the lotus columns.

As always, she is reticent about meetings with the Masters, yet does give us one incident. She was travelling in the desert with one of them (it will have been either Serapis or Tuitit), and they camped for the night under canvas. As they finished their evening meal, she remarked jokingly that what she would like now was a *café au lait*, as served in Paris at the Café de la Paix. He rose, went to the baggage-camel and drew from the water skin what she would have supposed to be water, but when he handed it to her, what was in the cup was coffee with milk. It was steaming hot and she smelled the mokkha. She was drinking it gratefully, when – what was this? It was only cold water. She thought he must have by his magic have turned the water into *café au lait*, and then turned it back again. He said it was not so. It had been cold water all the time. He had only created an illusion.[4]

He also showed her how one of the biblical plagues of Egypt could have been induced, by moving an electrified rod over a container full of water so as to cause unnatural multiplication of micro-organisms; this made it red, like blood.[5]

She was back in Cairo when, in the spring of 1872, Metrovitch came to see her. He had been in Odessa when her family received her letter saying she had been aboard the *Eumonia*. There had been a certain amount about the disaster in the papers. They were worried about her, and as Metrovitch was going to Egypt on some business of his own, had asked him to try to bring her back with him.[6]

It was, however, to himself that Egypt was dangerous. Probably because of his political activities, some Maltese monks had plotted to trap and kill him.

> Illarion warned me, then *bodily* in Egypt – and made Agardi Metrovitch come direct to me and never leave the house for ten days. He was a brave and daring man and could not bear it and went to Alexandria *quand même*, and I went after him with my monkeys.[7]

When she says Illarion was bodily in Egypt, she means that he could project in his astral body, but had come in his physical one. He seems to have worked with Serapis. Madame Blavatsky seems to have been accustomed to take rooms rather than a room – that is, a sitting-room as well as bedroom and bathroom – so that her having Metrovitch to stay was not so compromising as it sounds; but yet it attracted the interest of Miss Cutting.

After he had gone to Alexandria, despite his Master's advice, she received a telegram from a Russian friend she had made there, Countess Lydia Pashkoff, telling her he was ill at a hotel in Ramleh. So, encumbered by pet monkeys she had acquired and could not leave at the Hotel d'Orient, she went back to Alexandria, in the desperate hope of being able to cheat Illarion's prophecy that Metrovitch would die on 29 April. She planned to push him aboard the very steamer that had brought him, which was due to leave again. She found him, with a monk beside his bed, in a small hotel at Ramleh; he was suffering, a doctor said, from typhoid fever, though she thought it was from poison. Knowing how Metrovitch detested priests, she called for the police to remove the monk, who shook his fist as he was dragged away. She wrote 'I arrived too late'. He had gone to Ramleh on foot and had stopped on his way to drink a glass of lemonade at the hotel of a Maltese where was seen talking with two monks; when he arrived at Ramleh he fell down senseless. '. . . Then I took care of him for ten days – an agony incessant and terrible, during which he saw his wife apparently and called loudly for her. I never left him for I knew he was going to die as Illarion had said and so he did'.

No church would bury him. She appealed to the Freemasons. (As Garibaldi was a Freemason, so probably was Metrovitch.) They were, however, afraid, and in any case do not perform burials.[8] 'Then I took an Abyssinian – a pupil of Illarion and with the hotel servant we dug him a grave under a tree on the sea shore and I hired a *fellah* to carry him in the evening and we buried his poor body'.

One remembers that when she first stumbled over his seemingly dead body in Constantinople, it was by a Maltese that he had been stabbed. Malta had, during the time of Bonaparte, been captured first by the French then by the British. Then its last Grand Master, Baron Hompesch, had transferred it to British sovereignty. Obviously, there was a faction in it hostile to Garibaldi, and so to Metrovitch. He cannot have been a worthless man, or Illarion would not have concerned himself about him. The Venetian (of whom we shall hear more later), Serapis, and Illarion all worked together, in concord with the Brothers at Shigatsè. It was probably on Morya's suggestion that she had to make this tour of their Brothers in the Near East before returning to her family at Odessa.

This she now proposed to do, sending her monkeys direct by ship to her Aunt Nadyezhda as she would go the long way round, by land, in order to visit Palmyra and other ancient cities in Syria, Palestine and the Lebanon, where she would find the Druses.

Near Baalbek, at Dair Mar Maroon, between the Lebanon and the ante-Lebanon, she sighted another caravan, and as it came up she recognised Countess Pashkoff. Countess Pashkoff was, indeed, a noted traveller of Egypt, Palestine and Syria, and would later publish a book, *En Orient, Drames et Paysages* (*In the Orient, Dramas and Landscapes*) (1879). They camped that night together and after that the two Russian travellers joined caravans and for a while travelled everywhere together, until eventually Madame Blavatsky set her face once more for home.

As before, she walked in on her family unheralded. It was because her grandfather had died that the whole family had left Tiflis and grouped itself around Nadyezhda, in Odessa. Nadyezhda told her of the letter which had been handed her by a messenger who vanished:[10]

> It was only when I returned home that I told my aunt that the letter received from K.H. was no letter from a *Spirit* as she thought. When she got the proofs that they were living men she regarded them as devils or *sold to Satan*!!! I never speak with her about the Masters.

Nadyezhda was the dearest of her family to her, but one sees here the danger of trying to share a sacred experience with someone who is not ready. The sacred is rejected, with horror, indignation and total misunderstanding. The sacred has been profaned and no good done to the loved one. This is perhaps the hardest thing one has to learn to understand. It explains the insistence of teachers upon discretion. If Nadyezhda had been happy thinking it was an angel or a spirit purified by having passed through the portals of death who had given her the letter, it might have been better to let her go on thinking in the way that she, herself, had rationalised into acceptability, rather than, by revealing it was a living person who had this power, give her a psychic shock. How much to tell, and how quickly; that is always the question.

The letter is unsigned, perhaps to make it easier for Nadyezhda to believe in the little 'miracle'. It is in the hand of Koot Hoomi, though he will have written it for Morya, who must have been the one who delivered it, since he refers later to having seen Nadyezhda, and her description fits him.

In March or April 1873, Madame Blavatsky set out once more. She went first to Bucharest, to see an old friend, Frosya Popescu. With regard to the murder of Prince Obrenovich, Madame Popescu showed her a cutting from a Viennese paper about two persons who had been found dead, marked as though stabbed, though there was no puncture of their flesh. She said that the Serbian woman and gipsy girl whom Madame Blavatsky had met in Serbia had been partners in a sombre rite, the Serbian entrancing the gipsy and commanding her to seek the murderer or murderers of Michael Obrenovich and avenge the crime. Illarion told Madame Blavatsky what her Romanian friend told her was true, and suggested she make it into a story. Later, she did make it into one, under the title, 'Double murder'.[11]

Next she went to Paris, where she stayed with her cousin, Nikolai Gustavovich von Hahn, and his wife, formerly Countess Adlerberg, at 11 rue de l'Université. It was an excellent vantage-point from which to see the sights of the city, but a Dr L. Marquette, MD, who was a frequent visitor to her cousin's home, says that she seldom went out and spent most of her time drawing and painting.[12]

In June, a messenger came from Morya. Had she been staying in because she was expecting him? He handed her an enormous sum in French banknotes. It was not for her own use. She was to take it to the United States, and she would be told what to do with it when she arrived.

So instant was her obedience, she obtained her ticket and set out upon her journey the next day.

CHAPTER 14

New York

At Le Havre, on the quay, she noticed a woman sitting on the ground weeping, children around her. She asked the woman what was the matter. The woman said she had been going to join her husband, but the tickets, which she had bought in Hamburg, turned out to be false. The ship's staff did not recognise them and she had no money for others. Madame Blavatsky had time only to write to her father and ask him to send her money to wait for her at the Russian Consulate in New York. The little she was carrying would not buy tickets for this family. But what she had bought for herself was a first-class ticket. By exchanging this for a third, enough money was available for them all to travel steerage.[1]

Landing in New York on 7 July 1873, she went to the Russian Consulate and asked for the funds that would be awaiting her collection, but was told nothing had come. This was awkward, as she had now very little money, which made it imperative for her to live inexpensively and find something to do to tide her over until her father's draft arrived. She was directed to 222 Madison Street, New York, where about forty women were making an experiment in co-operative living. There, she was told of two Jews with a firm that might give her immediate employment. She called, and was interviewed by one of them, of whom she afterwards spoke with gratitude. He said she might start to work at once, with her needle, helping to make fancy articles for the shop.[2] At the co-operative she was found by a Miss Anne Ballard of the New York *Sun*, who wished to interview her because she was writing an article about Russians in New York. Madame Blavatsky said she had made wide travels: 'I have been in Tibet'.

She then received a further instruction from Morya, to take to Buffalo the banknotes with which she had been entrusted in Paris, deliver them to a certain person and obtain a receipt.

She was still at the co-operative when, on 18 October 1874, she received a cable from her half-sister Lisa. It was to tell her their father had died (on 27 June, Old Style). Lisa said they had had difficulty in contacting her, but that she would be receiving a draft for her share of the inheritance, 1,000 roubles. This arrived. The Assistant Librarian of the Bank of England (Miss M.A.L. Chapman) has worked out for me that, with 33.25p sterling equalling a rouble in 1874, the value of a rouble in terms of the purchasing power of the pound in Britain in 1984 would be £22.28½. Madame Blavatsky, therefore, received the 1984 equivalent of £22,285.

Soon afterwards, she encountered Countess Gerebko, whom she had known in Russia in 1866. Countess Gerebko persuaded her to invest $1,000 in the development of two plots of land, both in Suffolk County, Long Island, one in Huntington and the other in Northport, for chicken-farming and market-gardening. With the dollar at an average of £4.84⅝ in 1875, her investment would therefore have been, multiplying by the same figure as before to bring the dollar to the 1984 pound, very roughly about £11,000 today, half her total inheritance.

An agreement was signed on 1 July 1874, and Madame Blavatsky later went to live on the land, expecting to work it. On arrival, however, she felt that she was not being fairly dealt with, returned to New York and filed a suit for restitution of her investment.

In *The Sunday Graphic*, she read a series of articles by a Colonel Olcott concerning a farmstead at Chittenden, Vermont. Phantoms appeared there, and materialised. She went to see.

CHAPTER 15

Olcott

There now entered Madame Blavatsky's life a person so important we must try to know as much as we can about him.

Henry Steel Olcott was an all Anglo-Saxon, apparently eighth generation American, with a family tree traced to an ancestor who had arrived from England only about ten years after the Pilgrim Fathers in the *Mayflower*. He was born at Orange, New Jersey, on 2 August 1832. He was thus almost exactly one year younger than Madame Blavatsky. They were both Leos. His family was Methodist. We do not know where he went to school, except that it was in New York, but the curriculum included the beginnings of French, Latin, Greek and science. Thence he proceeded to the Columbia University of New York, where he was studying scientific agriculture when a crash in his father's business compelled him to break the course. For two years he worked a 30-acre farm in Elyria, Ohio, on a share basis. It was here that a friend, knowing he had been reading books on mesmerism, asked him whether he could relieve his daughter's pain while waiting for a dentist's appointment. He made passes, and they seemed to help. At 23 years of age he found himself known internationally for his work on a model farm at Newark, and the Greek government offered him the chair of scientific agriculture at Athens. This he declined, but he availed himself of a legacy to become co-founder of the Westchester Farm School at Mount Vernon. When he was 26 he visited Europe in the interest of agriculture, and his report was published in the New American Cyclopaedia of 1859. In the same year he had two books of lectures on agriculture published, the second by Yale. He became American correspondent to the *Mark Lane Express* (London), a journal of the corn trade, and agricultural correspondent to the *New York Herald Tribune*. The conscience of the country, in the north anyway, was becoming roused over the cruelty of slave-owning, and the *Tribune* was abolitionist. That was why Olcott volunteered to go as a reporter to the hanging of the abolitionist, John Brown.

The southerners were anxious to prevent northerners from being present, and it was despite some difficulty, even danger, that he succeeded in attending the unhappy event, in Charlestown, Virginia, on 2 December 1859. The eyes of John Brown met his and searched them, Olcott felt, with intense enquiry, just before he mounted the scaffold. Soon afterwards, a song began to be heard:

John Brown's body lies a–mouldering in the grave,
But his soul goes marching on.

On 26 April 1860, Olcott married Mary Eplee Morgan, a clergyman's daughter, conventional and not disposed to what became apparent, his growing interest in Spiritualism.

In April 1861, the Civil War broke out. Olcott took service with the Federal forces, that is, the forces of the north, the Yankees, and fought in the North Carolina campaign under General Burnside. He became a signals officer, but was invalided out with malaria and dysentery.

A chance observation he had made led to his being assigned to look into a question of illegal profiteering, through which the army was losing heavily. What had been intended as a fortnight's job, after which he would have returned to his unit, extended because of the scale of the malpractice he uncovered into a full time one. He was made a Special Commissioner of the War Department, with the rank of Colonel. Then, at the request of the Secretary of the Navy, Wells, he was lent to him as Special Investigator for the Navy, to do a like job for it.

On 14 August 1865, President Abraham Lincoln was assassinated. Secretary of War Mr Stanton sent for Olcott, and he was appointed to a three-man commission to investigate whether the assassin had acted alone or been supported by conspirators. He interrogated suspects, mounted a raid upon a suspect premises and arrested one major conspirator.

Later in 1865, he resigned his commission, and three years later he was admitted to the New

York Bar, in May 1868. Thereafter, he practised law from an office in New York, specialising in customs, revenue and insurance cases. His clients included the Treasury of the City of New York, the New York Stock Exchange, the Mutual Equitable Life and Continental Life Insurance Companies, the Gold Exchange Bank, the Panama Railway Company and the United Steel Manufacturers of Sheffield (England).

His professional life was therefore successful, but his marriage had not been happy. He was living at the Lotus Club, in the expectation of divorce papers. He may, therefore, have been feeling a spiritual void in his life when, one day in July 1874, as he sat in his office at 7 Beekman Street, New York, his mind ceased to be upon a case in which he had been retained by the City of New York, which had to do with the mechanical construction of water-meters. By no chain of reasoning that he could ever after recapture his mind came to be upon the fact that he had not paid sufficient attention to Spiritualism.[1] So strong was this feeling that he went out and round the corner to a newsagents, where he bought a copy of *The Banner of Light*. In it, he read that at a farmstead at Chittenden in Vermont phantoms appeared and apparently solidified. He took the train.

He could only stay for a few days in the first instance as his business called him back to New York. He went again in September, and wrote articles about the phenomena, which were printed in the *Daily Graphic*. Again he had to return to New York, and this time received from his wife's lawyers, Burrill, Davison & Burrill, her summons and complaint against him, dated 21 September 1874. He was summoned to appear before the Supreme Court of New York on 25 November 1874, to answer her complaint that he had on 3 May (this was later changed to 2 May) 1873, committed an act of adultery at a house of prostitution, 136 East 22nd Street in the City of New York, and had on earlier occasions had carnal intercourse with other women at diverse times and in various places unknown to the plaintiff. She was asking for a divorce against him, costs of the divorce proceedings and maintenance until the time of the proceedings and thereafter of $2,000 a year (that is £400 of that day, which, having to be multiplied by 20 to bring it to the purchasing power of the beginning of the 1980s, is about £8,000 today). This was to be paid to her each year in four quarterly instalments and was for her own maintenance alone, maintenance and education of their two sons, aged 12 and 14, to be paid for separately and additionally.[2]

Perhaps he succeeded in putting this to the back of his mind when he went again to Vermont on 14 October, the day of his destiny. He was afterwards able to recall and record that it was a sunny day, the whole country covered with a faint blueish haze, the beeches, elms and maples, which had been green, now turned by a touch of the early frosts to such a mottling of gold and crimson it looked as though the landscape were covered with royal tapestries.[3] Re-entering the farmstead of William and Horatio Eddy, he saw that there was amongst the curious come to gape at ghosts somebody new, a woman in a red Garibaldi shirt, standing out from among all the rest, who looked by comparison dull, her hair 'a thick blond mop, silken-soft and crinkled to the roots, like the fleece of a Cotswold ewe'.[4]

CHAPTER 16

Meeting in Vermont

He heard her speak a few words to another person in French, so when he saw her produce a cigarette, he stepped up, and summoning his own best French to the occasion, said as he offered her a light, '*Permettez-moi, Madame*'. In his own words, his relationship with Madame Blavatsky 'began in smoke, but it stirred up a great and permanent fire'.[1]

She said she hoped not to meet 'that Colonel Olcott', in case he wrote about her, but on his confessing he was that same, avowed it was his articles that had caused her to come.

He was impressed by her 'massive Calmuk face, contrasting in its suggestion of power, culture and imperiousness, so strangely with the commonplace visages about the room, as her red garment did with the grey and white walls and the dull costumes of the rest of the guests.'[2]

He felt they were of the same world, cosmopolitans, in closer touch with each other than with the rest.[3]

> It was the voice of common sympathy with the higher occult side of man and nature, the attraction of soul to soul, not that of sex to sex. Neither then, at the commencement, nor ever afterwards had either of us the sense of the other being of the opposite sex. We were simply chums; so regarded each other, so called each other.

By the end of the week, he was calling her Jack.

Olcott insists constantly that he felt her to be more like another man than a woman, but, while the women of that day were expected to be almost unrealistically feminine, and she, by contrast, had vigour and power, it was probably to emphasise the respectability of their relationship that he develops this point.

He could not know yet that it was the Master Morya who had steered him to his meeting with Madame Blavatsky, but he knew his relationship with her was not as with other women. 'Some base people from time to time dared to suggest that a closer tie bound us together. The same alleged she had been the mistress of other men.' This he never believed: 'her every look, word and action proclaimed her sexlessness'.[4]

The wound below her heart reopened while they were at Chittenden, and to consult him about it she showed it to him, explaining it was where she had been stabbed with a stiletto. She told him she had been with Garibaldi at Mentana, showed him where her left arm had been broken in two places by a sabre stroke, and made him feel, in her right shoulder, a musket-bullet, still embedded in the muscle, and another in her leg.[5]

As for the phenomena they were come to observe, William Eddy would go into a cupboard in a recess by the chimney, across which was drawn a curtain; a succession of human forms would then come out of the cupboard, be briefly visible and then vanish. As a private experiment of her own, Madame Blavatsky visualised certain spectacular types, a Muslim merchant of Tiflis, a Kurdish horseman with scimitar, pistols and lance, and a negro, to see if they would come out of the cupboard. They did. This proved to her two things, that the apparitions were not live people, fraudulently impersonating dead ones, and not dead ones either. Thus, in a letter published in the *Graphic* on 30 October, she defended the Eddys against the allegation of a Dr Beard that they were vulgar frauds who had merely dressed people up in white muslin and so on; but in a long letter to her sister Vera,[6] she explains the phenomena as psychic but unpleasant. The brothers, being mediums, drew (unconsciously) for the material of their phenomena upon the thought-forms generated by those assembled round them, and, worse, upon the reliquae of the dead, the decaying remnants of their astral bodies, which ought to have been allowed to follow the dense physicals into dissolution. Thus, bulked out by matter from the brothers' own subtle bodies, simulacrae of the dead were formed in the room; these simulacrae were recognised and greedily embraced by their living relatives, who drew the matter of them into their own living bodies, causing themselves to take on manners and characteristics of those they had loved – unfortunately, only the inferior ones. The immortal souls of the loved ones were not present. They were (happily) elsewhere. It is this phenomenon that, happening naturally, often causes the living to become like the relatives they have lost, but here the unwholesome process is induced.

At that date, the term 'Spiritualism' was still used as the simple opposite to materialism, but from this letter one sees that Madame Blavatsky never approved Spiritualism in the narrower sense to which it was later limited, of attempted communication with the dead through séances.

CHAPTER 17

A divorce comes through

Madame Blavatsky left Vermont in the latter part of October, and took rooms at 104 East 16th Street, New York. Olcott, who remained in Vermont, received letters from her signed 'Jack'. She moved to 16 Irving Place when he returned to New York at the beginning of November, then to 23 Irving Place, only a few doors from his club. She showed him various kinds of phenomena which she could produce at will, and explained to him that what were at work were not spirits of the dead but spirits of the elements. Tiny and invisible, they were all about them. The Kabbalists divided them into four main groups, spirits of the earth, water, air and fire; gnomes, undines, sylphs and salamanders.[1] It was the earth spirits that were the most used in magic, and these played (though the mediums were not aware of it) the biggest role in Spiritualistic phenomena. The role of those in water and air was more limited, though generally they were obliging with regard to what concerned their element. The fire elementals, however, dwelt, except where there was exposed flame, deep in the earth and were difficult to dominate. One must never be controlled by these creatures, but must control them. One must also beware of them, for, having no proper forms of their own, they were infinitively imitative, taking body in any form created by the human imagination, which, to see anything clearly, must be held at bay. They would take form as deities, devils or the dear departed – when the latter were not the decaying, empty astrals of the dear departed, which one should no more think to reanimate than the physicals in the grave. The immortal souls of the departed were elsewhere.

Those who had taught her were living men, Adepts or Masters, sages who could have entered Nirvana, but remained with humanity out of compassion. They were not, as Olcott at first thought, because of her travels, all orientals. One was a Copt, one a Greek, one a Venetian and one an English philosopher disappeared from the world's sight.[2] There were seven 'rays', and one would find oneself mainly the pupil of a teacher who was on one's own ray.

He asked her how these men lived, that he might try to be like them. She said they were total abstainers from sexual intercourse, alcohol and meat. He perceived that for him the way would be long and hard, yet resolved to set his feet upon it. He then became unwell through switching suddenly to a vegetarian diet. She owned that for her, too, that was the difficult point; she had not yet been able to renounce meat.

Meanwhile, his old life was still winding up. The case of Mary E. Olcott against Henry S. Olcott came up before the Supreme Court on 7 December. Mrs Olcott, having been sworn, said, 'I have not lived with the defendant as his wife since the 1st of January, 1873 and I have not cohabited with him since the discovery of the acts of adultery charged in the Complaint'. A Harry D. Walker, called for the plaintiff, then testified that he had known the defendant for eight or ten years, the plaintiff only since October 1872. On the evening of 2 May 1873, he and the defendant went to a theatre, and afterwards to a house of prostitution at 136 East 22nd Street. There they shared a bottle of wine in the waiting-room. Then the defendant went up the stairs with one of the women, who had descended to the waiting-room, and went with the woman into an upstairs room. The witness said that he himself waited below for a time, then went up the stairs and knocked on the door, to find if the defendant was ready to leave with him yet. Defendant was still dressing as he opened the door, and asked him to lend him money with which to pay the woman.[3]

Olcott did not defend, and on 28 December he received notification that judgment had been entered against him.

Probably it was a relief to have this over. He was free. Before concluding that Olcott was of habitual resort to prostitutes, one should notice the witness was his friend. It would be an odd friend who would accompany him to such a place, wait below and then tell his wife about it. It looks as though Olcott had asked the friend to come in order to be able to bear witness and enable his wife to divorce him. Olcott will later say he used to keep mistresses. Now that does not mean he patronised prostitutes. It may be that he had as a mistress a woman who was of respectable repute in the world, whose name it would be blackguardly to expose to citation in divorce proceedings if he did not intend, after them, to marry her. I would think it was to spare the name of some woman we have not heard of, yet to enable Mary to obtain her divorce against him, that he thought out the set-up in the brothel.

At any rate, Madame Blavatsky had nothing to do with it. Miss Williams, in her venomous book, represents Madame Blavatsky as enticing him from his wife,[4] and even Mr John Symonds, though without Miss Williams' venom, follows her, in writing, 'The details shall never be known; the Colonel omits in his *Old Diary Leaves* all mention of his wife, who, if she was a normal kind of wife, must have rued the day when the bulky figure of Madame Blavatsky appeared on the horizon.[5]

CHAPTER 18

Philadelphia

The turn of the year 1874–5 saw an ado in Spiritualist circles. In Philadelphia, a Mr and Mrs Nelson Holmes had been giving séances, at which there appeared to manifest a 'John King' and a 'Katie King'. Now an Eliza White had sold a newspaper the story that she had played the role of 'Katie'. Her confession was supported by a Dr Child, a member of the circle, yet was it true? One has to understand that there was an epidemic of Spiritualism in America at this time. Séances were advertised in the press along with conventional church activities. In as much as materialism was seen by the Masters as the chief bane of the nineteenth century, the new craze was to some extent encouraged by them, and the 'John King' who appeared in various mediums' circles, posing as a buccaneer of the reign of Charles II, was often a nature or elemental spirit employed by them to do this. On some occasions, however, he was the Master Illarion, who astrally projected in this disguise, and when Madame Blavatsky refers to 'John', she means sometimes the gnome or sylph and sometimes Illarion, the Greek or Cypriot Adept she had often met in the flesh.

But were the Holmeses mediums or frauds? Despite the fact that she had just slipped on a New York sidewalk and injured her knee, with what were to be serious consequences, Madame Blavatsky left for Philadelphia to investigate, and took rooms at 111 Girard Street. There, on 4 January 1875, Olcott joined her. He had brought mechanical aids for checking the phenomena; she used her clairvoyant sight. Her opinion one can gather from a letter she wrote to Professor Hiram Corson, who occupied the chair of Anglo-Saxon and English at Cornell University, Ithaca. He must have sought it, for we find her writing to him on 9 February, from Philadelphia, saying she blamed Mrs Holmes less than Dr Childs. Mrs Holmes, she thought, had at times mediumistic abilities, but she was not able to exhibit them always just when people were assembled, and so fell back upon trickery. Childs was in it only for money. Madame Blavatsky was furious, because people such as a 'poor old Robert D. Owen' had been given a hope of immortality by these séances; that hope was dashed by the exposé, and he now would never rise from his death-bed again. 'That is why I hate Childs so bitterly'.[1] In an *IMPORTANT NOTE*[2] in her hand found by Olcott after her death, she says that on one occasion, to 'save the situation', she had used her own power to bring 'out the faces of John and Katie King from the astral light, giving Mrs Holmes a terrible fright, for she knew that on that occasion the 'spirit' phenomenon was genuine'. She wrote again to Corson; she had been sent from her 'Lodge' to investigate western Spiritualism, and so far was not impressed. 'Alan Kardec and Flammarion, Andrew Jackson Davis and Judge Edmonds are but schoolboys trying to spell out their ABC . . .'[3] This letter is in the envelope of Betanelly & Co., Russian-American Commission Merchants, 3420 Sanson Street, Philadelphia, and postmarked February 26 1875.

On 24 March, Olcott returned, to join Madame Blavatsky at Betanelly's. He had gone from Havanna, New York, to Hartford, Connecticut, and thence come back to Philadelphia without stopping off at New York to collect his mail. He, therefore, went to the General Post Office and asked that any letters that might come which had been redirected from his office in New York to the Philadelphia Post Office might be delivered to him at 3425 Sanson Street.

Later that day, he was just going out when the postman arrived with letters, which he took straight from the postman's hand.

A letter normally carried two stamped dates, that imposed on the front by the office at which it was posted and that imposed on the back by the office at which it was received. A redirected letter should bear at least three frankings. These letters all bore the stamps of their origins, one, for instance, Louiseville and one abroad, but none of them bore a New York stamp. They had never been through New York. So who had crossed out the address of his New York office and re-addressed them? How had the Post Office officials – Post Official officials where? – known he would be at Philadelphia and re-addressed them? On opening them, he found that the margins and other blank spaces bore comments upon the writers and their motives, not always favourable, all in the same hand.

Though he would in the future witness many more marvellous phenomena, none impressed and mystified him more than this first.

CHAPTER 19

Betanelly

Olcott was aghast when Madame Blavatsky told him she was going to marry Michael C. Betanelly. He was a Georgian, who had written to Olcott after reading his articles in the *Graphic*. It was unfortunate that Vera had written to tell her sister that Nikifor Blavatsky was dead, depriving her of the answer in reply to his suit that she was married already. All she could say was that she did not wish to live as a married woman. To this he replied that he sought nothing but the privilege of watching over her in admiration of her intellectual grandeur. When Olcott expostulated that it would be folly to marry a man 'inexpressibly her inferior in mental capacity', younger than herself, whose mercantile business was not yet established, she said it was a misfortune she could not escape. Even if it was restful to have in him someone she could talk to in Russian, there is something here we are not going to understand. Her second marriage, like her first, remains a mystery. They were married on 3 April 1875, in the first Unitarian Church of Philadelphia, by the Rev. William Furness. Olcott did not attend the ceremony and is reported to have said it should have been two days earlier – on April Fools' Day, but on their return to Sanson Street he sat down with them to the wedding breakfast.

On 26 April she had to go to the Supreme Court of Suffolk County, at Riverhead, Long Island, for the hearing of her case against Madame Gerebko, which was heard before Judge Calvin E. Pratt. She was her own principal witness, and, giving her evidence in French, won her case, recovered $1146 (the whole of her investment in the poultry farm) and costs.

CHAPTER 20

Letters from Luxor

A book written by Olcott about his investigations into Spiritualist phenomena had now appeared, under the title *People from the Other World*. This brought him many letters, including one from Alexander N. Aksakoff, a Spiritualist of St Petersburg, asking if Madame Blavatsky, concerning whom it contained some paragraphs, would make a Russian translation of it which he could publish in St Petersburg.[1]

However, a note she wrote in their scrapbook reads:[2]

An attempt in consequence of orders received from T... B... through P., personating John King. Ordered to begin telling the public the truth about the phenomena and their mediums. And now my martyrdom will begin! I shall have all the Spiritualists against me in addition to the Christians and the Sceptics. Thy will, oh M, be done.

'T... B...' will be Tuitit Bey. 'P.' is a new initial, and must stand for the name given by the Masters to the elemental or sprite who called himself John King, a sort of Ariel of the Luxor Lodge. 'M.', of course, is Morya. In one way, it would be a relief to her no longer to have to prop up disagreeable Spiritualist phenomena, but she was right in apprehending that the Spiritualists would all now rend her. In retrospect, one can see it as unfortunate that she had been ordered to mix with Spiritualists, but the Masters must have thought that to redeem them was worth a try. Plainly, it was Morya who had now ordered her to make the break, and Luxor had accepted his decision.

There was a small paper, *The Spiritual Scientist*, edited and published from Boston, by Elbridge Gerry Brown, which seemed superior to other Spiritualist organs in that it showed the need for a philosophy. To encourage this idea, Olcott wrote a letter to the Editor. When the proofs came, he shuffled the paragraphs around to read better, then showed it to Madame Blavatsky, asking if she thought it should go out over his signature. She pointed out to him that the initial letters of the first words of the six paragraphs, 'The . . . Until . . . It . . . The . . . Instead . . . The . . .' spelled the name of an Adept, Tuitit. The letter was signed already. He had had no idea when he shuffled the paragraphs that it was under direction.[3]

Shortly after, Olcott received a letter in a black glazed envelope, addressed to him in gold ink:[4]

O.H.L., pour [sic] Messager Special
   Colonel E.S. Olcott,
      au No. 7 Beekman Street, New York,
      Etats Unis d'Amérique

aux bons soins de Madame Blavatsky
             C.O.S. R+

The address in French suggested postage from abroad, but why should it have been sent to him at his office c/o Madame Blavatsky who did not go to it? The letter within was headed 'The Brotherhood of Luxor', and addressed him as 'Brother Neophyte', beginning 'He who seeks us finds us. Try'. It was signed 'Tuitit Bey'.

On a copy of *The Spiritual Scientist* of 27 May 1874, Madame Blavatsky jotted:[5] 'At ... & Ill... passed thro' New York & Boston; thence thro' California and Japan back.' 'At...' was an Adept mentioned by Koot Hoomi, 'Ill...' was Illarion. Olcott, who craved to see an Adept, could therefore have done so, on the physical plane, but he was still at the stage of imagining high teaching always to come from the dead and disembodied.

Soon afterwards, letters from Serapis began to arrive; what seems to be the first opens,[6] 'Brother Henry – greetings' and bids him be courageous and hopeful.

Several of the following letters concern Madame Blavatsky's marriage, regarded by both Serapis and Illarion as a calamity. Betanelly was planning to flee the United States to avoid bankruptcy, leaving her responsible for his debts. The temptation to enter into this marriage came from something welling up, for which Serapis borrows from Bulwer-Lytton's novel, *Zanoni*, the term The Dweller. Very much later in life, Madame Blavatsky will explain to her pupils what The Dweller really is – not something external but within. As yet, she did not understand it herself, and was wrestling with it. Although Olcott was her pupil, Serapis had to ask him to help her:[7] 'The final result of the dreadful ordeal depends on her alone and on the amount of sympathy from her two brothers, Henry and Elbridge'.

Olcott is told that the cause rests:[8] 'entirely on the closest unity of you three – our Lodge's chosen triad'.

A Masonic Lodge always has three pillars, representing the three aspects of deity: power, love and creative mind.

The apparently intended third pillar, Elbridge Gerry Brown, however, was now hanging back, resisting and mistaking for conscience what was merely fear. There are occasions which wait for no man. Serapis wrote:[9] 'If he fails . . . the wisdom of the Lodge will provide otherwise'. This seems to mean that Helena and Henry will go on, and another will be found to accompany them.

Madame Blavatsky's ordeal had come to a head in a physical crisis. Unwisely attempting to move a piece of heavy furniture, she had hurt her knee again. Her whole leg had swollen up, with mortification around the knee. A Dr Pancost said the only way to save her life would be to have it amputated, but she felt she would rather die with two legs than live with one. She exerted her own will and slept for two nights with a white puppy, borrowed from a negro, which was persuaded to lie across her leg. This was a remedy mentioned 200 years before by Francis Bacon. In his *Historia Vitae et Mortis*, he explained that as the dog is a very 'hot' animal, especially while young, by cuddling a puppy to oneself one's deficiency is made good by the little companion's superabundance of vitality.

On the third day she was well. Soon after, she left Betanelly.

CHAPTER 21

The Theosophical Society

As they left Boston, Serapis expressed to Olcott anxiety lest Madame Blavatsky be tempted to return to Philadelphia, where Betanelly was still living. Serapis bade him take tickets for the two of them to New York and no further, to settle her there and help build around her a circle in which she would be appreciated:[1] '*Try* to have her settled by Tuesday eve – and wait'.

Olcott had perhaps been asking himself whether his own increasing proximity to Madame Blavatsky was entirely innocent and proper, for in another letter Serapis assures him:[2]

> . . . that where a truly spiritual love seeks to consolidate itself doubly by a pure, permanent union of the two, in its earthly sense, it commits no sin, no crime in the eyes of the great Ain-Soph, for it is but the divine repetition of the Male and Female principle – the microcosmal reflection of the first condition of Creation. On such a union angels may well smile. But they are rare, Brother mine, and can only be created under the wise and loving supervision of the Lodge . . . But even such must suffer, before they are rewarded.

This tender letter from the Master Serapis seems to sanction or recognise a spiritual marriage between Olcott and Madame Blavatsky, whilst warning of stresses and trials the relationship would have to undergo in its probationary stage.

He settled her at 46 Irving Place, very near his club, and, as bid, tried to draw to her people who would appreciate her gifts.

One of their guests was an Italian, Signor B., an artist who had been a Carbonaro. He and Madame Blavatsky were talking of Mazzini and Garibaldi, when he dropped the name of a Venetian gentleman. She started as though an electric current had passed through her, and looking him straight in the eyes asked, in Italian, 'What is it? I am ready'. Does this mean the Venetian was behind Mazzini and Garibaldi and she had performed missions for him? After Signor B. had gone, she told Olcott the Venetian was one of the great Masters, of the Brotherhood to which her Eastern teachers, the Copt Serapis and the neo-Alexandrine Greek Illarion, belonged. But if Signor B. knew a Master and possessed magical powers, the jealousy he began to show of Madame Blavatsky's powers disqualified him from becoming the third Founder.

William Quan Judge enters unnoticeably. Perhaps he had been one of those who called after Madame Blavatsky and Olcott first returned from Vermont. At 46 Irving Place, he was one of the regulars of their circle, without much note of his presence being taken. The son of Frederick H. Judge and Mary, née Quan, Methodists, he had been born in Dublin on 13 April 1851. He was therefore British by birth and of a Protestant minority in Catholic Ireland. When he was 7 years old he had some illness and the doctor even thought he was dead; on his unexpected recovery he showed interest in mystical subjects.

His mother died in giving birth to a seventh child, and when he was 13 he was brought by his father with the rest of the children on the *City of Limerick* to New York, where they landed on 14 July 1864. The family, which settled in Brooklyn, was not well off, but he finished his schooling and then, as he had to support himself, became a clerk in the office of George P. Andrews, attorney. On attaining his majority, he became, in April 1872, an American citizen, and a month later he was called to the State Bar of New York. Commercial law was his speciality. In 1873 he married Ella, née Smith, a partner more conformable to his family background than to his future. She was a Methodist, and seems not to have realised she was marrying a person who was becoming a mystic, for, though she remained with him to the end, she opposed the tendency he began so soon afterwards to exhibit to move out from Methodism into the Mysteries. So here he was, presumably unaccompanied, spending his evenings with Madame Blavatsky and Olcott at 46 Irving Place.

On 7 September 1875, at 46 Irving Place, one of their circle, George Henry Felt, gave a lecture on 'The lost canon of proportion of the Egyptians'. The subsequent discussion went on until after midnight. Afterwards, Olcott wished he had made a contemporary note of all who were there. They included a Dr and Mrs Hardinge-Britten; a New York judge, Signor Bruzzesi, and his wife; an English barrister and Freemason, Charles Carleton Massey; a bookseller, Charles Sotheran; and William Quan Judge. As the discussion deepened, Olcott scribbled on a piece of paper, 'Would it not be a good idea to form a Society for this kind of study?', and passed it to Judge, who was standing between Madame Blavatsky and himself. Judge passed it to Madame Blavatsky, and she nodded. This, surely, was the electric moment, the real moment of the foundation, though nobody took the time, and the name was not chosen till later.

Olcott put the suggestion to the company. Felt expressed enthusiasm, and, upon a motion of Judge, Olcott was elected to the chair.

There has been difference of opinion as to whether Judge was a principal Founder or not. Surely he was. His grooming had been short because he had been brought forward in haste to occupy the third point of the triangle left vacant by the hesitation of Gerry Brown. For a spiritual foundation, what is required is not a duo but a triad, to represent and transmit the three aspects of a spiritual downpouring; divine power, divine love and divine intellection. This trinity, in this foundation, was constituted by Henry, Helena and William. But, as in a Masonic Lodge, it is the second pillar beneath which the Master sits (because in this world to give pre-eminence to power would be dangerous), so Madame Blavatsky, who must in this context represent the second, was the inspirer.

As it was already late, the meeting was adjourned until the evening of 8 September, when Olcott was elected President. Judge was elected Secretary and Madame Blavatsky was elected a member, unencumbered by office. Other members were Charles Sotheran, Dr and Mrs Hardinge-Britten, Dr Charles Simmons, MD, H.D. Monachesi, Charles Carleton Massey, W.I. Alden (editorial writer on the *New York Times*), John Storer Cobb (an English barrister), George Felt, D.E. da Lara (a learned Portuguese Jew) and Henry J. Newton (a retired manufacturer).

On 13 September they met again to choose a name for the Society. Hermetic, Egyptological and Rosicrucian were suggested, yet did not seem right. Then they hit upon Theosophical.

Madame Blavatsky had arranged to spend the latter part of the month with the Corsons, at Ithaca, but returned for the next meeting, on 13 October. On 17 November, the Theosophical Society was constituted.

CHAPTER 22

The Lamasery

The frequency with which Madame Blavatsky changed her address suggests that she must have been living in furnished lodgings, and carrying only such possessions as could be packed into a bag. In November, she and Olcott took, briefly, suites of rooms one above the other at 433 West 34th Street. Here they extended their hospitality to an impoverished nobleman, the Baron de Palm, till he passed away in hospital, and, in accordance with his wishes, Olcott had to organise America's first cremation. Olcott's sister, Belle, came with her husband, Mr Mitchell, and children to take rooms above theirs, later returning to Orange.

In August 1876 Madame Blavatsky and Olcott jointly took an unfurnished apartment at 302 West 47th Street, for which they bought their own furniture. Apart from the usual offices, there were four rooms: her bedroom, his bedroom, a dining-room and a sitting-room, dominated by a noble chandelier.

A long central desk, across which they faced each other, was its essential feature, for Madame Blavatsky was now working with concentration on her first big book, begun in Philadelphia and continued at the Corsons'. Friends gave them a piano for her to play, an upright, on which stood images of the Buddha, a Siamese talapoin and curios. There were small, decorative Japanese cabinets, with their many drawers, and a Swiss cuckoo-clock. Olcott bought at a curiosity shop a stuffed lioness's head, with jaws open, which was strategically placed to impress visitors. He also bought a stuffed grey owl, which he perched on the top of the bookcase; small stuffed monkeys, which he made peep from above the curtain cornices; and toy lizards, which he stuck on the walls. In two of the corners he put palm-fronds, which touched the ceiling. He coiled a stuffed snake around the mirror over the mantlepiece. In one corner he stood a large stuffed baboon, which he decked with a collar, white cravat and a pair of his spectacles, pushing the manuscript of a lecture on Darwin's *Origin of Species* under one of its arms. This baboon he dubbed Professor Fiske, after an academic whose interpretation of the universe seemed to them narrowly materialistic. Madame Blavatsky contributed a live hen canary, Jenny, which she had bought in Philadelphia, and Olcott bought a mate for Jenny, Pip.

They breakfasted at 8.00 a.m., after which he went to his office and she sat down to write. Lunch he had at a restaurant near his office and she took alone, at home. When he came back from his office, they sat down to their evening meal. They had a maid to cook this, Madame Blavatsky not being domesticated. If for any reason the maid failed them, it was not she but he who stepped into the breach. He never got over having seen her try to cook an egg by placing it directly upon a coal in the fire. (He had probably taken for granted the housewifery of his mother and ex-wife, of middle-class American backgrounds, and did not quite appreciate that Madame Blavatsky, waited upon from childhood by serfs, had not been taught cookery or housewifery.) He taught himself to cook a little.

Guests were many, and long after the maid had gone home, someone would be sure to say it would be nice if they could have a cup of tea. Madame Blavatsky would agree, 'Yes, let's have some!' making no move towards the kitchen, as though it would just arrive. Olcott, after several times searching their shelves for milk and sugar without finding any, wrote out and pinned up a notice reading:

TEA

Guests will find boiling water and tea in the kitchen,
perhaps milk and sugar, and will kindly help themselves.

The question was what their many guests should call her. She hated, detested, loathed the title 'Madam', either by itself or coupled with Blavatsky; she did not like Blavatsky by itself, either, because it reminded her of a man she ought never to have married (although she had declined to change it for Betanelly). Neither did she invite anybody to use her Christian name. Olcott confesses he would have found it impossible to call her either Helena or Helen. It just would not have come naturally. From first to last, he called her 'Jack'. But other people could not be instructed to use this style. She asked them to call her 'H.P.B.'. This seemed oddly impersonal, like initials signing a newspaper article, but the initials, non-committal as to sex and status, were what she preferred.

It should be noted that to be at odds with one's name and style is to be so with some aspect of oneself. It was as if she had never really settled for being a woman and preferred it forgotten that nature had, inappropriately, made her one. Yet there is something married about her relationship with Olcott; a settled deep tie that she never formed with anybody else.

After their guests left, they settled down to their real work of the day, or rather night.

CHAPTER 23

The writing of *Isis Unveiled*

As soon as the last guest had gone, or directly after they had finished their evening meal if there were no guests, they sat down to the work they did together. They faced each other across the desk, and she would pass him the pages she had written during the day. This may have been the happiest period of her life. She was for the first time creative, engaged upon a big work, sharing it with a friend. Her pages were very untidy, several strips of paragraphs often pasted over ones they were to supplant.[1] Her command of English, though idiomatic, was not faultless; and he would read through, inserting punctuation marks, paragraphing, correcting awkward syntax and occasionally completely re-casting,[2] in which case he would read back to her, for her approval or criticism, the text he had substituted for hers.

Her manuscript was full of quotations, but where did they come from? They had a few books in the flat. Of some of these she made great use, Eliphas Levi's works, Jacolliot's twenty-seven volumes (on Krishna, Manu, the Bible in India and so on), Moor's *Hindu Pantheon*, Dunlop's *The Mysteries of Adonai*, *Sod* and *Spirit History of Man*, King's *Gnostics*, Jennings' *Rosicrucians*, Des Mousseaux's various attacks upon magic, etc., and the works of Max Müller, Thomas Huxley, J. Tyndall and Herbert Spencer.[3] These, because they were to hand, were frequently rummaged through, and references, with page numbers, were given in the normal way. But they had probably not more than a hundred books altogether, and though some of their friends brought her a few, which they lent her, these still did not add up to a great number. He did not think she went to any of New York's libraries.[4] She was indoors all the time, working round the clock, and could not be persuaded to leave the flat to walk, even for her health's sake. Naturally, she could, in the works to hand, have found quotations from other works, complete with the references she just took over; yet Olcott, working opposite her, was struck by the way she would be writing busily, then look up, shorten her sight as if to read an invisible book held or propped in front of her, then look down again to write, and up and down again, as if copying. The page that she afterwards passed over to him then did always bear a quotation. She told him she would see a book, open at the page required, 'in the astral light'.[5] She would ask him to go to some library where he could apply for the book in its physical form to check her quotation, and when he did so he came up against a difficulty only resolved when it dawned on him that the page numbers had sometimes been given to him by her in reverse. Thus, if she had given the reference as p.291 of some work and he did not find it there, it was worth looking at p.192, where it well might be. When he mentioned this to her, she said it was because in the astral light everything was presented as in a mirror. Though to read it involved some strain, as she became accustomed words became recognisable, but she sometimes forgot to turn numerals round.

She wrote in pencil, and had a habit of appropriating pencils, rubbers and penknives intended for their common use and putting them in her drawer. On one occasion he brought in two nice, soft pencils, made by Faber, giving her one and keeping one for his own use. In a short while she had mislaid hers and was asking him to lend her his. The thought flashed into his mind, 'If I lend her this nice pencil it will go into her drawer . . .'. It was only a thought, but as if she had read it, she dealt him a sarcastic look, reached out to the tray between them in which his was lying, handled it between her fingers for a second or so, and suddenly there were a dozen pencils, all of the same make, identical in every respect. He felt more shamed, more humbled than ever in his life, and felt the blood rushing to his temples.[6]

She had been writing in French when this happened, apparently under the close inspiration of someone who preferred to express himself in that language, for Olcott had afterwards to put it into English. He fancied that sarcastic look that was shot him came from a male eye, the eye of a being who was working through her and who had performed the phenomenon of the duplication of the pencils.

Much later, he was told that in duplications of this sort infinitesimally small particles of the object to be reproduced are detached and become the nucleus around which others are drawn from all that is in space, so that physical reproduction results.

If the duplication of the pencils was the work of Narayan, as she later called this helper, there were occasions when she seemed to perform something comparable unaided. Olcott's married sister, Belle, and her husband invited them up for Christmas to see the tree she had decked for the children. Madame Blavatsky felt she ought to have brought a present, and asked what the little boys would like. Belle said, 'A loud whistle'. Madame Blavatsky took from her pocket her bunch of keys, handled three of them, and in their place was hanging an iron whistle which she detached and gave Belle. Afterwards she told Olcott she would need to have duplicates made (presumably by a locksmith from his) as she had used the iron in hers to make the whistle.[7]

Olcott, seated opposite to her as she wrote, noticed that her handwriting was not always the same. The changes in writing corresponded with changes in the matter dealt with, and with a change in her look and manner. Particularly after she had left the room for a minute, she would come back looking like another person.[8] She was never entranced, yet said others wrote parts of the book through her. They were not, she assured him, the kind of 'spirit guides' mediums talked of, but living men, separated from them only by geography. Narayan, who had been 'in' her at the moment of the duplication of the pencils, lived in southern India. Sir Henry More, however, puzzled them both, because according to their books of reference he had died on 1 September 1687. They thought he must have become earthbound by his academic interests, astrally haunting libraries in which he continued the researches that had occupied him while he had his physical body, to the detriment of his spiritual evolution but to their benefit.[9] It was he who supplied the passages on Plato, and when he was writing Olcott did not have to correct the English. His comments on Jowett were caustic; he stigmatised the later Plato scholar as more interested in showing off his own knowledge than in Plato.

One evening, when it was time to begin, Olcott said to his chum 'Well, Old Horse, let us get to work!'[10] and found himself looking into the grave countenance of Narayan. It registered such surprise and startled dignity that the American was abashed. The image of two cart-horses, working together in traces, was evidently unfamiliar to the Indian who so strangely preferred to speak French.

There was another, very different entrant, who said he was by birth Hungarian. This was presumably he who would later be known as the Master Rákóczy. He shaded his eyes, and slightly turned down the lamp standing on the table, explaining that to enter a body was an exceedingly delicate process, involving fitting in with the circulation and breathing of the natural occupant, and the bright light on his eyeballs could push him out. Olcott thereupon turned the lamp right out and lit a burner in the chandelier overhead. The incomer at once placed a newspaper over his head, explaining that was worse.[11] (There are great mysteries concerned with this character, a key to which I have tried to provide in my book, *The Comte de Saint-Germain*.)

When some years later Olcott was told about the chakras, or wheels of subtle force within the body, he thought he understood that incident. The single jet of bright light would have been just above the coronal or bramarandra chakra, beneath the parietal bones.

Sometimes not only her voice but also her hair changed. Her own was a fair, crinkled floss, yet sometimes it went black and straight. She let not only him but Belle and Miss Emily Kislingbury, an Englishwoman who had come from London to meet them, cut these black locks from her head. Olcott preserved two, both coarser than her own, one more so than the other. She said one was Egyptian, the other Hindu.[12] The locks cut from her head retained their blackness and straightness; those that remained in her head reverted to their natural character.

Sometimes, as she wrote, Olcott would see her tugging an invisible moustache and twirling invisible side-whiskers.[13] These seemed to belong to the Master who had the strongest link with her. When she became disturbed by one of her inner tumults, none of the other Masters could come near her, but this one took no notice. If he was coming in, he came, and simply settled her.

One summer evening, when after they had finished their dinner there was still so much light in the sky they had not yet lit the gas, she was sitting looking out of the window. He was standing at the mantlepiece, not specially noticing her, when she said, 'Look, and learn!'[14] He looked, and saw a mist rise from her head and shoulders. This formed itself into the head and shoulders of a man, an Indian, in a white turban, with a moustache and side-whiskers. Then the figure vanished. She remained still for a minute or so, then gave a sigh.

He asked her to explain. She said she could not. She could only show him things.

When she played the piano, he was surprised at the power of her performance. She mentioned that at one point she had made a tour in Europe, giving concert performances under the name of Madame Clara; but he felt that she did not play for an audience but inwardly. It seemed to him that the very angels of music were pouring forth their harmonies. She was not what is called a beautiful woman, yet as he watched her hands passing over the keys they seemed to him beautiful.[15]

There was also phenomenal music – chimes of bells that would come as from very far off, then move about the room, from here to there. Imperiously, she would stretch out a hand and the sound would come from where she pointed, as if by command. He and others filled a number of glasses with water, to different levels, so that when struck they emitted notes of different pitch. These they arranged in a row down the table. Then they tapped them at random, challenging her to produce in space the notes they produced from the glasses. She always succeeded.[16]

He asked her to explain how she did it. She rejoined by asking him to explain to her how he whistled. He began to say that he pursed his lips and blew air through them. Then he realised that was not the whole of the art. He just *thought* a tune, and it came out without his knowing how he made it do so. She said that was how it was with the bells.

The writing of *Isis Unveiled* was a heavy physical labour. She seemed to have no sense of how to arrange her material so that it formed an organic structure. It was all passages about this and that, unorganised. Apart from correcting the English, Olcott endeavoured to give it a structure. He never interfered with anything he recognised as coming from a Master, but only with what he felt confident was from H.P.B. In ripping some passages from the places in which he found them, and putting them in what seemed to him more suitable places, he could have removed parts of quotations from her source references. This only occurred to him when the Spiritualist, Emmette Coleman, alleged that not all her quotations were acknowledged. It was Olcott who divided the whole mass into two books, which he labelled 'Science' and 'Theology', putting into the one all parts which seemed designed to answer the materialistic science typified by Huxley and Fiske, and into the other those which set out the differences between Theosophical teachings and the Church. It was he who made the table of contents with the descriptive sub-headings for each chapter of Book I, and Miss Kislingbury did the like for Book II.

One of their friends was Professor Alexander Wilder, whom Olcott had known from before the rebellion. Of all their visitors, it was he who attached least importance to Madame Blavatsky's exhibitions of phenomena, the authenticity of which he took for granted, and most to philosophical discussions with her, 'one long leg on the chandelier and the other on the mantlepiece'.[17] He wrote some notions on the value of Greek and Hebrew names which she included in the text with acknowledgement of his help. Now he wrote the introductory chapter, 'Before the veil', but declined to sign his name to it. He did not, however, write the glossary which ends the introductory chapter, but prevailed upon her to make it. It was Wilder, also, who, for a fee, made the index.

The proof-reading was appalling. Madame Blavatsky kept altering the text, adding to it, and rearranging and inserting sections, even after it was in plate. The publisher, J.W. Bouton, was most concerned, because of the augmentation of expense. Olcott received a letter from him dated 17 May 1877, saying the alterations had already cost $280.80, and:[18]

> by the time the book appears it will be handicapped by such fearful expense that each copy of the first 1000 will cost a great deal more than we shall get for it, a very discouraging state of affairs to begin with. The cost of composition of the first volume (with stereotyping) amounts to $1,359.69 and this is for one volume alone, mind you, without paper, press work or binding.

They had always thought that the book would be called *The Veil of Isis*. Only when it was in proof was the title changed to *Isis Unveiled*.

Isis Unveiled appeared in September 1877 and, to the surprise and gratification of J.W. Bouton, the entire first edition sold out within ten days of publication.

CHAPTER 24

Isis Unveiled

Though the form of *Isis Unveiled* may be discursive, it is not impossible to discern the theme. Book I, *Science*, looks in the first chapter at Darwin's *Origin of Species* and Thomas Huxley's *Physical Basis of Matter*. Madame Blavatsky does not object so much to the former as to the latter. All Darwin says really is that the many species have evolved from a few. This perhaps we can accept, if not in the detail in which he works it out, yet to the extent of accepting the idea there is evolution. He does not presume to say where the first few species came from, and this modest omission leaves a door open, through which spirit can enter.[1] Huxley closes it with his assertion that all came from protoplasm. This – which is more than Huxley can know – firmly shuts out the divine.[2] We are now suffering from a plague of scientists come in his wake who are 'soul-blind'.[3] At a certain stage, intellect develops at the expense of clairvoyant and psychic faculties possessed by animals (she is revolted by the notion that animals have no souls)[4] and by simple people. Without loss of intellectual capacity, these clairvoyant and psychic faculties need to be regained if we are to become wise. She examines many of the odd happenings related in the Bible and other ancient writings, and asserts that they are neither necessarily fictitious nor supernatural (which nothing can be), but explicable in terms of a science different from modern materialistic science. In Huxley's work she finds a quotation from David Hume,[5] 'A miracle is a violation of the laws of nature'. To this her reply, extended over 628 pages, is: quite; but there are laws of nature you do not understand.

In Book II, *Theology*, she challenges the Christian claim to unique revelation, and shows how its symbols have developed from those of earlier religions, particularly the Egyptian. Beneath every popular religion lies a wisdom doctrine, which is always the same. The eternal essence, ineffable, unknowable, upon which all speculation is vain, is sexless. There is no polarity, for the two poles are in one. When, periodically, it opposes its poles, a universe is formed. The feminine pole, the true Virgin Mother, is called in the Egyptian religion Isis. She from whom all the nebulae and stars were formed has become in the Christian Church identified with the mother of a particular prophet. Some representations of the Virgin Mary show stars dotted as gold points about her head, while the Madonna lilies she holds are but the European variants of the lotus sacred to Isis. That is how her child becomes the Son of God and Osiris and Horus become the Father and Son.[6]

For having turned Isis into the mother of Jesus, she blames principally St Cyril of Alexandria, though St Irenaeus, Tertullian, St Jerome and St Augustine played their part. Her sympathies are with Marcion, Origen, Plotinus, Porphyry and Iamblichus.

There have been good reasons why the schools of deeper knowledge have kept their doctrine for initiates who have passed the moral tests required for entry. Yet sometimes the prudence has seemed excessive, which has prompted a self-sacrificial individual to give out more to the many. Anybody who says, 'The Kingdom of Heaven is within you' is rendering the priests dispensable. There is a karma of divulgation.[7] (She may have sensed here what she and her own teachers who had sent her out as their missionary were drawing on their heads.)

It is through Buddhism that she sees the wisdom-doctrine shine most clearly. 'Buddhi' means light of wisdom, and when she speaks of Buddhism she does not of necessity refer to any text, for there were Buddhas before our Buddha, Gautama Buddha, as there is Maitreya Buddha to come. What she always means is the wisdom-doctrine as she has understood it from the Masters by whom she has been taught. She deplores the notion, derived from bad translations and unintuitive European orientalists, that the Buddhists' goal is extinction of their souls; phrases such as 'absorption into Deity' or 'reunion with the universal soul' do not mean annihilation; a spirit reaching such a state becomes a *part* of the infinite *whole*, but never loses its individuality for all that. The word '*absorbed*' . . . must necessarily mean intimate union, not annihilation.[8]

I will offer her an image, which I think she would accept. On my lap is curled my little cat, Bambina. The small lithe body that darted through the garden when the dusk was falling and I called her from the perils of the night has come to me. There is naught but the quietest breathing. She is in my bosom, one with me, her mother. Yet she has not ceased to be.

CHAPTER 25

Nathalie Blavatsky

One unexpected result of the publication of *Isis Unveiled* was that it drew the attention of the Dr A.L. Rawson who had known Madame Blavatsky during her first visit to Cairo. He was now in New York, and wrote:[1]

> Only last week a letter passed under my eyes containing enquiries . . . written in Aden, Arabia: Is the Mme. Blavatsky (who wrote *Isis Unveiled*) the real Madame Blavatsky who was so well known in Cairo, Aden and elsewhere a few years since? For if she is, she must have revived, for the real Mme. Blavatsky died at her friend's residence six or seven miles from that city in 1868. The real Mme. Blavatsky was a Russian lady of family and fortune, and of considerable literary ability and reputation . . .
> There comes upon the scene, as if by magic, Mme. Lydia de Pashkoff, a Russian Countess, member of the Geographical Society of France . . . Mme. Pashkoff fortunately knew the Mme. Nathalie Blavatsky who died at Aden, and also knows, and has known for many years, Mme. H.P. Blavatsky, having met her in Syria, in Egypt and elsewhere in the East.

Countess Lydia Alexandrevna Pashkoff was a woman of some distinction, the author of several books on travel; it will be remembered that it was her telegram that informed H.P.B., then in Cairo, that Metrovitch was ill at Ramleh and that later she and Madame Blavatsky joined caravans for a while in the Lebanon. It is fortunate indeed that she informed Rawson that she had also known the Madame Nathalie Blavatsky who died in Aden, thus confirming the latter as a person who really existed.

Olcott's enthusiastic account of Madame Blavatsky in his *People from the Other World* had provoked the jealousy of other mediums. On 5 March 1876, a Boston newspaper, *The Sunday Herald*, printed a very long letter from Dr G. Bloede of New Brooklyn, in which he cited extracts from letters written to himself by Daniel Dunglas Home, the controversial medium of chequered career. Home, transparently, had been riled by passages in Olcott's book extolling Madame Blavatsky; and he challenged Olcott's assertion that one of the Eddy brothers handed her the buckle with which one of her father's decorations had been pinned, and which had been buried with him. Russian decorations, as he had been assured by a friend, Baron de Meyendorff, were not buried in the grave but returned to the government. Olcott's text may have been confusing,[2] and had probably not been submitted to Madame Blavatsky; but his illustration, on p.357, shows a buckle and also an impression, derived from a portrait of Colonel Hahn, of how it would have looked with the ribbon from which the medal depended threaded through it. Madame Blavatsky, replying to the letter, pointed out that it was obvious from the illustration that the buckle only which was the object of Olcott's story.

But how had Meyendorff been brought in? Because she was a foreigner, Olcott seems to have thought he had to vouch for her antecedents, and has stated that he had persuaded her to show him her passport, the certified copy of her father's will which had come from Russia and personal letters addressed to herself, one from Prince Ferdinand W. (Wittgenstein) and one from Baron M. (Meyendorff).[3] It was a mistake on her part to have let Olcott see the letter from Meyendorff, since he was not a friend, but she had probably said to herself that at any rate it was proof of identity. Unfortunately, it was this mention of Baron M. which had given Home the idea of consulting Meyendorff, and his letter to Bloede went on to say, 'He knew her to his sorrow in 1858'. Bloede commented, 'If Mr Home's opinion of that eminent foreigner differs from that of Colonel Olcott in regard to her apparent mediumship . . . one must not forget the fact that he knew her in 1858'.

Bloede's letter to the *Boston Herald* has long been taken as proof that Madame Blavatsky, contrary to her own statement, knew Home in 1858; but if one reads the lines from Home cited, one sees that it is Meyendorff who (Home says) knew Madame Blavatsky in 1858; it is Bloede who has made his final quip upon the basis of a false reading of the text he himself cited.

But it was in any case not our Madame Blavatsky but Nathalie Blavatsky with whom Meyendorff had an affair. In an age when Christian names were not used except within the family or between persons very close, Home might be pardoned for supposing any Madame Blavatsky mentioned in any context must be the Madame Blavatsky of whom Olcott wrote – especially as, Russianised from the Ukranian 'Blavatko', it was probably a unique name. Yet Meyendorff obviously knew the difference very well indeed. Why did he allow confusion to arise? We shall come back to that.

First we ought to look at the career of Home (pronounced Hume). It began with his arrival in England in April 1855, when he gave a series of séances in Ealing. In 1866 he went to Florence, where those who came to his séances included Lord Lindsay and Robert and Elizabeth Barrett Browning. She thought his phenomena genuine, but Robert Browning could not bear him and made him into the fraudulent creep of his poem *Mr Sludge, 'the Medium'*. In Rome he was converted to the Catholic Church and said he did not expect the spirits to use him as a channel again. He moved in June to Paris, but gave no séances. In February 1857, however, the Emperor Napoleon III sent an emissary to enquire whether his powers had yet returned to him. The promise he must have made on his admission to the Church of Rome instantly forgotten, he gave a series of private séances to the Emperor and the Empress Eugénie. (Apart from the fact that Madame Blavatsky was then in India, she was never a member of this Court circle.) In September, somebody set in circulation a 'report' that Home had, under the table, removed his sock and put his bare foot into the Emperor's hand as being the hand of the great Napoleon I. However that may be, Napoleon III was always troubled by a rumour that he was the child of his mother's adultery with a Dutch admiral, and so had no title to his throne.[4] It may have been for this very reason that he sought the assistance of Home, hoping the medium would be able to act as a channel through which Napoleon I would materialise and assure him of his legitimacy. The Empress is said to have expressed herself immeasurably shocked by the 'foot' story, and we do not know what the Emperor thought.

In January 1858, Home went to Holland,[5] gave séances for the Queen, and left on 5 February for Brussels, where he was taken ill and returned to see his doctor in Paris; the doctor recommended a return to the sun of Italy. He arrived in Turin later in the month, then went on to Rome, where he met a Russian girl, to whom he became engaged. He returned with her to her relatives in Paris, only to find he had to go to Scotland to fetch his birth certificate. Thence he returned only just in time to travel with the family to St Petersburg for the wedding, on 1 August. He gave séances to the Czar and stayed through the winter. Madame Blavatsky arrived in Pskoff at Christmas (6 January 1858 by our calendar), to stay in the bosom of her family.

Home mentions a date in January 1859 when 'a friend, Baron de Meyendorff'[6] was present. Meyendorff was of the Czar's circle, but Home may have known him earlier, since his memoirs contain a reference to dining in Paris in 1857 with a Baroness de Meyendorff,[7] perhaps the Baron's wife.

Does her role show any light? A hostile biographer of H.P.B., Bechhofer Roberts, writes that the sister-in-law of Baron Nicholas Meyendorff supplied him with information. He was 'an ardent spiritualist and a friend of Douglas Home' and:[8]

> According to the Baroness he fell under H.P.B.'s influence after her return to Russia in 1858, and began a liaison with her. She bore a son, whom she assured the Baron was his. He and his brother doubted this assurance – presumably suspecting Metrovitch's paternity – but they undertook to provide for the child, who was sickly and a hunchback.

I wonder why Bechhofer Roberts assumes that a man who has been unfaithful to his wife necessarily tells her and the rest of his family the truth about it. Apart from the fact that Madame Blavatsky only returned to Russia in January 1859, she was for the next several years with her family at Pskoff, Rougodevo and Tiflis, her every move chronicled, and such an affair would have been impossible. It is, however, possible that Baroness Meyendorff, the wife, became aware that the Baron was paying maintenance for a child, perhaps when Madame Helena Blavatsky's letter about the child's death arrived. The Baron, trying to lessen his offence, may have suppressed his affair with Nathalie Blavatsky in Paris and represented to his wife that Helena Blavatsky was the mother, putting the paternity on to Metrovitch. Madame Helena Blavatsky's letter to Meyendorff, telling him the child was dead, by falling into the hands of his wife could have given her the wrong idea – and so given him an idea as to where he could shift the paternity.

Madame Blavatsky relieved her feelings by writing in the scrapbook:[9]

> It ought to be remembered that Mr D.D. Home who was twice tried for swindling . . .
> never – knew or even *saw* me in my whole life, but has certainly gathered most carefully
> all the dirtiest gossip possible about Nathalie Blavatsky.

This gives the lie to the reporting of an interview with her in *The Daily Graphic* of 17 November 1884. This contains innumerable mistakes, for instance, as in 'my grandmother, Mme. Bagration, she left me a fortune'. Princess Bagration-Muhransky was not one of her grandmothers, though certainly she was the godmother who left her a fortune. Then, in the story of the shipwreck, Spetsai or Spezza and Nauplia, which are both in Greece, have become Spezia and Napoli, which are both in Italy. These, obviously, are mistakes of hearing by the reporter which Madame Blavatsky would have corrected had she been given the chance to see the report before it went into print. More serious is the statement put into her mouth 'Home converted me to Spiritualism'. There is a type of reporter who will put things into one's mouth. Even if Madame Blavatsky made a protest to *The Daily Graphic*, it may have gone unheeded.

Home's life's itinerary shows he cannot have known Madame Blavatsky, and it is with good reason that she is not mentioned in his own memoirs or in the biography of him by his second wife. The assertion in the *Memoirs* of Count Witte,[10] that she was 'the right hand of the celebrated medium of the sixties, Hume' is false – as is the statement that she 'entered Cairo in a wet skirt', having swum from the wreck, which would be over 500 miles. That Count Witte, a minister in the government of the Czar who has been described as 'the most powerful politician in Russia', should begin his otherwise sober memoirs with a ludicrously inaccurate and libellous account of his first cousin and her morals may seem unlikely; the *Memoirs* were published posthumously, from text not wholly in his hand, and with posthumous memoirs there is always the suspicion they may have been spiced.

After Madame Blavatsky's death, Rawson would write:[11] 'Mme. Blavatsky was the victim of a cruel slander for many years and compelled me to silence when a word might have cleared her.'

Happily, Countess Pashkoff, who knew Nathalie, was now in New York. The *New York World* of 24 April 1879 carries an article by David A. Curtis, describing a dinner-party given by Olcott and Madame Blavatsky at the Lamasery, at which Countess Pashkoff was a guest. The two Russian ladies were talking with each other when Countess Pashkoff explained to the others gathering round them,[12] 'I was once travelling between Baalbeck and the river Orontes . . . and in the desert I saw a caravan. It was Madame Blavatsky's. We camped together'.

CHAPTER 26

A glimpse into Morya's background

Madame Blavatsky sent a copy of *Isis Unveiled* to her Aunt Nadyezhda, hoping it would not shock her too much and assuring her she would find in it nothing against her beloved Greek Orthodox Church. Apparently answering questions, she replies that she has known her Master for about twenty-six years, having first met him in London in 1851; he came, she tells her aunt, in the train of the 'Premier of Nepaul', and came again later with the Queen of Oudh. He also visited America once and gave there some talks on Buddhism. It is unfortunate she does not tell us under what name he did this, but she does give us some further glimpses of his background:[1]

> He is a Buddhist, but not of the dogmatic Church, but belonging to Shivabhavika, the Nepaul *so-called Atheists* (?!!!) . . .
> He who could be on the throne, according to the rights of birth, renounced all, to live quite unknown, and gave all his enormous income to the poor.

It had been British policy during one period to take over principalities considered to be ill administered, and the dethronement of the royal family of Oudh has been considered by historians to have precipitated the Indian Mutiny. Nevertheless, the royal family of Oudh was Muslim, which might seem to make intermarriage with Rajputs unlikely, though some Rajputs are Muslims. There does not stand out amongst those who would have been in the line of succession to Oudh a figure who could have become known to us as Morya. There are many Rajputs in Oudh, but they are mainly wealthy landowners. There are also Rajputs in Nepal, but Britain did not dethrone the royal house of Nepal. Has Madame Blavatsky got something wrong? Not necessarily. Oudh lies sandwiched between Nepal to the north east and Rajputana to the south west. That opens up another range of possibilities to which we shall find a clue later.

We have Madame Blavatsky's letters to Nadyezhda only in English translation made by a Dutchman from a translation into French made by a Pole, and she is made to refer to Morya throughout as her 'host'. This, I feel sure, is a mistranslation of the Russian word '*xosyayin*' or '*khosyayin*'. It means the lord or master of a household, the owner of a place, the boss. Like the French '*patron*', it has its downward extension to designate the host of a tavern, but also an extension upward as the informal title of the person who gives the orders, the chief, even a great chieftain. I wrote to Adyar asking if they could send me a photostatted copy of one of the letters so that I could see the original of this word in Madame Blavatsky's Russian handwriting. This did not arrive, but in a later letter from Morya to Sinnett, giving him a message for Nadyezhda, I notice the phrase[2] 'Tell her I (her niece's Khosyayin) . . .'.

Physically, Madame Blavatsky was after *Isis Unveiled* not the woman she had been. She had turned the scales at 17 st 7 lbs, and though this may in part have been caused by the lack of exercise while cooped up writing, Olcott's description of folds hanging round her ankles and wrists suggests what was later formally diagnosed, dropsy.

The door of the canaries' cage was kept open, and Pip and Jenny used to fly about the room. During the writing of *Isis Unveiled*, Jenny would wait on the desk, watching. Madame Blavatsky would shear off thin strips from the passages gummed over ones they replaced as though they were being specially prepared for Jenny; the bird would then fly with them to the gas-tube supplying the chandelier, where she was building a nest. Another building material was the Turkish carpet, with its fringed ends. She would stand and lean back to brace herself to pull the threads out, and Madame Blavatsky and Olcott had not the heart to stop her. Pip trilled his encouragement from above, and the arrival of little ones was expected by their human friends. Yet the weeks went by. At last, Olcott placed a chair upon the table and, while Madame Blavatsky held it steady, climbed up on it and looked in the nest. It was empty. Madame Blavatsky said sadly, 'Jenny has been sitting on her illusions.'[3]

Then, one sorrowful day, Jenny was found lying on the floor of the cage on her back. Olcott took her out and gave her into Madame Blavatsky's hand. Madame Blavatsky kissed and stroked her and made magnetic passes, trying to restore her vitality. Then, as the gasps only grew fainter, she opened her dress and put her in her bosom, against her heart. Olcott writes:

> The granite face of H.P.B. melted into tenderness . . . there was a last gasp and flutter of the birdie's heart, and then? Then, sharp and sweet and clear in the Akasha near us, rang out a fairy bell, the requiem of the passing life; and H.P.B. wept for her dead bird.

Bouton offered her an advance of 5,000 dollars if she would unveil Isis a little further, but she told him her teachers did not wish to give out anything more for the moment.

One day she told Olcott the Master wished him to do some business for him in another town. It sounded as if it would take weeks, and he was reluctant because of the amount of money he would lose through being out of New York for so long. She asked how much would he lose? He said $500 for each month. The dollar, during the years 1876 to 1879, stood at between 4.83 and 4.85 to the pound. That makes $500 nearly £100, but that has to be multiplied by 20 to bring it to the purchasing power of the beginning of the 1980s. Olcott was therefore at least a £25,000 a year man. But then, he was paying £8,000 in alimony, plus meeting the cost of the education and maintenance of his sons. Madame Blavatsky reflected and said he was not a pledged chela and Master could not order him to neglect his own business.

Nevertheless, he went. On his return, he called at his bank and asked to see how his account stood. A statement was brought to him. He saw two credits, each of $500 dollars, which he did not understand, and in case they had been entered in error asked where they came from. He was told both had been paid over the counter in cash by the same person, an unusually tall man, with brown skin, long, black, flowing hair and very piercing eyes. He had asked the receiving teller to fill in the deposit ticket for him as he was not sufficiently familiar with the language to understand what he had to write where.[4]

CHAPTER 27

Letters to Chintamon

It was by chance that an acquaintance told Olcott that a Hindu, Mooljee Thackersey, whom he had met on a voyage, was now a member of the Bombay branch of a society called the Arya Samaj. Olcott wrote to Thackersey, and gathered from him that this was an organisation for teaching the wisdom in the Hindu scriptures, of which the head was Swami Dyanand; the head of the Bombay branch was Hurrychund Chintamon. This is why we find Madame Blavatsky writing letters to the latter. For some reason, both she and Olcott had jumped to the conclusion that these people must be in communion with their own Masters in Tibet; this was not the case, but it explains the level on which she attempts to discuss things with Chintamon. On 9 February 1878, she asks him to send:[1]

> a good photograph of either a Fakhir or a Sanyasi sitting self-supported in the air . . .
> Learned Brahmins believe, no more than you or me, that devils or angels have to do with the marvellous phenomena exhibited by the fakhirs. But how are they produced? I *know*; perhaps you do also, and if so, you know it is no jugglery . . .

She refers to an article by a Professor Zollner, which she sends him, concerning what he calls a 'fourth dimension', and says what is involved is not quite that, but rather Akasa:

> It is eternal motion, the Narayan or spirit of Brahma moving on the waters of chaos . . ., or matter: It is not a dimension but a quality, the direct effect of spiritual force upon matter, and – it does exist. And, *if science proves it to exist*, then the permeability of matter (without denial) or passage of matter through matter must also be accepted.

This has interest in respect of a phenomenon she herself will later produce. She wanted the photograph in order to convince both materialistic scientists and Christians that the apparently impossible was neither stunt nor miracle, and also 'no transgression of natural law', if that law be understood.

Chintamon had apparently no such photograph to send her, but must have replied with a lamentation for the woes of India, for we find her writing next, on 4 May:

> What you say of the 'deplorable condition' of the native princes under your bastard [?] Empire gives me great pain. Had I the secret guidance of things, I think I should contrive to have the Russians drive the English into the sea, and then the Hindoos unite to a man and kick the Russians over the crest of the Himalayas in their turn, with the Musselmans in their company . . . and yet, much as I hate the English . . . I would far rather see them in India than my sweet Greek-Orthodox countrymen.

Very much later, after they had parted in bitterness, Chintamon would put it about that in a letter she had written him from New York she had urged him to help throw the British out of India in favour of her countrymen. This must be the passage referred to, but it does not bear this out. It is he who has been complaining about British rule. She makes a joke of it, and says wouldn't it be nice to throw everybody out; then adds, seriously, that, whatever may be the faults of the British, she would rather see them remain in India than have her countrymen in (Greek Orthodox is the correct name for what is sometimes called, in respect of Russia, the Russian Orthodox Church.) Not too much importance should be given to the words 'I hate'. She often used emotional as well as jokey language. The whole is a put-off. Couched, to humour him, in amusing language, it is nevertheless a warning that she will not help him bring the Russians into India.

In her letter of 9 May, she reveals that, contrary to received opinion, she could read Sanskrit a little, though not well:

We are all much disappointed that you should have sent us the rules of the Arya Samaj without English translation, as not one of our members reads or understands Sanskrit . . . Having devoted a whole day to decipher your rules I think I understand well enough to make myself a correct idea of them, and yet notwithstanding Col. Olcott's desire I *cannot* take upon myself the responsibility of giving forth your ideas, which after all I may have misunderstood more than once.

Her letters of 22 May and 21 August are largely about C.C. Massey and Miss Kislingbury, President and Secretary of the London Lodge:

C.C.M. is what you might call a *congenital mystic* and I feel sure that if Pundit Dyanand will write to him any request he will joyfully comply . . . Another true, loyal heart is Emily Kislingbury . . . her motives and character are as pure as gold . . . My devotion, love and enthusiasm for India has fired them both . . . but unfortunately I am but a white-faced idiot not a Hindu . . .

They both need help. For want of encouragement and teaching, Miss Kislingbury could still turn Catholic, whilst: 'Brother Massey is an uncompromising, devoted Spiritualist. He imagines that everyone must believe in *Ghosts* as he does, otherwise he takes them for skeptics and – drops them.'

What they needed was the philosophy the East could offer. She suggests that Chintamon should write each of them a letter – she drafts possible texts – and sign it with his name in Sanskrit. This may seem to him childish, but she feels sure the 'mystery' it will create will deepen the impression made by the communication.

It cannot be denied that in thinking out this little stratagem she is treating Massey and Miss Kislingbury a little bit as though they were children, needing to be coaxed with a touch of mystery. Massey was a barrister, so he must have been a sharp-witted man of the world, which would not, however, have prevented his seeming to her childish in the way he approached the occult. Just as she had, in the beginning, humoured Olcott's Spiritualistic supposition that the teachers must be people who had died, until he grew up sufficiently to be told that they were living; so she was humouring Massey's supposition that teaching must come from somebody with a brown face by having Chintamon write to him what she could perfectly well have written herself, so that he might be impressed by an Indian postage stamp and a signature in Sanskrit. Nevertheless, her attitude to what she evidently considers her spiritual charges is obviously one of pastoral care.

At one moment, she and Olcott had been so enthusiastic about the Arya Samaj they thought to merge the Theosophical Society with it. Olcott had been willing to stand down as President in favour of Swami Dyanand. It was the receipt of the rules that changed their minds. To have received a set of rules must in itself have been a surprise. In July of the previous year, Madame Blavatsky had written to her Aunt Nadyezhda, 'Arya Samaj has no religious dogma nor rules'.[2] Now, not only were there rules, but when the Sanskrit had been understood what emerged was that the organisation was narrowly Hindu. Moreover, exception was taken by Dyanand to their being simultaneously in correspondence with Bombay Parsees and Buddhists in Ceylon. The Theosophical Society being eclectic, it was now seen inappropriate that the societies be merged.

CHAPTER 28

Last days in New York

The year 1878 saw two changes in Madame Blavatsky's legal status. On 25 May her divorce from Betanelly was finalised. Judge had acted as her counsel.[1] On 8 July, her American naturalisation came through. Olcott went with her to the Supreme Court, where she had to forswear allegiance to the Russian Emperor and swear loyalty to the United States constitution; she was made a citizen of the United States and came home with her papers.[2]

Her feeling for America was genuine. The occasional observations of its history and peoples which filter through *Isis Unveiled* show an interest that is sympathetic; but by the time her papers came through she was already hankering to go to India again, longing as always to see or at least be nearer to her Master. Olcott was planning to go with her. He had been determined by an occult experience.

They had worked as usual until late, together, and then they retired to their respective bedrooms. Before going to bed, Olcott sat for a while in a chair, reading a book, Stephens's *Travels in Yucatan*. His chair was not far inside the door, to the left of it. He thus had the door on his right, and though he had his shoulder slightly turned away, it could hardly have opened without his noticing its movement, or indeed hearing anything. What he became aware of, in the corner of his right eye, was the gleam of something white. He turned his head to see, and in his astonishment dropped his book.

Towering over him was a tall oriental, in white garments except for an amber turban. From under it his black hair hung to his shoulders. His beard was parted on his chin vertically, Rajput fashion, the ends twisted up and carried back over the ears; his eyes were piercing yet benignant, the eyes of a judge, but yet of a father.[3]

> He was so grand a man, so imbued with the majesty of moral strength, so luminously spiritual, so evidently above average humanity, that I felt abashed in his presence, and bowed my head and bent my knee as one does before a god or god-like personage. A hand was lightly laid on my head, a sweet though strong voice bade me be seated, and when I raised my eye the presence was seated in the other chair . . .

This was on the other side of a small table, now between them.

The visitor said it rested with Olcott whether they should meet often, as co-workers for the good of mankind. A great work was to be done and Olcott had the right to share in it if he wished. A mysterious tie, the Indian told him, bound him to H.P.B., a tie which could not now be explained to him but which could never be broken, however much at times it might become strained. He told him things both about her and about himself, too deeply personal for publication. He stayed for perhaps half an hour, perhaps an hour. Then at last he rose. As Olcott wondered at his great height and at a kind of internal shining within him, a soft gleam as of an inner light, the thought suddenly entered his mind, 'What if this be but a hallucination . . .?' He wished some tangible object could be left with him as proof that the visitation had been real. The Master, reading his thought, unwound his turban and laid it on the table, benignantly saluted him and – was gone. He had not gone out by the door. He had vanished. The turban, however, had not vanished. It was still on the table. He took it into his hand and admired the embroidery in yellow silk floss, evidently done by hand.

He had long wanted to go to India, but had not felt he should leave America before his sons had entered their professions; nor had he seen how he could maintain even himself, let alone keep up the alimony if he abandoned the legal practice by which he earned his livelihood. Morya had assured him he would find a way and that his boys would be all right. Indeed, the elder soon found an opening in California and Judge found one for the younger.[4] Olcott then set about trying to arrange some kind of import–export business that he could manage from the Indian side. His idea was that he could sell Indian cultural objects to America, while acting as agent for American goods in India. Eventually, President Hayes gave him a signed letter of recommendation to all United States ministers and consuls, and the Department of State gave him a roving commission to report upon opportunities for America to trade with Asia. He was given a diplomatic passport.[5]

On the advice of his doctor, he had grown a beard to protect his delicate throat. It had grown to be about four inches long when one morning he woke feeling there was something under his chin. He unravelled it, which took him an hour, and found it to be a single lock of his beard, which had grown in the night to fourteen inches in length. When he showed it to H.P.B. she said Master had made it grow in the night, to provide a reservoir of his protective strength. As it was but a single lock, coming down to the pit of his stomach, it would have looked odd, so he tucked it under his collar and shirt, until, after years had passed, the rest grew to match it.[6]

They would sail to London, then take another ship from Liverpool to Bombay, where they would let Chintamon know they were coming. Two English acquaintences, Edward Wimbridge and Miss Rosa Bates, would come with them; the latter volunteered to keep house. On 22 October, Madame Blavatsky wrote in Olcott's diary,[7] '*Narayan* left watch – and in came *Sahib* . . . with *orders* from Serapis to complete all by the first days of December'. Sahib is Master Morya. She means that Narayan ceased to overshadow or be within her and Morya took his place. On 14 November she wrote,[8] 'Naray decamped and Morya walked in – broken finger and all. Came with definite orders from Serapis. *Have to go*; the latest from 15 to 20th Dec'. Does this mean she felt one of her own fingers broken, as his was broken, whilst his astral body coincided with her physical? Serapis wanted them gone by 17 December.

On 9 December, most of their furniture was sold by auction. On 13 December she wrote in their diary,[9] 'Kali suspects departure and thinks of arresting H.S.O.'.

Kali, Hindu goddess of destruction, was her name for Olcott's ex-wife. Did Mrs Olcott think he intended to welsh on the payments? And – in case anybody else thinks of it – did he? Once out of United States jurisdiction, he would be unlikely to be brought to court for default. Yet evasion of a court order would not be a good first step nearer to his Master. Suppose that this had been one of the moral and practical responsibilities concerning which he consulted the Master when he appeared? I am not sure that Morya would have considered that a wife who had obtained a divorce against her former husband in respect of breach of one of his marriage vows had thereby the right to keep him forever pegged down to a particular office, no longer according to his deeper destiny, solely to maintain her for the rest of her life at a standard far higher than that of the average of her countrywomen. Morya wanted Olcott in India, and might have considered it equitable that he should make an honest attempt to earn there as much as he had done in the United States and send back the same proportion of his income; but if his income fell in consequence of the move, he might have thought it right for Olcott to appeal for a reduction in the alimony he had to pay, proportionate to the fall in his income.

Madame Blavatsky became anxious about whether Olcott – on business in Philadelphia – would be back in time. He reappeared on the evening of 17 December, at 7.00 p.m., with tickets for the British steamship *Canada*, departing that night. She wrote in their diary '*consummatum est*'. Shortly before 12.00 they said goodbye to the chandelier and drove to the ship, boarding her a few minutes before midnight. Madame Blavatsky wrote in their diary, 'Master S had the best of us and we did leave the American soil on the 17th.'[10]

They had left the soil, but because of bad weather the ship did not leave the wharf, and Madame Blavatsky fretted, still fearful that 'Kali' could have Olcott seized and taken off the vessel.[11] Not until 2.30 p.m. on 18 December did the *Canada* leave her moorings and then, as she had lost the tide, she cast anchor off Coney Island. At noon on 19 December they weighed anchor and made for the open sea.

CHAPTER 29

Via London to Bombay

They entered the English Channel on New Year's Day 1879, anchored off Deal for three hours in a thick fog, then went on, reaching Gravesend the following morning, whence they took the train to London. Here they had been invited to stay with Dr and Mrs Billing, in the suburb of Norwood Park. Theosophists and others came to see them, including Stainton Moses. On 5 January, Olcott lectured to the Theosophical Society in London. Mrs Billing took Madame Blavatsky to the British Museum. Whilst it was probably the Egyptian antiquities she was most anxious to see, she was very struck by the colossal heads from Easter Island.

Olcott was walking down Cannon Street with two Theosophists when he heard one of them give a gasp. Turning, he was in time to catch the eyes, through a thick fog, of a very tall Indian, who had likewise turned his head. When he returned to Norwood Park, Mrs Billing told him the front door had been locked and bolted as usual when she came out of her sitting-room, meaning to go to Madame Blavatsky's room, and was startled to find in the hall, between the hall door and Madame Blavatsky's door, a very tall Indian, with peculiarly piercing eyes. He did not explain how he had entered, but said, 'I wish to see Madame Blavatsky'.[1] He was moving towards her door, as though he knew which it was, so Mrs Billing opened it for him and he went in. He saluted Madame Blavatsky Indian fashion, placing his palms together, and spoke with her in a language not known to Mrs Billing. She made to withdraw, but Madame Blavatsky motioned her to be seated.

Mrs Billing was a Spiritualist, a medium, but could not understand how a physical man could have passed through a closed physical door. Madame Blavatsky expressed her belief that what Mrs Billing thought of as her 'spirit guide', Ski, was in reality a living man, an Adept who communicated with her under this name.

On the evening of 17 January they caught the 9.40 p.m. train from Euston and spent the night at the Great Western Hotel in Liverpool. The following afternoon, at 5.00 p.m., they boarded the *Speke Hall* in a downpour of rain. During the night they remained at anchor, moving out at dawn.

The voyage was wild, wet and rough. Madame Blavatsky was pitched against the leg of a dining-table and her knee was badly bruised. All of them were sick. The only good moment was when, in the Mediterranean, as Olcott wrote with a flash of poetry; 'The rose-and-opal tinted shores of Africa, seen through a pearly haze, rose like a fair cliff out of the sea'.[2]

It was the morning of 15 February when they entered the harbour of Bombay, and three Theosophists climbed aboard to meet them. One of these was Mooljee Thackersey, whom Olcott had known before. On the quay was Hurrychund Chintamon, of the Arya Samaj. From New York, Olcott had asked him to engage a small, clean house with a minimum of servants. It was certainly small and soon flowed over with their Indian visitors.

Mr Ross Scott, with whom they had made friends on the boat, called and begged Madame Blavatsky to give him an exhibition of her power to produce phenomena. She did, and it was Olcott's impression that this made some of the Indians jealous. Time would add to his observation of Pharaseeism amongst the Brahmins. They believed in the existence of the Mahatmas, yet resented its being Madame Blavatsky to whom they had chosen to reveal themselves.

Hurrychund Chintamon presented them with an enormous bill for the rent of the house, which was one of his own, though to others he had been describing them as his guests; and to this were added sums for repairs, food, attendance and even for the hire of 300 chairs used at their reception (which they could have done without) and for a cablegram he had sent them before they left New York, urging them to come.

Moreover, they now realised that the money they had sent him for the Arya Samaj had gone no further than his own pocket. At a meeting of the Arya Samaj, Madame Blavatsky accused him.[3] He produced the money, but he never forgave her.

Meanwhile, where were their own Masters?

CHAPTER 30

The bungalow by the sea

On 7 March 1879, they moved into premises they found for themselves, at 118 Girgaum Road, in the native quarter. Within its compound, Madame Blavatsky and Olcott each had their own bungalow. Mooljee found them a native boy, of about 15 years, Babula, who was to prove their faithful servant. They soon had many Parsee and Hindu visitors, and Olcott received a letter from A.P. Sinnett, Editor of *The Pioneer*, one of the most influential papers of India, saying that he was hoping that if they came north they would visit him. What they did not find was much contact with the British in Bombay. This was probably, Olcott reflected in later years, because they had neglected to call at Government House.

But where was the Master Morya? On 29 March, Madame Blavatsky told Mooljee to fetch a buggy (a light carriage for not more than two persons). When it arrived, she mounted it with him, yet (Mooljee afterwards told Olcott) she would not tell him their destination but gave a particular direction at each road junction, right, left or straight on. So, they passed from the city into a suburb (recognised by Mooljee, his mother having been cremated there). They went on through a wood, often changing course, Madame Blavatsky never faltering in her directions. They came to the sea-shore and drove along it. Finally, they arrived at a private estate with a rose-garden in the front and a bungalow with spacious verandas in the background. She said the driver was to stop at the gate, climbed down and told Mooljee they were to wait for her there, impressing on him that he must not for the life of him follow her through the gate and up to the house.

He was mystified, not only by the warning but by the house itself, for it was strange to him that he, a Bombay resident, should not have known of the existence of so magnificent a property so near to the city. He watched Madame Blavatsky walk up to the front door, and saw it opened to her by a very tall Indian, dressed entirely in white. They both disappeared within.[1]

Then, as he saw some gardeners hoeing the beds, he called through the gate to them. They came up, but refused to tell him the name of the owner or anything about him. This was unlike the usual behaviour of servants, who are generally willing to chat about their employers.

After a considerable time, the door opened again. Madame Blavatsky reappeared, and also the tall Indian in white. As they stood for a moment on the step, one of the gardeners brought a bunch of roses he had just cut. These he gave the tall Indian in white, who gave them to Madame Blavatsky. Madame Blavatsky returned to the buggy, mounted and told Mooljee to tell the driver to take them home.

Back home, she handed the roses to Olcott, telling him Morya had said they were for him. The bungalow, she explained, belonged to the Masters, so that any of them could use it if they had occasion to leave their Tibetan fastness for Bombay. It was kept in order for them by a steward when they were not there. It was one of several houses they used in this way, and could not be found by anybody uninvited as it was protected by a *maya*. (Mooljee was convinced he could find it again, and took Olcott with him, but, though he entered the wood, and drove all about, he could never again come out at that bungalow by the sea.)

Madame Blavatsky explained to Olcott that a *maya* was an arrangement of the atmosphere such that the uninvited did not see what was before him but something else. All really sacred places, for instance, burial places of sacred treasure, were protected by such *mayas*. The person having no business to find sees a yawning ravine or other impassible obstacle, and turns away. If someone is meant to find, for him the *maya* disappears.[2]

Just after this, Olcott was working in his office when Babula came to say a gentleman had called and would like to see him in Madame Blavatsky's bungalow (there were two separate ones within the property they had taken). Outside it, Olcott saw the visitor's horse tethered. He went in and found waiting for him, in the flesh, the Master he had seen, as if in the flesh, in New York. He was immensely tall, 6ft 6in. or even 6ft 7in., dressed as before in white linen;

however, whereas before he had moved silently, now his footsteps sounded. He was in body. At one moment he placed his hand on Olcott's head. It was warm.

He had come in order to reprimand them for something they had done amiss. Madame Blavatsky was in another bungalow, from which they heard her voice. After perhaps ten minutes Morya extended his fingers in the direction of the sound and she came rushing in, to fall on her knees. After speaking with her, he left, on his horse.[3]

Soon after this she began to speak to Olcott about reincarnation. This would become so important in her later book, *The Secret Doctrine* that it comes as a shock to realise it did not figure in *Isis Unveiled*, save in a few lines dismissing it. In after years, people would ask Olcott why, if the Masters had told her not to reveal it there, she had not simply left it unmentioned. She told Olcott that the first her Master told her about it was when they reached India, in 1879.[4] Naturally, she had not lived so long amongst Hindus and Buddhists without hearing of it, but had always thought the stories told about it to be symbolic. Many of them obviously are, for instance, the Jataka Tales, in which the Buddha is represented as having incarnated as various animals. We do not go back to being animals. She had always understood we had been somewhere before we were born here, and went on somewhere after death, but she had thought it was from and to a higher plane. Now, Morya had told her we reincarnated many times here, sometimes as man, sometimes as woman, but always evolving, and he had given her information about races and cycles.

Why was the mistake in *Isis Unveiled* allowed to occur? My guess is that the Masters did not notice it till they saw the book in print, and they decided not to worry her about it until it was possible for Morya to see her face to face. That may have been the purpose of the summons to the bungalow by the sea.

CHAPTER 31

Karli to Rajputana

On 4 April 1879, Madame Blavatsky and Olcott set out, at Morya's suggestion, for the Karli cave temple, taking with them Mooljee and Babula. At their first train stop, they were joined mysteriously by an extra servant, Baburao, who was so distinguished that Olcott thought for years that Morya must have sent him; it was only when going through some old accounts that he realised it was Mooljee who had engaged Baburao. He brought the palanquins in which Madame Blavatsky and Olcott made the next stage of the journey, twelve bearers to each litter, the others riding. On the following day they caught a further train on to Khandalla, where Baburao met them again, with a bullock-cart which took them on to the government rest-house. Mooljee went back to Khandalla to speak with the station-master, and returned with a bouquet of roses. He had, he said, been on the platform when he heard his name called, and he saw, in one of the carriages of a train that had just come in, the tall Indian in white whom he had seen at the bungalow by the sea. The one from the bungalow gave Mooljee the roses, saying, 'These are for Colonel Olcott'.[1]

Olcott said that if a note could be delivered he would like to thank the giver. (He always avoids using Morya's name as to name a holy one is considered disrespectful.) To his thanks he added a question. Madame Blavatsky handed the note to Mooljee and told him to walk down the road with it. Mooljee protested that it bore neither name nor address, but she insisted. When he came back, his eyes were popping. The tall Indian in white whom he had seen carried out of the station on the Khandalla to Poona train was suddenly in front of him, took the letter from his hand, and said, 'Now, go back'.[2] He started walking back but looked over his shoulder. There was no one there.

The interest of this episode lies in that it shows a Master using ordinary public transport. But then, since he would not have been known for an Adept by the others in his compartment, his privacy would not have been invaded by their curious stares. They probably noticed nothing strange in his eyes closing for a few moments.

In the cave temple, Madame Blavatsky disappeared for a moment behind a slab of turning stone, which gave, as she explained on reappearing, on to a passage leading to a chamber of Morya's. On their way down from the cave, she told Olcott she had just received a mental impression from Morya they were to go to Rajputana.[3]

At Khandalla they parted from Baburao and took the train. Madame Blavatsky said she wished the instruction had been in writing as Miss Bates and Wimbridge would think it an excuse to go off on a tour leaving them to do the chores. She got out her pad, wrote on it in some characters she said were Senzar – an extinct language from which Sanskrit had derived – and beneath them, in English, a request for the instruction to be telegraphed,[4] and to let it be a test. She tore it off, folded it and was about to throw it out of the window when Olcott caught her hand to make sure it was still the same piece of paper; then she released it and it fluttered into the rush of air.

Mooljee wrote and signed a statement of what he had witnessed. None of them left the train till they reached Bombay; from there they drove straight home and found Miss Bates had signed for a telegram:[4]

> Time 2 p.m. Date 8.4.1879
> From Kurjeet. To Biculla.
> From Goolab Singh. To H.S. Olcott.
> Letter received. Answer Rajputana. Start immediately.

We do not know if the sender's name was really given as Goolab Singh.

They left on 11 April, stopping at Allahabad, where they chanced to meet Babula's former employer, a Frenchman who had been steward at the Biculla Club. At Cawnpore Olcott met a

Sanyasi, who told him that to multiply physical objects, as in the parable of the loaves and fishes (Olcott may have thought of pencils), what was necessary was that there should be 'a nucleus around which the adept can collect the matter of space'.[5]

They went on to Bhurtapore. Olcott writes, 'We were now on what was to my chum and myself classic ground, for it was associated with the splendid Solar race of Rajputs, to whom our own Teacher belongs . . .'.[6] At the rest-house, a Hindu gave Olcott a letter. The question he had asked was if he might give up his life in the world and go to live with the Masters forever, wherever they lived. The answer, couched in the kindest language, was that it was not what they wanted. His way to them was through service in the Theosophical Society.

They took the road to Jaipur or Jeypur and on 20 April 'passed the castle where my Father's mother was born long ago'. This is not a reference to Olcott's physical ancestry. He had become accustomed to refer to Morya as his father, even, in buoyant moments, as 'Dad'. Now, how old does one think Morya was, and how long ago does one think his mother was born? What women were in Jaipur Castle then? Much hangs on this.

What used to be called Rajputana (now Rajasthan) was never a single state but a group of little ones. The Moghul Emperor Akbar, 1542–1605, a contemporary of Queen Elizabeth, subdued all of them but one, Mewar. Absolute autocrat, ruling by decree, he showed enlightenment in that, Muslim by birth, he listened to exposition of the doctrines of all religions and gave positions of trust in his service to members of the conquered races who would accept his spiritual fatherhood, including Rajputs. While he reigned, the religions of India were harmonised. His successors, including Shah Jehan, who built the Taj Mahal, lost what he had gained, and as the Moghul Empire crumbled, so the Rajput states fell victim to Maratha attack and plunder until 1818 when they accepted British suzerainty. The British took over, in fact, what had become a mess.

But who did Morya's mother marry? Marriages of Rajput women were restricted by rules. They must not marry non-Rajputs, must not marry into a Rajput clan into which theirs had married before and must marry upwards. This made it so difficult to marry them that, as to have a daughter unmarried disgraced the family, the usual practice was to smother female children at birth unless the father expressly directed otherwise. This, combined with the practice of sati or sutti (widow burning), so reduced the number of women in Rajputana that some polyandry resulted. The Masters abhorred these practices. There is not quite enough information available at the India Office to identify Morya's parents, though one can come very near. He probably left the field to the British and forged a different destiny.

CHAPTER 32

First visit to the Sinnetts

They returned via Agra, so as to see the Taj Mahal. A British police agent and his servant followed them everywhere. At Cawnpore, Swami Dyanand Sarasvati called on them, told them he was recommending the expulsion of Hurrychund Chintamon, and invited them to a dinner given for them at the Arya Samaj. The police agent attended. As they returned to Bombay, Madame Blavatsky went up to him on the platform and thanked him teasingly for his escort. They then drove to the United States Consulate (Olcott had not neglected his commission from President Hayes) to ask for a protest to be made. The reply their Consul later gave him, from the Bombay government, was that no discourtesy was intended.

It was not much over twenty years since the Indian Mutiny, and the British authorities were probably anxious lest the strangers, who frequented mainly the Indians, were sowing seeds of ferment. Could they but have known it, they had in Madame Blavatsky a friend. Her Masters in Tibet had during the Mutiny sustained the British, precisely because they could see the Russians poised to step into their shoes should they be forced into withdrawal. (This will emerge gradually.) Whatever her personal feelings, Madame Blavatsky would never have gone against the orders of those whose word was law to her.

They bought a book on Hindi, but made little progress in it as all the Indians they met spoke English. One visitor was Shrishri Babu, editor of the *Amrita Bazaar Putrika*. Before leaving, he asked her to duplicate something so that he might understand her teaching 'as to the nature of matter and force'. She refused several times. He then picked up a mirror and beseeched her to duplicate it. She said she would, on condition of his not afterwards asking her to do anything else.[1]

> He consenting, she took the mirror in her hand, rose from her chair, turned her back upon us, and in another moment threw on the seat two identical glasses. Then, exhausted, she dropped into her seat and sat silent for some minutes to recover herself.

On 4 July, they decided to create *The Theosophist*, a monthly magazine. Olcott would look after the business side of it, and Madame Blavatsky would be the Editor. She had no taste for speaking from public platforms, but this work she could do in her bungalow.

On 3 August 1879, Damodar K. Mavalanka, a young Brahmin, arrived and asked to be initiated as a member. Wearing a white rubber waterproof, flapped cap, leggings cladding legs thin as pencils and with the rain streaming from the end of his long nose, he did not look impressive, but he was to prove one of the most devoted servants of the Masters. (Olcott used in those days to perform an initiation ceremony.) Applications were also received from a Lieut.-Col. (later Maj.-Gen.) and Mrs Gordon. These, also, would prove faithful.

On 11 August, Madame Blavatsky received a letter from Emma, née Cutting, formerly of the Hotel d'Orient, Cairo, saying she was now married to Alexis Coulomb, the son of the former owner. He had inherited the hotel but it had failed. They had come to India and started another hotel in Ceylon, which had also failed. They were stranded in Ceylon without money. If they came to Bombay, could Madame Blavatsky or Colonel Olcott find some employment for them? She enclosed a copy in her own hand of a letter she had written to the editor of *The Ceylon Times*, which had appeared on 5 June. In view of the importance Emma Coulomb will assume in the story, I will give this in full, since it has not appeared in full before:[2]

> On the 15th of May I happened to read an article in your paper concerning the Theosophical Society. I was surprised to find the bad opinion expressed in the article mentioned and really cannot understand from what source 'The Colonial Empire of the Star of India' obtained its information. I am not acquainted with any of the members of the said society, except with Madame Blavatsky. I have known this lady for the last eight

years and I must say the truth that there is nothing against her character. We lived in the same town and on the contrary she was considered one of the cleverest ladies of the age. Madame B. is a musician, a painter, a linguist and an author and I may say that very few ladies and indeed very few gentlemen have knowledge of things in general as Madame B. Now if Nature has endowed her with so much talent and if she is so well informed re every branch of education and instruction and at the same time possessing a spirit of investigation and a desire to dive into the mysteries of nature, I really do not see that for this she should be considered and spoken of as a person of an indifferent character. Madame Blavatsky's family is a very respectable one indeed. Nature as you know is very capricious, it grants to some every perfection and deprives others of the indispensable endowments. Madame B. has a masculine mind and a perfect understanding and I could write much more about her, which I feel convinced would command a good opinion of her.

E. Coulomb

For a woman not accustomed to writing, this must have represented a considerable effort in literary composition. Madame Blavatsky told Olcott that the writer had been good to her when she stayed at the elder Madame Coulomb's hotel in Cairo, and he agreed she should invite them to come. He would try to find something for the husband to do. They did not, however, arrive at once.

On 2 December Madame Blavatsky and Olcott left to pay their first visit to the Sinnetts at Allahabad, taking Damodar and Babula. Alfred Percival Sinnett met them at the station with his barouche and pair and two liveried footmen. Just under 40, he seemed older from the set pattern of his ways, and they were perhaps more at ease with his wife, Patience, who they felt at once was their friend. Madame Blavatsky had warned Sinnett she was a rough old hippotamus, but he appreciated at once that:[3]

No one with the least discernment could ever fail to see that her rugged manners and disregard of all conventionalities were the result of a deliberate rebellion against, not ignorance or unfamiliarity with, the customs of refined society.

Olcott warned him she was 'under great self-restraint so far'.

This was needed in respect of the smell of alcohol in the house. Madame Blavatsky was not merely a total abstainer; the smell of alcohol in any form upset her. In New York, Olcott had been able to warn their warm-hearted American friends on no account to bring a bottle of anything as their contribution to an evening at the Lamasery; but now that they began to be invited into the homes of the British in India, they found there were nearly always drinks in circulation. Sinnett drank a whole bottle of claret with his dinner and poured himself other drinks during the day and after dinner. Madame Blavatsky was trapped with the fumes for a whole fortnight.

A friend of the Sinnetts who came to call was Allan Octavian Hume, of the Board of Revenue for the district, and he arranged for Olcott to give a lecture on Theosophy at the Mayo Hall. Olcott did something amiss, and on the way home Madame Blavatsky's self-restraint broke upon her familiar partner-in-traces. Sinnett, amazed by the storm, wrote, 'one might have thought the aspirations of her whole life compromised . . . Colonel Olcott bore all these tantrums with remarkable fortitude'.[4]

Olcott comments, 'Of course: I loved her loveable qualities and out of gratitude for showing me the Path, and bore her savage temper because the good she was doing outweighed all sense of personal suffering'.[5]

The Sinnetts were anxious to see her perform some phenomena, but she seemed indisposed to do that. After much urging, she gave in so far as to produce some raps. She made them come upon the glass part of a half-glass door, held ajar, so that it could be seen from the other side that her hands, placed on the glass, were not moving.

Then she lifted the protective glass dome from one of those clocks of which one is meant to see the works, put it on the floor, removed her rings and placed her hands on it. The Sinnetts, by getting down on to their floor and placing a lamp so that it illuminated the palms of her hands, were able to see they were not moving, although raps occurred. She then produced the raps on her hosts' heads, making them feel as though they were receiving electric shocks.[6]

On 7 December, Mrs Gordon joined them. On 15 December, Madame Blavatsky, Olcott, the Sinnetts and Mrs Gordon made an expedition to Benares, where the Maharaja of Vizianagram placed his residence at their disposal. That evening, Sinnett suggested that if Madame Blavatsky had to limit the energy she expended upon phenomena, she should reserve it for men of science. Olcott agreed, but in the middle of India it was impossible to persuade her to reserve herself for the Royal Society.[7] The Sinnetts appear to have left for their home on the 18 December, the others staying on at Benares.

They went to visit a female ascetic, the Maji, who dwelt in a cave off the Ganges. To this cave many made their pilgrimage to bow before her. Two mornings later, the Maji came to visit Madame Blavatsky. This caused a local sensation. The Maji had never before been known to visit anybody,[8] saving, that is, her Guru.

Next day, Olcott paid his respects to the German Professor Georg Friedrich Wilhelm Thibaut, Ph.D, Principle of Benares College. He had translated the *Vedanta Sutra* in the series of *Sacred Books of the East*, edited by Max Müller.

That evening, Dr Thibaut returned the call, bringing with him Sanskritists from the College. Also present were Madame Blavatsky, Mrs Gordon, Damodar, Swami Dyanand with a pupil, Ram Rao, and a Babu, Pramadha Dasa Mitra, as orthodox as the Sanskritists. Dr Thibaut said his Sanskrit Pandits assured him that in ancient times there were yogis who really possessed the *Siddhis* (magical powers) described in the *Shastras* (sacred writings), 'for instance, they could make fall in a room like this a shower of roses; but now nobody can do dat'.

Madame Blavatsky swept her right hand through the air with an imperious gesture, and about a dozen roses fell amongst them. While others eagerly gathered them up, Dr Thibaut sat straight as a post. He asked if she would do it a second time. She repeated the gesture, and more roses fell, one upon Dr Thibaut's head, thence bouncing off on to his lap. He started, opening and shutting his eyes several times, then said, 'De weight, mooltiplied by de felocity, prooves dat it must haf come from a great distance'.[9]

Olcott does not tell us the height of the ceiling, but he does mention they were in a bungalow, so it would not have been high. Even if there had been an unperceived aperture in the roof through which they were thrown, it would hardly have been high enough to give Dr Thibaut the impression, from the impact one made upon his head, that the weight multiplied by the velocity proved it to have come from a great distance.

They were not done with the wonders of the evening. When Dr Thibaut rose to leave, Olcott pushed aside a curtain for him, and Damodar followed with a light. It was a student's reading-lamp, with a shade, a rod to slide upon and a ring at the top by which to carry it. Olcott shook hands with Dr Thibaut, who was starting out into the night, when, as Olcott turned, he saw Madame Blavatsky had risen, 'with that strange look of power which almost always preceded a phenomenon'. He called Dr Thibaut back. Madame Blavatsky took the light from Damodar, holding it by her left fore-finger through the ring. She pointed her right fore-finger at the flame, and said imperiously, 'Go up!' It rose higher. 'Go down!' It dwindled till it burnt small and bluish at the wick. 'Go up! I command you'. It rose again. 'Down!' It went down again. She returned the lamp to Damodar, nodded to Dr Thibaut without speech, and went back into the bungalow.[10]

Afterwards, she told Olcott it was nothing. An Adept had turned the wick up and down. He did not believe that. He believed she had achieved domination of the fire elemental. Long ago, she had said that earth, water and air elementals were usually disposed to serve; to get the fire elementals to do anything was much more difficult. He thought she did not wish to admit to having so much power.

CHAPTER 33

The arrival of the Coulombs

Madame Blavatsky and Olcott returned to the Sinnetts' at Allahabad on 22 December 1879, and on 26 December Olcott initiated the Sinnetts. When he asked if the Masters heard and approved the candidates' pledges, he heard a voice respond, 'Yes, we do'.[1]

They returned to Bombay where, on 15 January 1880, Madame Blavatsky found that a Russian newspaper, *Russki Vyestnik*, had accepted a semi-fictionalised Indian travelogue she had sent it pseudonymously. Later it was translated by her niece Vera Johnston under the title *From the Caves and Jungles of Hindostan*. Although it is the poetry of the country she stresses, she does not miss the horror. She salutes the British achievement in making the burning of widows illegal, but observes that the widows' relatives so humiliate them for surviving that they must often wish the flames had consumed them. She applauds the scholarship of H.H. Wilson in pointing out that a passage in the *Rig Veda*, cited by the Brahmins as justifying sati, does nothing of the kind, but is mistranslated by the Brahmins to the people. She deplores that the Brahmins forbid those of inferior castes to read the sacred scriptures for themselves, and even to learn Sanskrit and reprobates their inhumanity to those they eject from their caste. Caste is lost in innumerable ways, for instance by sitting down to eat in company with anyone of lesser caste, by accepting a glass of water from one of lesser caste and by boarding a ship. The unfortunate may then neither be given food or water nor sold them; so that he is reduced to theft or dealing with Europeans unless he undergoes the most revolting ceremony of penance, ending up with eating cow-dung. She often asked Brahmins why, rather than submit to such vexatious restrictions, they did not break caste deliberately and form a non-caste society; but generally they would not, except for the few really brave ones who became members of the Theosophical Society, incurring all the penalties.

On 28 January, the Coulombs arrived.[2] The French Consul had paid their fare from Ceylon, but they seemed now to be without means. Their clothing was wretched, but Monsieur Coulomb brought a box of tools. Olcott enquired amongst friends and was able to find him 'a machinist's berth in a cotton mill'. The understanding was that as soon as Coulomb obtained employment he and his wife would move out and set up their own household. Unfortunately, 'he fell out with the owner. I found him a man very quick-tempered and hard to please in the matter of employers, and, as no other opening occurred, he and his wife just drifted along with us . . .'.[3]

Coulomb possessed skills as a mechanic, carpenter and draftsman, so he became an unofficial odd-job man, who could also be called upon to make a fair copy of a diagram if one was needed for the illustration of an article. His wife started sharing in the household chores. They received nothing for their labours, save their accommodation and food. With hindsight, one can see this was not wise. If they had been paid the slenderest wage, their position as servants would have been defined. The lack of definition would enable Madame Coulomb to say later that they were guests whose willingness to labour unpaid was exploited.

Madame Blavatsky and Olcott had long projected a visit to the Buddhists in Ceylon, and they got together several issues of *The Theosophist* in advance so that they could go away. They had intended leaving Miss Bates in charge of the house, but Olcott had never had much opinion of her housekeeping; he hoped Madame Coulomb, having been in the hotel business, might do it better. For Miss Bates he created a sub-editorship of *The Theosophist*. Here one can see a second mistake. It was obvious that Miss Bates would resent the charge of the house being taken away from her and given to a newcomer.

Madame Blavatsky, Olcott, Wimbridge and Damodar boarded the coastal steamer *Ellora* on 7 May, and landed at Galle on 17 May. A crowd pressed around them and followed their carriages to the home of a Mrs Wijeratne, widow of a P & O contractor, with whom they were to stay. Yellow-robed Buddhist monks who had followed them from the boat flocked around Madame Blavatsky, pressing her for phenomena which she had not the heart to refuse.

On 25 May Madame Blavatsky and Olcott took *pansil* at a temple of the Ramayana Nikaya (that is, they were received into Buddhism).

They started north to pay their respects to the most sacred relic, at Kandi, in carriages freely supplied to them by fishermen of the very poor class from whom St François Xavier drew most of his converts. In further travels around the island, they founded in all seven new branches. A party of Buddhist monks came to ask Olcott for initiation into the Society and he initiated them.[4]

On 13 July, they sailed for home. At their first Indian port, Tuticorin, the fancy took them to weigh themselves to see whether they had lost or gained since leaving Bombay. Madame Blavatsky had unfortunately gained 8 lbs, now weighing 237 lbs (16 st. 13 lbs); Olcott had lost 15 lbs and was now 170 lbs (12 st. 2 lbs); Wimbridge had neither gained nor lost; but Damodar, who could least afford to lose weight, had lost 6 lbs and weighed now only 90 lbs (6 st. 6 lbs).

On returning to Bombay they were greeted with the sad news that Mooljee had died a few days before. Then Miss Bates alleged that Madame Coulomb was trying to poison her.[5] Olcott could not believe this, and warned Miss Bates of the gravity of making criminal charges she had no evidence to šbstantiate. He was probably right in his supposition that the sub-editorship of *The Theosophist* had not satisfied her. She seemed to be trying to increase her hold on that.

For four days Madame Coulomb and Miss Bates could be heard hurling charges and counter-charges at one another. The air seemed filled with their voices, which Madame Blavatsky sat trying not to hear. Wimbridge sided with Miss Bates. They demanded the expulsion of the Coulombs. Madame Blavatsky and Olcott refused, and she turned against them.

On 4 August, Madame Blavatsky called Olcott into her bungalow to present him to someone she had with her. It was the Egyptian Coptic Master, Serapis, from whom Olcott had received letters in America. Serapis dictated a letter that they were directed to send to an influential friend of theirs in Paris, and gave them some advice in the management of the Society. Then, Olcott was asked to withdraw, and so he did not see in what manner Serapis departed. The last he saw of him, he was sitting with Madame Blavatsky in her room.[6]

The following day Miss Bates turned violently against Madame Blavatsky. At a moment when Miss Bates's back was towards Olcott, as she stood abusing Madame Blavatsky, a note dropped as if from nowhere into Olcott's lap. It read:[7]

1 Assert your rights to the paper – it was established for you, none but you two have a right over it as directed by [symbol]
2 Never ask 'the maid' in question to do anything whatever. Dispense with her services as much as you can, and *altogether* if you can.
3 Do it in such a way however as not to lead to an open quarrel. Whenever convenient explain that the paper is neither yours nor H.P.B.'s but belongs to and is under the control of certain persons no one knows anything about except your two selves. Try to avoid bringing into the 'Office' that opposing, malevolent magnetism of the maid. You have lost 31 subscribers through that influence.
    More tomorrow.
Serapis

Miss Bates and Wimbridge were by this time taking their meals in one bungalow; Madame Blavatsky, Olcott and Damodar in the other. It is not explained where the Coulombs ate. It was arranged that Madame Blavatsky and Olcott should pay Miss Bates's fare back to New York, but in the end she and Wimbridge made their own arrangement and left. The Coulombs, unfortunately, remained.

The day of the split brought a letter from Sinnett asking Madame Blavatsky and Olcott to join them at Simla.

CHAPTER 34

The Simla phenomena

Madame Blavatsky and Olcott left Bombay for Simla on the evening of 27 August 1880, taking Babula. At Allahabad they broke their journey and saw Swami Dyanand again. Olcott said he had occasionally seen inanimate objects such as letters, coins, pencils and jewellery duplicated before his eyes (not mentioning it was Madame Blavatsky who had done this), and asked how it was done. Dyanand replied,[1] 'In the atmosphere are particles of every visible thing, in a highly diffused state. The Yogi, knowing how to concentrate these, does so by the exercise of his will, and forms them into any shape of which he can picture to himself the model'. This confirmed what Olcott had earlier been told by the Sanyasi of Cawnpore.

At Simla they were met with jampans – chairs borne by porters upon poles – sent by Sinnett, and were carried to his house. Madame Blavatsky was still unable to stop talking of the row between Miss Bates and Madame Coulomb, and Sinnett told Olcott that it worried him she could be so upset as English people associated 'true merit with calm self-control'. When 'flushed and voluble', she was not a good advertisement for the teachings she was giving.

However, Sinnett invited a succession of government officials to meet them, including the Major Henderson who had had them shadowed, presumably on instructions from higher up. On 27 September, Olcott wrote a long letter to the Secretary of the government in the Foreign Department, setting out the objects of the Theosophical Society enclosing some of its literature and also copies of his letters from President Hayes of the United States and the American Secretary of State; he asked that the surveillance of Madame Blavatsky and himself should cease.[2]

On 29 September, Madame Blavatsky and Olcott went with Mrs Sinnett to the top of Prospect Hill. H.P.B. asked Mrs Sinnett what was her heart's desire. She said it was to receive a note from the Brothers. Madame Blavatsky tore off a piece of pink paper (Sinnett says it was from a note she had received earlier in the day, but he was not there; Olcott, who was, says from 'her pocket-book'). On this, she traced some invisible signs with her fingers. Then she folded it into a triangle and walked about twenty yards, to the brow of the hill, and, facing west, made some signs and threw it up into the air. Mrs Sinnett had said, or said now, that she would like the reply to land in her lap. H.P.B. said it would not come there; it would be in a tree. She walked up to a tree, but found nothing in it. Then they all walked to one that was further away, which they had not previously approached. At first they could see nothing in that either. Mrs Sinnett then climbed up it a few feet and looked around among the branches. At first she could see nothing. Then, on turning or bending back her head, without otherwise moving, she saw immediately before her face where previously there had been nothing, transpierced by a sprig or rather the stalk of a leaf, a pink triangle of folded paper which looked like the one they had seen committed to the air. Brought down and unfolded, this was seen to bear a message reading 'I have been asked to leave a note here for you. What can I do for you?' or words to that effect (text slightly different in Olcott and in Sinnett).[3]

Neither Olcott nor Sinnett regarded this phenomenon as proof for the sceptic, since the note did not come in the place requested by Mrs Sinnett; the sceptic would allege that it was not the note they had seen thrown into the air which was found in the tree, and that the latter was a different one of similar appearance planted by Madame Blavatsky earlier. Against that, Sinnett insists, upon the authority of his wife, that the stalk upon which it was found spiked was still green and fresh and moist, as it would be if the leaf had only that moment been removed from it to make the spike; it was not beginning to dry and to shrivel as it would have been had the leaf been removed earlier in order to spike the note on it.

Sinnett now conceived the idea of writing a letter to the Brothers, if Madame Blavatsky could transmit it for him, and a note arrived from Hume (whom they had met at Allahabad), making the same request of her. She said it would be beyond her unaided power, but there was in Simla a 'half-developed Brother' and it depended on whether he would give her the help she needed. They all heard the sound as of a little bell ring out near her head, and she said that signalled it was all right, he would do it.[4] But, as she later explained, she had difficulty in finding one of the Brothers to accept correspondence with Sinnett or Hume. Her own Master (Morya) to whom she first applied, did not wish to be burdened with it, nor did those she next thought of. In the end, it was one with whom she had not been in touch for a long while, Morya's beloved Brother Master (Koot Hoomi), who volunteered to undertake it.[5]

On 2 October, Madame Blavatsky told them a Brother would be passing close and they might meet him on his way, at a certain spot. They all set out, but Madame Blavatsky did not know Simla and led them up one road which ran in the right direction only for a certain distance and lost the 'scent'; when she found it again, to follow it would have meant leaving the path to descend a valley 'as the crow flies'. They found it impossible, and gave up. It was not in order to see them that the Brother was in the vicinity and he would not wait for them. They returned disconsolate from the afternoon's missed opportunity and spent the evening in the house together, the two Sinnetts, Madame Blavatsky and Olcott.[6]

The following day, 3 October 1880, was that of the most famous of all the phenomena. All were up very early for another excursion. The Sinnetts' servants packed six hampers, for Madame Blavatsky and Olcott, the Sinnetts and Major Henderson and another woman (Mrs Henderson?). They were all ready to set out, the men riding on horseback and the women being carried in jampans, when another man rode up and was invited to join their party. Though they had an idea of where they wanted to go, there was more than one route to it and the route they took was not predetermined. They travelled down the valley for some hours till they felt it was time to breakfast. When the ladies were set down and the men dismounted, they were on a flat grassy slope 'on the comb of a ridge covered with green turf, and overshadowed by great trees'. The servants spread out the table-cloth, built a fire on which to heat the kettle to make the tea and coffee, and unpacked the hampers. It was then realised there were only six cups and saucers, for seven people. Olcott heard Mrs Sinnett scold the servants for not having put in another cup and saucer when they saw the party had increased to seven. She then turned to the others and said two would have to share a cup. Olcott suggested one should drink from a saucer. Someone suggested this was Madame Blavatsky's opportunity to produce an extra cup and saucer by magic.

She said it would be difficult and she would need somebody to help her by digging for it. (It will be remembered that, being so portly, she found it difficult to bend.) Major Henderson picked up a table knife and followed her about as she moved, turning her seal-ring to face this way and that. Presently, she indicated a spot and said, 'Please, dig there'. Major Henderson plied his knife, but found that 'beneath the grass, the ground was covered with a network of fine roots of the adjacent trees'. These he had to cut through, and they were 'tough and interlaced'. As he brushed away the soil he was loosening, something white appeared. He continued to excavate, and brought out a complete cup and saucer.[7]

Major Henderson said he would join the Theosophical Society if he could be admitted then and there. Olcott formally initiated him, but then there was the matter of the diploma, a roll of paper, which should be done up with string. Madame Blavatsky set them all to search for it in the undergrowth, and it was Major Henderson himself who found it, in a deodar shrub, already made out to him. This impressed Olcott more than anything, because it appeared to be in his handwriting, though he was sure he had not made it out.[8]

After the breakfast, they continued to descend the valley, camping for the second time at a little Tibetan temple or rest-house where, Madame Blavatsky told them, the Brother they should have met the previous day had spent the night; this made it full of his beneficent atmosphere. More coffee was called for, but the servants said there was no more water and held up the water-bottles to show that they were empty. The water in the stream was not good, so Mrs Sinnett told one of them to go to a nearby brewery. Olcott wrote a note for him to take, but he came back saying there were no Europeans there (it was a Sunday), and so he had returned with the bottles still empty.

By this time Major Henderson and the man who had last joined the party had gone off, so there were just the Sinnetts, Olcott and Madame Blavatsky. She got up, went over to the bottles and came back with one under the fold of her dress; it was found to be full of water. This, Sinnett was aware, had some likeness to a conventional conjuring trick in which one object is substituted for another, though the water tasted to him unlike that of Simla.[9]

They started homewards and were rejoined by Major Henderson and the last man, who said they had been back to the place where the cup had been found and now felt the possibility could not be ruled out that a tunnel might have been made from the far side of the slope and the cup and saucer pushed up under the roots of the tree from underneath. Would Madame Blavatsky do another phenomenon for them? Madame Blavatsky exploded in anger, derision and scorn, and would have no more of them.

So, the party made its way back to the house. Here there was to be made an investigation crucial to Mrs Sinnett. The set of cups and saucers was one that had been brought by the Sinnetts when they came out from England some years before. Some pieces had been broken, so that there were only nine left. She therefore immediately asked their principal kitmagar (head butler) to show the other three cups. These were found, put away upon a high shelf, out of use because their handles were broken off and they were otherwise dilapidated.

Sinnett does not make the comment, but to my mind this explains why the servants, when they saw there was a seventh guest, did not pack a seventh cup and saucer. My mother always used to tell me that Indian servants were very sensitive about their employers' china and would never produce an imperfect set. They would borrow, silently, from some other household. The Sinnetts' servants, because of the last minute arrival of the seventh guest, had no time to operate a borrowing of this sort; nor was there time to take all the six cups and saucers out of the packed hampers and substitute seven from a set that was not defective (Sinnett says they did have non-defective sets). They would have been confronted with a situation in which they probably preferred to appear merely forgetful.

What Sinnett does point out is that if, as they well might have, the servants had packed cups and saucers from a different set, the one produced by Madame Blavatsky would not have matched it. Also, it had been by chance that they took the route they did and unpacked where they did, and the decision to make the excursion was made only on the previous evening, after the failure of the attempt to meet the Brother.

As for the theory of a tunnel, who could have made it? Sinnett specifies that Babula, the only servant brought by Madame Blavatsky and Olcott, had an alibi. There was a door banging the previous night which worried Sinnett after he had gone to bed until, in the middle of the night, he got up and roused the servants to go and mend it. Babula was then seen. He slept in earshot of Madame Blavatsky (probably on the floor outside her door) and she had, he said, told him to go and see why people were moving around.

Apart from all this, any gardener will know how long it takes, even armed with a spade, to dig a big hole. Any attempt to make a tunnel would cause the earth to fall in from the top, unless wood or some other material were introduced to make a roof and sides were made to support it. And can one really picture the fat Madame Blavatsky burrowing like a dog with her hands throughout the night to make a tunnel big enough for herself to crawl through, so that she could push a cup and saucer up under the roots of a tree from beneath?

Finally, if such a tunnel had been made, it could not afterwards have been filled in so perfectly that no tell-tale disturbance of the earth could ever be found. Sinnett assures us that though there was no failure to make a search, the doubters who had put forward this theory were never able to find a tunnel or any trace of disturbed earth.

But the events of that day were not ended with the return to the house and the check on the kitchen china. That evening they were all invited to dine at the Humes', at their house higher up the hill. Allan Octavian Hume, CB (born 1829), educated at Haileybury and the University of London, was Collector of Taxes for the North-West Provinces and a magistrate; his hobby was ornithology, his dominating interest Indian nationalism. Whereas Sinnett was a Tory, Hume, son of the Liberal MP Joseph Hume, was a left-wing intellectual (destined eventually to become known as the 'Father of the Indian Congress'). They dined, a party of eleven, including Mrs Gordon and a Captain Maitland, about a round table; Madame Blavatsky was tired and unusually silent, seated next to Hume. In front of each guest was a plate-warmer upon which each plate of food would be set to keep it warm while the food was being eaten. Between courses she kept holding her hands over hers as though they felt cold. Mrs Hume asked her why she was warming her hands. H.P.B. suggested they all warmed theirs and see what would happen. This they did. Mrs Hume asked, 'What next?' Madame Blavatsky stretched across the person between them and took one of Mrs Hume's hands, asking if there was anything she wished for. Some of the others said Mrs Hume should ask for an object, but nobody suggested what this should be. Mrs Hume said she would like to have brought back to her a brooch, given her by her mother, which she had lent to another person who had let it pass from her possession. Madame Blavatsky asked Mrs Hume to form in her mind as clear an image of the brooch as she could. Mrs Hume said it was a breast-brooch, made to contain human hair and set around with pearls. Mrs Hume made a drawing of it. Madame Blavatsky took two of the cigarette-papers which she always carried, wrapped them around a coin attached to her watch-chain and put it inside her dress. She said she hoped the brooch would be delivered during the evening. At the close of the meal she said the cigarette-papers were gone. They moved into the drawing-room, and a little later she said the brooch would not be brought into the house but would be found in the garden. She had seen it fall into a star-shaped flower-bed. Mr Hume led the way out to a bed of that shape, at some distance from the house. Everybody was carrying lanterns, with the aid of which they searched. It was Mrs Sinnett and Captain Maitland who found among the nasturtiums two cigarette-papers, within which there seemed to be wrapped some object. Olcott, hurrying up when he saw that they had got something, called to the others to come and watch while it was unwrapped. Madame Blavatsky had been searching in company with Mr Hume; now they and all the others gathered round. Mrs Sinnett gave the object, still in the cigarette-papers, to Mr Hume; he unwrapped them and found within a brooch such as Mrs Hume had described.[10]

Sinnett and Hume drew up an account of what had taken place, whilst they were all still present and their memories fresh; this was read over to all and agreed as correct. Then all signed it.[11]

In his book, *The Occult World*, Sinnett gives the signatures as:

A.O. Hume,	Alice Gordon
M.A. Hume	P.J. Maitland
Fred. R. Hogg	Wm Davidson
A.P. Sinnett	Stuart Beatson
Patience Sinnett	

Presumably it was only from oversight that Sinnett ommitted Olcott's signature.

The account was published in *The Pioneer*, which resulted in a great flurry of endeavours to explain the incident away. Mrs Hume, on being questioned, said the person to whom she had some years previously lent the brooch was her daughter, who had lost it. When it emerged that the daughter on her way to Europe had passed through Bombay, where she met Madame Blavatsky, there were people who then alleged the daughter must have given the brooch to Madame Blavatsky. The subsequent testimony of the daughter, Maria or Minnie Hume, that it was not so and that she lost the brooch before she went to Bombay or met Madame Blavatsky, appeared not to weigh with these scoffers. Olcott is positive that Madame Blavatsky had not been in the Humes' garden before and that the star-shaped flower-bed was not visible from the drive along which they arrived. She had been carried on a jampan, which did not set her down except for her to enter the house.[12] Indeed, for the theory of fraud to be credible, the required confederate is Mrs Hume with or without the complicity of Mr Hume, but with their daughter as accessory after the fact. Only Mrs Hume could have asked for a 'lost' brooch to be restored to her, knowing full well that she or her husband had buried it in the garden before their guests arrived. But why should the Humes have behaved in this way?

Sinnett adds, on Madame Blavatsky's explanation to him, that the brooch should not be imagined as having been brought through the air as a solid object. It would have been 'disintegrated, carried on the currents in infinitely minute particles, and then reintegrated at its destination'.[13]

CHAPTER 35

The Mahatma Letters:
introductory series, 1880

On 15 October, Sinnett found upon his writing-table his first letter from a Mahatma. It started straight off with a comment on the suggestion made by Sinnett in his, that if a copy of his newspaper could appear on the day of its publication thousands of miles away (instead of after the delay caused by carriage on ship), that would prove a convincing phenomenon:[1]

Esteemed Brother and Friend.

Precisely because the test of the London newspaper would close the mouths of the skeptics – it is unthinkable . . . everyone who would thus be made a witness to the occurrence would be thrown off his balance and the results would be deplorable. Believe me, it would be so – especially for yourself who originated the idea, and the devoted woman who so foolishly rushes into the wide open door leading to notoriety . . . You say half London would be converted if you could deliver them a *Pioneer* on its day of publication. I beg to say that if the people believed the thing true they would kill you before you could make the round of Hyde Park; if it were not believed true – the least that would happen would be the loss of your reputation and good name . . .

Experimental knowledge does not quite date from 1662, when Bacon, Robert Boyle and the Bishop of Chester transformed under the royal charter their 'Invisible College' into a Society for the promotion of experimental science. Ages before the Royal Society found itself becoming a reality upon the plane of the 'Prophetic Science' an innate longing for the hidden, a passionate love for and the study of nature had led men in every generation to try and fathom her secrets . . . *Roma ante Romulum fuit* [Rome was before Romulus] – is an axiom taught to us in your English schools. Abstract enquiries into the most puzzling problems did not arise in the brain of Archimedes as a spontaneous and hitherto untouched subject . . .

. . . As for human nature, it is the same now as it was a million of years ago . . . What then would be the results of the most astounding phenomena, supposing we consented to have them produced? However successful danger would be growing in proportion to success. No choice would soon remain but to go on, ever crescendo, or to fall in endless struggle with prejudice and ignorance . . . Test after test would be required and would have to be furnished; every subsequent phenomenon expected to be more marvellous than the preceding one . . . It may be an easy matter to increase the original number of believers at Simla to hundreds and thousands. But what of the millions who could not be made eye-witnesses? . . . First notify the public of the note, the cup . . . and let them digest these. Get them to work for an explanation . . . Isolated as it is, the case under notice in the *Pioneer* becomes less than worthless – it is positively injurious for all of you – for yourself as the Editor of that paper as much as for anyone else . . .

Koot' Hoomi Lal Singh

It was not the sort of letter Sinnett had expected to receive from Tibet. Except for the salutation, nothing bespoke the oriental. Madame Blavatsky explained to him that Koot Hoomi had been sent as a youth to Europe to receive a western education. Later he had returned, then gone to live in Tibet. The spelling of sceptic with a 'k', 'skeptic', was not, she said, in his case the effect of American influence but some fad of his own.

We do not have Sinnett's letters but the content of his next can be sensed from the reply to it, which he found, again upon his writing-table, on 19 October:[2]

Much Esteemed Sir and Brother,

We will be at cross purposes in our correspondence until it has been made entirely plain that occult science has its own methods of research as fixed and arbitrary as the methods of its antithesis physical science . . . and he who would cross the boundary of the unseen world can no more prescribe how he will proceed than the traveller who tries to penetrate to the inner subterranean recesses of L'Hassa – the blessed, could show the way to his guide . . . Your desire is to be brought to communicate with one of us directly, without the agency of Mad. B. or any medium . . . either by letters – as the present one – or by audible words . . . You seek all this, and yet, as you say yourself, hitherto you have not found 'sufficient reason' to even give up 'your modes of life' – directly hostile to such modes of communication . . .

Now what are your motives? . . . They are (1) The desire to receive positive and unimpeachable proofs that there really are forces in nature of which science knows nothing; (2) The hope to appropriate them some day . . . so as to enable yourself (a) to demonstrate their existence to a few chosen western minds . . .

To our minds then, these motives, sincere and worthy of every serious consideration . . . appear – *selfish.*

. . . And supposing you were thus to come – as two of your own countrymen have already – as Mad. B. did and Mr O. will – . . . Of these two persons one has already given three-fourths of a life, the other six years of manhood's prime to us, and both will so labour to the close of their days . . . would it not be a palpable injustice to ignore them as proposed in an important field of Theosophical effort?

. . . Neither of them has the least desire to interfere with the management of the contemplated Anglo-Indian Branch . . . But, the new society, if formed at all, must . . . be, in fact, a Branch of the Parent body . . .

Koot' Hoomi Lal Singh

One sees what has happened. Sinnett has proposed to cut Madame Blavatsky and Olcott out. He wants direct communication with the teachers of Madame Blavatsky so as to be able to do without her and to set up a new society, composed of his own friends, of which he will be the president so as not to be under Olcott.

If Koot Hoomi's reply was severe, yet there was consolation. That night, Sinnett woke to see what he believed to be Koot Hoomi in his astral body, then another Adept who, from the description he gave, Olcott later told him must have been Serapis, 'the youngest of the chohans'. (So the elderly Copt Madame Blavatsky met when she first went to Cairo will not have been Serapis himself.)

It had been planned that they should on the morrow make a picnic excursion to Prospect Hill, and when he came down in the morning Sinnett found on the hall table a note:[3]

My Good 'Brother',

. . . I hope to prove to you my presence near you last night by something I took away with me. Your lady will receive it back on the Hill. I keep no pink paper to write upon, but I trust modest white will do as well for what I have to say.

Koot' Hoomi Lal Singh

The reference to 'pink paper' alludes probably to the pink paper Madame Blavatsky had torn from her pocket-book for the note phenomenon.

Before they set out, Sinnett wrote a note to Koot Hoomi thanking him for his note and promise of a phenomenon, and gave it to Madame Blavatsky to send in her own way.

They all set off up Prospect Hill, the ladies carried as usual on jampans. At lunch, Madame Blavatsky said Koot Hoomi asked where Mr Sinnett would like to receive the object he would send. Sinnett first thought of on a tree or under the ground as in the previous instances, but then, to try something different, said, 'Inside that cushion', pointing to the cushion in the jampan of one of their guests. Madame Blavatsky was just accepting that place when Mrs Sinnett cried out, 'Oh no, let it be inside mine'. Madame Blavatsky told her to take the cushion from behind her and place it under her rug. This was Mrs Sinnett's usual jampan cushion, upon which she had been leaning all the way. She put it beneath her rug as requested, and after about a minute exposed it again when Madame Blavatsky said she could. It was a firmly made cushion of worsted cloth and velvet. Sinnett took a knife and cut it open, stitch by stitch. When he had ripped the outer cover he found that there was an inner one, also stitched, enclosing the feathers and he had to rip this, too. Inside it Mrs Sinnett found a brooch of her own, which she had last seen where she left it, on her dressing-table, but which now had the initials 'K.H.' scratched on it, and a triangularly folded note, reading:[4]

> My 'Dear Brother', – This brooch No. 2, is placed in this very strange place, simply to show you how very easily a real phenomenon is produced . . .
> The difficulty you spoke of last night with respect to the interchange of our letters, I will try to remove. One of our pupils will shortly visit Lahore and the N.W.P. and an address will be sent to you which you can always use; unless, indeed, you really prefer corresponding through – pillows? Please to remark that the present is dated not from a 'Lodge' but from a Kashmir valley.

Sinnett was positive that Madame Blavatsky could in no wise have got at that jampan cushion or, as Koot Hoomi calls it, pillow. It was a drawing-room cushion which Mrs Sinnett kept on her sofa except when she went out in the jampan, when it was picked up and taken with her. The Sinnetts were positive that Madame Blavatsky, who had been within their sight from earliest morning, had had no opportunity surreptitiously to do anything to it; and in any case she could not have foreseen that Sinnett would ask for the phenomenon to be produced within a cushion. But for his wife's interjection, it would have had to be produced in that on which one of the other ladies was reclining in her jampan, where Madame Blavatsky had indeed just signified the Master's willingness to produce it; Mrs Sinnett interrupted by asking for it to be in hers instead. The reintegration of her brooch (presumably taken from her dressing-table the night before though she had not noticed its disappearance); the materialisation or reintegration of paper belonging to Koot Hoomi; and the writing (which appears to be in ordinary ink) upon it, must, Sinnett emphasises, all have been accomplished in the seconds between asking for it to be in her cushion and his ripping the stitching.

It may here be pointed out that if the phenomenon is to be viewed as fraudulent, the required confederates are the two Sinnetts: Mr Sinnett to make up the whole story about having seen Koot Hoomi in the night and found the note from him on the table in the morning; Mr or Mrs Sinnett to have unpicked their own cushion and sewn into it her brooch and the note (written by whom?) found with the brooch; and Mrs Sinnett to interrupt after Mr Sinnett had pretended to want to find the phenomenon in somebody else's cushion, so as to give him the pretext to re-open their own cushion, within which they both knew they had placed the things to be discovered. Yet if Sinnett was acting a charade, might he not have avoided including in the second letter to himself the criticism of his motives as 'selfish'? Olcott adds his observation that the thread with which the pillow was sewn was hardened with time, and the seam oversewn with silk cord.

Even if one conceives of both the Sinnetts and the Humes as confederates, still, how with all their confederacy could they have produced the cup and saucer phenomenon without the involvement of Olcott also? Note that nobody has ever alleged that Olcott, the Humes and the Sinnetts were, in fact, confederates.

The note found in the pillow had made no mention of the 'thank you' note, and at dinner that evening there fell from Sinnett's table-napkin as he unfolded it a further note, reading:[5]

> A few words more: why should you have felt disappointed at not receiving a direct reply to your last note? It was received in my room about half a minute after the currents for the production of the pillow-*dak* had been set ready and in full play . . .

Sinnett regarded the interest of this as lying in the glimpse it afforded of occult mechanism. The precipitation of the note and brooch into the place chosen could have occupied only seconds, but the 'currents' required had had to be prepared beforehand. (Might one suggest comparison with the operation of a gun or camera? It takes only a second to trigger the shot, but before that the instrument has to be manufactured, loaded and positioned. Should one picture Koot Hoomi watching the scene from his Kashmir valley, waiting for the moment to 'shoot'?)

With the ending of the hot weather, the British in Simla began to leave for their homes and work. Madame Blavatsky and Olcott left on 21 October for Amritsar, where, having settled into the bungalow lent them, they left Babula to cook and drove straight out to see 'the Golden Temple of the warlike Sikhs'. The edifice housing the Amrita Saras, the fount of immortality, comprised a fluted dome, rising from four arches. The whole rose from an island in a pool of crystal clear water, to which there was access by a narrow causeway, floored, like the pool and all other pavings, with finest marble. The upper parts were overlaid with gold, resplendent against the strong blue sky. They heard the *akalis* chanting verses from the Sikh holy book, the Granth.

Sinnett wrote another letter to Koot Hoomi and posted it to Madame Blavatsky at Amritsar, just before he and his wife left Simla for Allahabad. When they arrived at Allahabad he found waiting from him a letter from Madame Blavatsky enclosing the envelope in which he had sent his to her, postmarked by the Amritsar Post Office 27 October, and a telegram from Koot Hoomi, stamped by the Post Office 27.10.80 – the same date. Against 'From (Station)' was written by the Post Office clerk 'Jhelum' and against 'From (Person)', was written 'Koothoomi Lal Singh'. In fact, though he signs his letters 'Koot Hoomi' or 'K.H.', when Koot Hoomi has occasion to refer to himself in the third person he habitually writes 'Koothoomi'. Sinnett asked the Post Office for the original of the message. The original was in Koot Hoomi's hand. It was the proof for him that the Koot Hoomi letters could not have been written by Madame Blavatsky.

A few days later, Sinnett received a long letter from Koot Hoomi headed 'Amrita Saras, Oct. 29', in which he referred to their recent exchange:[6]

Received at Umritsar [Amritsar] on the 27th inst., at 2 p.m., I got your letter about thirty miles beyond Rawal Pindi, five minutes later and had an acknowledgement wired to you from Jhelum at 4 p.m. on the same afternoon.

Koot Hoomi said he had been occupied with two crises, one in the Society and one in Tibet:[7]

Russia is gradually massing her forces for a future invasion of that country under the pretext of a Chinese War. If she does not succeed it will be due to us.

He was again at Amritsar because, as he was on his way home to Tibet, he heard Madame Blavatsky's voice appealing to him to come back to India:

I was coming down the defiles of Kouenlun – Karakorum you call them – and saw an avalanche tumble. I had gone personally to see our chief to submit Mr Hume's important offer, and was crossing over to Ladak on my way home . . . Just as I was taking advantage of the awful stillness which usually follows such a cataclysm, to get a clearer view of the present situation and the disposition of the 'mystics' at Simla, I was rudely recalled to my senses. A familiar voice, as shrill as the one attributed to Sarasvati's peacock . . . shouted along the current, 'Olcott has raised the devil again . . . The Englishmen are going crazy . . . Koot Hoomi, *come quicker* and help me.' . . . What could I do but come? Argument through space with one who was in cold despair, and in a state of moral chaos was useless. So I determined to emerge from the seclusion of many years and spend some time with her to comfort her as well as I could. But our friend is not one to cause her mind to reflect with the philosophical resignation of Marcus Aurelius . . .

How had Olcott blundered? He had received a letter from H.M. Durand, Officiating Secretary to the government of India, thanking him for the papers he had sent him, which had been filed at the Foreign Office, and promising that so long as the Theosophical Society kept within its stated objects, the surveillance by which the founders had been annoyed would be discontinued. Olcott had written a jubilant but unguarded letter about this to an acquaintance who had, without his permission, made it available to *The Times of India*, where its publication had sparked new vexations.

Koot Hoomi continued his reply to Sinnett:

Colonel Olcott is doubtless 'out of time' with the feelings of English people of both classes; but nevertheless more in time *with us* than either. Him we can trust under *all* circumstances, and his faithful service is pledged to us come well, come ill . . . Where can we find an equal devotion? He is the one who never questions, but obeys; who may make innumerable mistakes out of excessive zeal but never is unwilling to repair his fault even at the cost of the greatest self-humiliation; who esteems the sacrifice of comfort and even life to be cheerfully risked whenever necessary; who will eat any food, or even go without; sleep on any bed, work in any place, fraternise with any outcast, endure any privation . . .

He agreed that Olcott should not be concerned with the Anglo-Indian Branch which Sinnett and Hume wished to create, except as overall President of the Theosophical Society. Nevertheless, he had been somewhat startled by the revelation of the extent to which Sinnett was put off by the slightly different manners of an American, of his own Anglo-Saxon race, and suggested he ask himself why he was so ready to submit himself to dictation by an Indian, whose ways, should he meet him in the flesh, he might find even more alien.

Our best, most learned, and holiest adepts are of the races of the 'greasy Tibetans' and the Punjabi Singhs – you know the lion is proverbially a dirty and offensive beast . . . and which of our holy *Shaberons* has had the benefit of even the little university education and inkling of European manners that has fallen to my share?

CHAPTER 36

The Sikhs: Morya and Koot Hoomi

Koot Hoomi had not been favourably impressed by everything he had seen whilst at Amritsar,[1] 'I have seen some of our proud old Sikhs drunk and staggering over the marble pavement of their sacred Temple . . .'. He means the marble floor of the Golden Temple, and Sikhs should be total abstainers. He says 'their' sacred temple, yet when he wrote to Sinnett above of 'the Punjabi Singhs . . . the lion is proverbially a dirty and offensive beast', surely he was associating himself with them, otherwise the stab would have been rude. Why is he Koot Hoomi Lal Singh? Singh is the Sikh name.

The Sikhs are a religious group broken away from Hinduism. Founded c. 1510 by Nanak, a Hindu influenced by the Sufi strain within Islam, the Sikhs believe in reincarnation, but dislike images of anthropomorphised deities and reject the caste system. This last is most important. In orthodox Hinduism there are four castes, sprung from four parts of the body of Brahma: the Brahmins, the top or priestly caste; the Kshatriyas, the caste of princes and warriors; the Vaisas, the commercial caste; and the Shudras or Shoodras, the labouring caste. For those born at the bottom there is no hope of rising. They are not the equals of those above them and never will be. Those who have lost their caste are Untouchables. In 1609, the Sikh Gobind Rai gathered to him five Sikhs (Sikh means 'disciple'), who being members of the four castes (was the fifth an outcaste?) drank nectar from one bowl, after which he called each of them Singh (lion). They then called him Gobind Singh. This drinking from one bowl and taking a new name was spiritually a tremendous revolutionary act.

The lion's name and the sense of spiritual fearlessness lent them extraordinary courage in battle. Moreover, as Sikhism became the dominant religion of the Punjab which breeds very tall men, they had their height to help make them impressive.

During the Indian Mutiny of 1857, the Sikhs supported the British. This is in line with Koot Hoomi's preference for a British presence. It is not that he thought the British wonderful. He has some sharp things to say of some of their behaviour. Simply, he saw the many peoples of India as too far sunken and divided to be able to form a self-standing nation at that time and the British presence as keeping out worse.

Prince Ranjit Singh, the cricketer, was only a child at this time (he was born in 1872); but he was to be sent to Trinity College, Cambridge, and, of course, later played for England. His nephew would go to Cheltenham. Did Koot Hoomi belong to this family of Singhs? His classical allusions suggest an education in England such as only a princely family could afford. In this connection, I would not pay too much attention to Koot Hoomi's reference to a conversation he had with G.H. Fechner.[2] Gustav Fechner (1801-87) graduated from Leipzig, and first made a reputation as a translator of French scientific work into German. This won him a teaching appointment in physics, though his interest shifted to metaphysics and it was in physiology that he obtained his eventual professor's chair at Leipzig. From 1851 onwards, he was making the neurological experiments now seen as preparing the way for modern psychology, but by which he was striving to prove the materialist interpretation of the universe false.[3] This may well have interested Koot Hoomi, but it would have to be a very strange Sikh family that sent its son to Leipzig to be educated. The Sikhs have no contact with Germany or continental Europe. Their natural links are all with the British. What seems to me more likely is they sent him to Oxford or Cambridge to read classics, and that he used the vacations to visit some of the continental centres of culture and learning. He does not say he was a student of Fechner, only that Fechner asked him what would be the Hindu view of something he, Fechner, had written. (To most Europeans, all Indians are Hindus.)

Koot Hoomi elsewhere remarks that on about a dozen occasions he attended meetings of a secret club, composed of a dozen or so people, collected together by Bulwer-Lytton for experiments in magic at a house in London. Amongst them was Eliphas Levi. Koot Hoomi says he did not expect anything good from it as the approach was wrong. Yet again, he has provided a detail that can be checked. I wrote to Miss Flower. She knew of no formally constituted club and did not think Bulwer-Lytton would have created one as he was most secretive about his interest in occultism. On the other hand, he did refer to meetings or séances at a Mrs Milner-Gibson's house in London as 'our little club'. Eliphas Levi was in London in 1854, in a hotel in Gower Street, Bulwer-Lytton being at 1 Park Lane and at Knebworth. This pin-points a year during which Koot Hoomi must have been in England, perhaps making journeys down to London from his university. It also tallies very well with the period during which Fechner's experiments must have prompted Koot Hoomi to make a call on him at Leipzig.

Two odd points stand out. In England today, Sikhs are not seen on motor-bicycles because they fear to lose their Sikhhood by removing their Sikh turbans in order to put on the regulation crash-helmet. Koot Hoomi, at any rate in the ravine near Shigatsè, went about bare-headed, his uncut hair (they must not cut it) floating all around him in the wind – except when, as a courtesy to the Panchèn Lama, he wore the Gelukpa yellow hat. I think the answer here is that there is a point in every mystic's evolution at which, whatever the orthodox religion in which he started, he transcends its outward observances, living in the truth that has no name.

The other odd point concerns his name, Koot Hoomi. In the Oriental Department of the British Museum they told me that the words were not Tibetan, though they thought they might be Mongolian. I wrote to the Mongolian Embassy and had a note back, 'These words are not Mongolian'. I sent them to the School of Oriental and African Studies of the University of London, asking if their assemblage of experts could think of anything more likely than Kuthumi, in the *Vishnu Purana* (in Wilson's translation, Book III, p.60), perhaps split down the middle to prevent English people from pronouncing the 'th' as in 'thumb'. I received a reply, signed C. Shackle, Head of Indology and of the Modern Languages and Literatures of South Asia, saying my letter had been seen 'by colleagues both in the Far East Department and in this Department, and none of us can còme up with a better explanation than the one you suggest'.

Indeed, where the Master refers to his name in the body of his letters he writes it in one word, as though the Sanskrit form were more natural to him. It is only in the signature that we find it split, and often reduced to the initials K.H. We cannot know why the Master did this – and as I write these words, another thought comes to me – did he? The earliest of the letters, as we know, were all precipitated by Djwal Khool, including the signatures; to the signatures he added 'Lal Singh', which was considered by the Masters to be an amusing but inappropriate invention, and also a spelling of the same in Sanskrit characters, with mistakes, which appears beneath. These include, notably, omissions of the *virana*, a slash required after a consonant when not followed by the sound of 'a', as in reciting the alphabet. We know the Sanskrit is Djwal Khool's, not only because of the mistakes but because it includes the 'Lal Singh' which the Master would not have allowed. Is it possible that Djwal Khool, not knowing Sanskrit very well, thought the name ought to be split as are many of the names in his native Tibetan? In that case, the Master, knowing it to be wrong, may have adopted it, with amusement, because the boy's ignorance had created for him the appearance of a first and second name, with initials that could be used as in English. Kuthumi, according to the *Vishnu Purana*, was one of the sages who helped to spread the knowledge of certain sacred scriptures. Our Master may have taken the name as his mystic one in Tibet because, after all, he tried to help spread knowledge, or possibly because he had been Kuthumi in a previous incarnation.

On the strength of the name Kuthumi, Mohini Chatterjee (see *infra*) tells us his Master was 'a Kashmiri Brahmin'. This overlooks certain considerations. Olcott says that when Madame Blavatsky and he went again to the Golden Temple:[4]

> at the shrine where the swords, sharp steel disks, coats of mail and other warlike weapons of the Sikh warrior-priests are exposed to view in charge of akalis, I was greeted to my surprise and joy with a loving smile by one of the Masters, who for the moment was figuring as one of the guardians, and who gave each of us a fresh rose, with a blessing in his eyes.

Olcott has too much respect ever to name a Master in print, but this sounds like Koot Hoomi, who was in Amritsar at that time and went to the Golden Temple. A Brahmin could not have been officiating at the Sikhs' most sacred temple.

Morya was a Rajput. The Rajputs are Kshattriyas, not the second caste, as in the Brahmin system, which they scorn, but a noble race. Some Rajputs have become Sikhs, but the Rajputs have a much more ancient tradition. There are four tribes of Rajputs, descended from the sun, the moon, the fire and the great snake. Morya was a Rajput descended from the sun. The sun and moon tribes are the important ones. There was an Indian Emperor, Chandragupta Maurya, probably a Buddhist, contemporary with Alexander the Great. The third ruler of his dynasty, known as the Mauryas, was his grandson, the great Buddhist Emperor Asoka, who reigned over practically the whole of India 272–32 BC, bringing the blessing of Buddhism to his whole Empire. The Mauryas or Moryas, Madame Blavatsky tells us, were descended from a tribe related to the Sakya tribe, into which Gautama Buddha was born.[5]

Master Morya never signs his name in full. He signs an M, followed by something that could almost be a C, though I think it is the right-hand tail of the M continued and carried upwards, with three dots round it, in a manner reminiscent of a mystic symbol consisting of two or three dots flanking a slanting line. One asks oneself, therefore, whether Madame Blavatsky spelled his name by ear, unaware of the spelling 'Maurya' usual in English histories and encyclopaedias and of the Sanskrit underlying it. That is not necessarily so. In *The Cambridge Shorter History of India*, one reads, 'Buddhist tradition asserts that the Mauryas were descended from an ancient noble family, the Moriyas, who play a prominent part at the time of Buddha'.[6] Since Madame Blavatsky is asserting the Buddhist tradition as she understood it from her Master Morya, it is orderly that she should represent the pronunciation he would have given her as the true one. It was natural for this family to be the defenders of the Buddhists against the Brahmins, who attacked by declaring them to be descended from Shudras, though they later adopted a more flattering tune when seducing waverers back into the Hindu fold. Today there are few Buddhists in India, in contrast to Sri Lanka, Siam, Burma, Tibet and the Far East. There subsists an ancient prophecy that before the end of time the Moryas will restore the Kshattriyas and a Chandragupta will once more reign. Madame Blavatsky warns against taking this too literally, yet now we can understand the significance of the mystic name taken by her Master, and how he and Koot Hoomi could, without breaking with the Sikhs, think of themselves as essentially Buddhists and settle as neighbours of the Panchèn Lama.

There is, however, a complication. In the *Annals and Antiquities of Rajasthan*, by James Tod, Table I sets out the 'Vansavali or Genealogies of the Races of Soorya and Chandra from Icshwaca and Boodha to Rama and Crishna'. Surya (Soorya) is the sun, and Chandra the moon. Both races descend from Narayan or Vishnu, but the solars claim in their tree Vaivasvata Manu and Ishvara, and the lunars claim the Buddha. Table II, continuing the dynasties up to AD 700, shows 'Chandra Mori or Chandragoopta' and his grandson 'Asoca' as the founding and third members of a lunar dynasty (the fourth). Indeed, as Chandra means 'moon', it seems logical that they should be lunar. But then, either Olcott was mistaken in believing his 'Father' to be of the solar dynasty, or the Master Morya was a Rajput physically descended from the sun, who felt himself spiritually descended from the great rival whose link was with the Buddha.

Tod gives the states ruled by the lunar dynasty as the Kingdom of Magadha and Indaprestha (Delhi), and the states of the solar dynasty as Ayodia, Saurashtra and Mewar. Mewar was the only one of the Rajput states which Akbar was unable to conquer.

If the Buddhic connection is appropriate in one way, so, perhaps, is Mewar, in another.

CHAPTER 37

A controversial letter

There had been formed at Allahabad an all-Brahmin Lodge, the only Lodge of the Theosophical Society to omit from its objects the following: 'To form a nucleus of the Universal Brotherhood of Mankind', presumably because a Brahmin, unable even to sit at table with a non-Brahmin, could not call a non-Brahmin 'brother'. Now they had protested to Sinnett that they had not received messages from the Masters and did not understand why not, seeing that 'beef-eating, wine-drinking Englishmen' had been so favoured. It was in these circumstances that Madame Blavatsky wrote to Sinnett from 'Dehra Dun. Friday 14th' (no year),[1] 'Saw at last M. and showed him your last . . . I wrote this under his dictation and now copy it'.

Morya announced, somewhat roughly, that because Koot Hoomi and he had opened a correspondence with two men it did not give everybody else a claim to hear from them, especially such as had 'never given up caste . . . their exclusive selfishness', and none of that group would hear from them. H.P.B.'s letter continues:[2]

> . . . unless he is prepared to do as D. Mavalenkar did, – give up entirely caste, his old superstitions and show himself a true reformer – (especially in the case of child marriage) . . . It is useless for a member to argue 'I am one of a pure life, I am a total teetotaller and an abstainer from meat and vice . . .' There are 100 of thousands of Fakhirs, Sannyasis and Saddhus leading the most pure lives, and yet being as they are, on the path of *error*, never having had an opportunity to meet, see or even hear from us . . . Mr Sinnett and Hume are exceptions. Their beliefs are no barriers to us for they have *none*. They may have had influence around them, bad magnetic emanations the result of drink, Society and promiscuous physical associations (resulting even from shaking hands with impure men) . . . which with a little effort we could counteract . . . Not so with the magnetism . . . proceeding from erroneous and sincere beliefs. Faith in the Gods and God and other superstitions attracts millions of foreign influences, living entities . . . we would have to use more than ordinary exercise of power to drive them away . . . unprogressed planetaries who delight in personating gods. There are . . . 'Chohans of Darkness', who have never been born on this or any other sphere . . .

There seems to be a warning here that the polytheistic religions, unless their symbols are kept very pure, risk degenerating into the cult of nameless entities which, when not indeed demons, can, by inhabiting the thought-forms engendered, form distracting company. I knew a Catholic lady once, who was convinced that all hits at religion in the *Mahatma Letters*, including it seemed this one, were at the Christian Church. Well, if the cap is felt to fit there may be no harm in anybody's wearing it, but it was not for her Church this was intended. Perhaps the Muslims, who forbid all personifications of deity, keep to the safe side.

After Madame Blavatsky's death, G.N. Chakravarti, who had influence with Annie Besant, complained about this letter and she, and Olcott (to whom she passed the complaint although he did not see the letter), averred that it could not be genuine.[3] Yet it is now in the British Museum and it is in Madame Blavatsky's handwriting. Annie Besant and Olcott misunderstood the letter to be an attack on the Hindus, whereas it was the Brahmins' contempt for others that called forth the Master's rebuke. In any case, neither seems to have taken the point that the Moryas or Mauryas were the historic and legendary enemies of the Brahmin caste.

Damodar had, by breaking caste in sitting at table with Theosophists, forfeited his inheritance; his father made an alteration to his will.[4]

CHAPTER 38

First instruction concerning karma

Hume also had written to Koot Hoomi, and he lent Sinnett a reply he had from him, which we have to take from Sinnett's transcription. There are some interesting passages about the difference between the Adepts' science and physical science:[1]

> you . . . see no difference between the energy expended by the traveller who pushes aside the bush that obstructs his path, and the scientific experimenter who expends an equal amount of energy in setting a pendulum in motion. We do; for we know there is a world of difference between the two. The one uselessly dissipates and scatters force, the other concentrates and stores it . . . in the one case there is but brute force flung out without any transmutation of that brute energy into the higher potential form of spiritual dynamics, and in the other there is just that . . . No fact . . . is interesting except in the degree of its potentiality of moral results . . . Cosmic energy is something eternal and incessant; matter is indestructible . . . And yet even these scientific facts never suggested any proof that Nature consciously prefers that matter should be indestructible under organic rather than inorganic forms, and that she works slowly but incessantly towards the . . . evolution of conscious life out of inert material. Hence their [the scientists'] ignorance about the scattering and concretion of cosmic energy . . . we see a vast difference between the two qualities of two equal amounts of energy expended by two men, of whom one . . . is on his way to his daily quiet work, and another on his way to denounce a fellow-creature at the police-station . . . And why? Because the thought of man upon being evolved passes into the inner world, and becomes an active entity by associating itself, coalescing we might term it, with an elemental – that is to say, with one of the semi-intelligent forces of the kingdoms. It survives as an active intelligence – a creature of the mind's begetting – for a longer or shorter period proportionate with the original intensity of the cerebral action which generated it. Thus a good thought is perpetuated as an active, beneficent power, an evil one as a maleficent demon. And so man is continually peopling his current in space with a world of his own, crowded with the offspring of his fancies, desires, impulses and passions . . . which reacts upon any sensitive or nervous organisation which comes in contact with it, in proportion to its dynamic energy. The Buddhist calls this his 'Skamdha', the Hindu gives it the name of 'Karma'. The adept involves [sic, evolves?] these shapes consciously; other men throw them off unconsciously . . . the building ant, the busy bee, the nidificent bird, accumulate each in its own humble way as much cosmic energy in its potential form as a Haydn, a Plato or a ploughman turning his furrow, in theirs; the hunter who kills his game for pleasure or profit, or the positivist who applies his intellect to proving that $+x+ = -$ are wasting and scattering their energy, no less than the tiger which springs on its prey. They all rob Nature instead of enriching her, and will all, in the degree of their intelligence, find themselves accountable.

Here is a world of statements to ponder. All the creative activities, such as nest-building or home-making, and food collecting, actually build us up, it seems, gathering and storing energy for us at a higher level, for higher use; while the destructive actions actually break us down. The tiger has its karma, but less than the karma of the man who acts in a predatory and destructive way, because its thought is less. One seems to find here set out a scientific basis for a moral law, by which, in a poetically just universe, all get their deserts. In this passage alone there is enough to live by.

Unfortunately, Hume seemed less interested in this profound teaching than in some passages in Koot Hoomi's letter to Sinnett, which Sinnett showed him in return for Hume's showing him his; picking up the reference to the Russian menace, Hume says that if he thought Russia would govern Tibet and India better than the British he would work for it, though it seemed to be a corrupt despotism. He goes on to say, 'I should not object . . . to dear old Olcott's supervision, because . . . Sinnett and I are both quite capable of shutting him up . . . But . . . we both know that we are intellectually his superiors'.[2]

Neither of these points was well received by the Brothers. The first earned him – but only a long time afterwards – the animadversion from Koot Hoomi 'You pride yourself upon *not* being a "patriot" – I do not'. As for the patronising yet contemptuous manner of accepting Olcott as President of the Theosophical Society, this went down even less well in Tibet. This letter of Hume's, being examined there, laid the basis of an opinion by Koot Hoomi, Morya and their chief, or Chohan, that Hume was cold, conceited and proud to the point of arrogance; this was an opinion which, though they were allowed to persevere with him for the present in case he improved, was with time and closer acquaintance to become more settled.

Koot Hoomi's next letter to Sinnett begins:[3]

> I have your letter of November 9th, abstracted by our special *osmosis* from the envelope at Meerut, and yours to our 'old lady' in its half empty registered shell safely sent on to Cawnpore, to make her swear at me . . . But she is too weak to play at the astral postman just now.

It appears Sinnett had written a letter to Koot Hoomi and sent it enclosed in one to Madame Blavatsky with the request to 'post' it for him astrally, and Koot Hoomi had saved her the trouble by abstracting it from the envelope before she received it. *Osmosis* means pushing or percolation of fluids through porous partitions. Koot Hoomi regrets that through her weakness she had given Sinnett one message from him incorrectly 'I often neglect to give her an extra rub over her poor sick head' – he had not asked her to tell Sinnett an Anglo-Indian Branch would come to nothing, but that it would do so with Hume in it.

Sinnett must have said that he had written that Olcott was out of 'tune' not 'time' with the English, for Koot Hoomi continues:

> Did you write 'tune'? . . . out of 'time' or out of 'tune' is all one . . . you ought to adopt my old-fashioned habit of 'little lines' over the 'm's'. Those bars are useful, even though 'out of tune and time' with modern calligraphy.

This explains the horizontal lines to be found above the letter 'm' throughout Koot Hoomi's writing. Morya does not use it, neither does Madame Blavatsky or Sinnett, despite the recommendation.

Koot Hoomi does not think Madame Blavatsky will really be able to help the Anglo-Indian Branch with much instruction in practical occultism.[4]

> I am afraid she has remained too long a time outside the *adytum* to be of much use for practical *explanations* . . . she is sadly in need of a few months of recuperative *villagiatura* on the glaciers with her old Master [Morya] before she can again be entrusted with such a difficult task. Be very cautious with her in case she stops with you on her way down. Her nervous system is terribly shaken, and she requires every care.

What is meant by the *'adytum'*? Koot Hoomi must mean that inner, holy place within Tibet where he and Morya live.

There is an undated letter from Madame Blavatsky to Sinnett which gives an important clue. Speaking of a portrait of Morya (not the Schmiechen one, which was not done until much later) she says;[5] 'it does not look at all like him, since he never wears now his white *puggery*, but simply sticks a yellow saucer on top of his head like K.H.'. A puggery is a light kind of muslin turban. He would wear a white turban again later. Perhaps, like anyone else, he could change his attire. But 'a yellow saucer' can only refer to the Tibetan Yellow Hat order, the Gelukpa, called Yellow Hat to distinguish it from the Red Hats. The Gelukpa (virtuous ones) were a reformed order instituted by the Tibetan Lama Tsong-ka-pa (1357–1419). Tsong-ka-pa (of whom more later) was disgusted by what appeared to him to be the perversion of the Buddhist teaching under the influence of the old Bön religion of Tibet.

Madame Blavatsky and Olcott were making their way down from the hills slowly. In Lahore, she succumbed to Punjab fever. Olcott sat up with her all night and the doctor prescribed quinine and digitalis.

On 1 December they arrived together at the Sinnetts' house in Allahabad. Olcott left for Benares on 3 December, Madame Blavatsky joining him there on 11 December, 'and we were as glad to see each other as if we had been long separated'. They both returned to Allahabad and stayed with the Sinnetts until 28 December.

During this time Sinnett received, on about 10 December, another letter from Koot Hoomi, saying:[6]

> . . . of course I have to read every word you write . . . whether it be through my physical or spiritual eyes the time required for it is practically the same. As much may be said of my replies. For whether I 'precipitate' or dictate them or write my answers myself, the difference in time saved is very minute. I have to *think* it over, to photograph *every* word and sentence carefully in my brain before it can be repeated by 'precipitation' . . . to sit with your lady is more than useless. Your magnetisms are too similar and – you will get nothing.

Madame Blavatsky – who had a sudden attack of rheumatic fever, which had now abated – and Olcott reached Bombay on 30 December, where they spent the New Year 1881 at the new bungalow they had taken, the Crow's Nest.

On 30 January Sinnett received a further letter from Koot Hoomi, not occultly delivered but enclosed in a letter from Madame Blavatsky sent to him through the post, saying their 'venerable Hobilgan' had told him he had no right to encourage Sinnett, held back as he must be by 'previous and most sacred duties'.[7] Does he mean that Sinnett cannot leave his family to come to Tibet, if that is what he has in his mind?

On 19 February, Illarion, passing through Bombay on his way to Tibet, called on Madame Blavatsky and Olcott.[8] This must explain a passage in a letter from Koot Hoomi received about 20 February, in which he contrasts Sinnett, as a cool thinker, with Madame Blavatsky and Olcott, who are enthusiasts and quick thinkers – the latter disposition having its liabilities. A chela of his, called Disinherited, was that morning dictating something to Madame Blavatsky. He was called that by Koot Hoomi because he had been disinherited by his grandfather, who did however pass on to him a stock of notepaper, some of which he made available to Koot Hoomi. Suddenly Madame Blavatsky picked up another voice, that of 'one of ours who is passing through Bombay from Cyprus, on his way to Tibet' and tried to listen to both at once, becoming confused. (This must surely have been before Illarion's physical arrival at the Crow's Nest.)

In an interesting passage, Koot Hoomi assures Sinnett that:[9]

> . . . we (or most of us) are far from being the heartless, morally dried up mummies some would fancy us to be. 'Mejnoor' [sic] is very well where he is – as an ideal character of a thrilling – in many respects truthful story. Yet, believe me, few of us would care to play the part in life of a desiccated pansy between the leaves of a volume of solemn poetry.

Koot Hoomi's allusion is to a character, Mejnour, in Bulwer-Lytton's novel, *Zanoni*, representing what seems to be Lytton's idea of the impassive Adept, drained of all human emotions. In an earlier letter, Koot Hoomi has assurred Sinnett that so far, indeed, he has not, because of being an Adept, found the ties of friendship, blood and country become less dear. The tie of blood may refer to his sister, of whom we hear occasionally, and her child.

He gives Sinnett permission to quote from his letters in a book he would like to write.

Koot Hoomi says he is leaving space at the foot to 'accommodate' the chela known as Disinherited, who wants to write a note, but endorses it with his own initials. The footnote warns Sinnett of the 'friend' mentioned in a letter he has received from Lord Lindsay:[10]

> It is Home – the medium . . . He is the bitterest and most cruel enemy O. and Mad. B. have, though he has never met either of them . . . I feel it my duty to warn you, for this one is an exceptionally bad man – hated by the Spiritualists and mediums as much as he is despised by those – who have learned to know him. Yours is a work that clashes directly with his . . . He is no man to stop before a slanderous accusation – however vile and lying.

CHAPTER 39

The Mahatma Letters:
Morya takes over

Madame Blavatsky and Olcott had only recently received, through Koot Hoomi, a reprimand from his and Morya's Chohan for becoming obsessed with phenomena, and they had been admonished that what the Brothers wanted was not a magic parlour in Simla but a brotherhood of humanity. Now, Illarion told them the same thing. But they had redrafted their objects two days before, on 17 February, so that the first object was now 'To form the nucleus of a Universal Brotherhood of Humanity'.

On 23 April 1881, Olcott left for another tour of Ceylon, and for some months we lose his eye-witness account of Madame Blavatsky's daily movements.

The Sinnetts went early in the year to Paris and London, where his book *The Occult World* appeared. It was an account of the phenomena produced by Madame Blavatsky in his presence, with extracts from Koot Hoomi's letters. Whilst in London, Sinnett received a letter from Koot Hoomi through the post, addressed to him in the Master's hand 'c/o J. Herbert Stack, Esq., 30 Kensington Gardens, London' but bearing a French stamp and postmarked Nantes, Loire Inferieure. We shall later realise that precipitation required expense of energy proportionate to the distance to be covered and also to the auric fitness of the recipient for it to be of any help in reception. Sinnett's being nil, Koot Hoomi had presumably precipitated the letter to another Master (or senior pupil) who was at that moment in France, with the request to put a stamp of the country on it and commit to the post. It arrived the next day, 26 March, and read:[1]

It is from the depths of an unknown valley, amid the crags and glaciers of Terich-Mir – a vale never trodden by European foot since the day its parent mount was itself breathed out from within our Mother Earth's bosom – that your friend sends you these lines . . . A letter 'from the abodes of eternal snow and purity' sent to and received 'At the abodes of vice' . . . Queer, *n'est-ce pas*? [is it not?] . . . As Spiritualists of today have degraded 'Spirit', so have the Hindus degraded Nature by their anthropomorphic conceptions of it. Nature alone can incarnate the Spirit of limitless contemplation . . . But you can hardly be expected to enjoy the above *phanerosis* of our teachings . . .

Phanerosis is Greek for manifestation, here used in the sense of exposition: *osmosis, phanerosis*. It is noticeable that Koot Hoomi likes Greek-based words. One doubts if Sinnett – or Madame Blavatsky – would have known what they meant. He concludes: 'Our hapless "Old Lady" is sick. Liver, kidneys, head, brain, legs, every organ and limb shows fight and snaps its fingers at her efforts to ignore them'.

As Sinnett's book is entirely about Madame Blavatsky and her phenomena, one would have expected him to share his royalties with her, but that does not appear to have been the case.

The Sinnetts returned to India and asked Madame Blavatsky to join them at Allahabad; then they all went together to spend the hot weather at Simla, this time as the guests of the Humes.

This stay cannot have been a happy one, for we find a letter from Koot Hoomi to Hume and Sinnett received (how?) during it:[2]

I am painfully aware of the fact that the habitual incoherence of her statements – especially when excited – and her strange ways make her in your opinion a very undesirable transmitter of our teachings. Nevertheless, kind Brothers . . . this unbalanced mind, the seeming incongruity of her speeches and ideas, her nervous excitement, all that in short, which is so calculated to upset the feelings of sober-minded people, whose notions of reserve and manners are shocked by such strange outbursts of what they regard as her temper . . . is intimately connected with her occult training in Tibet, and due to her being sent out alone into the world to gradually prepare the way for others . . . After nearly a century of fruitless search, our chiefs had to avail themselves of the only opportunity to send out a European body upon European soil to serve as a connecting link between that country and our own . . . remember what she tried to explain . . . the seven principles in the human being. Now, no man or woman unless he be an initiate of the 'fifth circle', can leave the precincts of Bod-Las [Tibet] and return back into the world in his integral whole . . . One at least of his seven satellites has to remain behind for two reasons: the first to form the necessary connecting link, the wire of transmission – the second as the safest warranter that certain things will never be divulged. She is no exception to the rule . . . to hold her responsible for her purely physiological excitement, and to let her see your contemptuous smiles, was positively *cruel*.

Sinnett was still full of the people he had met in London, including the Spiritualist Stainton Moses, and that is the reason why we now find Koot Hoomi answering what seems to have been a question as to the identity of Moses's 'spirit guide', whom he called Imperator. Koot Hoomi says that he worded an earlier reply to this question guardedly as 'I had no right to divulge the "*secret of a brother*"'[3]. This surely means that Imperator is not, as Moses imagines, a spirit, and it may be that Koot Hoomi is referring to Morya, whom he elsewhere describes as 'an imperious sort of chap'. The trouble with Stainton Moses, he says, here and *passim*, is that it is impossible to open his eyes; he talks sense when Imperator is speaking through him, but as soon as he is left to himself, he relapses into his habitual illusory notions. We shall find much the same said of Mrs Billing, the most honest of the London mediums; her Ski is sometimes Morya, sometimes one or other of his fellow Brothers. She never notices the difference. This renders her liable to betray, unintentionally, since unless guarded she could be taken over by one of the Brothers of the Shadow, without detecting that she was not hearing the voice of the Ski she had learned to trust. All mediums are liable in this way. In the present letter, Koot Hoomi warns Sinnett:[3]

All of you have been more or less imprudent . . . Notwithstanding the purity of motives, the Chohan might one day consider but the results, and these may threaten to become too disastrous for him to overlook . . . Very soon I will have to leave you to yourselves for the period of three months. Whether it will be in October or January will depend on the impulse given to the Society . . . The brandy atmosphere in the house is dreadful.

A note marked as received in October refers further to the coming retirement. As nothing is settled, Koot Hoomi will have to forgo his projected journey to Bhootan (Bhutan) and Morya will go in his place:[4]

My chiefs desire me . . . to be present at our New Year's festivals, February next, and in order to be prepared for it I have to avail myself of the three intervening months. I will, therefore, bid you now good-bye . . .

The Tibetan New Year is celebrated at the new moon of February, or sometimes of March.

The next letter is from Morya. He had not wished to correspond with Sinnett or Hume, but now took up the burden at his Brother's request. His letters are rougher than Koot Hoomi's. The ink is red, and whereas Koot Hoomi's hand is upright and somewhat rounded, Morya's is slanting and bears more resemblance to the hand one finds written by Indians. That is to say, there is the slight awkwardness of a hand not really practised in writing English. Indeed he confesses to that, and Koot Hoomi says elsewhere that Morya hates writing letters. Something Hume has said has displeased him, for he delivers himself of some opening sarcasms:[5]

We of the Indo-Tibetan hovels . . . we ignorant Asiatics of Tibet, accustomed to rather follow the thought of our interlocutor or correspondent than the words he clothes it in – concern ourselves generally but little with the accuracy of the expression . . .

A few days before leaving us, Koot Hoomi speaking of you said to me as follows: 'I feel weary of these never ending disputations. The more I try to explain to both of them the circumstances that control us and that interpose between us so many obstacles to free intercourse, the less they understand me! . . . It is as though we were hallooing to each other across an impassible ravine . . .'

Two days later when his 'retreat' was decided upon in parting he asked me: 'Will you watch over my work, will you see it falls not into ruins?' I promised. What is there I would not have promised him at that hour? At a certain spot not to be mentioned to outsiders, there is a chasm spanned by a frail bridge of woven grasses and with a raging torrent beneath . . . it hangs like a spider's web and seems to be rotten and impassible. Yet it is not; and he who dares the trial and succeeds – as he will if it is right he should be permitted – comes into a gorge of surpassing beauty of scenery – to one of our places and some of our people, of which and of whom there is no note or minute among European geographers. At a stone's throw from the old Lamasery stands the old tower, within whose bosom have gestated generations of Bodhisatvas. It is there, where now rests your lifeless friend – my brother, the light of my soul, to whom I made a faithful promise to watch during his absence over his work. And is it likely, I ask you, that but two days after his retirement I, his faithful friend and brother would gratuitously show disrespect to his European friends? . . .

Mr. Hume prides himself in the thought that he has never had 'a spirit of veneration' for anything but his own abstract ideals. We are perfectly aware of it. Nor could he possibly have any veneration for anyone or anything, as all the veneration his nature is capable of is – *concentrated upon himself.* This is a fact . . . he is simply . . . *the embodiment of pride.*

It did not matter that in a letter written to Olcott, Hume had made 'an insulting fling at me', but 'My Rajput blood will never permit me to see a woman hurt in her feelings'.

Nevertheless, Morya does appreciate what Hume is trying to do for the millions of the native peoples of India, particularly the weak and oppressed, which is in the spirit of the Society's first object.

He must refuse Sinnett's persistent request for more phenomena: indubitably proving the Masters' existence:

I wish I could impress upon your minds the deep conviction that we do not wish Mr. Hume or you to prove conclusively to the public that we really exist. Please realise the fact that so long as men doubt there will be curiosity and enquiry, and that enquiry stimulating reflections which beget effort, but let our secret be more thoroughly vulgarised and not only will sceptical society derive no great good but our privacy would be constantly endangered and have to be continually guarded at an unreasonable cost of power . . . I close the longest letter I have ever written in my life . . .

      M

Hume had taunted Olcott that he had given up the world without becoming an Adept. Olcott wrote from Ceylon on 30 September 1881:[6]

For six years . . . I have known perfect happiness. It has seemed to you 'the saddest thing of all' to see me giving up the world and everything that makes the happiness of those living in the world; and yet, after all these years . . . not made an adept . . . But if you will only reflect for one moment what it is to transform a worldly man, such as I was in 1874 – a man of clubs, drinking parties, mistresses . . . into . . . a BROTHER, you will cease to wonder . . .

Indeed, he had come a long way, though there had been setbacks:

Most of all I regret a certain Magyar philosopher, who had begun to give me a course of instruction in occult dynamics, but was repelled by an outbreak of my old earthly nature. But I shall win him back . . .

This refers to the Hungarian Adept, later called the Master Rákóczy.

Olcott now received a letter, dated August 1881, from Judge, telling him his ex-wife was now re-married, to a southerner called Cannon. This was probably a relief.

With the coming of the cold weather, the Sinnetts returned to Allahabad and Madame Blavatsky to Bombay; on 19 December Olcott also returned to Bombay.

Ross Scott had married the Humes' daughter, Minnie, and the couple came to stay. Together with Madame Blavatsky, Olcott and others, they were sitting on the balcony one moonlight December night when Ross Scott, his chair facing into the house, saw through the darkened library into a lighted room beyond, when to his surprise an Indian in white dress with white turban of a Rajput entered. He stood by a table, writing something on it. Ross Scott recognised him from the portrait he had been shown of Morya, and they all made towards him, but he vanished – at a point where there was no door. On the table was a note in the familiar red writing. A statement of this phenomenon was drawn up instantly and signed, 'Ross Scott, B.C.S.; Minnie J.B. Scott; H.S. Olcott; H.P. Blavatsky; M. Moorad Ali Beg [an Englishman who had embraced Islam]; Damodar K. Mavalankar'.[7]

Early in 1882, Madame Blavatsky received a letter from Hume (it is dated 'Jan. 4th, 1881', but the text makes it plain he had forgotten to change the year at the beginning of it.) It began:[8]

My dear Old Lady,
  And tho' I am desperately inclined at times to believe that you are an impostor, I believe I love you more than all of them . . .

Against this is written in Morya's hand:

As there are perverted natures which come to love physical deformity as a contrast to beauty, so also there are those who find a rest in the moral depravity of vitiated persons. Such would consider *imposture* as *cleverness*.

Hume refers to Koot Hoomi's explanation:

that you are a psychological cripple, one of your principles being in pawn in Tibet – if so the more shame to them keeping other people's property to the great detriment of the owner. But . . . It ain't the Hoola sariram, the body . . . It can't be the linga sariram as that can't part from the body . . . it ain't the kama rupa . . .

Morya comments:[9]

Very clever – but suppose it is neither *one of the seven* particularly but all? Every one of them a 'cripple' and forbidden the exercise of its full powers? And suppose such is the wise law of a farseeing power?

It will later be explained the seven principles are themselves each sub-divided into seven, so it could be a layer from each of them.

Hume says he is writing a pamphlet in which he first puts the arguments against Theosophy then those for it. He is drawing for the latter upon a letter written him by Olcott from Ceylon, omitting a passage 'which the world would at once hit upon as pointing to a transcendental flirtation between Morier [Morya] at this "most exquisite specimen of perfect womanhood", K.H.'s sister . . .'

Morya comments:[9]

As for the sentence about my brother's sister, no one with any delicacy would have thought of giving it to the public. The public, represented so brutally indecent in thought, that even one of its most accomplished leaders could not read of the pure sisterly friendship of a holy woman for her brother's lifelong brother in occult research without descending to the grovelling thought of a sensual relationship must be but a herd of swine.

Hume asks, 'When is our dear old Christ – I mean K.H., again to appear on the scene – he is quite our favourite actor . . .' Morya comments, 'The man blasphemes! K.H. will never be an *actor* for the gratification of anyone'. Morya added that on 5 January he had both written to and projected himself before Ross Scott: 'Whoever else will see us it will *never* be Mr. Hume. He can retire but Mr. Sinnett need not break with him'.

Hume's pamphlet in its current form was not approved.

On 17 February Olcott left on another tour, and on 6 March Madame Blavatsky joined him in Calcutta. There they stayed with Colonel and Mrs Gordon until 19 April, when they embarked on the *India* for Madras. They arrived on 23 April and attended a formal reception for them organised by T. Subba Row (Rao). The Hon. Humayam Jah, a survivor of the family of Tipu Sultan, the Tiger of Mysore, last Moghul Emperor of southern India, read to them an address of welcome bound in red morocco and placed garlands about their necks.

On 30 April, Madame Blavatsky and Olcott boarded a houseboat for a trip up-country by the Buckingham Canal. There was only one small cabin, with a mattress on each side of it. It was the first and only time they shared a sleeping-chamber. He writes in retrospect,[10]

> I see a picture of H.P.B. in her shabby wrapper, sitting opposite me on her locker, her huge head with its brown crinkled hair bent over the page she was writing on, a look of introverted thought in her light blue eyes, her aristocratic hand driving the pen swiftly over the lines, and no sound to be heard save the liquid music of ripples against the boat's sides . . . Dear, lamented friend, companion, colleague, teacher, chum . . . I believe we have worked in lives before, I believe we shall work in lives to come, for the good of mankind.

On 8 May they landed at Muttukur, whence they proceeded overland by palanquin, at one point fording a river so deep that the coolies bearing them, up to their armpits in water, had to balance the palanquin poles on their heads. Olcott, going first, heard H.P.B. wailing from the palanquin behind that she was being upset; he called back that she was too fat to sink.

Everywhere they gave talks. Most of the people were very welcoming, but when a Brahmin Pundit of the Vedantin School turned up they felt he hoped to catch H.P.B. out in argument. He was, says Olcott, worsted by her, and thereafter became their enemy.

They had long had it in mind to find a permanent home for the Theosophical Society, and when on 31 May they were shown a property on the Adyar River, they knew at a glance their 'future home was found'.[11] Negotiations for purchase were put in hand at once, and meanwhile they returned to Bombay.

In June they accepted a joint invitation to Baroda. On 15 July Olcott left again for Ceylon. H.P.B. remained in Bombay. She did not, this year, join the Sinnetts or the Humes either in Allahabad or in Simla, yet the most important of all the Mahatma Letters arrived there in her absence.

CHAPTER 40

The Mahatma Letters
further teachings

The Masters' letters began to contain more teaching, and some was given _ Sinnett orally by Madame Blavatsky. Thus, in his *Esoteric Buddhism*, he was able to give the constitution of man:[1]

1 The Body – *Rupa*
2 Vitality – *Prana* or *Jiva*
3 Astral Body – *Linga Sharira*
4 Animal Soul – *Kama Manas*
5 Human Soul – *Manas*
6 Spiritual Soul – *Buddhi*
7 Spirit – *Atma*

'Astral' was a term taken over from European mediaevalists (Besant and Leadbeater will transfer it to mean 4). At death, 1, 2, 3 and 4 disintegrate. *Manas* in union with *Buddhi* is the 'true individuality', which 'assimilates to itself the eternal life-power residing but in the 7th. The chief object of our struggles and initiations is to achieve this union while yet on this earth. Those who succeed will have nothing to fear in the Fifth, Sixth and Seventh Rounds. Our beloved K.H.' continued Morya, 'is on his way to this goal – the highest of all beyond us in this sphere'.[2]

What are these Rounds? The Earth, also, has seven principles. Koot Hoomi presents an image of a chain of seven beads, the fourth the lowest and heaviest. This is Globe D, our Earth. The life-wave, having descended from A, the lightest, to D, the heaviest, reascends to G, which is as light as A. (These globes must not be confused with the other planets of the solar system.)

Morya gives us an image:[3]

Go to your fortepiano and execute upon the lower register of keys the seven notes of the lower octave – up and down. Begin *pianissimo*; *crescendo* from the first key and having struck *fortissimo* on the last *lower* note go back *diminuendo* getting out of your last note a hardly perceptible sound – '*morendo pianissimo*' (as I luckily for my illustration find it printed in one of the music pieces in K.H.'s old portmanteau). The first and last notes will represent to you the first and last spheres in the cycle of evolution – the *highest*! The one you strike *once* is our planet. Remember you have to reverse the order on the fortepiano and begin with the seventh note, not with the first.

He means that nature is forever playing through our necklace of worlds, including the worlds of effects which follow each world of causes, ti, la, soh, fa, mi, re, doh, re, mi, fa, soh, la, ti.

The Rounds are desperately difficult to understand. Even Koot Hoomi, referring to a very detailed exposition in the Chinese books of the *Kiu-te*, avers they are almost incomprehensible, while 'Their commentaries are worse still'. (Madame Blavatsky will later tell us there are both the ordinary exoteric *Kiu-te* and very secret esoteric *Kiu-te*, but for a long time not even the former could be found. Now a bibliography of them has been issued.)[4]

It is dangerous to turn to Sinnett for simplication, since in his *Esoteric Buddhism* he committed the momentous blunder of making Mars and Mercury the C and E globes of our chain, in which he was followed by Leadbeater and A.E. Powell. We do not have three physical bodies; why should the Earth have three? Madame Blavatsky had to correct this in *The Secret Doctrine*, and it would seem safest not to go beyond the clues in the *Mahatma Letters*:

we are agreed to call the passage of a monad from globe 'A' to globe . . . 'G'
the encasement in all or each of the four kingdoms . . . as a mineral, a vegetable,
animal and man or the deva kingdom.[5]

. . . in our string of globes it starts at globe 'A' of the descending series and passing
through all the preliminary evolutions and combinations of the first three kingdoms it finds
itself encased in its first mineral form (in what I call race when speaking of man and what we
may call class generally) of class I there. Only it passes through seven instead of 'through
the thirteen spheres' even omitting the intermediate 'worlds of results'. Having passed
through its seven great classes of inmetalliation (a good word this) with their septenary
ramifications – the monad gives birth to the vegetable kingdom and moves on to . . . 'B'?[6]

This is Koot Hoomi explaining, but Morya says,[7] 'Each man of us has gone this ceaseless
round and will repeat it for ever and ever'. Always rising to something higher, that is.

On this globe, Globe D: Root Races I and II were aetherial; III, the 'Lemurian', began as a
semi-solid, primitive androgyne, belonging to the Jurassic age of the great reptiles. Only
towards its end did it develop skeletons. Indeed, the Australian aborigines and African pygmies
were its remnants. Its habitat was a vast continent in the southern Indian and Pacific Oceans, of
which Australasia, Ceylon and some parts of Africa were constituents. (More of this later.) It
will already strike some that the reference is to what some modern geologists call Pangaea.

Those who form the most evolved of the human race did not, however, pursue the course of
evolution we have been tracing. Having attained on a previous chain to an evolution too high
for this to be appropriate, they began to incarnate here only after Lemuria had broken up by
volcanic action and in the gigantic rearrangement of the land-masses a new continent appeared
where now there are the north and south Atlantic Oceans.

This is where the more highly evolved souls began to join in, the total number of souls
pursuing their evolution on this earth being limited despite the apparent growth of population.
This has relevance to the perplexity of Theosophists concerning the very long time Koot Hoomi
makes people spend in their worlds of effects between incarnations. Some feel they have been
incarnated so recently as to suppose very much shorter intervals. Now, one point to be observed
here is that if the animic population remains always the same, then when the physical
population was small the queue for incarnation must have been very long. As the population
grows, there is the possibility of coming back very much more quickly.

There is further an all-important 'Annotation' to the fourth edition of *Esoteric Buddhism*,
which, being tucked away in such an inconspicuous place, has not received proper publicity:[8]

There are such things as artificial incarnations accomplished by the direct intervention of
the Mahatmas when a *chela* who may not yet have acquired anything resembling the
power of controlling the matter himself is brought back into incarnation almost
immediately after his previous physical death, without having been suffered to float into
the current of natural causes at all.

The word 'artificial' seems ill-chosen, but what is meant is that those of a certain evolution, if
willing to do without a long lie-up in the heaven world (*devachan*), are brought back as soon as
can be arranged, both to pursue the course of their own evolution and to be lamps to those
around them. Masters always come back at once.

The Fourth Root Race was the Mongolian, of which practically only the earliest and last sub-
races survive, the Chinese, Tibetan and Japanese comprising the latter. In the middle period, its
prime, in the early Eocene Age, it attained to an immense sophistication, and to the discovery
of the universal power of '*vril*' imagined by Bulwer-Lytton as to be discovered in the future. Yet
the tremendous development of the fourth principle, *Kama Manas* (desire mind) entailed a fall
into evil. This will be explained more fully in *The Secret Doctrine*. It was, after all, the Fourth
Root Race of the Fourth Round, the nadir of the whole cycle of evolution on this chain. Few of
us escaped involvement. The break up of Atlantis began in and continued through the Miocene
Age, the once vast continent disappearing in a series of calamitous submergences, to end with
that of the last small remaining island, of which Plato speaks in the *Timaeus*. Plato's source was

Solon, and the date given to Solon by the priests of Sais, 9,000 years before his (Solon's) time, was, says Morya, no fancy one. Writing in October 1882, Morya says the submergence of which Plato tells was 'just 11,446 years ago', therefore, 13328 B.C.'. Naturally, the Egyptian priests knew that it was only the final event of the long series in which a vast continent had disappeared over an age, but they did not wish to divulge to Solon their secret chronology. (The Master salutes Donnelly, only, he says, he confused Atlantis with Lemuria; certainly both went down, but with a world of time in between.)

Even during the period of the greater catastrophes, some people had been picked out and escorted to an island in what is now the Gobi Desert, where, about a million years ago, they were moulded into the nucleus of the Fifth Root Race. The first sub-race of this was that of the original Aryan Indians, the fifth sub-race, 'yourselves, the white conquerors'.

The Fifth Root Race will in its turn have to be destroyed 'to arrest its progress towards absolute evil',[9] but that will not be for a long time yet, and when the continents of our present world go down, the seventh sub-race of the Sixth Root Race (which has not appeared at all yet) will be found flourishing upon Lemuria and Atlantis, which will in the great convulsions of the earth have reappeared, cleansed. We may be there.

By the end of the Seventh Round, 'men will have become *Gods* and animals – intelligent beings'.[10]

That is written by Koot Hoomi. Morya writes:[11]

> The last seventh round man having passed on to a *subsequent* world, the precedent one with its mineral, vegetable and animal life (except man) begins to gradually die out, when with the exit of the last animalcula it is extinguished, or as H.P.B. has it snuffed out (minor or partial pralaya). When the spirit-man reaches the last bead of the chain and passes into *final* Nirvana, the last world also disappears or passes into subjectivity. Thus there are among the stellar galaxies births and deaths of worlds, ever following each other in the orderly progression of natural Law. And . . . the last bead is strung upon the thread of Mahayuga.
>
> When the last cycle of man-bearing has been completed by that last fecund earth; and humanity has reached in a mass the stage of Buddhahood and passed out of objective existence into the mystery of Nirvana – then 'strikes the hour'; the seen becomes the unseen, the concrete resumes its pre-cyclic state of atomic distribution.
>
> But the dead worlds left behind the on-sweeping impulse *do not* continue *dead* . . . The thrill of life will again re-unite the atoms, and it will stir again . . . though all the forces have remained *statu quo* and are now asleep, yet little by little it will – when the hour re-strikes – gather for a new cycle of man-bearing maternity, and give birth to something still higher.

Madame Blavatsky explained in different words in a letter to Sinnett;[12] 'The fact is, after our exit from here, the Planet gets ready to receive another group of humanity coming after us'.

The 'heart and brain of our pigmy universe'[13] is, of course, the sun, 'our Father-Mother'.[14] Koot Hoomi refers to *La Résurrection et la Fin des Mondes* (*Resurrection and End of Worlds*) by C. Flammarion, and says that the French astronomer's intuition led him towards the occult doctrine of solar Pralayas and Manvantaras, only he erred in thinking Earth would end by falling into the sun. The sun would be the first member of the system to disintegrate. Again, Flammarion supposed the ruin of the solar system to be spread over a long time. 'We are told that it occurs in the twinkling of an eye but not without many preliminary warnings'.[15]

Nature follows the same groove, from the 'creation' of a universe down to that of a mosquito'.[16] This makes it possible to use the key of analogy, to understand things outside our experience.

The second generation Theosophy of Mrs Besant and Leadbeater will make a great deal of the 'Solar Logos'. The term does not occur in the writings of Blavatsky or the Mahatmas, though the words 'heart and brain' seem indeed to imply that vast ball of fire we call the sun to be the physical body of a being. But it is not God. Moreover, it did not create us. When we come to *The Secret Doctrine*, it will look as though it scooped us up, along with other multitudinous life-germs in the oceans of Chaos. It may be unfair to blame it for crudities in the system; they may be vestiges of Chaos it has not been able to bring to order yet.

In his notes for Hume, Koot Hoomi gives an all-important explanation of the causes of Manvantara (the coming into physical state or existence of a universe) and Pralaya (its return to Nirvanic state). It is to do with the atoms. It is when the positive and negative polarities begin to act again that there is generation of matter and worlds; but past a certain point the contrary process begins:[17]

> As the forces move on and the distance between organised and unorganised matter becomes greater, a tendency towards the reverse begins to take their place. The powers of attraction and repulsion become gradually weaker. Then a complete exchange of properties takes place, and for a time equilibrium is restored in an opposite order . . . There comes a time when polarity ceases to exist *or act*, as everything else. In the night of mind, all is equilibrised in the boundless cosmos in a state of non-action or non-being.
>   . . . Cosmic matter can no more be non-molecular than organised matter, 7th principle is molecular as well as the first one but the former differentiates from the latter, not only by its molecules getting wider apart and becoming more attenuated, but also losing *its polarity*.

> . . . As the molecules go on rarifying, so in proportion they become attenuated . . . the greater the change in their polarity, the negative pole acquiring a stronger property of repulsion, and the positive losing gradually the power of attraction.[18]

Hume wrote a question: When the entire universe goes into pralaya (what is your Tibetan word?) how can anyone know anything about it?' Koot Hoomi replied:[19]

> Maha bar do – the period between death and regeneration of man is so called – also Chhe bar do.
>   They can know for this is but *our scan*, or as you say by analogy.

In *The Tibetan Book of the Dead*, Evans-Wentz tells us, '*Bar-do* literally means "between (*Bar*) two (*do*)" ie between two states',[20] while Tucci's *Religions of Tibet* gives '*che*' as meaning greater.[21] Both books appeared long after Madame Blavatsky's death.

Hume asks, 'Who are the artificers of the world?' and is answered,[22] 'Dyan Chohans – Planetaries' (the spelling is more often 'Dhyan'). Referring to Pralaya, Hume asks, 'Can the planetaries in any way cognise the passive non-being portions of the universe?' He is answered,[23] 'They can'.

Sinnett asks a good many questions about death, and is told that a man's last thoughts can affect his future rebirth. 'No man dies insane'. However he may have lived, even if he has passed away in *delirium tremens*, he has his 'instant of perfect lucidity at the moment of death', in which he sees what he has done with his life, though this may be after he appears dead:[24]

> . . . from the last pulsation, from and between the last throbbing of his heart and the moment when the last spark of animal heat leaves the body – the *brain thinks* and the *Ego* lives over in those few brief seconds his whole life again. Speak in whispers, ye, who assist at a death-bed . . . especially have you to keep quiet just after Death has laid her clammy hands upon the body. Speak in whispers, I say, lest you disturb the quiet ripple of thought, and hinder the busy work of the Past casting its reflection upon the veil of the future.

This means that where an organ transplant is carried out, it is while the donor is doing the most important thinking of his entire life, and nothing should disturb him.

Any attempt to bring the departed back, through a medium, can only harm him. It is impossible for the real being to descend between incarnations. There is only one possibility of communication with the departed. It sometimes happens that the bereaved has a beautiful dream, in which it seemed the loved one came down. What has really happened is that the link of love drew the living person up, to spend a few moments with the departed in the heaven (*Devachan*).[25]

Sinnett was having difficulty in understanding what the being that reincarnated was, for he asked if A.P. Sinnett was 'a new invention'.[25]

Koot Hoomi says that on the contrary, Sinnett is the child and karmic progeny of his antecedent personal self:[26]

> Nonius Asprenas, Consul of the Emperor Domitian – (AD 94) together with Arricinius Clementus, and friend of the Flamen Dialis of that day (the high priest of Jupiter and chief of the Flamenes) or of that Flamen himself – which would account for A.P. Sinnett's suddenly developed love of mysticism.

Is Koot Hoomi saying that he himself was the Flamen Dialis? If so, there may be an implication that because he then submitted to answering questions, so far as his vows would allow, he finds himself doing the same again now for the benefit of the same interrogator?

There are mistakes in the passage, though not so many as in his editor's transcription. He sometimes fails to dot an 'i', so that Barker has rendered 'Dialis' as 'Dealis'. Also, on the printed page, one reads 'Asprena', but when one looks at the original, one sees that the name occurs at the end of a line and that the 'a' is going off the paper. The final 's' doubtless went on to the desk or whatever the paper was placed on. Finding in the *Oxford Classical Dictionary* only two persons of the name of Nonius Asprenas, both of whom lived in the reign of Augustus, I wrote to a classical scholar, a specialist in Roman history, and asked whether there was a Nonius Asprenas who was Consul in AD 94, and if anything was known of him. He replied that there was a Nonium Torquatus Asprenas who in 94 was Consul Ordinarius, i.e. from 1 January (by this time Consuls no longer served for a whole year but only for two to four months); beyond that nothing was known of him. His colleague, however, was a T. Sextius Magius Lateranus. Yet there was an Arrecinus Clemens (he bade me note the spelling of both names), who served in 73 and again in 85 as Consul Suffectus, i.e. from a date later than 1 January.

Even with the mistakes, the passage could only have been written by a person with close knowledge of Roman history. Madame Blavatsky, for instance, would not have known where to look for the names of Consuls so obscure nothing save their names was known. The passage is written by the Master from memory; is it from memory of classical studies in an English university thirty years back, or from memory of an existence 2,000 years back? Perhaps he was then sought by two individuals who stuck to him like burrs, both asking questions all the time, both of them *profani* and both Consuls – with the result that he slipped into thinking of them as having been Consuls together. Was Arrecinus Clemens once again now known to both of them – was he perhaps Hume?

Sinnett's twenty-nine numbered questions have obliged Koot Hoomi to give an immensely long reply, much of it on pink paper. Madame Blavatsky could have given him her pad at Amritsar, but it could have been taken in another way. Earlier, Sinnett must have expressed surprise at receiving a letter written to him by the Master on *The Pioneer*'s notepaper. Koot Hoomi replied in explanation, 'The several "privations" of such sheets of notepaper'[27] were obtained in Calcutta, where somebody was in the atmosphere of Mrs Gordon, who had with her letters she had received from Sinnett. These provided the link with the blank paper in his box, from which was 'disintegrated particles', around which it was possible to form the duplicate sheets used in writing to him. The stock given him by the Disinherited had, presumably, run out, so he abstracts particles from the paper of his correspondent or other friends.

Replying to some of Sinnett's new set of questions, Koot Hoomi says, answering the eighth, that the great ice ages are not caused primarily by fluctuations in the heat of the sun. That does vary, but what is more important is that the whole solar system, as it moves through space, passes at times through great clouds of meteoric dust, which prevent our receiving the warmth the sun is radiating.[28] Koot Hoomi anticipates by 100 years a theory published in 1982 by the astronomers Clube and Napier.[29]

Even more remarkable, answering the fourteenth question, he says that in the twentieth century;[30] 'Science will *hear* sounds from certain planets before she sees them. This is a prophecy'. This refers forward to the Great Dish at Jodrell Bank and the whole science of radio astronomy.

CHAPTER 41

Reunion in Sikkim

Meanwhile, Madame Blavatsky had been left in Bombay, ill. Rats had 'devoured my poor little canary bird' (presumably a successor to Pip), as she wrote on 4 August 1882 to Sinnett, and she was very low. Her doctor warned her she could 'kick the bucket any day in consequence of *an emotion*'. Then she heard from Morya that he was willing to see her again:[1]

> Boss wants me to prepare and go somewhere for a month or so towards the end of September. He sent a chela here Gangya Deva from Nilgiri Hills and he is to take me off, where I don't know, but of course somewhere in the Himalayas. Boss is fearfully mad with Hume . . .

She often calls Morya 'Boss'.

News that she was about to see her chiefs again somehow spread through her entourage, necessitating some strategy regarding concealment of her departure and route to throw off followers not invited to attend her to the sacred precincts. All hoped for a glimpse of the Master, but that was a rare privilege.

That she did meet Morya again, and Koot Hoomi with him, we gather in the course of a very long letter written by Koot Hoomi and received by Sinnett in October 1882. Apropos of the suspicion voiced by C.C. Massey, of Mrs Billing's circle, that some of H.P.B.'s phenomena might, through excess of zeal, embody deceptions, Koot Hoomi says she has never in the smallest degree deceived with regard to the phenomena; but sometimes she has attributed to the Brothers phenomena produced by herself. (One may remember Olcott's conviction that it was not an adept standing by but she herself who controlled the flame in the lamp through the fire elementals.) Koot Hoomi says:[2]

> If she ever became guilty of real, *deliberate* deception, owing to that 'zeal' it was when in the presence of phenomena produced she kept constantly denying . . . that she had anything to do with their production personally. From your 'European standpoint' it is downright deception . . . meant for the benefit of the 'Brothers' – yet . . . a sublime, self-denying, noble and meritorious – not dishonest – zeal . . . She could never be made to realise the utter uselessness, the danger of such a zeal; and how mistaken she was in her notions that she was adding to our glory, whereas, by attributing to us very often phenomena of the most childish nature, she but lowered us in the public estimation . . . But it was of no use. In accordance with our rules, M. was not permitted to forbid her such a course, in so many words. She had to be allowed full and entire freedom of action, the liberty of *creating causes* that became in due course of time her scourge, her public pillory. He could at best forbid her producing phenomena, and to this last extremity he resorted as often as he could, to her friends' and Theosophists' great dissatisfaction. Was, or rather is, it lack of intellectual perception in her? Certainly not. It is a psychological disease, over which she has little if any control at all. Her impulsive nature . . . is always ready to carry her beyond the boundaries of truth, into the regions of exaggeration; nevertheless without a shadow of suspicion that she is thereby deceiving her friends, or abusing of their great trust in her. The stereotyped phrase, 'It is *not I*; I can do nothing of myself . . . it is all they – the Brothers . . . I am but their humble and devoted slave and instrument' is a downright *fib*. She can and did produce phenomena, owing to her natural powers combined with several long years of regular training and her phenomena are sometimes better, more wonderful and far more perfect than those of some high, initiated chelas, whom she surpasses in artistic taste and purely Western appreciation of art – as for instance in the instantaneous production of pictures: witness her portrayal of the 'fakir' Tiravalla . . . compared with my portrait by Gjwal Khool. Notwithstanding all the

superiority of his powers . . . his youth as contrasted with her old age; and the undeniable and important advantage he possesses of having never brought his pure unalloyed magnetism in direct contact with the great impurity of your world . . . yet do what he may, he will never be able to produce *such* a picture, simply because he is unable to conceive it in his mind and Tibetan thought. Thus, while fathering upon us all manner of foolish, often clumsy and *suspected* phenomena, she has most undeniably been *helping us* in many instances; saving us sometimes as much as two-thirds of the power used, and when remonstrated – for often we are unable to prevent her doing it on her end of the line – answering that she has no need of it, and that her only joy was to be of use to us. And thus she kept on killing herself inch by inch, ready to give – for our benefit and glory, as she thought – her life-blood drop by drop . . . No doubt she has merited a portion of the blame; most undeniably she is given to exaggeration . . . and when it becomes a question of 'puffing up' those she is devoted to, her enthusiasm has no limits. Thus she has made of M. an Apollo of Belvedere, the glowing description of whose physical beauty made him more than once start in anger, and break his pipe while swearing like a true – Christian; and thus, under her elegant phraseology, I, myself had the pleasure of hearing myself metamorphosed into an 'angel of purity and light' – shorn of his wings. We cannot help feeling at times angry, with, oftener – laughing at her. Yet the feeling that dictates all this ridiculous effusion, is too ardent, too sincere and true, not to be respected or even treated with indifference. I do not believe I was ever so profoundly touched by anything I witnessed in all my life, as I was with the poor old creature's ecstatic rapture, when meeting us recently both in our natural bodies, one – after three years, the other – nearly two years absence and separation in the flesh. Even our phlegmatic M. was thrown off his balance, by such an exhibition – of which he was the chief hero. He had to use his *power*, and plunge her into a profound sleep, otherwise she would have burst some blood-vessel including kidneys, liver and her 'interiors' . . . in her delirious attempts to flatten her nose against his riding-mantle besmeared with the Sikkhim mud!

There is a letter from Madame Blavatsky to Sinnett:[3]

Darjeeling, October 9th

How did you know I was here?

Sinnett must have reproached her with stealing away secretly, for she explains that had she not done so, she would never have managed to leave the railway without being followed into Sikkim (some twenty or thirty miles);[3]

and would not have seen M. and K.H. in *their bodies* both . . . Oh the blessed two days! It was like the old times when the bear paid me a visit. The same kind of wooden hut, a box divided into three compartments for rooms, and standing in a jungle on four pelican's legs; the same yellow chelas gliding noiselessly; the same eternal 'gul-gul-gul' sound of my Boss's inextinguishable chelum pipe; the old familiar sweet voice of your K.H. (whose voice is still sweeter and face still thinner and more transparent) the same *entourage* for furniture – skins, and yak-tail stuffed pillows and dishes for salt tea etc. Well when I went to Darjeeling sent away by them – 'out of reach of the chelas, who might fall in love with my beauty' said my polite boss . . .

This is the only description we have of an interior within which she met her Masters. The hut in Sikkim will have been, like the bungalow near Bombay, retained by the Masters for occasional use. One wishes she had given some description of their clothing, but a description is supplied from an unexpected source. She was mistaken in thinking she had shaken off all followers. Sorabji B. Ramaswamier wrote on 7 October to Damodar that he had followed her, in so far as he was able. On 5 October he crossed the river dividing British territories from Sikkim, heading in what he hoped was the direction of Tibet, for which he supposed her to be making. When darkness fell he found shelter in a wayside hut, and in the morning of 6 October he went on again:[4]

It was, I think, between eight and nine a.m., and I was following the road to the town of Sikkim whence, I was assured by the people I met on the road, I could cross over to Tibet easily in my pilgrim's garb, when I suddenly saw a solitary horseman galloping towards me from the opposite direction. From his tall stature and the expert way he managed the animal, I thought he was some military officer of the Sikkim Rajah. Now, I thought, am I caught! He will ask me for my pass and what business I have on the independent territory of Sikkim, and, perhaps, have me arrested and – sent back, if not worse. But – as he approached me, he reined the steed. I looked at and recognised him instantly . . . I was in the awful presence of him, of the same Mahatma, my own revered Guru whom I had seen before in his astral body, on the balcony of the Theosophical Headquarters. It was he, the 'Himalayan BROTHER' of the ever memorable night of December last, who had so kindly dropped a letter in answer to one I had given in a sealed envelope to Madame Blavatsky – whom I had never for one moment during the interval lost sight of – but an hour or so before! The very same instant saw me prostrated on the ground at his feet. I arose at his command and, leisurely looking into his face, I forgot myself entirely in the contemplation of the image I knew so well, having seen his portrait (the one in Olcott's possession) a number of times. I knew not what to say: joy and reverence tied my tongue. The majesty of his countenance, which seemed to me the impersonation [*sic*, for personification] of power and thought, held me rapt in awe. I was at last face to face with 'the Mahatma of the Himavat' and he was no myth, no 'creation of the imagination of a *medium*' as some sceptics suggested. It was no night dream; it is between nine and ten o'clock of the forenoon. There is the sun shining and silently witnessing the scene from above. I see HIM before me in flesh and blood; and he speaks to me in accents of kindness and gentleness. What more do I want? My excess of happiness made me dumb. Nor was it until a few moments later that I was drawn to utter a few words, encouraged by his gentle tone and speech. His complexion is not as fair as that of Mahatma Koot Hoomi; but never have I seen a countenance so handsome, a stature so tall and so majestic. As in his portrait, he wears a short black beard, and long black hair, hanging down to his breast; only his dress was different. Instead of a white, loose robe he wore a yellow mantle lined with fur, and on his head, instead of a pagri, a yellow Tibetan felt cap, as I have seen some Bhootanese wear in this country. When the first moments of rapture and surprise were over . . . I had a long talk with him. He told me to go no further . . . I should wait patiently if I wanted to be an accepted *Chela* . . . The Mahatma I found speaks very little English . . . and *speaks to me in my mother tongue – Tamil*. He told me that if the Chohan permitted Madame B. to go to Pari-jong next year, then I could come with her . . .

Before he left me, two men came on horseback, his attendants I suppose, probably *Chelas*, for they were dressed like lama-gylongs, and both, like himself, with long hair streaming down their backs. They followed the Mahatma, as he left, at a gentle trot. [Gylongs are monks.]

It will be remembered that Madame Blavatsky earlier wrote to Sinnett that Morya no longer wore a white *puggery* as in his portrait, but 'sticks a yellow saucer on top of his head like K.J.'. Now, a saucer is not a cap, but if one consults *The Religions of Tibet*, Giuseppe Tucci (Routledge, 1980), one finds on p.133 a half-page of drawings of 'hats worn in summer while riding a horse': (a) 'reserved for incarnates' has a very wide, shallow brim, turning up a little only at the edge, so that the crown does present the appearance of a cup within a saucer; (b) for 'government officials', is also a cup within a slightly smaller saucer. Turning to p.136, we find drawn an assortment of 'hats worn while riding a horse in winter'. Here we find (c) 'yellow in colour, reserved for dGelugs pa great lamas while riding', a Phrygian cap, coming well down over the ears, with tails, perhaps meant to tie under the chin. This would provide warmth which the saucer would not. Morya was certainly riding a horse, and, in October, since he was in a fur-lined mantle, felt it was winter.

Also happening to visit Darjeeling at just this moment, October 1882, was an aspirant chela, the young lawyer Mohini M. Chatterjee (also hoping to glimpse Madame Blavatsky's meeting with her Masters?). He met no Mahatma, but, while in company with some others he met there who said they were chelas, he saw a Tibetan pedlar selling nicknacks, and asked him if there were really beings who possessed extraordinary powers. The pedlar, whose name was Sundook, replied that there were, but that they were not ordinary lamas; something much higher, they lived secluded in the mountains beyond Lhasa and Shigatzè. Just about a year before, in October 1881, he himself had seen, at Giansi, about two days south of Shigatzè, a group of gylongs gathered around one who was evidently their Guru. The Guru was unusually light in complexion. He asked them who they were, and was told they were 'Koot-hum-pa'.[6] One of Mohini's companions showed him a portrait of the Master Koot Hoomi, with one arm bare. Sundook exclaimed that that was indeed the man.

Sundook was then shown a rosary belonging to Madame Blavatsky. (How did they come to possess this? Had one of them borrowed it from her, or was what he was shown a photograph of her in which she was holding it?) Sundook said that the rosary could only be a gift from the Trashi Lama. It was in no other person's power to bestow, and could not for any money have been bought anywhere.

After this, Mohini looked in a Tibetan dictionary, and found the meaning of 'pa' given as 'man' or 'men', as Bod-pa, 'men of Tibet'. (According to the article on Tibetan language in the current *Encyclopaedia Britannica*, it means 'pertaining to'. This would better explain its apparently divergent uses: Peling, European, Peling-pa, Europe; Bod, Tibet, Bod-pa, Tibetan; Koot Hum-pa, pupils of Koot-Hoomi.)

CHAPTER 42

The Chohan Rimbouchy

Morya and Koot Hoomi have a chief. Koot Hoomi expresses himself as,[1]: 'a worm of yesterday before our "Rock of Ages". My Cho-khan'. More often the name is written in one word, 'Chohan'. Madame Blavatsky sometimes calls her Master's Master the 'Paramahaguru'.[2] Koot Hoomi refers to him as 'my great Master'. It is only by his permission that Morya and Koot Hoomi are able to enter into communication with the two Englishmen, which they would have to break off should he so order them. It is the Chohan who has forbidden them to use power in connection with Hume's *Eclectic*.[3] Koot Hoomi later has a story to tell. A letter written him by Sinnett, with an enclosure from C.C. Massey, was handed to him by the messenger when he was near Pari-Jong. Being at that moment occupied with other matters, he simply broke the seal of the bulging envelope to form an idea of what it contained, then put it, as he thought, into the travelling bag he wore across his shoulder. In reality, it fell on the ground behind him, scattering its contents. He was mounting the steps to the library when a gylong (monk) who was looking from a window called to him to look round, and he saw that a goat was devouring the pages. He could have used power to restore them, but had noticed the matter had to do with the *Eclectic*. He was already resolving that he must ask an exceptional permission from the Chohan, when:[4]

> I saw his holy face before me, with his eye twinkling in quite an unusual manner, and heard his voice: 'Why break the rule? I will do it myself'. These simple words, *Kam mi ts'har* – 'I'll do it' contain a world of hope for me.

It was the Chohan who forbade Morya to bring Madame Blavatsky into Tibet in 1882,[5] because she was more needed in India, which was why he and Koot Hoomi went to Sikkim to meet her briefly.

Modern Theosophists have followed Leadbeater in supposing the Chohan to be an Indian. I believe they are mistaken. Several times, Koot Hoomi refers to him as 'our venerable Chohan'. He refers also to 'our venerable Hobilgan'.[6] Sinnett is told that it is actions, not words, that may one day open 'a secret door to the heart of the sternest of Hobilgans'.[7] He may be stern, yet in some circumstances he can laugh more easily than Koot Hoomi – who was vexed when he read a ribald paragraph concerning the brothers in an English newspaper. However, 'the Hobilghan, to whom I showed the passage, laughed till the tears streamed down his old cheeks'.[8] Surely the Hobilgan and the Chohan are one and the same person; but who is he?

A clue comes in an unexpected manner. Olcott had seen that Madame Blavatsky could precipitate. Some of the letters he received in the familiar red writing might therefore have been precipitated by her (as Djwal Khool precipitated for Koot Hoomi). In such cases, Olcott realised she would be authorised to use Morya's signature, and possibly even to compose a text with Morya's injunction behind it; yet he felt this would not be the same thing as a letter precipitated by Morya himself and wished he could know which ones were wholly from the Master.

Having been in Ceylon since mid-July, he returned to Bombay on 1 November. On 25 November, Madame Blavatsky, Ramaswamier and others, having broken their journey from Darjeeling to see the Sinnetts at Allahabad, also returned. Ramaswamier then gave Olcott a private message, from Morya.[9] When the words 'Chohan Rimpochey' appeared in a letter, it came straight from himself; when these words were absent, it came through Madame Blavatsky.

In *The Religions of Tibet*, by Giuseppe Tucci, one finds in the index '*Rin po che*' or '*Rimpoche*', meaning 'Precious', used as the title of 'Incarnate Lamas',[10] especially of the Panchèn Lama. Further, in *The Religions of Tibet*, by Helmut Hoffman, one finds the term '*hubilganic succession*'[11] used of the succession of incarnating lamas, generally restricted to the Dalai and Panchèn. This explains 'our venerable Hobilgan'. Is the Chohan, then, the Panchèn?

Before jumping to that conclusion, one should note a snag. Our Hobilgan had 'old cheeks', but His Holiness the Panchèn Lama Jè Pèdèn Chökyi Trakpa Tènpé Wangchuk, died of smallpox on 30 August,[12] 1882, aged only 28 or 29. Sarat Chandra Das walked in the funeral procession which on 13 September bore his mortal remains from Tobgyal to Trashi Lhünpo.[13] A party of mourners on foot preceded more than 100 nobles on horseback, who made the way for the sedan which brought his coffin to the place where it would be preserved in a great tall tomb with a gilded roof. Moreover, he came of two original Tibetan families.[14]

This was not the case with our venerable Hobilgan, the Chohan. Though he was of more advanced age than Morya and Koot Hoomi, he is referred to as giving orders governing what they might or might not do in years subsequent to this funeral and there is an indication he was of mixed blood. There is a reply from Madame Blavatsky to a correspondent who had gathered from Sinnett that all the really high Adepts were orientals, saying that it will have slipped from Sinnett's mind that:[15]

> among the group of Initiates to which his own mystical correspondent is allied, are two of European race, and that one who is that Teacher's superior is also of that origin, being half a Slavonian in his 'present incarnation', as he himself wrote to Colonel Olcott in New York.

The two of European race will be the Hungarian and the Venetian (she may think of Illarion as belonging with Serapis in Egypt). Sinnett's 'mystical correspondent' is Koot Hoomi, whose superior is our venerable Hobilgan, the Chohan. There have always been Russians about in central Asia. I would think it was the father who was a Russian and wandered down from Siberia or Sinkiang into Tibet, where he left with a Tibetan lady this precious souvenir of his passage. Even though he had been brought up Tibetan so that they had to talk in English, the fact that he was half of her blood may have rendered him the more pleased to welcome Madame Blavatsky to the neighbourhood of Shigatsè. Further, it seems fitting that this high teacher who was so concerned with the transmission of the wisdom to the West should have been half of European blood.

But can there have been two Hobilgans at Shigatsè? To probe the mystery behind this question, it will be necessary to go right back to the origin of the incarnating lamas, Dalais and Panchèns. That means going back to Tsongkapa.

CHAPTER 43

Tsongkapa and the Hubilganic succession

Tsongkapa or Tsong-ka-pa lived from 1357 to 1419. To place this period relative to western history, the reign of King Richard II of England fell within it. Tsongkapa may be hardly known in the West, but in Tibet he is holy, and for Madame Blavatsky's teachers he ranks with the Buddha.[1] Indeed, it will dawn on us that, for them, he was not merely overshadowed by the Buddha, he was the Buddha. Renouncing Nirvana, he had kept a watch on the world. He saw the teaching which, seventeen centuries before, he had given on the banks of the Ganges degraded, especially in Tibet; there it had become mixed with the pre-Buddhistic Bön religion, in which demons were worshipped, humans and animals sacrificed and sex used in peculiar ways. To cleanse it, he descended into rebirth. He was born into the black yak-hair tent of a nomad family. Too poor to afford a house, they had a small flock of sheep, about twenty goats and perhaps a yak or two, and were settled on plains near a ravine through which ran fresh water. It was in the province of Amdo, in the Tsongka region in the extreme north east, where Tibet meets Mongolia and China, not far from the salt Lake Koko Nor (or Kuku Nur), Mongolian for Blue Sea. Except for coarse grass near its edge and in the ravines, the land, destitute of vegetation, rolled red and ochre, 'vast and melancholy plains' relieved, in Bain's poetic prose, solely by 'Koko Nur's blue, lovely sheets of sapphire, scattered like fragments of a broken mirror to spot earth with the colours of the sky'.[2]

The day of his birth (converted into the Gregorian calendar) was 21 November; the time, as given by his nephew or grand-nephew to Khèdrup Jè, his disciple and first biographer, was 'at dawn, when the great star had arisen'. Professor Wayman, in his translation, puts after 'great star', in brackets, '(i.e. Venus)'.[3] I checked with an ephemeris for 1357 and found that Venus on that date was an evening star, and would not have risen until after the sun, when it would have been invisible. I wrote to Professor Wayman about this, and he replied saying he supposed the birth must have been a little later than when the grand-nephew told Khèdrup Jè it was. But I do not see how the tent-dwellers could know Venus had risen when they could not see it. I feel that, in the poetic mind of Khèdrup Jè, 'the great star' was the sun itself, the great orb, golden and glorious on the horizon.[4]

Tsongkapa attracted interest from the first, as he appeared to have been born fully conscious.[5] Although he was the fourth child in a family of six,[6] the Abbé Huc was told at Kumbum that no man had to do with his begetting. His mother Shingmo Acho, went down to the stream to draw water, and as she climbed up the ravine again, carrying her pail, she stumbled over a flat stone and fainted. When she came round, she felt a pain in her side, saw that on the stone was incised a saying of the Buddha, and realised she had been impregnated by the Holy Scripture.[7] From the ground where her blood fell in his birth sprang a wonderful tree, its leaves imprinted with the sacred characters. Indeed, Huc and his companion, the Abbé Gabet, were shown a tree, around which had been built the monastery of Kumbum, meaning place of Ten Thousand Images, with reference to the characters on the tree. Huc made drawings of the tree, *in toto* and in detail. It looks squat, the bole wide for the height. The branches push not upwards but straight outwards, in layered tiers of bushy clumps, with space between them; the leaves are narrow and tapering, slightly broader at the base, serrated and bear markings, in light or darker green, shaped like Sanskrit characters. The bark, he says, is like that of a plane, but reddish and exuding a sweet scent, akin to cinnamon. The two Abbés were told that in the summer it bore large red flowers,[8] but these they did not see as they were not there in that season. They had come to try to convert Tibet to Catholicism, but when Huc's book was published, he found his account of the tree and of the marvels said to have attended the birth of Tsongkapa had brought him into trouble with his own Church – which provoked Madame Blavatsky to say poor Huc was defrocked for telling the truth. She does not tell us if she saw the tree (Major Cross was told she was heading for Kumbum), but the tree may already have been sealed off. When Huc saw it, it was protected only by a silver canopy upon slender supports, erected at the expense of the Chinese Emperor Khang Hsi,[9] a larger enclosure in brick round that having a door which anyone could open. The present Dalai Lama's brother, Thubten Norbu,[10] writes that about a century ago this was sealed, and when he was at Kumbum, even though he became its Grand Lama, he would have needed the formal consent of every member of the governing body of the monastery to break the seal. There was one monk who had the privilege and duty of entering the enclosure to tend the tree and keep the silver pagoda clean and shining; and Thubten Norbu was told that some seventy years before, the monk in attendance, as he came out of the enclosure, was seen to have on his shoulder a leaf that had fallen from the tree. That was all the the monks were able to see. It was fresh and green, and bore a marking in the shape of a Sanskrit character. Huc's description[11] of the whole tree, Thubten Norbu informs us, was accepted at Kumbum as correct.

As soon as the infant Tsongkapa could utter words, they were those of a sage. At the age of 3 (that is, 2, for Tibetans count as one the first year), he was allowed to take his vows as an upasaka. His mother shaved his head for him. From the ground where she laid the locks she had shorn from him is said to have sprung a second tree, an old and sprawling juniper in the ravine. Thubten Norbu says he often sat by it and smelled it; it smelled of human hair.[12]

It was noticed that from the first, Tsongkapa forbade himself the consumption of flesh.[13] The Tibetans, even monks, had fallen back into meat eating.

News of the marvellous child travelled, and in the year his head was shaven the Mongol King Togol Temir (1333–68) sent his Ambassador to visit him, presumably both to pay homage and report back. In the following year there arrived a lama who wished to assume his tutorship. Assent was given. The little boy learned with extraordinary rapidity. In the autumn of 1373, close to his sixteenth birthday, he left to pursue further studies in central Tibet. It was noticed that as he went he did not look behind.[14]

The people of the region where he had been born were taller, with longer heads and faces than those of the people of central Tibet, so it is likely he was of this type, and would have had the sense of coming among a different people when he came to the new area.

The political constitution of Tibet at this time was confused. Anciently, Tibet had had kings. Then the kingdom broke up into small, warring factions, with a tendency for local kings to recur. In 1207, invasion by the Mongol Genghis Khan was averted by timely submission. In 1247 the Sakya monk, Pakpa, was summoned to Mongolia, where he converted Kublai Khan, and so Mongolia, to Buddhism. Pakpa was counted upon to rule the four provinces into which Tibet was divided, Ü, Tsang, Amdo and Kham, on behalf of the Mongol dynasty. This worked for a while, but then the power of the Sakya dynasty of monks was challenged by monks of different sects, one of which, dedicated to the overthrow of the Mongol overlordship, under the leadership of one Changchub Gyaltsen, had by 1358 effectively replaced the Sakya hierarchy. Tibet was effectively independent by the time of his death in 1364, and it was his successors who formed the dynasty of monks or 'kings' when Tsongkapa arrived from Amdo in the central province of Ü.

Tsongkapa abstained from involvement in politics. He had his studies to complete. He had been invited to take up residence at the monastery of Brigung, to the north east of Lhasa, where he studied medicine and therapy, but afterwards moved from one monastic college to another. At the same time, people were beginning to listen to him,[15] though it was not until later that he assumed in a formal manner the instruction of others in non-Tantric Buddhism. He kindled in their hearts the desire to return to the Buddha's teaching in its purity, to abjure the use of skulls and bones (survivals of the old Bön religion), and to deem needless the Tantric sexual practices and representations of deities coupling with their shaktis. The idea of positive and negative polarities could be understood in a more abstract way. Of monks he required a return to celibacy and abstinence from liquor.[16] At first he had only eight pledged disciples, but soon hundreds, taking flame from his flame, were fired to form themselves into a new body, the Gelukpa, the purified or reformed ones. Popularly they were dubbed the Yellow Hats, because whereas the lamas of the other sects wore hats of red or black, the Gelukpa distinguished themselves with yellow ones. Golden yellow has always been the colour of Buddhism, standing both for sunlight and the golden light of the Buddhic plane.

At the same time, there was resistance to the reform, falling into two categories, those who rejected it totally, of whom the most notorious were the Dugpas, and those known as the semi-reformed, such as the Sakyas, who thought it too hard to wean the people from the deities and demons beloved of them, and that a compromise should be made by ascribing to them more elevated and symbolic meanings. The weakness of this strategy lies in the liability of the old meanings to come through.

When he felt his time drawing near, Tsongkapa passed his hat and cloak to a disciple who had helped him in the founding of Ganden, Gyètsap Darma Rinchèn (1364–1430).[17] He was only seven years younger than Tsongkapa, and it is thought that it was envisaged that he would hand on, as indeed he did, to the younger disciple Khèdrup Jè (1385–1438). Tucci tells us, 'Along with their master, these two form an indivisible triad, known as *yab sras gsum*, i.e. the master and his "spiritual sons"; they are always presented as three'.[18] This, then, was the founding triad of the Gelukpa, which the Theosophical triad of Helena, Henry and William was doubtless picked to represent in the outer world. Dr Philip Denwood, Lecturer in Tibetan at the University in London, informs me that the term or phrase, unpronounceable when literally transliterated from the Sanskrit characters, is pronounced 'yapsè sum'. Waddell presents a drawing of what must be a typical painting of the yapsè sum: Tsongkapa top centre, Gyètsap Darma Rinchèn and Khèdrup Jè just beneath him, at his right and left knee respectively; all three wearing their yellow hats and haloes; all three sitting cross-legged upon the petals of opened lotus flowers, upon and amongst clouds in the sky.[19] Below, centre, is a table set with an incense-burner, with smoke rising, a vase of flowers and a shell. Bottom right is a small person, his hands raised in prayer. I am not sure about a demon who appears bottom left. Is that 'dweller' meant to be there, or was it some back-slider's hand that put him in?

Tsongkapa left this life as he had entered it, at dawn, fully conscious. Seated cross-legged, his hands were level with his breast in a holy gesture, when just as the sun rose he ceased to breathe.[20]

That was on 15 December by our Gregorian calendar, and it is still kept a holy day in Tibet. His body was still at Gandèn and the monks there told Das it was still uncorrupted.[21] Naturally, the profane are not allowed to view. There is a popular legend that he will remain there till the end of the world, when he will go to join the other holy ones at Shamballa. The Tibetans do not doubt that this is a real city, but they do not know where it is, except that by tradition it is in a land north of Tibet, guarded from mortal eyes.[22] (Madame Blavatsky says it is in the Gobi Desert.)

Gyètsap Darma Rinchèn indeed handed on to Khèdrup Jè. Khèdrup Jè was succeeded by Gédun Druppa, from Drèpung. He was either the nephew or the great-nephew of Tsongkapa, and his dates are 1390 or 1391 to 1475. He extended the order's presence from Ü to Tsang and in 1445 or 1447 founded the monastery of Trashi Lhünpo, at Shigatsè, with about 3,000 monks. According to Mr Shakabpa, Gédun Druppa died at Trashi Lhünpo at the age of 84.[23] Writing in exile, Mr Shakabpa may be without his papers. At any rate, he is at variance with Hoffman, who says Gédun Druppa died at Drèpung (which sounds more likely), having installed as the first Abbot or Grand Lama of Trashi Lhünpo Sönam Chöklang, 'who was then regarded as the reincarnation of mKas grub je'.[24] mKas grub je is Khèdrup Jè. Waddell gives Sönam Chöklang's dates as 1439–1505,[25] which confirms Hoffmann. It was now understood, says Hoffmann, that Khèdrup Jè would continually reincarnate at Trashi Lhünpo, and that Gédun Druppa would continually reincarnate (at Drèpung). This seems to fix the latter as the grand-nephew (not nephew) of Tsongkapa, born after his death, for surely the meaning has to be that both Khèdrup Jè and Gyètsap Darma Rinchèn have renounced Nirvana, continually to reincarnate respectively at Trashi Lhünpo and at Drèpung. One would expect to see the reincarnations of Gyètsap Darma Rinchèn to represent the first aspect of the trinity, or power, and the reincarnations of Khèdrup Jè the third aspect, of divine ideation or learning. Indeed, we shall see this come about. The second aspect probably remains vested in Tsongkapa at Shamballa (unless projected at Urga, see below). Gédun Druppa was succeeded by Gédun Gyatso

(1475–1542). The title 'Gyatso', which he was the first to use, means 'Ocean' (i.e. of Wisdom). Gédun Gyatso was succeeded by Sönam Gyatso (1543–1588). Beset by the Red Hats, Sönam Gyatso went to Mongolia to beg help. He was well received by Altan Khan, to whom he recalled earlier days when he had been Pakpa and had converted to Buddhism Altan Khan, who had then been Kublai Khan. This moved Altan Khan, who conferred upon Sönam the title 'Talè' (Englished as Dalai), which is the exact Mongolian translation of 'Gyatso', 'Ocean of Wisdom'. Retrospectively, the title of Dalai Lama was now conferred on Gédün Druppa and Gédün Gyatso, now known as the First and Second Dalai Lamas, Sönam Gyatso being the Third. After Altan Khan had helped him establish his power against the Red Hats, he made a return visit to Mongolia, in the course of which he died. His reincarnation was now found in a grandson of Altan Khan, Yongtan Gyatso (1589–1617), the Fourth Dalai Lama. The Mongolian people became so attached to him they kept him as long as they could, and when he had to depart for Tibet, he left with them, to console them, Lama Maidari Hutuhtu (or Hutukhtu), who would be inspired by the future Buddha, Maitreya.[26] He would take up his residence at Urga, (on modern maps Ulan Bator) on the far side of the Gobi Desert, where the land begins to rise towards the Siberian border, ever to reincarnate there amongst them, a Hubilgan of their own. (This distinction for Mongolia made China jealous.)

The two Mongolian terms, 'Dalai' and 'Hubilgan', were thus brought into Tibet by Yongtan Khan, the Mongolian Dalai Lama.

He was succeeded by the 'Great Fifth', Nabang Lopsang Gyatso (1617–82). He was initiated and enthroned at the age of 7 by the Abbot of Gandèn, Lopsang Chogyèn (1570–1662). In the seventh year after his enthronement, therefore c.1631, he created this monk, Lopsang Chogyèn, Grand Lama of Trashi Lhünpo, with the title of Panchèn Lama. Tucci writes:[27]

> In this case, too, retrospective validity was conferred upon the theory, and the series was held to begin with mkas grub rje (Khèdrup Jè), so that Blo bzang Chos kyi rgyal mtshan (Lobsang Chokyen) became the fourth reincarnation.

But if Khèdrup Jè (1385–1438) was the First, Sönam Chöklang (1439–1505) the Second and his successor, Wensapa (1505–70), the Third, then there is a gap. So far as I am concerned, the whole of the mystery lies in this gap. Was Trashi Lhünpo for sixty years without a Grand Lama, and if so why does nobody mention it? Was a strange and unexplained vacancy now being filled by the induction of new blood, or was a Grand Lama quietly put aside as though he did not exist?

Thubten Norbu, brother of the present Dalai Lama, writes:[28]

> . . . the office of Panchèn Rimpoche was brought into being because the fifth Gyalwa Rimpoche [Dalai Lama] wished to show his gratitude to his teacher, Losang Chogyan, a highly influential and venerated incarnation of Opagme. It was claimed that the great teacher was in fact a reincarnation of Kha-drup, Tsong Khapa'a disciple, further enhancing his prestige.

This is one way of putting it, but it is puzzling. Opagme is an aspect of Buddhahood, as Chinresi (overshadower of the Dalai Lamas) is another aspect of Buddhahood (see Blavatsky's *Theosophical Glossary*), but the first three Grand Lamas of Trashi Lhünpo had been incarnations of Khèdrup Jè, so how could the new induction (who came from Gandèn) be the same individual? Was he, or was he not?

Thubten Norbu's assertion is that the Panchèns owed everything to the Dalais. Madame Blavatsky's view is the inverse of this; she insists passionately upon the Panchèns' seniority. Unfortunately, she overshoots the mark, following Markham's introduction to the narrative of Bogle's mission to Trashi Lhünpo into the mis-statement that the Dalais were the creations of the Panchèns.[29] I imagine that because it was totally in keeping with the feeling of true seniority at Trashi Lhünpo, she did not stop to check with the Masters that it was factually correct. Boris de Zirkoff was obliged to point out the error in an editorial footnote (though he fails to recognise its source), but he goes on, unfortunately, to expound the Lhasan point of view, blandly replacing her contradiction of it with what it was her intention to contradict – because he has not understood her standpoint. This editorial footnote of de Zirkoff has, in its turn, provoked abusive comment by Mr Walter Carrithers; his language may be intemperate, but he has the right to be infuriated.

Mr Shakabpa, representing the view of the present Dalai Lama's government in exile, writes:[30]

> It is to be noticed that while the Tibetan government regards the present Panchen Lama as the seventh in line, the attendants of the Panchen Lama claim him to be the tenth reincarnation. The difference stems from a disagreement concerning whether the first three rebirths are to be counted or not.

Quite so. In this aside, the game is given away. The Dalais recognise only their own creation.

Mr Carrithers, in his bitter paper,[31] reveals himself the only one to have scented the real trail. Yet there is a twist in it that even he has not seen. Before indicating this, I must sketch some intervening history.

At Trashi Lhünpo they were having trouble with Red Hats. According to Mr Shakabpa, a Red Hat King:[32]

> built his own Kar-ma-pa monastery at Shigatse at a place overlooking Tashi Lhunpo monastery of the Ge-lugs-pa. His monastery was known as Tashi Zilnon, meaning 'The Suppressor of Tashi Lhunpo'. The stones for this monastery were collected from the hill above Tashi Lhunpo, and the workers deliberately rolled boulders down on the Ge-lugs-pa monks' quarters, killing a number of them. Tashilhunpo monks were harrassed whenever they passed the kar-ma-pa monastery on their way to Shigatse.

At Lhasa, also, there was harrassment.

In 1638, the Dalai Lama received a courtesy visit from the Qoshot Mongols, headed by Gushri Khan. The Dalai Lama honoured the Khan's subordinates with Tibetan titles, and the Khan honoured the Dalai Lama's subordinates with Mongolian titles. It was in this way that Mongolian titles such as Dzaza, Teji, Ta Lama, Dayan[33] and others came to be used in Tibet – for, naturally, it was courteous to Mongolia to use the Mongolian titles bestowed.

Following this exchange of courtesies, Gushri Khan attacked the Red Hats, deposed their King, and, in 1642, proclaimed the Dalai Lama ruler of all Tibet.[34] This not only brought Trashi Lhünpo within his temporal realm, but created for him an entirely new status. The Fifth Dalai Lama Ngawam, proclaimed Lhasa to be the capital of Tibet, and, since he was no longer merely the Grand Lama of Drèpung, decided he should move his personal quarters out from there and into a new residence commensurate with his new dignity. He had the Potala built, atop the Potala Hill, on the legendary site of the palace of the ancient kings.

Ngawam was a strange man. He now began to show interest in the Red Hat teachings. This may have been partly political. Since he had to rule the whole country he had to know the whole of the people. This must be the origin of the theme one now finds repeatedly reiterated in the writing of members of the present Dalai Lama's entourage, that the Dalai Lama is above 'sectarianism' and that the Red and Yellow sects are equal in his sight. This, it must be observed, marks a departure from the aim of Tsongkapa. This new view may only have been formulated since the Chinese invasion that sent the present Dalai Lama into exile and placed a premium upon the idea of national unity in exile. In Ngawam's time, probably all that was noticed was that Ngawam had taken to reading the Tantric books of the Red school. He was also believed to have broken his vow of celibacy.

In McGovern's book there is a detail I find disturbing. He went into the temple at Lhasa. At the ground level he saw 'two statues of Maitreya, the blessed saint who now dwells in the Tushita Paradise waiting for the time to come when he will descend to earth to be incarnated as the next Buddha',[35] a statue of Gautama Buddha, as a young Prince before he had forsaken the world, and a statue of Tsongkapa. Then he went up the stairs and found himself in the presence of a most hideous black goddess or demon, eating brains from a skull.[36] What is she doing there? She must have survived from the old Bön religion, from admixture with which Tsongkapa was trying to purify Buddhism. The temple is older than Tsongkapa's reformation, so perhaps the Gelukpa found her when they took it over. But why did they keep her? When the Third Dalai Lama, Sönam Gyatso, went to Mongolia to see Altan Khan, he urged him to have all images of pre-Buddhistic deities broken up and got rid of.[37] Surely, this was meant to have been done at home, too. Mr Heinrich Harrer says she is the guardian of Lhasa, and is on occasions carried around by a procession. I have heard it said that the gargoyles on mediaeval cathedrals are to frighten the Devil away, but I hope nobody worships them.

The only way in which I could understand Tibet's 'wrathful deities' would be as representations of those sleeping dragons within us, the liabilities to temptations, often unconscious until aspiration to spiritual development calls them out into disconcerting manifestation, threatening to swamp us unless and until they are dissolved in our new understanding. I still think it is dangerous to conserve upon any pretext images of the darkness which may provide footholds for it. In any case, they can be dangerous for Europeans, who contact the Tibetan religion at too low a level. Not everything is holy that is Tibetan.

When Ngawam (the Great Fifth) died in 1682, his successor was found most inauspiciously in a Red Hat family.

The fragility of the Hubilganic succession lies in the need correctly to identify the child in whom the late lama has reincarnated. There are tests to be made. Ideally, his body should show certain physical characteristics. He should at least recognise somebody or something with which only the late departed was familiar, thus demonstrating continuity of memory. But suppose a mistake is made? The Sixth Dalai Lama, Tsang Yang Gyatso (1683–1705) behaved most unlike a Gelukpa monk. He visited women and wrote them verses, which might have been considered charming but for who he was supposed to be. He performed a curious sexual gymnastic on the balcony of the Potala. Madame David-Neel has suggested, as if in extenuation, that he was performing Tantric sexual exercises, but this does not make it better at all for these were precisely what Tsongkapa had forbidden. In the end, he renounced his vows before the Panchèn Lama, and it was declared that the Ocean of Wisdom was not in him. Lhazang Khan, who had succeeded Gushri Khan, summoned him to come and attend criticism of his failings. Mongolia was by then under Chinese influence, and, under escort, somewhere along the road to either Mongolia or China, he expired in unknown circumstances.

If a succession like this once goes wrong, can it be redeemed? Presumably the real holy one is still reincarnating, but will he be found and enthroned again? The Chinese produced an adult man as the Seventh Dalai Lama (1707–57); the ordinary people of Lhasa rejected him and civil war ensued. The Eighth Dalai Lama (1758–1805) saw his country invaded by Ghurkas and called for help from the Chinese. They integrated the Koko Nor region in their own Empire and stationed in Lhasa two resident Chinese Ambams. These were never after got rid of.

The Ninth, Tenth and Eleventh Dalai Lamas all died in their teens, and when Huc was in Lhasa, 1845–6, he found the people in gloom because a long-lasting Regent had just been forced by the Chinese to confess to having three times caused the Dalai Lama prematurely to transmigrate, the first time by strangulation, the second by suffocation and the third by poisoning.[38] Mr Shakabpa, the official historian for the present Dalai Lama's government in exile, says nothing at all about this, and what is puzzling is that at the time Huc's book was published the Eleventh was still living, in his minority, as indeed Huc mentions. Did the first offence against him relate to his eighth incarnation? Anyway, the eleventh also died in his teens, and so did the Twelfth, in whose case Mr Shakabpa admits to there having been some rumours that the transmigration was improperly expedited.[39]

According to Sarat Chandra Das, it was Panchèn Jè Pèdèn Chökyi Trakpa Tènpé Wangchuk who identified the Twelfth infant as the true incarnation, and fixed the day for his enthronement,[40] 31 July 1879, but he was not invited by the Regent and his Council to attend it – Das says because it was because it had been learned that the Panchèn had accepted his ordination from a monk of one of the Red Hat schools. This sounds unlikely, seeing that he was the protector of our Masters, Yellow of the Yellow. What I would think more likely is that he had been warned not to trust himself into the hands of the officials surrounding the infant Dalai Lama, who in fact survived his enthronement only two years and fifteen days.

At the time that our story has reached the Thirteenth Dalai Lama, Thubten Gyatso, destined to survive – by dint, he would afterwards say, of taking infinite pains not to be poisoned or otherwise done away with – was still an infant.

But who was 'our Great Master', the 'sternest of Hubilgans'? My tentative submission is that when the 'Great Fifth' Dalai put his own tutor in as Grand Lama of Trashi Lhünpo, with the title of Panchèn, there were some at Trashi Lhünpo who were faithful to the old one, the one they had already. As a spiritual man, he would not resist the imposition of the new arrival; but, while maintaining his ground and continuing to reincarnate, he would become recessive, more withdrawn, and those who gathered round him, for whom he was the real one, would form a group within a group, probably coming to be thought of as ascetics.

Madame Blavatsky refers to 'the Chief of the Archive Registers of the secret Libraries of the Dalai and the Ta-shu-hlumpo Lamas-Rimpoche . . . the latter, moreover, is a "Pan-chen" or great teacher',[41] and, again, to 'the Venerable Chohan-Lama – the chief of the Archive Registrars of the libraries containing manuscripts on esoteric doctrines belonging to the Ta-loi and Ta-shühlumpo Lamas Rim-boche'.[42] The title of Chohan has puzzled many people, and enemies of Madame Blavatsky, notably Lillie, have suggested she made it up. Yet, when Dr Wright of the Manuscripts Department of the British Museum consulted their Oriental Department about it for me, he was able to tell me it was thought, there, to be Mongolian, and meant spiritual teacher (Indian 'Guru'). Though used in Tibet, there was not a settled Tibetan spelling. (It was probably one of the Mongolian titles introduced in 1638.) Madame Blavatsky is in error in giving it in her *Theosophical Glossary* as 'Tib'. She will have thought of it as Tibetan because she heard it in Tibet.

I wrote to Mr Hugh Richardson, for many years British Representative in Lhasa and author of a history of Tibet, asking if he knew the name of the Keeper of the Dalai and Panchèn Lamas' Libraries c.1868–1884 and the name of the tutor or Regent of Panchèn Jè Pèdèn Chökyi Trakpa Tènpé Wangchuk during his minority. He replied regretting that he was unable to answer any of these questions with certainty, and said he doubted if there was a living Tibetan who could. There was an official at the Panchèn's whose title meant literally 'High Steward responsible for the lama's food'. The Regent (he was not sure if this term was appropriate in the case of the governor of the infant Panchèn) was usually the senior tutor. There would have been several tutors, but the senior tutor and the 'librarian' was probably one and the same person. That had been my thought, but coming from me alone it could not have constituted an informed guess.

So there we have it. The Chohan was probably the Regent or governor of the infant Panchèn Jè Pèdèn Chökyi Trakpa Tènpé Wangchuk, who remained after the enthronement of his charge as his most senior and trusted adviser. Further, if, as Madame Blavatsky hints when she calls him 'a' Panchèn, he was the Grand Lama of the displaced or true Hubilganic succession, our Masters may have thought of him as the reincarnation of Khèdrup Jè.

CHAPTER 44

Maitreya

But was the Mahachohan, the Chohan Lama Rimbouchy, the final head of the school or hierarchy to which Morya, Koot Hoomi and the other Masters of Wisdom belonged? No. About the higher reaches both Madame Blavatsky and Olcott are naturally very reticent. The highest human being on our planet, they explained, was Gautama Buddha or Tsongkapa, in respect to whom Morya and Koot Hoomi felt themselves less than the dust beneath his feet. But though he had renounced Nirvana to help humanity, he had not, since his reincarnation as Tsongkapa, walked about bodily. There was, however, a person to whom only passing reference has been made, his eventual successor and the Buddha to be, Maitreya. Being in the process of preparation to take over in the far future, he would have to be incarnate. But where? He would be doing something with his time, but what?

Olcott has been groomed to discretion, yet an allusion slips from his pen. It was while he was trying to do something for a blind man, Badrinath Babu, with his magnetic passes, that the latter began to say he saw a 'shining man', though it was through closed eyelids. He then described what seemed the unlikeliest person, an individual with:[1]

> blue eyes, light flowing hair, light beard and European features and complexion, for surely I have not found among the Brahmins any legend of such an adept. Yet the description . . . fitted exactly with a real personage, the Teacher of our Teachers, a *paramahaguru* . . . who had given me a small coloured sketch of himself in New York, before we left for Bombay.

No name is named. But then, no Adepts' names are ever mentioned by Olcott in the whole of his published *Old Diary Leaves*. There is no Morya, no Koot Hoomi, nor Serapis, Tuitit or Illarion. It is only from his manuscript scrapbook or other sources that we can sometimes tell when 'an Adept' means M., K.H. or another. There is, however, in the Theosophical Society a legend that a portrait of Maitreya was precipitated to Olcott and is possessed at Adyar. It is, moreover, asserted that the features and colouring are as described above.

It is not actually stated by Olcott of what race the being is. One cannot rule out that a Celt or other fair European could be living somewhere in Tibet or some more desolate part of Asia, though Olcott's sense of mystification almost seems to suggest a blue-eyed, fair-haired Indian. As blue eye and fair hair genes are both recessive, there seems to be no absolute reason why this should not be possible. A recessive gene, being masked by a dominant dark eye or dark hair one, could remain, so far as is known, for innumerable generations, and then suddenly reappear, mysteriously. For a mundane explanation, it might be remembered that Alexander the Great led an army into north-western India, which could have caused blue eye and fair hair genes to be recessive in some Indian families. Again, the explanation may be quite other.

What is interesting is that it will have been noted that Maitreya has a Hobilgan at Urga, in northern Mongolia. That, if genuine, would make a kind of outpost of his consciousness in a place other than that in which he was incarnate. But is the outpost in such an out-of-the-way place to be considered as the only one? The doctrine has implications for the eventual drama of Krishnamurti.

In any case, it should be remembered that the Gelukpa have always seen it as their most sacred duty to prepare the way for Maitreya Buddha, when, in the far, far future, he relieves our actual Buddha.[2]

As a footnote to Olcott's story, it is interesting to notice that some forty years later, McGovern, describing his travels in Tibet, writes about 'Maitreya', the compassionate . . . the next Buddha':[3]

He is frequently portrayed almost as a European. I have sometimes seen representations of him with white skin and blue eyes, and in nearly all cases his image is sitting on a chair in European style as opposed to the Oriental cross-legged attitude . . .

It is a pity that he does not give us the date of these representations. Unless they are so recent as to portray Maitreya in the body of his incarnation in Madame Blavatsky's and Olcott's time, does it mean that he has brought the blue eyes over from incarnations in the blue-eyed races of the West, or that it will be in a blue-eyed body that he will assume his eventual Buddhahood?

CHAPTER 45

Adyar

On 17 December 1882, Madame Blavatsky and Olcott left together for Adyar. She cannot have been feeling well, for on 29 December he wrote in his diary, 'She made me promise that if she should die no one but myself should see her face. I am to sew her up in a sheet and have her cremated'.

Soon, however, she was planning her new quarters, which she decided to have not in the big room on the ground floor, which could be used as a convention hall, but in a superstructure on its flat roof. This she would divide with a curtain into bedroom and sitting-room, but now that at last there was the space, she thought of having a separate room for whatever concerned the Masters, an occult room. Olcott therefore directed Coulomb to build for her an extension on the bedroom side.[1] A bricked-up window to this he had Coulomb demolish, to give her access. The existing door to it was superfluous, since there were two other doors to the terrace and staircase, and the recess gave her the idea of having a cabinet made to hang in it that would be a shrine. It had small folding doors, behind which she placed the portraits of the Masters and one or two specially sacred or beautiful objects. Beneath the shelf on which these stood was a little drawer in which the Masters could place any letters they chose to precipitate. The whole recess, with its shrine, was then made more private with further curtaining.

It should be noted that this shrine has no relation to what we have come to know as *The Mahatma Letters*, that vast collection to Sinnett, which embodies the Masters' teaching. Only one note to him was sent through Madras, and that because Koot Hoomi did not know on what date Sinnett was sailing.

Sinnett was sailing for England because the proprietors of *The Pioneer* had dismissed him as they did not like the new tone of the paper. Koot Hoomi was trying to organise the foundation of another paper, *The Phoenix*; this would have Indian proprietors but Sinnett would be editor, and it would be devoted to 'the Indo-British nation',[2] a phrase Sinnett had used in one of his editorials. The Rajas, however, were too apathetic to subscribe the share capital. Koot Hoomi thought Sir Courtenay Ilbert's proposed Bill, to enable Indian judges to try Europeans, 'untimely'. Violently resisted by many of the British, it was inflaming feeling against Indians, and so creating a climate unfavourable to the start of a new paper dedicated to the conciliatory concept of an 'Indo-British nation'. *The Englishman* told its readers that the government was on the eve of a crisis as grave as that of the Indian Mutiny; racism was suddenly frantic. The only offer of capital came from an embarrassing quarter, from the Zemindars, with the condition that the new paper should oppose the Bengal Rent Bill. The Zemindars were tax farmers, to whom the permanent settlement of 1793 had given too much power to squeeze money out of the ryots, or peasant cultivators. It has been speculated that half the members of the House of Commons who passed the measure, hearing the Zemindars continually spoken of as farmers, thought they farmed the land and so confused them with the peasant cultivators. A bill to lessen their power to extort from the latter was needed, but the new paper was needed also. Koot Hoomi suggested that Sinnett could accept the backing and meet the condition, in as much as the Bill, as it stood, contained real flaws, which he could point out. Pointing them out would not prevent the Bill from being passed, and would indeed make it better. The Bill once having been passed, as it must be, the Zemindars would no longer bother Sinnett about it. The Zemindars would see a financial return for their investment in the paper, and India would be provided with a conciliatory paper dedicated to the Indo-British nation. Sinnett replied that to accept the Zemindars' backing and to appear to oppose a needed Bill, destined to be passed, would lower his reputation, yet he would do it and cast the responsibility upon Koot Hoomi. Koot Hoomi replied that he could not do that since it was not an order that he was giving, merely a suggestion that he was making; so that the karma of acting on it would be Sinnett's. Further, on reflection, he withdrew the suggestion, because '*your* standing . . . must not be jeopardised.'[3]

The failure to find the capital elsewhere was in part occasioned by unhelpful letters from Hume. Koot Hoomi had followed Morya into loss of patience with Hume. During the previous autumn, he had written that Hume would advocate 'Sutee' if it were his only means to get his hands warm. (Sutee, otherwise sati or sutti, is widow-burning.) Back in 1881, Morya had referred to Hume as 'the evil genius of the Society',[4] and said it was against not only his own advice but the Chohan's that Koot Hoomi sacrificed himself in the endeavour to teach him. Koot Hoomi confessed:[5]

> . . . the Chohan permitted himself to be over-persuaded by us, into giving sanction to my intercourse with Mr. Hume. I had pledged my word to him that he had repented, – was a changed man. And now how shall I ever face my Great Master, who is laughed at, made the object of Mr. Hume's wit, called Rameses the Great and such like indecent remarks? And he used terms in his letters, the brutal grossness of which prevents me from repeating them, which have revolted my soul when I read them . . . words so filthy as to pollute the very air that touched them, and that I hastened to send to you with the letter that contained it, so as not to have those pages in my house, full of young and innocent chelas, that I would prevent from ever hearing such terms.

We do not know what caused him to write,[6] '. . . the situation is thrown into serious danger by wild indiscretions and the Khobilgan deeply incensed . . .'; but it was Hume he was talking about when, in connection with his actions over *The Phoenix*, he referred to,[7] 'the Dugpas, under whose influence he has now placed himself altogether'.

In the one letter sent Sinnett through Adyar, he refers to,[8] 'our ex-friend Mr. Hume – (now entirely in the hands of the Brothers of the Shadow)'. The terms 'Dugpas' and 'Brothers of the Shadow' are synonymous. The Dugpas are one of the Red Hat orders that refused the reformation of Tsongkapa, and are mainly found in Bhutan. In another passage Koot Hoomi refers to 'the Red Capped Brothers of the Shadow'.[9] When a chela, the Disinherited, slipped on the edge of an abyss, Madame Blavatsky wrote that Morya said it was 'a fiendish Red Cap'[10] who had deliberately caused the accident.[11] 'They put upon certain paths bits of rag soaked in evil magnetism. If anyone trod on one, the "psychic shock" could cause him to lose his footing and fall down the precipice'. They were the committed enemies of the Gelukpa, and constantly sought the ruination of all works tending to spirituality. They take hold of weak-minded persons or persons who by nursing dark and hate-filled emotions grant them foothold.

But we had begun to describe the arrangements at Adyar. Olcott had instructed Coulomb to make a little kitchen for Madame Blavatsky, so that Madame Coulomb could prepare a meal for her in her own apartment if she did not feel like coming downstairs.

Entrance to Madame Blavatsky's rooms was solely by an exterior staircase, off which Damodar and Babula had rooms. This staircase was closed to outsiders by a door at the bottom, which made it very private.

Olcott had his quarters in a bungalow below. He had left in February on a tour of Bengal, but was back in June. Wondering whether he should next accept invitations to Colombo or Allahabad, on 6 June he put one of the invitations into the shrine, and opened it to find that there was already an answer. 'It was done while I stood there and not half a minute had elapsed'. It was from Illarion (or as Olcott writes it, Hilarion) and was in French, beginning, '*Maha Sahib avec qui je suis pour le moment m'ordonne de dire . . .*'[12] (Maha Sahib with whom I am at the moment orders me to say . . .) Maha Sahib is not the Maha Chohan but an Adept whom Olcott knows as S. If Jinarajadasa is right in taking him to be Serapis, it looks as though Serapis was now in Tibet too.

That this was in fact the case appears to be confirmed in a letter written later by Madame Blavatsky to a friend. Refuting the idea that the Masters or Mahatmas of the school in Tibet of which she was a pupil all originated there, she said:[13]

> One of their highest Mahachohans lived in Egypt and went to Tibet only a year before we did (in 1878) and he is neither a Tibetan nor a Hindu; this 'Occult Brotherhood' has not originated in Tibet, nor is it *only* in Tibet, now; but what I always said and maintain to this day is, that most of its *members and some of the highest* are, and move constantly, in Tibet, because of its isolation . . .

The Master who had always lived in Egypt must, surely, be Serapis, the Egyptian Copt, who first wrote to Olcott from Luxor but must have gone ahead of them – and of Illarion, so much associated with him – to Tibet.

This does not mean Serapis and Illarion stayed in Tibet for ever. That Illarion would be returning to Greece was implied in Koot Hoomi's hint that he would be starting an esoteric school in Greece, and Serapis is always associated with special wardenship of Africa. They went to Tibet for a while to learn from the highest of all.

The letter, which is the first of six short ones Olcott received from Illarion during the first half of June, said he could go to Colombo immediately, but only for a few days as there were places nearer to their new home, in the Presidency of Madras, which he would do well to visit; he could go to Allahabad later.

In London, Sinnett received another letter from Koot Hoomi in July, saying that although a certain Sir Charles Turner might twit him with having his grey ventricles 'surcharged with the Tzigadza Akasa',[14] he was helping to 'build a bridge over which the British metaphysicians may come to within thinking distance of us'. Sir William Crookes, of 'radiant matter', was putting a foot across the Theosophical threshold. A letter of 13 June from Illarion had urged Olcott to put his 'whole soul' into writing a letter Sinnett could show Crookes.[15]

Koot Hoomi adds that the reason most scientists do not make contact with them is that their power is confined to Manas. Commenting on a mistake he finds on p.202 of Rhys David's *Buddhism*, and also on the Christian mysticism of Anna Kingsford, he explains:[16]

The supreme energy lies in *Buddhi*; latent – when wedded to *Atman* alone, active and *irresistible* when galvanised by the *essence* of *Manas* . . . Avolokita Iswar . . . means 'the Lord that is seen' . . . the Atman or seventh principle ridded of its mayavic distinction from the Universal Source – which becomes the object of perception for and by the *individuality* centred in *Buddhi*, the sixth principle . . . Avalokiteswara is both the unmanifested *Father* and the manifested *Word*, Logos, the Verb . . . the real *Christ* of every Christian is the *Vach*, the 'mystical voice', while the man Jeshu was but a mortal like any of us, an adept more by his inherent purity and ignorance of real Evil, than by what he had learned with his Initiated Rabbis and the already (at that period) fast degenerating Egyptian Hierophants . . . in Chinese . . . Kwan-Shai-yin or the universally manifested voice – is active – male . . . It is Kwan-yin that is the female principle . . . correct rendering of our Avalokiteswara and Kwan-shai-yin . . . would simply amount to showing Christendom the true and undeniable origin of the 'awful' and incomprehensible mysteries of the Trinity, Transubstantiation and Immaculate Conception, as also whence their ideas of Father, Son, Spiritus, and – Mother . . . Pythagoras had a reason for never using the finite, useless figure 2 – and for altogether discarding it. The ONE can, when manifesting, become only 3. The manifested, when a simple duality, remains passive and concealed . . .

Madame Blavatsky was invited by Major-General and Mrs H.R. Morgan to spend the hot weather with them at Ootacamund, a hill resort in the Presidency of Madras, called Ooty by the British. The property was an enormous dairy farm and market garden, stretching for miles. Mrs Morgan had bought it with her own money, early in their marriage, so that when her husband eventually retired, as he now had, he could take up the management. The garden of the house was planted with roses and heliotropes and with air-freshening eucalyptus trees, grown by Mrs Morgan from a packet of seeds from Australia.

The Morgans talked to Madame Blavatsky about the Indians who worked on the estate. Both were convinced some of them possessed powers not known to western science, which was why they were interested to know what Madame Blavatsky would say about instances they mentioned. They also told her of a mysterious tribe in the Nilgiri or Blue Mountains, of tall men, held in such awe by all others that their name was never pronounced. The unspeakable name was Toda. They took Madame Blavatsky on an excursion to a Toda village. Here her sex was against her, as the Toda men reserved their secrets from the women. Nevertheless, she made out some things. They worshipped the buffaloes it was the business of their lives to tend, and could undertake healing, but they would not exercise their powers for the benefit of anyone who took alcohol. They told her the story of their race, as it had been told them by the buffaloes. It intersected the *Ramayana at several points. This puzzled Madame Blavatsky, for the Todas could not read Sanskrit, or indeed read at all. She believed the Ramayana*, at whatever the date it was first written down, embodied a story of happenings in Atlantis. However old then, were the Todas? To have played a role in the events of the *Ramayana*, they must be remnants of an Atlantean race. This, her deepest thought about the matter, she kept back from the account she wrote in Russian for her usual paper. Only after her death was it translated into English, when it ran in *The Theosophist* from May 1909 into 1910, under the title 'Mysterious tribes: three months in the Blue Mountains near Madras'.

On 1 August, General Morgan had to go into Madras on some business. Madame Blavatsky told him that if he called at Adyar he might see the portraits of the Masters. The shrine was opened for him by Madame Coulomb, who knocked from a shelf a saucer, which fell to the floor and broke. The General asked Coulomb to get some glue. He said he would fetch it from his bungalow, about 100 yards away. The General then remarked that if the Mahatmas thought it sufficiently important, they might mend it. Damodar, who had all the time been sitting watching, said 'There is a message'. He re-opened the shrine, and took from the bowl a letter addressed to them. He then re-opened the cloth in which the pieces had been wrapped and found the saucer intact. Coulomb had been absent for perhaps three to five minutes. Madame Coulomb then wrote a letter dated 13 August 1883, to Madame Blavatsky, which will be interesting to recall in the light of her future assertions. It is in English:[17]

> The General found the portraits admirable, but I wish I had never gone up, because of my opening the 'Shrine', I, Madame Coulomb, who never cares either to see or to have anything to do in these matters, as you well know, must needs go and open the Shrine, and see before her eyes, and through her fingers pass, the pretty saucer . . .

On 27 August, a far-away volcano, Krakatoa, blew its top, creating the loudest sound ever heard on earth. Did Madame Blavatsky sense an omen?

In September, Olcott rejoined her at the Morgans'. He wrote, 'My old chum seemed really overjoyed to see me and rattled on in her affectionate way . . . the champagne-like mountain air set her blood leaping'.[18] The English at Ooty received them well. They dined with Mr C.P. Carmichael, Secretary to the government, and his wife; and Colonel Kenney-Herbert, retired Military Secretary to the government of Madras, invited them to tiffin. He had cooked it himself, making it, in their honour, a vegetarian meal. It was the first Olcott had ever enjoyed.

From Ooty, they went south to Pondicherry, the diminutive French possession, where the Governor's band met them at the station, playing 'God save the Queen'. At the lodgings to which they were conducted, Madame Blavatsky gave Olcott a look, nodding her head in a particular direction. To his astonishment, he recognised amongst those surrounding them one of the faces that had sometimes appeared through hers in New York, while she was writing *Isis Unveiled*, the one who had been 'in' when she duplicated the pencils and who communicated in French.[20] Olcott wanted to go over and speak to him – for he was sitting at the back – but though Narayan smiled, his eyes forbade approach. Presently he rose, saluted them both with folded palms and withdrew.

On 23 September they returned to Madras, and reached Adyar on the same afternoon. On 27 September, Olcott left again, for another tour of the north of India; he took with him Damodar and William T. Brown, Bachelor of Laws of the University of Glasgow, who had only just joined the Society but had been granted a letter from Koot Hoomi through the shrine.

On the day he left, Madame Blavatsky wrote to Sinnett:[21]

Adyar,
Sept. 27

Just arrived from Ooty through Pondicherry . . .

You use very extraordinary words . . . Olcott as *nominal*(!!) *head of the whole Society* . . . he is not a *nominal* but the *actual* head of the Society, if you please . . . I would consider myself the meanest of creatures to read how you lower down poor Olcott – whose shoes none of your *cultured* Theosophists is worthy to untie – and not tell you what I think of it. I say you are unjust and unfair . . . forgetting Olcott's rare devotion, unselfishness, blameless and pure life, his great philanthropy and most precious qualities you see in him only one thing! He is an American, a Yankee, while your English sympathies have been during the war for the South, and whom I verily believe, you hate and cannot forgive only for their being Northern Yankees . . . Olcott is a thousand times *higher* and *nobler* and *more unselfish* that I am or ever was . . . your remark that he ought to answer *himself reverentially* every line of the London Secretary has cut me to the deep.

19 November found Olcott in Lahore, with Damodar and Brown. He was asleep in his tent when a touch woke him. Starting up, he clutched the arm of what might have been an assassin, and heard a sweet voice saying, 'Do you not know me?'[22] It was Koot Hoomi whose arm he was gripping. The Master took Olcott's left hand in his left, gathered the fingers of his right into the palm and stood quietly, his face illuminated by a lamp on a packing-case. Olcott felt something form within his palm, wrapped in silk, a letter in the well-known blue writing. Koot Hoomi placed his hand on his forehead for a moment in blessing, then, leaving him to read the letter, went through the flap dividing his part of the tent from Brown's.

Hearing an exclamation from Brown's side of the tent, Olcott went in after a few minutes and found Brown clutching a K.H. letter wrapped in silk. Brown said that when the Master came in and gave it to him, he realised that he had seen him earlier in the day, in broad daylight.

Olcott's letter, besides giving personal counsel, mentioned that the Master would come again on the following evening. At about 10.00 p.m. the following evening they were all three together when an Indian came in and said the Master would like to speak to Damodar. Then Koot Hoomi entered. Damodar went forward and stood speaking with Koot Hoomi in the sight of the others. Koot Hoomi saluted all three with folded palms, and withdrew. Olcott heard his footsteps on the ground. He was in body.

CHAPTER 46

The Kiddle incident

On 1 September 1883, the Spiritualist paper, *Light*, carried a letter from Mr. Henry Kiddle saying that one of the letters printed by Sinnett in *The Occult World* contained phrases which were in a talk on Spiritualism he had given in August 1880; that had been printed in *The Banner of Light* later that month.

The phrases common to both publications were:

> . . . ideas rule the world; and as men's minds receive new ideas, laying aside the old and effete, the world . . .

> crumble before their onward march . . . when the time comes, as to stay the progress of the tide.

As to the material before, after and in between these common phrases, Koot Hoomi's text played upon the ideas in Kiddle's, but from an opposite point of view.

Madame Blavatsky, Olcott, Judge and Subba Row all picked up their pens in defence of the Master. Koot Hoomi wrote to Sinnett, giving him an explanation, which, however, he forbade him to publish, for, 'One does not cease entirely, my good friend, to be a *man*, for being an *adept*'. He must have felt it would be undignified to defend himself against Kiddle, but to Sinnett he confided:[1]

> The letter in question was framed by me while on a journey and on horseback. It was dictated mentally, in the direction of, and 'precipitated' by, a young chela . . . who had to transcribe it from the hardly visible imprint.

When he reached home, the chela asked him if he would look it over, but having been for forty-eight hours in the saddle he was too tired, and said it would not matter if some of it were missed. When he awoke, the chela had already precipitated the letter. He gave it no further thought and when Sinnett asked his permission to print his letters, he forgot there was this one. If Sinnett had sent him the book in proof, he would have corrected it. As soon as the commotion amongst his defenders reached him 'across the eternal snows', he 'ordered an investigation into the original scraps of the impression'. He had begun, 'Plato was right to re-admit every element of speculation which Socrates had discarded . . .'. There had followed three sentences the chela missed; then, 'Hear some of them [the Spiritualists] reasserting the old axiom that "Ideas rule the world" . . .'.

A few months before, he had made a clairvoyant survey of American Spiritualism, to see what was now being said by its leading figures; without becoming aware of Kiddle as a person, had picked up some of the phrases used by him, as typifying 'the pernicious intellectual tendency of the movement'. Unintentionally, he had transmitted his recollection of this verbiage more sharply than his reflections on it, and the sharp etchings were what the chela recorded. 'Had I looked over the impressed *negative* there would have been one more weapon broken in the enemy's hand. Having neglected this duty, my Karma evolved . . .'.

CHAPTER 47

Anna Kingsford

Madame Blavatsky, during this time, was still at Adyar. Her letters to Sinnett, and also those of Koot Hoomi, are largely concerned with a Dr Anna Kingsford, author of *The Perfect Way or the Finding of Christ*, who, though not previously a Theosophist, had been brought into the London Lodge as its President. All her interest was in the Graeco–Egyptian Hermetic and Gnostic Christian traditions and seemed almost anti-Tibetan, so that Sinnett, who had come to London full of all he had learned from Tibet, was put out, as was Madame Blavatsky. The new development was, however, welcomed by the Great Chohan, because, although it dashed Sinnett's hope of becoming President in London, it could bring to the Society a broader basis and help to spread the essential wisdom among English people who would feel as alien a theosophy that seemed to have a solely Indo–Tibetan basis. That Mrs Kingsford should remain, wrote Koot Hoomi to Sinnett and to the London Lodge as a whole, was:[1]

the express wish of the *Chohan himself*. Mrs Kingsford's election is not a matter of personal feeling . . Nor is it a matter of the slightest consequence whether the gifted President of the 'London Lodge' of the Theos. Soc. entertains feelings of reverence or disrespect toward the humble and unknown individuals at the head of the Tibetan Good Law, – or the writer of the present, or any of his Brothers . . . Hermetic Philosophy is universal and unsectarian, while the Tibetan School, will ever be regarded by those who know little, if anything of it, as coloured more or less with sectarianism. The former knowing neither caste, nor colour nor creed, no lover of Esoteric wisdom can have any objection to the name . . . The Egyptian Hierophant, the Chaldean Mage, the Arhat and the Rishi were bound in days of yore on the same voyage of discovery and ultimately arrived at the same goal though by different tracks. There are even at the present moment three centres of the Occult Brotherhood in existence, widely separated geographically, and as widely exoterically – the true esoteric doctrine being identical in substance though differing in terms . . Mr Sinnett and Mrs Kingsford are both useful, both needed by our revered Chohan and Master . . . But both cannot be Presidents . . . Mrs Kingsford's views . . . by reason of their association with the names and symbols familiar to Christian ears and eyes . . . Mrs K is . . . more adapted to lead the movement successfully in England . . . Her constant and not altogether unsuccessful strife in the cause of anti-vivisection and her staunch advocacy of vegetarianism are alone sufficient to entitle her to the consideration of our Chohans . . . hence our Maha-Chohan's preference in this direction.

K.H.
December 7th, 1883
Mysore

The place from which this is dated may cause surprise; but it is confirmed by a letter from Koot Hoomi from Madras, dated 17 December, to Brown,[2] denying a meeting and saying he had already left Mysore for China, whence he will return home. That means he will have sailed, probably from Colombo, on a boat with ordinary people. He would not, however, have booked his passage in the name of Koot Hoomi (which means his passport cannot have been in that name); they would not have connected him with the Mahatma Letters and his privacy would have been secure.

The three great Brotherhoods of which he speaks will be those centred at Shigatsè, Luxor and –? It is a long time since we have heard of either the Hungarian (Rákóczy) or the Venetian; though as Sinnett was returning through Venice, Koot Hoomi asked him to send him three pebbles from a canal near the Doge's Palace, preferably from under the Bridge of Sighs,[3] packed so as not to spoil the magnetism. (Koot Hoomi also mentions that Illarion was starting a school in Greece⁴ which was to be kept secret, though that sounds more like a twin for the Theosophical Society than the centre of the third great Brotherhood.)

Olcott, reaching Adyar just before Christmas, wrote, 'Home never seemed more delightful, nor my old Chum more dear'.⁵

The turn of the year found Madame Blavatsky still writing to Sinnett about the London Lodge. Some one had told her that Anna Kingsford wore too much jewellery, yet it was the Chohan who wanted her, so if she did not turn out well, it was 'the Chohan's karma'.⁶

In the same letter, she mentions that Mrs Kingsford had written to her, saying that the advertisements for 'Bradlaugh's and Besant's literature' in *The Theosophist* would impede its circulation in England. Madame Blavatsky, probably bridling at the interference, applied to Koot Hoomi for a ruling; he sustained Mrs Kingsford,⁷ 'Write to the *Seeress* of the London Lodge that you are ready to take out that *obnoxious* avertisement . . . but that you will not stop advertising free thought literature in general'.

Sinnett must also have written to Koot Hoomi about the matter raised, for we find Koot Hoomi writing back to him in a letter he received in January 1884:⁸

> I am sorry you took the trouble of posting me about Bradlaugh. I know him and his partner well . . . He is *not* immoral, nor could anything that might be said against or for him by Mrs K., or even yourself, change or even influence my opinion of both himself and Mrs Besant. Yet the book published by them – '*The Fruits of Philosophy*' is infamous and *highly pernicious* in its effects, whatever and however benificent and philanthropic the objects that led to the publication of the work . . . I *have not* read the work – nor ever will; but I have its unclean spirit, its brutal aura before me, and I say again in my sight the advices offered in the work are abominable; they are the fruits of Sodom and Gommorah rather than of Philosophy, the very name of which it degrades.

What was the book, published by Annie Besant and Charles Bradlaugh? We shall gather more about this later.

In the same letter, Koot Hoomi wrote further of Mrs Kingsford:⁹

> Suffice it that you should know that her anti-vivisection struggle and her strict vegetarian diet have entirely won over to her side our stern Master. He cares less than we do for any outward – or even inward – expression or feeling of disrespect for the 'Mahatmas'. Let her . . . be true to her principles and all the rest will follow in good time.

Again, in a subsequent letter:¹⁰

> Mrs Kingsford's ignorance of our real character, our doctrines and status (underlying as they do all her uncomplimentary remarks in connection with the present writer and his colleagues) made them of not even the weight of a flake of cotton in the matter of her re-election.

This letter begins by saying that since his telegrams to Mrs Kingsford and Sinnett from Mysore may not have been understood, 'I was ordered by the Maha-Chohan to advise the postponement of the annual election . . .'. They did not wish to force Mrs Kingsford's election; they merely wanted their attitude to be understood before a free ballot was taken. They advise that it be postponed until the arrival of Olcott, who knows their mind. It is signed,

> '(By order of my Most Venerated
> Guru Deva Mahatma K)',

followed by a triangle with a point in the centre and Sanskrit characters, and then '. . . K.H.'. The Indian words are further titles, 'Guru Deva' meaning the same as 'Chohan', 'Spiritual Teacher', and 'Mahatma' meaning literally 'Great Soul'; but we do discover, at last, in the initial K, the first letter of the Great Chohan's real name.

Olcott decided to go to London to try to sort things out, and because the climate of Madras was getting Madame Blavatsky down¹¹ she went with him. Olcott appointed a Board of Control, to be in charge during their absence. The European members were Dr Franz Hartmann, physician, German by birth, American by naturalisation, who had come to them from

Colorado; St George Lane-Fox, electrical engineer, newly arrived; and W.T. Brown. The principal Indian members were Subba Row, Screenivas Row and Damodar. As Madame Blavatsky had not been comfortable in her bedroom, Olcott instructed Coulomb to build her a new one, on the roof, while they were away; as an afterthought he added him, but not his wife, to the Board of Control. As Damodar had shifted his sleeping quarters downstairs, the superstructure upon the flat roof was now deserted except for the Coulombs, who were given the key.

Madame Blavatsky and Olcott left Adyar in February and were accompanied as far as Bombay by Hartmann and Madame Coulomb. They broke their journey to stay with an Indian Raja, Prince Harisinghi Rupsinghi, and Madame Coulomb repeated an attempt she had made during the convention in December to borrow 2,000 rupees from him. Madame Blavatsky, suddenly becoming aware of this, reproached her for pestering him.[12]

On 21 February, Madame Blavatsky, Olcott and Babula boarded their ship, being seen off by Hartmann and Madame Coulomb, who remained aboard until the last bell warned non-passengers to leave. Hartmann says that as Madame Coulomb and he stepped into the small boat that would take them back to the quay, Madame Coulomb said to Babula, 'I shall be revenged on your mistress for preventing me from getting my 2,000 Rupees'.[13]

CHAPTER 48

London Lodge

With them on the *Chaundernagore* they took the young Bengali Brahmin, Mohini C. Chatterjee, by now a chela of Koot Hoomi, and Sorabji J. Padshah, an aspirant poet. Koot Hoomi wrote to Padshah, 'A true seer is always a poet, and a poet can never be a true one – unless he is in perfect unity with occult nature'. They took also Babula.

On 12 March 1884, they docked at Marseilles, then Mohini and Padshah went on to Paris, while Olcott and Madame Blavatsky (with Babula) went to stay at the Palais Tiranty in Nice with the Countess of Caithness, Duchesse de Pomar. Their hostess, who had long begged Madame Blavatsky to come and see her, invited everyone of distinction to meet them, including the French astronomer, Camille Flammarion, who had joined the Theosophical Society. (For Olcott, it was a first taste of continental high life.)

On 27 March they left for Paris, where the party that met them in the early morning of the next day included Judge. He had perhaps been neglected in favour of Sinnett, but he had been given Damodar with whom to correspond, and at last one of the latter's letters had arrived bearing a precipitation in red, 'Better come. M.'.[1] So here he was, en route for India, ready to escort them to 45 rue Notre Dame des Champs in the artists' quarter, where Lady Caithness had taken a suite for them. Their arrival had been heralded in Victor Hugo's journal, *Le Rappel*, with a three-column leader on the Buddhist mission to Europe.

Madame Blavatsky wrote Sinnett a fractious letter, passing on the Chohan's instructions regarding Mrs Kingsford – with obvious disapproval:[2]

> She has to remain President . . . since it is the Chohan's desire. Ye Gods! Why is it the Chohan wants her at all! Is it for our, or your sins? . . . But it seems a fatality that the old, venerable gentleman who *never* meddles in anything theosophical least of all European, should have thrown his eye upon her! . . . Is it that the Chohan Rimbouchy wants to disgust you all . . . They [Morya and Koot Hoomi] are *forced* to tolerate her on account of and out of deference for the wishes of the Chohan – His name be blessed.

Nowhere does the occasional conflict emerge more clearly between Blavatsky the woman, with sometimes ungoverned feelings, and the orders for which she was the agent – even those from her Master's Master.

The correspondence also now contains references to Mrs Laura Holloway, an American medium, who was occasionally able to hear the voice of Koot Hoomi. He had inspired her to come to London, where he had set her to work with Mohini (because they had co-operated in past lives) upon a book to be called *Man*. They were expected to work in Mrs Arundale's house,[3] 77 Elgin Crescent, where Mohini had now arrived, but Sinnett wanted her to work for him. Koot Hoomi had not wished her to spend too much time at Sinnett's house, 7 Ladbroke Gardens (because of characteristics of the house, of which we shall learn later), but now Sinnett was staying in Windsor and wanted her to come out to him there. Mrs Holloway had written to ask Madame Blavatsky if she should. Madame Blavatsky replied saying that she supposed there was no reason why she should not take a holiday from her work on *Man*, but she wrote to Sinnett, saying that Koot Hoomi's instruction had been that Mrs Holloway should sleep and in fact live at Mrs Arundale's. She had been brought over by the Master for a precise work, and if Sinnett diverted her from that work it would block his own line of communication with the Master.

Olcott left for London on 5 April. He and Mohini had a carriage to themselves all the way, and he was reading when there dropped from above a letter in Koot Hoomi's writing:[4]

> . . . Do not be surprised at anything you may hear from Adyar . . . You have harboured a traitor and an enemy under your roof for years, and the missionary party are more than

ready to avail of any help she can be induced to give. A regular conspiracy is on foot. She is maddened by the appearance of Mr Lane-Fox and the powers you have given to the Board of Control.

Long before, Olcott had upset Miss Bates by taking the housekeeping away from her and giving it to the newly arrived Madame Coulomb. Now, in putting the newly arrived Lane-Fox on to the Board but not Madame Coulomb, he had made the same mistake, though in reverse.

In London he had to move fast. The election of officers of the London Lodge was on 7 April. With the Sinnett/Kingsford opposition threatening, he went first to see the party he did not know, Dr Kingsford. She told him she had decided not to stand for re-election. He offered her a charter for a separate branch of her own, the Hermetic Theosophical Society, which she accepted.[5]

The meeting of the London Lodge was at the rooms in Lincoln's Inn of a member who was a barrister, Mr G.B. Finch. Olcott chaired the meeting. Mr Finch was elected President, Mr Sinnett Vice-President and Miss Francesca Arundale Treasurer. In the middle of everything, Madame Blavatsky, thought to be in Paris, appeared at the door. Mohini – who had been told by his Master to show her particular respect during the tour as the Chohan would take advantage of her being in Europe to view the scene through her eyes – prostrated himself.

Through Mohini's action, Leadbeater realised who she must be.[6] The Rev. Charles Webster Leadbeater, born in Stockport, aged 30, was a curate at Bramshot, Hampshire. He saw her being conducted to the platform, where the retired Anna Kingsford and the newly elected officers were introduced to her. Amongst those on the floor was Mr F.W.H. Myers, from the newly formed Society for Psychical Research, who wanted to know about Adepts' astral projection. Madame Blavatsky motioned Mohini to answer him.

She repaired with Olcott to the Sinnetts', where she stayed a week. Amongst new people who came to see her were Countess Wachtmeister and Archibald and Bertram Keightley, of whom more later. Professor William Crookes, who had been elected to the Council, invited her to his laboratory to see his radiant metal experiments, and on 15 April she was accompanied back as far as Boulogne by Frau Gebhard, who had been a pupil of Eliphas Levi.

Olcott still had business in London. On 9 April he attended the first meeting, at C.C. Massey's, of Mrs Kingsford's new branch. Her idea was that its members and those of the London Lodge should be able to attend each other's meetings, but he thought this would lead to competition. He introduced a new rule, that members should belong only to one Lodge. This was surely a mistake. Thus separated, the Hermetic Society broke away from the Theosophical Society, bringing about that loss to it of Anna Kingsford and the Hermetic element which the Chohan had hoped to avoid.

Olcott had also an embassy for the Sinhalese Buddhists. He called at the Colonial Office, where he was received by Mr R.H. Meade. Olcott put to him a number of entreaties, such as that marriage according to Buddhist rites be recognised; and that Buddhists might be allowed to have as their holiday the birthday of the Buddha, celebrated at the full moon that usually falls in May, Wesak, in place of one of the Christian holidays. Meade advised him to address these petitions to the Earl of Derby, as Secretary of State for the Colonies. This he did, and almost all of them were granted.[7]

He had, therefore, the feeling that he was doing not too badly. Neither did he see any danger in accepting a suggestion made him by Myers, at a lunch in the Junior Atheneum, that he should call and see his friends in the Society for Psychical Research. He met them in Cambridge on 8 May and in London on 11 May. Present were Myers, Edmund Gurney, Frank Podmore and J.H. Stack. They were not interested in Theosophy, only in phenomena, particularly astral projection. He told them of some experiences of Damodar,[8] which they took down, and he mentioned, as a phenomenon, that a letter had fallen to him while in a train. They also saw Sinnett once, Padshah once and Mohini twice, on 9 and 10 June.

Mohini also told them about the letter that had dropped to Olcott in the train.[9] It had been about half an hour before they reached Calais. The train was travelling at normal speed. They occupied corner seats, facing each other, and the window was closed. Suddenly he saw the white letter fall to Olcott. Stack suggested to him he was mistaken as to the window's being closed, and that somebody in the country through which they were passing could have thrown the letter in. Mohini said he thought the rush of air would have prevented the letter from being thrown in. Asked if there was space between the walls of the compartment and the ceiling of the train, he said there was not. Asked whether, as they entered the train in Paris, any other person had entered with them, he said only the porter had come in, to put the luggage in. Asked if Olcott could have brought the letter in himself and suddenly thrown or jerked it up into the air, so that it fell down to him, he said that if Colonel Olcott had done that, he must have seen him do it. 'I was looking in front of me.' It was he who had picked the letter up and handed it to Olcott. Asked if he had seen the Master Koot Hoomi in the flesh, he said he was not at liberty to answer. He said that before leaving Adyar, he had seen a white mist form which became the figure of the Master Koot Hoomi, but only for a few moments. It had been in Madame Blavatsky's sitting-room and she and Damodar had been there.

Before they left Bombay, in December 1882, he had been on the balcony with Nobin Krishna Bannerji, Deputy Collector at Nerhampore, Moorshedabad, Bengal; Ramaswarmier, District Registrar of Madura, Madras; and Pundit Chandra Sikir of Bareilly. They saw outside a shining substance which became a human being and looked like Colonel Olcott's Master (Morya), in the portrait of him, and remained for perhaps four or five minutes, not on the ground but floating. A day or two later, he had been sitting by himself on a rock outside the house when he saw another man, whom he could not identify but who could not have been ordinary for his footsteps made no sound, and indeed he did not walk but floated.

While this interviewing was going on in London, the drama in Adyar, of which Olcott had been warned, had been unfolding.

CHAPTER 49

The expulsion of the Coulombs

According to Hartmann, Madame Coulomb:[1]

> was not only the independent master of all the household affairs at the head-quarters, but was suffered to 'boss' Madame Blavatsky and Col. Olcott, and woe to him who would accidentally step on her toes.
>
> Imagine a weird witch-like creature, with wrinkled features, a stinging look and an uncouth form. Her duty was to patronise the servants, to nurse like a mother a decrepit old horse and several mangy dogs that were unable to walk. She seemed to consider it her especial purpose of life, to pry into everybody's private affairs, pick up stray letters here and there that were not addressed to her . . . she attempted to wriggle herself into the confidence of newcomers, and had a way of finding out their secrets by pretending to tell their fortunes by means of a pack of cards; while at the same time she would try to awaken the sympathies of strangers by her tales, how from a life of luxury she had sunk down to servitude, and if she found a willing ear she would never hesitate a moment to insinuate that the whole society was a humbug, the phenomena produced by fraud, and that 'she could tell many things, if only she wanted to do so'.
>
> She would tell the aspirant for theosophical honours kindly and confidentially that Col. Olcott was a fool, who was led by the nose by Madame Blavatsky. If asked to explain herself, she would say: 'My mouth is shut up, I cannot talk against the people whose bread I eat'.

How far was this unattractive portrait influenced by the experience of later events? To hold against her the shelter she gave to an abandoned horse and stray dogs – one of the problems of India – was surely unfair. Olcott writes that he had noticed she was 'a gossip and tale-bearer, and gabbled too much about religious matters she did not in the least comprehend'.[2] On the other hand, she kept the place tidy and he never doubted her devotion to Madame Blavatsky, who was perhaps not altogether easy to serve, sometimes asking for meals at odd times and at a moment's notice.

Hartmann describes Monsieur Coulomb more briefly as:[3]

> a ghostly looking Frenchman with the complexion of an ash-barrel, Mr Coulomb held nominally the office of librarian and man of all work . . . and while Madame Coulomb's talk was listened to as the innocent twaddle of a cranky old woman, her appendix was treated with great civility to avoid having him go into a fit of hysterics or epilepsy.

Hartmann was sure Madame Coulomb made money out of the housekeeping at Adyar, and decided (apparently without consulting Madame Blavatsky and Olcott) that they would do better without her and her husband. At a meeting of the Board (date not given) it was decided 'to impeach them in a formal manner'.[4] They were drawing up the charges when Damodar withdrew for a moment, and returned with a letter which he said had been handed to him by one he knew as a chela of the Master Koot Hoomi. It read:[5]

> So long as one has not developed a perfect sense of justice, he should prefer to err rather on the side of mercy than commit the slightest injustice. Mad. Coulomb is a medium and as such irresponsible for many of the things she may say or do. At the same time she is kind and charitable. One must know how to act towards her to make of her a very good friend. She has her own weaknesses, but their bad effects can be minimised by exercising on her mind a moral influence by a friendly and kind feeling. Her mediumistic nature is a help in this direction, if proper advantage be taken of same.

It is my wish therefore that she shall continue in charge of the household business, the Board of Control of course exercising a proper supervisory control and seeing, in consultation with her, that no unnecessary expenditure be incurred. A good deal of reform is necessary, and can be made rather with the help than the antagonism of Madame Coulomb. K.H.

In the light of all that happened after, some Theosophists have tended to feel a little bitter about this letter, wondering if the Master for once lacked percipience. Not necessarily.

My mother told me that when she went out to join her father in India in 1910, one of the first things he told her was that the accounts she received from the servant she deputed to buy for the kitchen would always show each item as having cost more than it did. If she was wise, she would do as the native Rajas and appear not to notice this silent commission upon each purchase. Newly arrived English people who taxed their servants with dishonesty, humiliating them, never had good servants and were liable to all manner of troubles, as though the country were getting back at them for crossing its grain. Madame Coulomb was not an Indian servant, but Koot Hoomi, as an aristocratic Indian, may have found it shocking that the Board at Adyar so grudged her the margin by which she made a little money on the purchase as to intend impeaching her. She and her husband still received no payment for their services. They received their accommodation and food free, and might take what they needed for their clothing and so on from the Society's funds. This informal arrangement had the double disadvantage that, on the one hand it enabled them to assert that they were not servants but friends who obliged out of their goodness, and on the other that they had no independence, no spending money to use as they would, unless indeed they drew a quiet profit on the housekeeping. Some of this profit may have gone on the upkeep of the superannuated horse somebody had turned out to die and on the stray dogs. We know that charity to animals was a quick way to a corner in the Chohan's stern heart, and that may have contributed to Koot Hoomi's advice to the Board to abandon impeachment and explain to Madame Coulomb in a friendly way that the Society could not afford expenses at the current level.

Hartmann now tried a different tack. He offered Coulomb a quarter share in, and charge of, a silver mine, in Colorado, USA, if he and his wife would go there. A route via Hong Kong and San Francisco was agreed, but then the Coulombs thought to improve upon the occasion by asking for a golden handshake of 3,000 rupees, adding that unless this was forthcoming they had compromising letters from Madame Blavatsky to Madame Coulomb which they could give to be published. Subba Row wrote to Madame Blavatsky asking if she had ever written letters to Madame Coulomb best not published, and if they should buy them at any price.[6] Madame Blavatsky replied that she had never written anything to Madame Coulomb publication of which would matter in the least. Payment was therefore refused, and the Coulombs refused to leave.

Next came a severe warning from Morya, dropped to Damodar, in Ootacumund, where he and Lane-Fox were staying for a while:[7]

April 26, 1884 – For some time already the woman has opened communication – a regular diplomatic *pourparler* – with the enemies of the cause, certain padres – She hopes for more than 2,000 Rupees from them if she helps them ruining or at least injuring the Society by ruining the reputation of the founders. Hence hints as to 'trap-doors' and tricks. Moreover when *needed* trap doors *will be found*, as they have been forthcoming for some time. They are the sole masters of the top story [*sic*]. They have full entrance to and control of the premises . . . They hate you with all the hatred of failure against success; the Society, Henry, H.P.B., theosophists, and aye the very name of Theosophy . . .
    Keep all said above in strictest confidence, if you would be strongest. Let her not suspect you know it but if you would have my advice be prudent. Yet act without delay. M.

Olcott also received, under anonymous cover and postmarked Madras, a strange letter, dated 28 April, purporting to be from Hartmann to Madame Coulomb in which he represents himself and Lane-Fox as believing Madame Blavatsky to be a trickster, despite Madame Coulomb's assurance of her innocence, and Olcott also to be of dubious character. The syntax was that of an uneducated writer, as were mis-spellings,[8] 'beleived', 'arrieval' and 'sayd', of which Dr Hartmann would have been incapable. On the back of it was written in red,[9] 'A clumsy forgery, but good enough to show how much an enterprising enemy can do in this direction. They may call this at Adyar – a pioneer – M.'.

It seemed obvious that one or other of the Coulombs had composed this, with the intent of putting Madame Blavatsky and Olcott against Hartmann and Lane-Fox and making them think the Coulombs were their loyal supporters. Olcott took it so.

Madame Blavatsky next received letters from both the Coulombs, written on the same date, 7 May. The husband wrote (I use the Adyar translation):[10]

> Dear Madame, My wife has just returned [from Ooty] . . . She tells me that it is the general rumour that if Mr Lane-Fox should take your place, your Society, which has cost you so much to build up, will suffer. 'Our dear Colonel and our dear Madam' say the majority, 'can never be replaced by others'.
>
> I beg you to give no credence to anything bad they may report to you about us before you hear us, and we have had a chance to explain the truth. Those who are attacking us are only using it as a pretext for a covert attack on you. *And all they are doing is simply to make themselves masters of the situation and overthrow you* . . .
>
> Your devoted friend, A. Coulomb

Madame Coulomb wrote (Adyar translation):[11]

> I may have said something in my rage, but I swear on all that is sacred for *me* that I never said *fraud, secret messages, trap-doors*, nor that my husband had helped you in any way. *If my mouth has uttered these words . . . I pray the Almighty to shower on me the worst maledictions in Nature.*

What we cannot know is what Madame Blavatsky and Olcott made of all these missives that were reaching them. Coulomb's allegation that there was a plot between Lane-Fox and the others to overthrow them suggests he was the author of the forged Hartmann letter which was contrived to suggest that theme. Hartmann says he received from Madame Blavatsky a letter saying she would not return so long as the Coulombs were still 'infecting the place'. This does not sound like her language, and the letter has not been produced.

On 13 May notice of a meeting of the General Council was issued, and on 14 May, at 6.00 p.m., the Coulombs were arraigned before Subba Row (in the chair), Dr Hartmann, Screenivas Row, Lane-Fox, W.T. Brown, V.V. Naidu, M. Singaravelu Mudalyar and Damodar (as Secretary).[12]

Hartmann read the charges. Against Madame Coulomb, these may be summarised as:

> I four affidavits that she said both to Members and outsiders that the object of the Society was the overthrow of British rule in India (two of these were by Brown and Lane-Fox);
> II nine affidavits that she had said the objects were inimical to what she believed good and true (one of them by Damodar);
> III ten affidavits that she had alleged the phenomena fraudulent (one of them by Damodar);
> IV three affidavits that she had attempted to extort money from members of the Society;
> V three that she had wasted the funds of the Society;
> VI that she was guilty of backbiting (in all the affidavits);
> VII one that she had slandered H.P.B.;
> VIII two that she had dissuaded people from joining the Society;
> IX all agreed that her continued presence was against the interest of the Society;
> X letters proving she had sent a blackmailing letter to H.P.B.

Against her husband were:

I Aiding and abetting his wife in the above machinations;
II Disobedience to the Board of Control.

Hartmann writes, 'Only the first three charges against Mrs C were tried and Mrs C neither admitted nor contradicted them, but the evidence was of such a conclusive nature that no doubt about their truth was possible'.[13]

That is probably so, yet the form of this trial (and he does in his pamphlet call this chapter 'The trial'), in which the prosecutor was one of the judges and some of the witnesses for the prosecution were amongst the judges, the accused being unrepresented, was not right. It could not have been so in a court of law, and Brown as a lawyer should have so advised Hartmann.

Madame Coulomb was expelled and her husband was asked to resign. He wrote asking why he should, and it fell to Damodar, as Secretary, to point out to him the impropriety of his remaining after the expulsion of his wife, and, as he still refused to resign, to inform him that he was expelled, too. They still refused to go – they probably had nowhere to go to – or give up the key to Madame Blavatsky's rooms (which included the shrine), into which they both now moved, cooking and eating up there and keeping others from entering. However, it could only be a question of time before their food ran out. Coulomb had said he had been given custody of the room by Madame Blavatsky and would only leave on orders from her. Hartmann must have cabled Madame Blavatsky, for she cabled back in the sense required by the Board. This was probably the biggest mistake of her life.

Coulomb now said he would hand over the key, but only in the presence of witnesses. Accordingly, on 18 May, Hartmann, Subba Row, Screenivas Row, Brown, Damodar and others trooped upstairs. Coulomb now demonstrated to them a hole from Madame Blavatsky's room to the occult room (through the anciently plastered-up place where the door had been), and sliding panels in the back of a cupboard placed against it on the one side, and in the back of the shrine on the other. The workmanship looked to Hartmann and the others very new, and when an attempt was made to make the panels slide they did so only with difficulty and noise.

The Coulombs still lingered, presumably in the hope of some overture. As none was made, after a day or two Coulomb came down to Hartmann's room and asked for 10,000 rupees not to ruin the Society. His wife, hovering behind him, called out to him not to compromise himself. No rupees being forthcoming, the couple left Adyar on 25 May.

Hartmann, in his pamphlet, regards the absence of both the Founders in Europe as providential, since had they been present Madame Coulomb needed only to have shed some tears and she and her husband would be there still. Even after all that happened later, he seems still to congratulate himself on having rid Madame Blavatsky of them. But to let them go in this way, without references and without money, made them very dangerous. Lacking everything except their hatred, where should they turn save to the Society's enemies?

There is no contemporary comment by the Masters available, but years later, in August 1888, a letter was precipitated to Olcott by Koot Hoomi, in which, referring to someone Olcott must have asked about, he says he has not been abandoned (as he imagines), although he has made mistakes:[14]

> in helping thrust out of the Headquarters house one who deserved a more charitable treatment, whose fault was the result of ignorance and psychical feebleness rather than of sin, and who was a strong man's victim . . . tell my devoted though mistaken 'son' that it was most theosophical to give her protection, most untheosophical and selfish to drive her away.

Jinarajadasa says he is unable to think of any incident to which these lines can refer. I suggest the reference is to the expulsion of Madame Coulomb, the 'strong man' being her husband, and the 'son' being Brown, whose part in the events cut him off from his Master. It would explain one of the minor mysteries: why Brown, having been shown much favour in the beginning, was later apparently left in the cold and so turned sour.

CHAPTER 50

Enghien: the Massey-Billing affair

In retrospect, one can see the worst might have been avoided had both the Founders returned to Adyar at once, but it seemed to them that they were spending their time well in Europe, making the Society known to interesting people. Olcott met Robert Browning and lunched with Sir Edwin Arnold at his home. He was also invited to the country seat of Lord Borthwick, Ravenstone, in Wigtonshire, Scotland; from there he went on to Edinburgh to talk and to found a Scottish branch.

Madame Blavatsky, after visiting friends in Boulogne-sur-Mer, went on 13 May to spend a fortnight as the guest of the Comte and Comtesse d'Adhemar de Cronsac, in their beautiful house, Château Ecossais, on the Lac d'Enghien (Seine-et-Oise) near Paris. Judge and Mohini were included in the invitation, as were later Bertram Keightley, Cooper-Oakley and Countess Wachtmeister. Judge furnishes an idyllic description of the view from the drawing-room over the garden and lake. Once, when they were at table, he placed in a tumbler a rosebud he had picked and the sister of their hostess asked if Madame Blavatsky could cause it to open into a flower while they sat there; before they had finished their meal it did so. He quotes also from a letter subsequently written by the Comtesse d'Adhemar, recalling an occasion when H.P.B. went to the window, raised her arm in a commanding gesture and 'faint music broke into lovely strains and filled the drawing-room where we were all sitting'.[1]

This was the rest in the country which the Masters had prescribed for the recovery of her health, but it was broken into by the arrival of a letter from C.C. Massey about what has become known as the Massey-Billing affair. This is made much of by her enemies, but it should be appreciated that most of the primary documents in the case have vanished. We can only try to glimpse what happened through the argument over it.

It went back to 1879. Massey, President of the London Branch, had craved some token the Adepts existed, above all a letter from an Adept. In July of that year, there was a response. That it was Illarion who wrote to him we gather from a letter from Koot Hoomi, in 1883, to Sinnett, who must have asked him about it:[2]

... about Mr Massey's difficulty as regards the letter our brother H[ilarion] then in Scotland sent him circuitously through 'Ski'. For not only once but twice has he had such occult relationship – once with his Father's glove, sent to him by M through 'Ski', and once again with the note in question, for the delivery of which the same practical agency was employed, though without an equal expenditure of power.

Illarion, however, did not precipitate his letter direct to Mrs Billing for reprecipitation by 'Ski'. He precipitated it to Madame Blavatsky, in Bombay. Why Illarion used this circuitous way we are not told. He could have posted his letter from Scotland to Massey in London direct. It seems he did not sign it or furnish any clue to his nationality. Madame Blavatsky, then, was faced with a letter, precipitated by Illarion for Massey, to forward to him. In a further letter to Sinnett, Koot Hoomi explains,[3] 'Madame B. was therefore left to send it by post, or if she preferred it, to go by "Ski" – M. having forbidden her to exercise her own occult means'.

If she had posted it from Bombay direct to Massey with a covering letter saying the enclosed had been written by a Master to him, a host of vexations would have beeen avoided. Unfortunately, she wished Massey could receive it in the same way that she had, as a precipitation, which would seem to him more wonderful than arrival by post, and so she opted for 'Ski'. Olcott, with whom she discussed it first, saw no harm in it. 'Ski' was the name under which Mrs Billing knew Morya. Morya, though not willing to precipitate it from Madame Blavatsky's desk in Bombay to London, for the same reason that he forbade Madame Blavatsky to use her own power – namely that it would require the expenditure of energy disproportionate to the occasion – was willing to precipitate it the shorter distance from Mrs

Billing's home to Massey's. That was why Madame Blavatsky wrote a letter to Mrs Billing, asking her to give to 'Ski', for transmission to Massey, the letter she was enclosing.

There was, however, a complication. Massey was doubtful of the 'entity' of 'Ski', not altogether without reason, because the entity communicating through Mrs Billing as 'Ski' was not always Morya. Koot Hoomi explains that Mrs Billing was medium to more than one communicator and never noticed when the communicator changed. This made her dangerous in that, though good and loyal, she could be taken over by a dark power, unawares:[4]

> Mrs Billing is a medium, and when that is said all is said. Except this, that amongst mediums she is the *most honest* . . . loyal . . . She also, unless closely watched by 'Ski' can *turn a traitor* – precisely because she is a medium . . . withal she is incapable of either deceit or falsehood in her normal state . . . 'Ski' has more than once served as carrier and even mouthpiece for several of us; and in the case Mr Massey alludes to, the letter from 'a Scotch Brother' was a genuine one . . .

It was because Massey had had some experience of a 'Ski' who was not a Master of Wisdom speaking through Mrs Billing that Madame Blavatsky, in her letter, warned Mrs Billing not to go near Massey herself as she did not want him to connect 'Ski' with the letter. As she knew in advance that 'Ski' would, on this occasion, be Morya, she saw no harm in this.

It happened, however, that Mrs Billing had to give the Minute Book to Massey, and in it he found Illarion's letter. Koot Hoomi, however, says Mrs Billing did not know it was there,[5] 'Had she known that "Ski" had placed the letter inside that book there are 99 chances out of 100 that she would not have brought it to him herself'. As a professional medium of twenty years' standing, she would not, Koot Hoomi points out, have courted ridicule and suspicion by presenting a communication from her 'control' in such a way that she herself could obviously have placed it where it was found.

Further, Koot Hoomi goes on to sow a doubt about whether Mrs Billing ever received the letter which Madame Blavatsky wrote to her or knew anything about its enclosure. He also talks about the relationship between Mrs Billing, Dr Billing, her husband, and another woman, as though it were germane to the circumstances in which Dr Billing became possessed of Madame Blavatsky's letter to his wife:[6]

> Dr Billing, the husband of that good, honest woman . . . whom he married for her few thousand pounds, ruined her during the first year of their married life, went into concubinage with another medium, and when vehemently reproached by H.P.B. and Olcott – left his wife and the Society and turned with bitter hatred against both women . . . Let C.C.M. put all these facts together; fathom the mystery and trace the connection between his *informants* and the two innocent women . . .

> Mr Massey is not even to this day sure that Dr Billing did not intercept the Simpson letter to his wife, keep it to use against her at a fortunate time and actually use it in this instance? Or, even allowing the letter to have been delivered to the addressee, know what was the answer – if any written? Has the idea struck your observant friend that, at that very time there was a womanly – worse than that – medium's spite far worse than the *odium theologicum* between the Simpson and Hollis-Billing . . .?[7]

Is Mrs Simpson (she is later referred to as 'Mrs') the other medium with whom Dr Billing went into concubinage? Had she the opportunity to intercept a letter to Mrs Billing – perhaps addressed to her at some club used by mediums – and to take a copy of it, even if it was allowed to reach her later?

It was Dr Billing who showed Massey in May 1882 what purported to be the letter written by Madame Blavatsky to the wife he had abandoned, without explaining how he came into possession of it, and who allowed Massey to take a copy of two paragraphs.

The alleged text, copied by Massey, rightly or wrongly, from whatever was shown him by Dr Billing, reads:[8]

28 June, 1879

My dear good friend – do you remember what Ski told or rather promised to me? That whenever there is need for it, he will always be ready to carry any message, leave it either on Massey's table, his pocket, or some other mysterious place? Well now there is the *most important need* for such a show of his powers. Please ask him to take the enclosed letter and put it into Massey's pocket or in some still more mysterious place. But he *must not know* it's Ski. Let him think what he likes, but he must not suspect you have been near him with Ski at your orders. He does not distrust you, but he does Ski.

Also if he could treat L.L. with some Oriental token of love it would be right, but none of them must suspect Ski of it, therefore it is more difficult to make it do it than it would otherwise be were it to be produced at one of your séances . . .

It must be understood that Ski is a non-existent entity. 'He' is a concept in Mrs Billing's mind, a thought-form, animated at times by Morya, at other times by others, but thought of by Mrs Billing as a departed spirit.

However, if this was a real letter from Madame Blavatsky to Mrs Billing, if Mrs Simpson stole the original and gave it to Dr Billing, then Mrs Billing would never have known it had been written and could not have acted on any instruction or suggestion in it. Indeed, when asked about it by Massey, after being shown it by Dr Billing, Mrs Billing told him she had never received any such letter, and had never seen the letter said to have been enclosed in it, before it was discovered by Massey in the Minute Book she gave him.[9] Mrs Billing's statement, therefore, bears out that of Koot Hoomi. So, what seems to have happened is that although Mrs Simpson stole Madame Blavatsky's letter to Mrs Billing and gave it to Dr Billing, Morya whisked Illarion's letter out of it, so that it should not pass into profane hands and placed it in the Minute Book. But was the original tampered with before Massey saw it? Madame Blavatsky now wrote to Massey:[10]

Enghien, Friday

All I have the honour of telling you is – on my *theosophical word of honour* – that I am the author of the first part of the letter you quote . . . down to 'He does not distrust you but he does distrust Ski'. What follows after has never been written by me . . . *It is forged* – that's all I know . . .

She could not see anything dreadful in what she had written in the paragraph she recognised:

I have not, nor have I had in writing it, the smallest or faintest notion I was thereby *deceiving you*, trying to *impose upon you* etc. Do you call *withholding facts* one has no right to enter upon – deceiving? The letter forwarded to you was genuine, from as genuine a 'Brother' as ever lived.

One sees a problem here. One can sympathise with Massey's feeling that in trying, as it were, to catch hold of an Adept who was he did not know where, he was playing at blind man's buff. But for Madame Blavatsky, as for the Masters, all that mattered was that the letter he received was genuine. It should not concern him by what route it came. He was too junior in his understanding of the occult world for it to be appropriate to explain to him the astral mechanics involved in the precipitation from Scotland 'circuitously'. She had no right, even now, to go into these things.

Perhaps Madame Blavatsky was too quick in accepting the whole of the first paragraph as hers. Koot Hoomi had already written to Sinnett that the words 'mysterious' and 'or some other still more mysterious place' were introduced by the copying, while the second,[11] 'half of the letter *is* a forgery and a *very occult one*', the whole thing being a typical Dugpa composition.

Does he mean that Mrs Simpson's jealousy, as woman and as medium, so opened her to possession by dark powers that instead of giving Dr Billing the original letter she had stolen, she copied it in part, weaving into her copy invented matter? This was intended by her to damage Mrs Billing in the eyes of Dr Billing, but intended by the Dugpas to damage Madame Blavatsky. I think that is the meaning.

As early as 3 March 1882, Morya had warned Sinnett,[12] 'Only look out sharp: the Dugpas and Gelukpas are not fighting but in Tibet alone, see their vile work in England among the "Occultists and seers" '.

The Dugpas, ever defending their kingdom of the shadow against the intrusion of the light, were skilled magicians. If forging 'Blavatsky' letters was a tactic they had now begun to use in their endeavour to ruin the work of the yellow-hatted Masters of Wisdom, then more forged 'Blavatsky' letters might be expected to follow.

The Dugpa letter shown by Dr Billing to Massey has never been made publicly available and its fate is unknown. Illarion's letter to Massey cannot be inspected, either. Massey destroyed it.

CHAPTER 51

Russians in Paris

When she returned to Paris, Madame Blavatsky found Nadyezhda and Vera had come from Russia to see her. The latter had now re-married and was Madame Zhelikhovsky. In French, she signed her name 'Jelihovsky', but the 'j' should be pronounced as in French '*je*', not as in English 'jelly'.

They were joined by another Russian, Vsevolod Sergeyevich Solovioff. He was a novelist, but held a position in the service of the Czar. He had read her Russian articles, *From the Caves and Jungles of Hindostan*, which was the reason why he called and introduced himself.

On the morning of 11 June, Madame Blavatsky and her visitors were sitting with the sitting-room door open, so that everybody saw Babula answer the ring at the door and take a letter from the hand of a postman. It came from Russia. Although Vera had noticed that it now tired her sister to produce phenomena, she could not restrain herself from exclaiming that it would be a perfect occasion for her to read the contents before the seal was broken. Madame Blavatsky did so, writing the text on a spare sheet of paper, and said she would cause the signature to be ringed with the double triangles of the Theosophical seal, as she had done on her copy. To do this, she placed the copy on the original for a moment, a look of concentration on her face. Then she removed her hand and the envelope was opened. The text was correct. In the double triangles enclosing the signature was a slight imperfection in the drawing, matching that which Madame Blavatsky had drawn.

An attestation of this phenomenon was drawn up and signed by all:[1]

Vera Jelihovsky
Vsevolod Solovioff
Nadyezhda A. Fadeyeff
Emilie de Morsier
William Q. Judge
H.S. Olcott

21 June, 1884

Madame de Morsier was the Secretary General of the French Société Théosophique. The interesting thing is that Solovioff signed it. Further, he wrote a letter to the St Petersburg *Rebus*, detailing it, and ending:[2]

> . . . the circumstances under which the phenomenon occurred in its smallest details, carefully checked by myself, do not leave me in the smallest doubt as to its genuineness and reality. Deception or fraud in this particular case are *entirely out of the question*.

It is dated 10 June 1884, Old Style (that is, 22 June).

CHAPTER 52

The Society for Psychical Research

On 29 June 1884, Madame Blavatsky travelled to London, this time to stay with Francesca Arundale and her mother, Mary Anne Arundale, at their home, 77 Elgin Crescent, Notting Hill – then suburban.

She found herself an object of interest to the Society for Psychical Research, and on 5 July was visited by four members, Myers and Gurney (of a special committee appointed to this investigation) plus F.W. Thurstan and Professor Barrett. Concerning this visit, Gurney reported to the Society for Psychical Research that it took place in the morning, and that:[1]

We were sitting in a brightly lighted room, Madame Blavatsky being in an arm-chair completely in view, without any table in front of her. The only other person in the room was Colonel Olcott. In the middle of the conversation the attention of Mr Myers and myself was caught by a very distinct sweet, musical sound, resembling somewhat the sound which can be made with the nail of a finger against a finger-glass, but differing in that there was less sharpness of 'attack'. The sound, as I perceived immediately on its occurrence, had been synchronous with a gentle, forward movement of Madame Blavatsky's right hand – a gesture similar to a gentle, 'mesmeric' pass. The sound was not loud; it was soft enough to fail in attracting the attention of Professor Barrett, who was engaged at the moment in eager conversation with Colonel Olcott, and was further from Madame Blavatsky than Mr Myers and myself. Professor Barrett heard the sound, however, when it was repeated (as it was immediately) for his satisfaction. (He also heard it after Mr Myers and I had left.) It was notably a free sound, such as could not be produced by any object whose vibrations were in any way damped or checked. I should say, for instance, that it would be difficult, if not impossible, for such a sound to be produced by any mechanical arrangement concealed in a dress or up a sleeve.

Thurston specified that:

the tones of the bells were unmistakable, coming out distinct and slowly, in two or three notes, as if from a musical instrument of very sonorous vibrations. They seemed soft, yet clear, and to my hearing to be sounding from up in the air, and from the spot on which Madame B's eyes were fixed, some five or six feet from her.

On 26 July, Myers, Gurney and Thurstan came back, and there were also present Mrs and Miss Arundale, Keightley, Mohini and Mr Ionides. On this occasion, in Thurstan's words:

We were all engaged in earnest conversation relative to Koot Hoomi. Some of the visitors present had ventured to criticise his literary and scientific abilities, and Madame Blavatsky was vehemently defending her Mahatma, when I heard one, or it may have been two, deep sonorous tones. Not expecting anything particular, I hastily put it down to some very musical-toned clock in another room striking, and was not thinking of mentioning anything about it, when someone else of us visitors remarked, 'Did we not hear some chime?' Another visitor said, 'Oh, it was only the clock striking the half-hour'. Miss A. then pointed out that it wanted a minute or so to the half-hour (12.30 p.m.) by the clock on the mantlepiece in the room, and that it would strike in a minute, and we would notice the tones were very different. Madame B. (I think it was) said, 'It was the Mahatma, and she had heard him speaking'. Then the clock in the room struck, and we noticed the difference of sound, as different to the former as a chapel bell to Big Ben, of Westminster. We then resumed conversation, and a few minutes after Madame B. suddenly stopped her conversation, and looking upwards, fixed her face and gaze for a minute. This fixed and focussed the attention of all the rest of us; it may be thereby

His Excellency Jung Bahadur, Prime Minister of Nepal. see p.7.
London Illustrated News, 8 June 1850

Madame Blavatsky. Photograph by Enrico Resta at his studio in Coburg Place, Bayswater, London, 8 January 1889 *Theosophical Society in England*

The Ravine in Tibet. Morya riding to his house. see p.24. *Theosophical Society, Adyar*

The Monastery of Trashi Lhünpo. Shigatsè, Tibet. see p.26. *Royal Geographical Society*

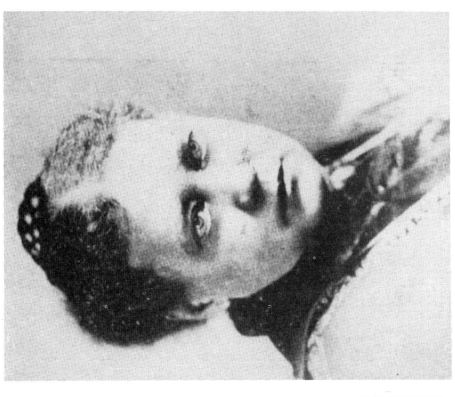

Madame Blavatsky in "Lamasery" days, New York, c.1877–8. see p.46.
Theosophical Society, Adyar

"The Lamasery", New York, today. *Photograph by Norbert Krapf*

Morya, a picture presented by the Master to S Ramaswamier, inscribed to him "in commemoration of the event of 5th, 6th and 7th October 1882, in the jungles of Sikkim". *Artist, unknown*

Madame Blavatsky, a casual snap, India or Ceylon, 1880. *Theosophical Society, Adyar*

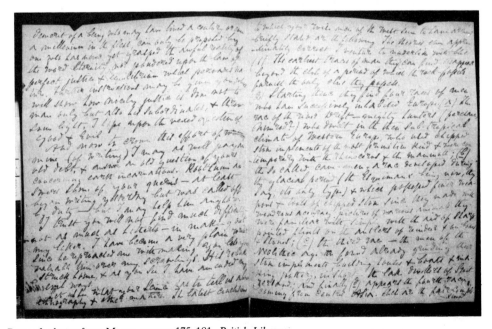

Page of a letter from
Koot Hoomi.
see pp.175–181.
British Library

Page of a letter from Morya. see pp.175–181. *British Library*

Madame Blavatsky and Colonel Olcott, 17 Lansdowne Road, London, October 1888. see p.195. *Theosophical Society, Adyar*

Panchèn Lobsang Tub-ten Chog-gyi Nyima. see p.231. *H P B Library, Canada*

causing a sort of expectant attention amongst us, which seems to favour any manifestation from the metaphysical world.

Gurney reports this:

On Saturday morning, July 26th, 1884, the phenomenon recurred. Besides Mr Myers and myself there were present Mrs and Miss A., Mr Thurstan, Mr Ionides, Mr Mohini and Mr Keightley. We were all seated round the table, and animated conversation was proceeding, when suddenly I heard the same musical note. There was a clock ticking in the room, and for an instant I remained unimpressed, assuming that the sound was the striking of the half-hour after eleven; but when others exclaimed, and when I saw Madame Blavatsky wake up (so to speak) from a few seconds of *recueillement*, I looked at the clock, and found that the time for striking had not yet arrived. I then at once perceived the identity of this sound with the previous ones. The half-hour struck two or three minutes afterwards, and the sound then was markedly different – poor and clacky in comparison. On this occasion, Madame Blavatsky connected the phenomenon with an impression or message conveyed to her by Mahatma Koot Hoomi, relative to the conversation which had been going on, and of which he had been the subject. The sound was repeated after a few minutes' interval.

Myers reports:

My recollection as to the two interviews agrees with Mr Gurney's and Mr Thurstan's. Of the two independent accounts of the second interview, Mr Thurstan's is on two points more precisely in accordance with what I remember –

(1) The clock struck, I should say, less than a minute after the bell sounded. I watched it till it struck, in order to be quite certain as to its not having struck when he heard the bell. The 'bell' might have been compared to the sound of a hammer striking a peculiarly sweet gong, such as is sometimes placed in ornamental clocks. But the clock in question does not strike as a gong.

(2) As to the *second* bell on July 26th, Mr Thurstan's account seems to me the more precise. Mr Gurney, I think, was speaking at the time, but Mr Thurstan and I, who were at opposite sides of the table, instantly exchanged first looks and then words, and found that we had heard it simultaneously, and localised it in precisely the same tract of air, over the middle of the table. I will add one or two remarks as to the *freedom* and the *localisation* of the sound.

(3) I have experimented with the conjurer's trick called 'Is your watch a repeater?' and have of course heard repeating watches, in and out of waistcoat or other pockets. I think that in all cases there is something of deadened quality when the origin of the sound is concealed about the person. I was alive to this point, and I could not discern any deadening in the clear, tingling sound of the bell.

(4) Again, as to localisation. The localisation of sound is a proverbially uncertain thing. But in each of the cases the persons who heard the sounds did all of them, as I understand, though Mr Thurstan's evidence is not quite clear on the point, localise these *sounds* in the same places. In the case of the bell, which we were inclined to refer to the *clock*, it is noticeable that the clock was behind and above Madame B., nearly in the place where a human being might have spoken had he been behind her and wishing to address her specially. When the second sound came on July 26th, which was in response to a request of my own, it did not appear to anyone to proceed from the direction of the clock, but, as already said, from the centre of the table in front of me. Madame B. made no observable movement *before* either of these bells of July 26th, though she started and looked preoccupied *after* the first of the two.

The tone of these reports made to the Committee being friendly, so, presumably, was that of their makers to Madame Blavatsky and doubtless she felt that whatever eventually appeared in print would be helpful, rather than otherwise.

CHAPTER 53

Francesca Arundale

Born into a low church family, Francesca Arundale had been converted first to the Episcopalian Church of England, then to Catholicism, then to Spiritualism; this was before she heard of Madame Blavatsky from Mrs Billing and joined the London Lodge of the Theosophical Society, in the time of Dr Wyld. Her recent election as Treasurer had been capped by Olcott's making her Assistant Treasurer to the Theosophical Society as a whole, with sole responsibility as Treasurer for Europe. In the story of Madame Blavatsky she occupies but a background place. In her memoir, she tells us she brought her guest early morning tea at 7.30 a.m. and, at the other end of the day, would usually sit talking with her before they said goodnight; she was present when the people from the Society for Psychical Research came and heard the astral bell ring; and she was present when another guest, who had been playing their piano, was putting on her things to leave, at which point the last bars of the piece sounded again, in the air.[1] Yet there may be something suppressed.

When she had renewed her subscription to *The Theosophist*, her letter to Madame Blavatsky of 8 September 1882 had arrived endorsed by Koot Hoomi, 'A good *earnest* Theosophist, a mystic whose co-operation ought to be secured by you'.[2] From Paris, Madame Blavatsky had written to her,[3] 'You ought to be a little firmer, Sister Teresa, lest from a saint you should tumble down into a sinner'. Olcott later began a letter to her, 'Dearest Teresa'.[4]

This may explain why I have heard it said in French Theosophical circles that Francesca Arundale was Santa Teresa de Avila (born 5.00 a.m., 28 March 1515; died 4 October 1582). If so, she was told this privately and kept it to herself, for it has never become general Theosophical property, yet in this light it is interesting to consider a letter from Koot Hoomi given to her by Madame Blavatsky the day after she came to Elgin Crescent:[5]

> I have watched your many thoughts. I have watched their silent evolution and the secrets of your inner soul . . .
> To your mother, who has trodden with you in many stony paths . . . you owe a great duty. Not a blind and unjust obedience, whose consequences may be most harmful to her as to you; but a dutiful assiduity, and loving help . . .
> To you, personally, child, struggling thro' the darkness to the light, I would say that the Path is *never* closed; but in proportion to one's previous errors so is it harder to find . . . Your acts in the past have been the natural fruit of an unworthy religious ideal, the result of ignorant misconception. They cannot be obliterated, for they are indelibly stamped upon the record of karma, and neither tears nor repentance can blot the page. But you have the power to more than redeem and balance them by future acts . . . You have much to unlearn. The narrow prejudices of your people blind you more than you suspect . . . You are not yet able to appreciate the difference between inner purity and outer 'culture' . . . Try, child, hope, and accept my blessing.

Koot Hoomi will not have meant the Christian ideal was unworthy, but that Teresa's conception of it was. One would have liked to see his analysis of Teresa's life in detail. To non-Catholics, all three of the Spanish mystics seem unbalanced. Teresa's junior, the Venerable Maria Vela, of the Convent of St Anna, Avila, tried to endear herself to Christ by living without any food at all.[6] Wearing a hair-shirt and scourging oneself with nettles were so general one can hardly see them as special to Teresa. What all who practise mortification of the flesh have to learn (including Indian fakhirs) is that tormenting one's body does not make one more spiritual. She founded the Discalced (unshod) Carmelites. As a mystic, she describes ecstasies, raptures and transportations,[7] which, occuring during prayer after long fasting, suggest fainting with at least partial disengagement from the body. As for the horned devils which beset her,[8] the small ones even leaping on to her prayer-book, one remembers Morya's observation that thought forms can become animated by elementals. As a Prioress she was probably not more severe than others, though the cases of melancholia amongst the nuns suggest not all had a vocation and her advice in respect of one, 'perhaps if you would whip her too she would stop crying out as she does now',[9] is alarming. In giving instructions to do silly things, such as planting a rotten cucumber, to test obedience, she was following St Francis of Assisi, who gave instruction for cabbages to be planted upside down; yet obedience at the expense of common sense cramps the mind and could lead to sin if the superior were in it. Further, she disliked her nuns to read – even the Bible.[10] They had to take everything from her. That was mental tyranny. Yet, curiously, music was at least once heard in the air, near her.[11] Though the nuns decided that as there was no physical source it could only be the sound of angels playing their harps, it parallels the music heard in the air near Madame Blavatsky.

One question remains. Why did Olcott no sooner look at Francesca Arundale than he made her Treasurer for Europe and Vice-Treasurer of the whole of the Theosophical Society? Teresa, though she sought poverty, proved herself a shrewd administrator of the funds of her order.[12]

CHAPTER 54

Cambridge to Elberfeld

During these London days, Olcott enquired about portrait painters and was put in touch with Hermann Schmiechan. He not only painted a portrait in oils of Madame Blavatsky, but also painted professional portraits from the amateur ones which Harrisse had made of Morya and Koot Hoomi in New York, from Olcott's description of them.

On 25 July, Olcott left to stay with the Gebhards at Elberfeld, in Germany. Dr Hübbe-Schleiden, for many years President of the Society in Germany, travelled with Olcott on 1 August to Dresden. The other people in their compartment of the train were unknown to them. A ticket inspector came in. Schleiden leaned forward to present his ticket and Olcott drew to his attention that there was something white behind his back.[1] It was on his far side from where Olcott was sitting, and it was a letter from Koot Hoomi, answering a letter Olcott had written to Madame Blavatsky on 29 July. (Olcott had posted it, but Madame Blavatsky, when told of the incident, said she had never received it.)

Madame Blavatsky, Miss Arundale and Mohini were invited to Cambridge on 9 August, to meet Professor Sidgwick, President of the Society for Psychical Research, and his wife, Eleanor. They took rooms near the Union Society. Miss Arundale saw a note flutter down, bearing comments on people they were to meet.[2]

The sole record we have of the meeting is in Sidgwick's journal for 10 August 1884:[3]

Our favourable impression of Madame Blavatsky was maintained; if personal sensibilities can be trusted, she is a genuine being, with a vigorous nature intellectual as well as emotional, and a real desire for the good of mankind. This impression is all the more noteworthy as she is externally unattractive – with her flounces full of cigarette ashes – and not prepossessing in manner. Certainly we like her, Nora and I. If she is a humbug, she is a consummate one: as her remarks have the air not only of spontaneity and randomness but sometimes of an amusing indiscretion.

On 15 August, Madame Blavatsky, Mrs and Miss Arundale, George (Francesca's nephew and adopted son), Bertram Keightley and Mohini left London from Charing Cross. They sailed from Queensborough, Kent, to Flushing, Holland, whence they took the train to Brussels and changed for Elberfeld, where they arrived on 17 August. Their hosts were the Gebhards.

Madame Fadeyef now came to Elberfeld too. Solovioff and a Mademoiselle Glinka (who had recognised one another while changing trains at Brussels) arrived from Paris. These two both claimed to have seen the Master Morya while at Elberfeld, but Solovioff wrote to the Society for Psychical Research about it for both of them, and as regards himself, at least, the claim may be doubted as according to Madame Blavatsky Morya rejected him at sight.

Koot Hoomi wrote to Sinnett, suggesting he join the others at Elberfeld. He also explains why he had not wished Mrs Holloway to stay at his house in Ladbroke Gardens:[4]

Your house, good friend, has a colony of elementaries quartering in it, and to a sensitive like her, it was as dangerous an atmosphere to exist in as would be a fever cemetery to one subject to morbific physical influences. You should be more than ordinarily careful when you get back not to encourage sensitives in your household . . . not to admit more than can be helped the visits of known mediumistic sensitives . . . burn wood fires in the rooms . . . ask Damodar to send you some bundles of incense-sticks . . . These are helps; but the best of all means to drive out unwelcome guests of this sort, is to live purely in thought and deed.

Sinnett was much put out by this letter. (Later in life he persuaded himself it must have been written by Madame Blavatsky, from jealousy of Mrs Holloway. The Master's concern, however, is plainly with the atmosphere of the house.) The next letter he received from Koot Hoomi has a warning tone.[5]

> You forget that he who approaches our precincts even in thought is drawn into the vortex of probation . . . There is such a thing when understood allegorically as treasures guarded by faithful gnomes and fiends. The treasure is our occult knowledge that many of you are after – you foremost of all; and it may not be H.P.B. or Olcott . . . who have awakened the guardians thereof, but yourself . . . it is absolutely necessary that those who would have that knowledge should be *thoroughly* tried and tested . . . We found Mrs H. in America, we impressed her to prepare for the writing of the book she has produced with the aid of Mohini . . . The effect of her coming to your house has been described to you . . . in resenting what Mohini and H.P.B. were saying to you and Mrs H. you have been . . . in my way, in her development . . . My friendly regard suffered a shock from the hearing of your 'ultimatum' which may be condensed thus:– 'Either Mrs H. passes a week or two at our house, or I (you) leave the L.L. to get on as best it can' . . . My friend, this is treading upon dangerous ground. In our mountains here, the Dugpas lay at dangerous points, in paths frequented by our Chelas, bits of old rag, and other articles best calculated to attract the attention of the unwary, which have been impregnated with their evil magnetism. If one be stepped upon a tremendous psychic shock may be communicated to the wayfarer, so that he may lose his footing and fall down the precipice . . . Friend, beware of Pride and Egoism, two of the worst snares for the feet of him who aspires to climb the high paths of Knowledge and Spirituality. You have opened a joint of your armour for the Dugpas – do not complain if they have found it and wounded you there . . . this makes my position still more embarrassing before my Chief, who, of course, has had the 'ultimatum' put on record . . .
>
> Some, most unjustly, try to make H.P.B. and H.S.O. solely responsible for the state of things. Those two are, say, far from perfect – in some respects quite the opposite. But they have that in them . . . which we have but too rarely found elsewhere – UNSELFISHNESS, and an eager readiness for self-sacrifice for the good of others . . . It is a true manhood when one boldly accepts one's share of the collective karma of the group one works with and does not . . . throw all the blame upon some one 'black sheep', a victim specially selected.

This appears to have been the last Mahatmic letter received by Sinnett. The inference must be that the chink in the armour had grown wide enough to let the Dugpas find their foothold.

CHAPTER 55

Reply to Lillie

The issue of the Spiritualist paper, *Light*, for 6 September 1884, contained an article full of muddled allegations against Madame Blavatsky, but the letter to the Editor she composed at Elberfeld in reply affords us some useful statements:[1]

> I had never known, nor even seen a medium, nor ever found myself in a séance room, before March, 1873, when I was passing through Paris on my way to America . . . I never held séances in my life. It was not at *my* séances, but those of William Eddy . . .

She is irritated because he assumes every Adept or person she mentions to be Koot Hoomi. One whom she had referred to as, on one occasion, robed in white, was 'a Greek gentleman whom I have known since 1860, whereas I had never seen Mr Sinnett's correspondent before 1868'. Moreover, Lillie's sarcasm, 'a curious costume . . . for a Tibetan monk' is doubly misplaced, as the subject of reference (Illarion) was Greek, not Tibetan, and anyway, Koot Hoomi was not a Tibetan monk. Further, she continued, 'What authority has Mr Lillie to connect the Kutchi gentleman mentioned in *Isis* . . . with Mahatma Koot Hoomi? Nothing but his insatiate desire to find me at fault . . .'. Indeed, Lillie cannot have known much about Tibet, or he would have known what Kutchi were – Lhasa's Muslim population, with their own mosque and Governor.

She says Lillie is taking his idea of Buddhists in Tibet from the Abbé Huc, whereas her statements are based on her own knowledge:

> . . . our Mahatmas . . . are neither 'Hermits' (now), for they have done with their 'practice' of yoga; nor 'Wanderers', nor 'Monks', since they tolerate, but would never practise, *exoteric*, or popular, Buddhist rites. Least of all are they 'Renegades'.

Lillie's eventual book about her did not appear until after her death. It is a medley of misunderstandings and misrepresentations that, like a jumbled ball of string, seems to have no end from which to begin to sort the muddle out. Yet he is a Spiritualist, and the nub of his trouble becomes evident in an almost pathetic chapter in which he recapitulates the traditional story of how the father of the Buddha, fearing his son's becoming an ascetic, tried to hold him to this world by ordering that all its delights should constantly surround him; whereas he who would become the Buddha put them all aside, for he heard the voices of the Buddhas of the past reminding him that in his past existences he had vowed to become the next Buddha. Lillie makes the pathetic and give-away comment that here it is the living who preach worldliness and the dead who give the spiritual message, not as in (his misunderstanding of) Madame Blavatsky's teaching, wherein it is only proper to learn from living teachers, as the dead become tempting demons (!).[3] He misunderstands completely. Madame Blavatsky disapproved of seeking instruction from the astral forms produced by mediums in séance rooms, because these were not real people but simulacra composed from the decaying astrals of the departed and from the medium's and sitters' own astrals. What she insisted upon was that her teachers were real people, as she knew because she had met them in the flesh. The past Buddhas whose voice Gautama Buddha heard were likewise real people – who came *in propria persona*, of their own volition. The Buddha was not a client of mediums. But Lillie was a spiritualist, and it was a point he did not want to understand.

Much of his sarcasm is misplaced, as where he says the word ' *"Chohan"* is not to be found in any Sanskrit dictionary'.[3] Naturally not; it is Mongolian.

CHAPTER 56

The Coulombs' revenge

The September issue of the Madras *Christian College Magazine* carried an article entitled 'The collapse of Koot Hoomi'? It was by the Editor, the Rev. George Patterson, a Wesleyan Methodist, and based upon information given him by Madame Coulomb. Koot Hoomi did not exist. He was a dummy face and shoulders, made in cloth, cut out and sewn by herself, and painted with eyes and a mouth on instructions of Madame Blavatsky. It was carried on a bamboo pole when it was to be seen in the distance, as if floating; for close up presentations, requiring the full-length figure, it was worn by her husband, over his own head and shoulders. When not in use, it was kept in a box. She was unable to exhibit it as in a fit of disgust she had destroyed it. There was not one of Madame Blavatsky's phenomena that she failed to 'explain', all were tricks performed with the utmost ingenuity most often by Monsieur Coulomb and herself.

After their expulsion from Adyar in May, the Coulombs had gone to the missionaries, who had charitably given them lodging. When she saw Patterson on 9 August, to give him her information, she handed him a bundle of letters said to be from Madame Blavatsky to herself and her husband and containing instructions as to the frauds to be perpetrated.

The Times correspondent in Calcutta cabled the substance of the attack, and it may have been from its columns, of 20 September, that Madame Blavatsky learned of it, after some delay, at Elberfeld. At once, she wrote to *The Times* on 9 October:

> Sir,
> With reference to the alleged exposure at Madras of a dishonourable conspiracy between myself and two persons of the name of Coulomb to deceive the public with occult phenomena, I have to say that the letters purporting to have been written by me are certainly not mine. Sentences here and there I recognise, taken from old notes of mine on different matters, but they are mingled with interpolations that entirely pervert their meaning. With these exceptions the whole of the letters are fabrications.

She returned to London, where she gave interviews to the *Pall Mall Gazette* and other papers, saying she was going back to Madras to sue the *Christian College Magazine* and the Coulombs.

Mohini, who had at his interview with the Society for Psychical Research declined to answer the question whether he had met Koot Hoomi, now wrote from Elberfeld to the *Pall Mall Gazette*, saying that he had had knowledge of him even before meeting Madame Blavatsky, 'and I met him in person when he passed through the Presidency of Madras last year'.

Olcott had gone ahead. So had Babula, whose wife was ill. Madame Blavatsky booked a passage for herself on 1 November.

On 30 October, she received a visit from the curate, Leadbeater. He told her he had, on 3 March, written a letter to the Master Koot Hoomi and given it to a medium but had received no reply. She told him that when he returned to Bramshot he would find one. Returning the next morning, at 1.00 p.m., he found an envelope in the blue handwriting, addressed to 'The Rev. C.W. Leadbeater, Liphook, Hants'. A capital E, obviously intended to start the word England, had been crossed out, probably with the thought that as the letter was being precipitated to Madame Blavatsky, she would post it from within England. The envelope was postmarked 'Kensington, OC. 30, 84'. Notting Hill is in North Kensington. Madame Blavatsky, when she received it, probably just put an English stamp on it and dropped it in the nearest letter-box.

The letter told Leadbeater that his had not been received, nor was it likely to have been considering the nature of the messenger. Nevertheless, he was replying to the substance:[1]

> It is not necessary that one should be in India, during the seven years of probation. A *chela* can pass them anywhere . . . Force any one of the 'Masters' you may happen to

choose; do good works in his name and for the love of mankind . . . and you will have *forced* that 'Master' to accept you.

Koot Hoomi suggested Leadbeater might spend a few months at Adyar. He rushed back to London on the evening of 31 October, to give to Madame Blavatsky a letter saying he would come. She bade him keep close to her until a further message came for him, and so he accompanied her when she went to see Mr and Mrs Cooper-Oakley, who would be sailing with her on the morrow. It was in their drawing-room, in their presence and that of Dr Keightley and Miss Laura Cooper (Mrs Oakley's sister), that he saw one of Madame Blavatsky's hands suddenly jerk forwards, palm upwards. Within it formed a white mist,[2] which condensed into a letter,[3] '. . . Sail on the 5th if possible. Join Upasika at Alexandria.'

It was after midnight. Later in the morning of 1 November, Madame Blavatsky and the Cooper-Oakleys left by train for Liverpool, where they boarded the SS *Clan Drummond*, bound for Port Said. Leadbeater resigned his curacy and left by train from Charing Cross, seen off by Miss Arundale and Mohini, to catch the SS *Erimanthe*, which sailed from Marseilles on 5 November.

CHAPTER 57

At the Hotel d'Orient

When Leadbeater caught up with Madame Blavatsky and the Oakleys, it was to see all three of them sitting on the veranda of a small hotel in Port Said.[1] Madame Blavatsky told him that they were going to occupy the interval created by the need to change steamers by visiting Cairo, and would see if they could pick up any information about the Coulombs.

There was no train from Port Said to Cairo, only a train to Cairo from Ismailia. They therefore boarded a small packet-boat, to take them thus far down the Suez Canal. The boat was infested with bugs and cockroaches. Mrs Oakley and Leadbeater were deterred by them from even attempting to use the cabins, and were pacing about in the night when they heard cries from Madame Blavatsky's cabin. Mrs Oakley darted in and found her in pain, asking for something not to be had aboard the boat. When the boat stopped at Kantara, they persuaded the Captain to wait while they took her ashore for a few minutes. There was neither wharf nor gangway, but somebody produced a plank down which Oakley and Leadbeater helped her, and later they helped her back.[2] Was the visit to a chemist's shop, if there was one?

At Ismailia they landed thankfully, and ate some breakfast at a hotel. Then they took the train. Madame Blavatsky was recovering from her attack of the night before but, weary and gloomy, she began painting for the new disciples a rather dauntingly dark picture of the trials with which they would find the way beset. The train was one of those lit at night by smoky oil-lamps, to accommodate which were round holes in the roofs of the carriages. As it was daytime, there were no lamps. Oakley and Leadbeater, in their respective corners, were leaning back, idly looking up at the blue of the sky through the empty round hole in the ceiling of their carriage. Suddenly, both of them saw a white mist begin to form in it, which became denser and assumed the form of a piece of folded paper; this fell down on to the floor of the carriage. Leadbeater picked it up and handed it to Madame Blavatsky. She unfolded it, read, flushed and tossed it to him, saying, 'That's what I get for trying to warn you people of the troubles that lie before you'. The note said that when one had earnest candidates it was a pity to give them such a gloomy view of a path leading to joy unspeakable. It concluded with a particular message for each of the three, and was signed Koot Hoomi.[3] Leadbeater gave it back to Madame Blavatsky.

At Cairo they engaged a carriage and directed the driver to take them to Shepherd's Hotel, where most English people went. Oakley was just engaging rooms for them when Madame Blavatsky stopped him to say that they should stay at the Hotel d'Orient 'which had been kept by the Coulombs'.[4] The Hotel d'Orient was on Ezbekeeh Square. They all four took rooms in it and stayed for several days.

Leadbeater was in Madame Blavatsky's room, sitting on the floor sorting out some papers for her, when he was startled to see standing before them a man who had not entered by the door, 'which was straight before me all the time, and had not opened'. He jumped up. Madame Blavatsky laughed, said he would not go far in occultism if he was so easily startled, and introduced him to 'Djwal Kul'.

Leadbeater met three acquaintances from her earlier days in Cairo. The Russian Ambassador, Mr Mitrovo, called at the hotel and sent Madame Blavatsky flowers each morning. The Prime Minister of Egypt, Nubar Pasha, invited her and her three friends to dinner. In the Boulak Museum she introduced them to Maspero, the Curator and Egyptologist.

She had not been wrong in thinking they might pick up something about the Coulombs at the Hotel d'Orient. Leadbeater says she obtained:[5]

> from the present host and hostess of the hotel, and from some servants who had worked in the house for many years, numerous evidential details of unreliable and discreditable conduct on the part of the previous occupants.

Before boarding their new ship, the *Navarino*, at Suez, Madame Blavatsky cabled Olcott, 'SUCCESS COMPLETE. OUTLAWS. LEGAL PROOFS. SAIL COLOMBO, NAVARINO'. The meaning, as he realised when he read the statements she had procured, was that the Coulombs had fled from Egypt to avoid arrest for fraudulent bankruptcy.[6]

CHAPTER 58

The Language
of the Coulomb letters

Before we go further, let us look closely at the letters alleged by Madame Coulomb to have been written to her by Madame Blavatsky. There is one which is dated Simla, saying that as she is translating a book of Russian statistics for the Foreign Office (presumably at the local office of the British government), she will not be back until 25 October. If it becomes necessary to move their headquarters from Bombay, it will probably be to Calcutta or Ceylon. This, if genuine, was then written in 1881. After this practical start, it ends mysteriously:[1]

Oh mon pauvre Christofolo! Il est donc mort et vous l'avez tué. Oh ma chère amie si vous saviez comme je voudrais le voir revivre . . . Ma bénédiction à mon pauvre Christofolo. Toujours à vous,

H.P.B.

I translate from the French:

Oh my poor Christofolo! He is dead then and you have killed him; oh my dear friend, if you knew how much I would like him brought back to life . . . Blessings on my poor Christofolo. Ever yours,

H.P.B.

Even if Madame Blavatsky had written this passage, it would not in itself incriminate her. It might refer to the death of a pet, possibly another canary, or to an ornament, a porcelain shepherd or clay gnome broken in the dusting. Madame Coulomb adds a footnote, 'Christofolo was our "occult" name for the doll (Koot Hoomi); I had burnt him in a fit of disgust at the imposture'.

There is no proof of this assertion. Madame Blavatsky could create Indo-Tibetan compounds (so do Tibetans) but could hardly have conceived anything so Italian as an occult name for Koot Hoomi,

Then, there is a long letter, alleged to have been written by Madame Blavatsky from Poona in October 1883, which ends:[2]

Now dear, let us change the programme. Whether *something* succeeds or not I must try. Jacob-Sassoon, the happy proprietor of a crore of rupees, with whose family I dined last night, is anxious to become a Theosophist. He is ready to give 10,000 rupees to buy and repair the headquarters; he said to Colonel (Ezekiel, his cousin, arranged all this) if he only saw a little phenomenon, got the assurance that the *Mahatmas* could hear what was said, or give him some *other sign of their existence* (? . . .) Well, this letter will reach you the 26th, Friday; will you go up to the shrine and ask K.H. (or Christofolo) to send me a telegram that would reach me about 4 or 5 in the afternoon, same day, worded thus:–

'Your conversation with Mr Jacob Sassoon reached Master just now. Were the latter even to satisfy him, still the doubter would hardly find the moral courage to connect himself with the Society.

'Ramalinga Deb'

If this reaches me on the 28th, even in the evening, it will still produce a tremendous *impression*. Address, care of N. Khandallavalla, Judge, Poona. *JE FERAI LE RESTE* [*I WILL DO THE REST*] . . .

Yours truly
Signed H.P.B.

Madame Blavatsky will repudiate this entirely, as being a substitute for a letter she actually wrote to Madame Coulomb from Poona. One wishes it could be known whether the words '(or Christofolo)', were an editorial interpolation or present in the purported original. As it has never been produced, there is no way of knowing.

In the following, I translate from the French:[3]

> My very dear Friend,
> You do not need to wait for the man 'Punch'. So long as it is done in the presence of some respectable persons *besides* our own familiar *muffs*. I beg you to do it at the first opportunity.

The italicised words '*besides*' and '*muffs*' are in English in the purported text. We have never heard of 'Punch'.

Again, I translate from the French:[4]

> Dear Monsieur Coulomb,
> This is what I think you need. Try, if you think you can succeed in having a larger audience than our domestic imbeciles [*imbeciles domestiques*] only. It is worth trying for the Adyar saucer can become as historic as the Simla cup . . .

In both this and the above it seems to be assumed that performances or séances were given for which an 'audience' was gathered together. But we know of nothing like this in the history of Madame Blavatsky. Her phenomena occurred all over the place, sparked for the most part by chance remarks and requests, in circumstances which precluded the 'audience' having been got together by Madame Coulomb. Who could the 'domestic imbeciles' be? There are not known to have been any servants at Adyar, apart from the Coulombs themselves and Babula, Madame Blavatsky's personal attendant. Otherwise, the Indians at Adyar were mainly aspirant chelas. Note that the French for 'audience' is '*assistance*', not '*audience*' as appears incorrectly in the French text.

Next we have a suggestion that Madame Blavatsky, writing from Ootacumund, asked Madame Coulomb to produce a phenomenon for General Morgan when he called. I translate from the French:[5]

> Dear Madame Coulomb and Marquis,
> . . . beg K.H. whom you see every day or Christofolo to sustain the honour of the family . . . For the love of God [*per l'amor del Dio*] or what you will, do not let this occasion slip, which will not repeat itself. I am not there, which is what is fine . . .
> Luna Melanconica

The Coulombs maintained that Marquis was a nickname for Monsieur Coulomb. Perhaps odder is the transition from French into Italian. The words 'of God' are in French '*de Dieu*'. '*Dio*' is Italian; 'of' by itself in Italian should be '*di*', '*del*' is Italian for the combined form 'of the'. 'For love' is, in French '*Pour l'amour*', in Italian '*Per l'amore*'. The final 'e' is dropped if the next word begins with a vowel, which here it does not (and it can be dropped in verse for the sake of the rhythm). I cannot find an instance of Madame Blavatsky's thus dropping into Italian. Could the lapse explain where one of the Coulombs had passed some part of their drifting life?

We get the same effect again towards the end of the same letter:

> Turn the General's head. He will do anything for you if you are with him at Christophe's moment. I send you one [one what?] in case – *e vi saluto*.

Presumably the last means, 'and I salute you', but the French would be '*et je vous salue*'. The form, '*e vi saluto*', for 'I salute you' is Italian, but there is a complication, for the 'you' form is avoided in conventional usage. The polite form would be 'her' (as if the person one is addressing might have a title such as 'Her Excellency' or something like that). Manuals on the Italian language, if they give the 'you' forms warn against their use, which could give offence.

There is another odd phrase in the same letter, where it is said a phenomenon would be worth '*son pesant d'or*', presumably meaning 'its weight in gold', but the French for that would be '*son poids en or*'; '*pesant d'or*' means literally 'heavy of gold'. Even if the omission of the accent over the e of '*pésent*' is the printer's fault, the phrase is not proper French. Again, '*Je reviendrai au milieu de Septembre*' (I shall return in the middle of September) at the end of the letter, reads oddly. The usual French phrase for 'middle' when meaning the middle of a month, is not '*milieu*', which is spatial, but '*mi*', half-way through.

There are two brief extracts in English concerning cigarette-papers and a hair, designed to give the impression that Madame Blavatsky did fraudulent tricks with cigarette-papers.

Another letter in French runs as follows; I translate:[6]

> I think the handkerchief trick has failed. Let us leave it. But all the instructions that they rest [*qu'elles restent*, perhaps 'let them rest'] *statu quó* for the Maharajas of Lahore and of Benares. Both [*tous*] are mad keen to see something. I will write to you from Amritsir or Lahore, my hairs will do well on the old tour of Sion and you will put them in an envelope, a curious sachet, and hang it, hiding it, either at Bombay – choose the place well – and – Write to me at Amritsir *poste restante*, then towards the 1st of the month at Lahore. Address your letter to my name. Nothing more for S – he has seen enough. For fear of missing the post, *à revoir*. [*sic*] Have you put the cigarette on the little cupboard of Wimb–. Do something for the old man, Damodar's father [*il padre di Damodar*].

There is no Maharajah of Lahore, as Madame Blavatsky had pointed out in her letter to *The Times*, 'The fabricators must have been grossly ignorant of Indian affairs since they make me speak of a Maharajah of Lahore, when every Indian schoolboy knows that no such person exists'.

There are also the linguistic mistakes: *statu quó* for *status quo* (Italian words sometimes end in 'ò', not 'ó'; '*tous*' (all) for '*tous les deux*' (both); Amritsir for Amritsar (twice, which precludes its being a printer's error); and finally '*à revoir*' for '*au revoir*'. It is this last which seems to me the most damning. Of all the expressions in French '*au revoir*' is perhaps the most widely known because no other language has a phrase quite so short and neat for 'till we meet again'; it has become international. It has found its way into the *Oxford English Dictionary*. Every English person knows it. That Madame Blavatsky did not know it is inconceivable. It needed a French-speaking person of a rare degree of illiteracy to write it '*à revoir*'. That the printer has not simply dropped off the 'u' is shown by the presence of the accent, which belongs to the 'a' only when it is standing by itself. Even for the most uneducated of French persons, it is a mistake of very unusual and unnatural kind and suggests the influence of some other language – perhaps an aural reminiscence of Italian '*arrivederci*', which has the same kind of short front vowel at the beginning and the same meaning – certainly not of Russian, in which the equivalent expression is '*do svidanya*'.

Even more surprising, and revealing, is the ending, '*le vieux, il padre di Damodar*'; '*le vieux*' is French for 'the old man', but the French for 'the father of' is '*le père de*'. The words '*il padre di*' are the Italian for 'the father of'. The use of '*à revoir*' for '*au revoir*' is in itself a mistake so singular as to disprove the authorship of Madame Blavatsky, '*il padre di*' points to a person whose natural language is Italian.

There is a letter in which Madame Blavatsky is made to seem to ask Coulomb's help in impersonating Koot Hoomi to deceive Hume (I translate from the French):[7]

> My dear Friends,
>   . . . I cannot and dare not write anything. But it is absolutely necessary you should understand that something must happen in Bombay while I am there. The King and Dam must see and receive the visit of one of our Brothers while I am here and it is possible the former should receive a letter which I will send. But to see them is still more necessary. It must fall on his head, like the first, and I am begging 'Koothoomi' to send it to him . . . Act independently of me, but in the clothes and customs of the Brothers . . . Oh dear M. Coulomb, save the situation and do what they ask . . . Does he not see [*ne voilà-t-il pas*] that Mr Hume wants to see Koothoomi, *astrally* from a distance . . . Here is a problem [*Enfin en voila d'un probleme*] . . . *Enfin à revoir* . . .

Apart from the obvious absurdity of the whole, here are further linguistic mistakes. '*Ne voilà-t-il pas*' is not French. There is the well-known French expression '*Voilà*', meaning 'See there', but what the writer means is '*Ne voit-il pas?*' (Does he not see?) The '*là*' is intrusive, and so is the '*-t-*', the 't' sound being naturally present in the ending of '*voit*'. This is the error of some uneducated person having no sense of the parts of speech. Then, one sees again at the end the fatal '*à revoir*'.

There is a curious snippet,[8] 'Will you O Sorceress of a thousand resources ask Christofolo when you see him to transmit the enclosed letter by astral post . . . I embrace you. Yours faithfully'. The last two words are added in English. The writer did not perhaps know they constitute the formal termination of most impersonal business letters.

There is another oddity (I translate from the French):[9]

Dear Marquis,
. . . Show or send him the paper or slip (the little sacristi, not the big one which should repose next to its author in the mural temple) [*temple mûral*] . . .

Whatever may be meant by this, there is no such word as '*mûral*'. There is '*mur*' (wall), whence 'mural' (without circumflex); there is also '*mûr*' (ripe) and '*mûre*' (mulberry); from a memory of one of the last two the writer would seem to have transported the accent. The letter goes on:

. . . I have received a letter which has forced our dear K.H. to write his orders to Damodar and others. May the Marquise read them . . . Ah if I could have my dear Christofolo here . . . Dear Marquis I bequeath to you the destiny of my *children*. Take care of them and make them make miracles. Perhaps this one should be made to fall on his head.

In another letter we have:[10] '. . . Let Screenivas Row prostrate himself before the *shrine*, and whether he asks it or not I beg you to pass him this reply by K.H. for he counts on it there; *I know what he wants*'. In yet another she is made to say that some Indian wants to place something in the temple:[11] 'In case he does, here is the reply of Christofolo. For God arrange that . . . I embrace you *e vi saluto*'. Notice again the Italian '*e vi saluto*'.

Another letter starts:[12]

Too late [*Tropo tardi*]
Dear Marquis, If what Christofolo had in hand had been given in reply at the right moment it would have been fine but it is too late now . . . I may return with the Colonel . . . but I may stay here until October. In that case, during the few days the Colonel is in the house, *you must send me the keys of the shrine*. Send it to me by the underground route. I will see it put away safely; but I do not wish the luna melanconica of the cupboard to be examined in my absence, and it will be examined if I am not there.

One should look at the first two words. The French for 'too late' is '*trop tard*'; '*troppo tardi*' is the Italian, but in the letter '*tropo*' appears. Madame Blavatsky was a pianist, and one cannot go far as a pianist without becoming familiar with the appearance on musical scores of such instructions as '*Allegro ma non troppo*'; the correct spelling would be imprinted on her mind. As for Olcott's having to be kept away from the shrine in Madame Blavatsky's absence, it seems plain from his own account that he went to it when he wished, without troubling her.

Another of the letters ends:[13] '*Oh Dio Dio!*' What a pity. '*Dio*' is the Italian for 'God'; the French is '*Dieu*'. In another letter, there is '*à revoir*' again.[15]

In a letter said to have been written by Madame Blavatsky from Simla prior to their move to the Crow's Nest, asking Madame Coulomb to choose another bungalow for them, she is made to say:[16] '*que la vostra camera si trova sopra la testa d'un certo Signore Pres. e – altra roba*'. This is meant to be French for 'Let your own room be over that of a certain Mr Pres.[ident] [i.e. Olcott] – and the other dress'. The only French words in the sentence are, however, '*que*' and '*un*', and '*la*' is common to French and Italian. All the rest are Italian. The French would be '*Que votre chambre se trouve au dessus de celle d'un certain Monsieur Pres. – et l'autre robe*'. '*Vostra*' is Italian for '*votre*' (your); '*camera*' is Italian for '*chambre*' (room); '*si trova*' is Italian for '*se trouve*' (finds itself); '*sopra*' is Italian for '*sur*' (on) or '*au dessus de*' (above); '*la testa*' is Italian for '*la tête*' (head); '*certo*' is Italian for '*certain*' (certain); '*Signore*' is Italian for

'*Monsieur*' and '*altra roba*' is Italian for '*autre robe*' (other dress). Curiously, the last enigmatic phrase has spilled over into Madame Coulomb's English translation, in the facing column, which appears as '*Ed altra roba*'. 'Ed' is the correct form for Italian 'and', 'e' when the next word begins with a vowel.

Equally interesting, or almost more so, is the 'French' attributed to Madame Blavatsky in a letter in which she is made to appear to be begging the assistance of Madame Coulomb to produce some phenomenon mechanically:[17] '*Per l'amore de San Jiuseppe fatte l'affare bene*'. Against this, Madame Coulomb's English translation is, 'For the love of St. Joseph do the thing well'.

Here the only French word is '*de*'. '*Per l'amore*' is Italian for '*Pour l'amour*' (French 'For the love'). Italian for 'of' would be '*di*', the '*de*', as has been noted, is French. '*San*' is short for '*Santo*', Italian for 'Saint' (the same in French and English). The Italian form of Joseph (used in French and English) is Giuseppe (the 'Gi' being pronounced as English 'J'). '*L'affare*' is Italian for French '*l'affaire*' (the affair); and Italian '*bene*' replaces French '*bien*' (well).

This extraordinary composition makes it quite plain that we are not looking at international quotations from Italian. What we have before us is the work of a person in whose mind the French and Italian languages are inextricably mixed, so that one comes out when the other is intended and hybrid forms occur.

Madame Coulomb attributes to Madame Blavatsky the words uttered by word of mouth, 'Do you know that you are a great "Secatura"?' Since she places it between quotation marks, she perhaps thinks of it as being Madame Blavatsky's French breaking through; but '*secatura*' is an idiomatic Italian expression for a dry, boring person. There is no French equivalent for it.

A letter about 'putting the reply of Christofolo' in the shrine ends in another Italian '*e vi saluto*'.[18]

A letter about buying furniture contains a curious phrase:[19] '*Maintenant – c'e la moneta . . .*'. '*Maintenant*' is French for 'now'. '*C'e*' (the 'c' pronounced as in 'church', a sound which does not occur in French), is a very idiomatic Italian phrase, meaning 'there is' in the sense 'there is no lack of' or 'there is sufficient'. It has no French or English equivalent. '*Moneta*' is Italian for 'money'. In her English translation opposite, Madame Coulomb gives, 'Now – we have the money'; but the French for 'money' is '*argent*'. (There is a French word '*monnaie*' but it means 'money' only in the sense of the money given in change.) The French for 'we have the money' would be '*nous avons l'argent*', and '*c'e*' is not an expression that would come to the mind of a person who did not customarily think in Italian.

A letter alleged to have been written by Madame Blavatsky from Suez contains another example of '*Ne voilà-t-il pas*'. A paragraph ridiculing Olcott for having turned away an offer from the rich Lane-Fox to endow the Society ends:[20] '*O Dio! a t'on jamais vu un – – – semblable*', meaning 'O God! [in Italian again; French would be '*O Dieu*'] Has one ever seen such a – – –?' In a footnote it is stated: 'Consideration for the feelings of my French readers forbids me to print the word omitted. Suffice it to say it is used only by the Marseille sailors'.

This is interesting. Marseille is a great port, and there are sailors there from all countries, including Britain. Like Port Said, it is thought of as somewhat of a sink, full of brothels and of hotels and restaurants of doubtful character. If apart from the international traffic there is some kind of a fleet manned by French sailors living in Marseille, plying to and from places within near reach, a foul word peculiar to its men could hardly become known to a woman, unless she was related to one of them or employed in one of their resorts. The intention is plainly to defame Madame Blavatsky, but since the passage is the work of the person whose Italian background keeps breaking in, the question is how that person knew it.

Having now found so many Italianisms, I think we may include among them '*audience*', noticed earlier. There are a great many words which, both in English and French, end in 'ence' or 'ance', but in Italian end in 'enza' or 'anza', for instance, English and French 'elegance', Italian 'eleganza', English and French 'prudence', Italian 'prudenza', English and French 'vigilance', Italian 'vigilanza'. Thus, an Italian-speaking person might be forgiven for supposing that to convert any Italian word of such termination into French, it was only necessary to change 'za' into 'ce', hence, Italian '*auddienza*' into French '*audience*'. However, the French do not use the word '*audience*' except in the special sense of to be received in audience by a sovereign or the Pope. The audience gathered in a theatre to see a play is the *'assistance'*.

It should be noted that Madame Blavatsky wrote beautiful French. One has only to look at the letters she wrote to Madame Corson to see the fluency and elegance with which she commanded the French language. She writes *'au revoir'*, not *'à revoir'*. She had been in a great many countries, Italy amongst them, but her letters do not degenerate into unconscious Italian.

The letters are the work of a person bilingual in French and Italian. Bilingual is a term used of persons who have grown up with two languages, usually because their parents speak, for ease, in different languages from each other, or because they live in a country not their own. Whether it should be considered an asset or a misfortune is questionable, for in the majority of cases it means that neither language is commanded perfectly, each being spoken or written with unintentional admixture of the other. The victim of this condition cannot get them apart. I would say that in the case we are looking at the intention was to write French but the Italian kept coming through; therefore Italian was probably the basic language of the writer. A basically Italian speaker would more easily attempt to Frenchify 'Giuseppe' as 'Jiuseppe' than a French person to commit the barbarity of writing 'Joseph' as 'Jiuseppe'. The 'i' is needed in Italian only to show that the 'G' (which otherwise would be hard) should be pronounced soft. French 'J' is soft.

We do not need to ask whether either of the Coulombs had a past in which the Italian language had some part. In her pamphlet Madame Coulomb obligingly lets slip that they did not go direct from Cairo to Ceylon but went first to Calcutta, where she gave Italian lessons to Lady Temple. (Why did no one apply to Lady Temple for a character of Madame Coulomb?) Further, in a list of staff reproduced in Josephine Ransom's *Short History of the Theosophical Society*,[21] seven assistants to the Corresponding Secretary are detailed, each with the language or languages professed, thus 'Damodar . . . – Marathi and English' and 'Mme Coulomb – French and Italian'.

Where could she have come from? Corsica has an Italian population under French rule; but I tend to think of the French Riviera, which gets both Corsicans and Italians from across the border, plus the sprinkling of British needed to provide the maiden name of Cutting. Perhaps she herself has given us the clue in her intimate reference to Marseille.

CHAPTER 59

Gribble's Report and the handwriting of Coulombs

It is infinitely to be deplored that the forged letters used to mount the attack upon Madame Blavatsky have disappeared from the world without ever having been seen by it. Not only was she, herself, denied the sight of these papers, by which her reputation was said to have been destroyed and which her accusers kept sedulously close amongst themselves, but they have never been reproduced in facsimile. Now, nobody knows where they are, and it is feared they may have been destroyed. All we have is a verbal description of them by J.D.B. Gribble,[1] to whom they were submitted by the *Christian College Magazine* shortly after their publication in its columns; he was an occasional contributor to the magazine. It does not appear that he was a professional handwriting expert, but he was a retired civil servant, late Officiating Judge of Tranquebar, Nellore and Cuddapah. He takes as what he calls the 'test letter' the long one dated as from Paris on 1 April 1884, and compares the 'disputed letters' with it. One could wish he had not taken as his 'test letter' one of the collection presented by the Coulombs. He assumes it to be genuine because it would be a strain on a forger to produce anything of such length and it contains nothing incriminating, yet the forger may have copied out a genuine letter so as to provide a comparatively innocent 'control'. He may be comparing Coulomb with Coulomb.

Details he finds common to the 'test letter' and the 'disputed letters' include capital letters, particularly 'F' and 'T' in which an upward starting stroke precedes the downstroke;[2] small 'a', 'o' and 'g' in which the gap appears sometimes on the left;[3] small 'd' in which the upstroke curves left;[4] and terminal 'ez' formed like 'y', French words *'assez'*, *'devez'*, *'achetez'* *'manquez'*, *'addressez'*, *'suffrirez'*, *'tournez'*, *'Sentez'* and *'saviez'* looking like *'assy'*, *'devy'*, *'achety'*, *'manquey'*, *'addressy'*, *'suffriry'*, *'tourny'*, *'Senty'* and *'saviy'*; and *'vous'* abbreviated to *'vs'*.[5]

Gribble has seen some of Madame Coulomb's writing, and tells us:[6]

> It is what was known about twenty years ago as 'a lady's hand' . . . It has not one feature in common with that of the disputed correspondence. Madame Coulomb's writing is that of a lady who had been somewhat imperfectly educated a great many years ago. It is essentially feminine. The disputed letters, on the other hand, are written in a bold, free running masculine hand.

He thought it would be too difficult for Madame Coulomb to copy out, let alone compose in, a hand so different from her own. As Monsieur Coulomb's English was too imperfect for him to have composed the letters that were in English, he did not apparently think it worth while to ask to see his hand. Here, Gribble was at fault. He did not consider the possibility of a joint husband and wife job.

I wrote to Adyar asking if they could send me photostats of any writing they might possess in the hands of Madame and Monsieur Coulomb – the former in French if possible. They had nothing in French by Madame Coulomb, but sent me the handwritten original of her letter to the *Ceylon Times* and the letter from Monsieur Coulomb (in French, of course) of May 1884. (These are quoted above in Chapter 32).

As to the letter by Madame Coulomb, I saw at once what Gribble meant, and except for one detail I agree with him. It is the precious, slow hand of a woman not accustomed to writing a great deal, taking pains to produce an elegant writing. It nevertheless has the leftward curving vertical stroke to the 'd' which Gribble thought special to the 'test' and 'disputed' letters.

But when one turns to Alexis Coulomb's hand one sees something far more swiftly running and aggressive. There is no capital 'F' or 'T', but all the capital 'J's have a strong upward starting stroke. His small 'a' is nearly always wide open at the top, but sometimes open a little to the left – notably in '*Ma*' of 'Ma femme' (My wife) at the beginning. Here the left-hand gap is as much as in the examples taken from Madame Blavatsky's hand in the later Hodgson Report. His small 'd' does not curve leftwards but, on the other hand, his small 'n' does. At first sight I took his '*en*' (of it) for the English word 'and', and on the second page his '*on*' (one) ends with a similar flourish upwards and left. His '*vous*' is twice abbreviated to '*vs*', and he writes '*venez*' (come) so that it looks like '*veny*' and '*sachez*' (know) so that it looks like '*sachy*'. In each case, the 'e' has no loop and there is no nick in the downstroke of the 'z' to distinguish it from a 'y'. Gribble, I feel sure, would recognise what he has described.

Given that Coulomb was a draughtsman, accustomed to looking at shapes in order to copy them, and that his own hand possessed certain features akin to Madame Blavatsky's, it should not have been too difficult for him to have cultivated the rest. I think Madame Coulomb composed the text with all those Italian words in what was supposed to be French, and that he copied it into 'Madame Blavatsky's' hand.

Where the longer letters are concerned, they may have been able to utilise pages of Madame Blavatsky's own letters, so saving the labour of copying all but the page on which some 'incriminating' matter was to be interpolated. Here, it would have been interesting to see the paper and the manufacturer's watermarks. People may write on different pads at different times, but if the pages bearing the 'incriminating' passages were on paper different from the rest of the letter supposed to contain them, that would be significant. In just one instance, that of the long letter from Poona, Gribble does mention that the first two pages are on grey paper and the last page on pink. In this letter, all the 'incriminating' matter, concerning the purported plan to deceive Sassoon, is at the end. Did the Coulombs simply use the first two pages of the genuine letter, destroy the last page, and, not having any more of the grey paper she used, compose a new end to the letter on pink? The photostat I obtained from the Society for Psychical Research of their copy of Madame Coulomb's pamphlet (reprinted from the *Christian College Magazine*), unexpectedly showed marginal comments in the hand of Madame Blavatsky. Beneath the first part of this letter she has written, 'This letter appears to be genuine', but against the last part she was written 'This is an addition . . . Never wrote it'. These comments she made without being allowed to see the alleged originals on the differing paper. Gribble noted the differences because pink looks so different from grey, but would he have noted the difference between, say, two white papers, perhaps only distinguishable on holding them up to the light to look for the watermark? On the Simla letter, Madame Blavatsky has written in the margin against the first part, about their changing headquarters, 'Likely to be genuine', but against the Christofolo passage '?!!'. Again, the original end to the letter may have been destroyed and a new one composed and added to the original page or pages. This procedure would greatly reduce the amount of labour.

With this clue, one can see why the 'incriminating' passages tend to be either at the end of very long letters or else in very short ones, as well as why – and this is very significant – the Italianisms and other faults in French occur only in the 'incriminating' passages, or so close to them as probably to have been on the same sheet.

There is a sinister detail. Gribble tells us that in two of the letters there is a dash over an initial 'm' – in '*mouchoir*', '*manquent*', 'simply', 'more' and 'mistranslations'. Koot Hoomi never fails to place a horizontal mark over his 'm', wherever placed. Madame Blavatsky never does it. The forger was trying to engender the suspicion that Madame Blavatsky wrote the Mahatma Letters.

Nevertheless, in a postscript to his Report, Gribble says that when shown what purported to be messages from the two Mahatmas and a chela, he saw 'three different hands', none of them having the characteristics to which he had alluded in his Report.

CHAPTER 60

Back to Madras

When Madame Blavatsky landed at Colombo, she found Olcott and Hartmann had come to meet her. With her were Leadbeater and the Oakleys. They all sailed on another boat to Madras, where they landed on 20 December 1884, to a tumultuous welcome for H.P.B. from Theosophists come to the pier. Thence they were escorted back to Adyar, where they found that Mr Richard Hodgson, from the Society of Psychical Research, had arrived two days earlier, on 18 December. There had been some trouble because Hodgson had wished to be admitted, at once, to see the occult room and the shrine. The occult room being within Madame Blavatsky's private living quarters, Damodar told him he could not admit him in her absence and in that of Colonel Olcott and Dr Hartmann. This seems to have riled him, though no caretaker or steward could have taken on himself to admit a stranger without authorisation. Then the two Founders arrived home with Hartmann, and Hodgson at once wanted to know where the shrine was. This was what Madame Blavatsky, returning to her rooms after a ten-months absence, was herself asking. At first there seemed to be no answer forthcoming. Then Damodar said that on 20 September about midday it had been removed to his own room, where it had remained during the night. About 9 a.m. the following morning he saw that it was no longer there. Further enquiry elicited that, in the presence of Dr Hartmann, it had been burned. Also, presumably also on instructions from the Board of Control, the hole bored from the occult room into Madame Blavatsky's room had been plastered up.

Madame Blavatsky had returned in order to sue for libel. Olcott writes, 'From the day she landed, she kept urging me to take her to a judge, or solicitor or barrister . . . for her to file her affidavit and begin our action, but I positively refused'.[1] It reads as though she did not understand how proceedings are instituted in the British system, wherein one goes only to a solicitor. But why did Olcott refuse? He was not impressed by the statements she had collected in Cairo and says that acting without legal advice, she had 'made a mess of the affair'. Probably she should not herself have approached the persons from whom she had obtained statements. In any case, written statements, even affidavits, are not accepted in British courts; witness can only be given from the box. He continues:[2]

> I told her that within the next few days the Convention would meet, and that our paramount duty was to lay her case before the Delegates, have a special Committee formed, of our ablest lawyers, and let them decide what steps she should take . . . She fretted and stormed and insisted, but I would not stir from my position, and, when she threatened to go by herself and 'wipe this foul stain off her character', I then said I should, in that case, resign my office and let the Convention decide between us . . . She then yielded.

The Convention met on 27 December. Olcott told the delegates that Madame Blavatsky wished to go to court, but their resolution was:[3]

> That the letters published in the *Christian College Magazine* under headline 'Collapse of Koot Hoomi' are only a pretext to injure the cause of Theosophy; and as these letters necessarily appear absurd to those who are acquainted with our philosophy and facts, and as those who are not acquainted with those facts could not have their opinions changed even by a judicial verdict in favour of Madame Blavatsky, it is the unanimous decision of this Committee that Madame Blavatsky should not prosecute her defamers in a Court of Law. Signed by Norendro Nath Sen, Chairman [Editor of *Indian Mirror* and Honorary Magistrate, Calcutta]; A.J. Cooper-Oakley, Secretary; Franz Hartmann, M.D.; S. Ramaswarmier; Naoroji Dorabji Khandalavala [note that he was the judge alleged in one of the faked letters to have been deceived]; H.R. Morgan, Major-General;

Gyanendranath Chakravati; Nobin K. Bannerji [Deputy Collector and Magistrate]; T. Subba Row [Rao] BLL. [Pleader, High Court, Madras]; P. Screenivas Row [Rao] [Deputy Collector, Madras]; P. Iyaloo Naidu (Deputy Collector, Ret.); Rudolph Gebhard, R. Raghoonrath Row [Rao]; S. Subramania Iyer [later justice of the High Court of Madras, and knighted].

Judge Khandalavala had dismissed the letter in which he was mentioned as 'a perfect forgery'; and General Morgan had asserted the whole lot were forgeries as it was impossible that Madame Blavatsky could compose such bad French (even he did not recognise it was bad in that it was part Italian). The Indians, however, were appalled at the idea of proceedings which could cause the sacred names of the Masters to be spoken aloud in court, which would be to desecrate them; and the lawyers told Madame Blavatsky that if the judge ordered her to answer questions about the Mahatmas which the Mahatmas forbade her to answer, the judge could have her imprisoned for contempt. Even that might have been better than the inaction they forced on her.

On 14 January 1885, Olcott left for Burma, where King Thibaw III had invited him. With him he took Leadbeater.

Just after they had gone, Madame Blavatsky was taken ill, and made her will. Except for her dresses, which she left to her nieces, and keepsakes for Damodar, Babaji, Ananda, Hartmann and Olcott's sister, Louise (Belle?), she left everything to Olcott. Olcott and Damodar were the executors. The will was signed on 31 January 1885, and witnessed by P. Screenivas Row, H.R. Morgan (Major-General), T. Subba Row and C. Rama.

Olcott was at the Burmese Court when, during the night of 28 January, he was awakened with a telegram from Damodar: 'RETURN AT ONCE UPASIKA DANGEROUSLY ILL'. ('Upasika' was the Masters' name for Madame Blavatsky; it is a Buddhist term, meaning female lay disciple or sister who has taken eight vows.) Olcott left Leadbeater in Burma and by 11 a.m. was on the steamer *Oriental*, bound for Madras. During the voyage, he wrote in his diary:[4]

> My poor Chum, and is thy life of adventure, of anguish, of violent contrasts and of unswerving devotion to Humanity ended? Alas, my loss will be greater than if thou hadst been wife, or sweetheart, or sister; for now must I carry alone the immense burden of this responsibility with which the Holy Ones have charged us.

The ship reached Madras on 5 February, and he rushed to Adyar, to find Madame Blavatsky still breathing. 'She was so delighted to see me that she put her arms around my neck, as I came to her bedside, and wept on my breast'.

With her were Drs Mary Scharlieb and Hartmann. They said she was suffering from congestion of the kidneys, enfeebled action of the heart, rheumatic gout and alarming loss of vitality.

Then he found that earlier on that same day, Hartmann and Lane-Fox had presented for her signature a paper, which was 'simply my setting aside'[5] (so the Coulombs, when they alleged them to be plotting the overthrow of the Founders, were evidently not wide of the mark). The paper provided for 'the transfer of the governing power to a Committee, composed mainly of themselves' (more exactly of five persons, of whom four were white, the only Indian being Subba Row). Further, both Madame Blavatsky and Olcott were to convey, 'our *Theosophist* and its book business to the Society without compensation, and without reserving out of the property we had ourselves created, without a rupee's help from the Society, even the pittances needed for our modest support'. H.P.B. and he had within the past twelve months given the Society 9,000 rupees from the *Theosophist* fund, and of the gross profits of the magazine to date, 15,000 rupees, they had given the Society over 14,000 rupees.

She had already signed the paper:[6]

> Believing that this new arrangement is necessary for the welfare of the Society, I approve of it, so far as I am concerned.
>
> H.P. Blavatsky

He went over it with her, and asked her if it was just that:[5]

I who had watched over and built up the Society from its first germ until now, should be turned out on the road to go hang, without a word of thanks or even so much as the 'chit' or character certificate one gives to the rest-house keeper after a night's stay . . . she moaned out that she had signed something they had brought to her dying-bed, and which they said was very important for the Society, and that she repudiated any such ingratitude. She told me to tear the papers . . .

She had also now received a copy of what must have been the *Private and Confidential First Report of the Society for Psychical Research*, published at the end of 1884 (Olcott refers to it as though it were a copy of the final or Hodgson Report, but that had not yet been made). In it she had written:[7]

Madame Blavatsky, who will soon be dead and gone, says this to her friends of the P.R.S.: After my death these phenomena, which are the direct cause of my premature death, will take place better than ever. But whether dead or alive, I will be ever imploring my friends and Brothers never to make them public; never to sacrifice their rest, their honour, to satisfy public curiosity or the empty pretext of science. Read the book. Never, throughout my long and sad life, never was there so much of uncalled for, contemptuous suspicion and contempt lavished upon an innocent woman as I find here in these few pages published by so-called friends.

H.P.Blavatsky

Adyar, Feb. 5, 1885
on my death-bed.

Olcott can be forgiven for having slipped into taking this as her comment on the Hodgson Report, for actually the earlier one was, at least in comparison, benign, and it is unfortunate that it was not published. This was because the SPR wanted to make further enquiries and possibly because publication would not be liked by Damodar. It seems a pity that the passages about him could not just have been left out. Indeed, Olcott should probably not have talked to the Committee about Damodar's feats of astral projection without first asking Damodar whether he wished these to become public; and the Report is not the stronger for including hearsay evidence of this sort, especially given 'off the cuff' without access to contemporary notes against which to check recollections. The interviews with Olcott and Mohini are printed from the stenographer's record, and favourable written testimonies from General and Mrs Morgan, Mr and Mrs Ross Scott, Hübbe-Schleiden, Prince Harisinghji Rupsinghji and many others are printed. An account of the interview with Sinnett is omitted. The oddest and in retrospect most sinister, thing is that the testimonies of their own representatives, Myers, Gurney and Thurstan, as to their having visited her and heard the bell phenomenon, are entirely omitted. In the list of interviews given to the Society at its headquarters in Cambridge appears 'Aug. 9th Madame Blavatsky and Mohini'. This may or may not be the meeting mentioned by Sidgwick in his journal. There is not even a mention of three of their representatives having, before that, been twice received by her in July at the Arundales.

My knowledge of the omitted passages, first discovered by Mr Walter Carrithers, comes from Mr Leslie Price, who sent me a draft of the lecture given on 12 April 1983, since published as *Madame Blavatsky Unveiled?*, London 1986. According to this, 'Stack had lived in India and felt it to be an environment in some respects conducive to fraudulent phenomena . . . Stack emerges as the "hard man" of the Committee in a memorandum he sent Sidgwick after reading the preliminary report'. Stack, in his memorandum to Sidgwick, recommended deletion from the Report of the testimony of Myers, Gurney and Thurstan concerning the bell, as being 'a very small fact to be so elaborately and solemnly recorded . . . the sole outcome of the *research* into these Oriental phenomena. The rest is the collection of depositions more or less trustworthy – the immense mass Indian testimony'. Here one sees the anti-Indian bias and, perhaps, racial prejudice. Now, it may be prudent to regard with caution testimonies of people from a far distant land, whose status there and antecedents are less easily checked up on than those of people of one's own sort, but that makes a strange basis for excluding the testimonies of three Englishmen, well known to them, members of their own Society.

Stack added in his covering letter to Sidgwick, 'I tried to convert Myers and Gurney yesterday; I am afraid my arguments had not much effect; they are still under the spell of Madame Blavatsky'. Sidgwick wrote, 'Agreed, Omit bell'. The testimonies of Myers, Gurney and Thurstan, though they had been set in type, were then deleted, in the galley-proofs, from the text of the report to be published.

It is Mr Leslie Price who adds in his paper:[8]

This memorandum seems to me of significance in the history of psychical research, since it was the first time, possibly, that an SPR Committee decided not to publish eye-witness testimony to a phenomenon by the person being investigated. Possibly HPB produced other phenomena which were witnessed but not reported by the Committee. Certainly the decision not to publish this one, even to SPR members, had been taken before Hodgson arrived in India. Had they published this one, instead of concealing it, Hodgson in his turn might have witnessed more in India.

Perhaps some sixth sense of these machinations behind the scenes told Madame Blavatsky that Hodgson's visit boded no good to her. He came to see her several times and was very anxious for a specimen of her handwriting. She soon felt he was unfriendly. He showed her an envelope addressed by herself to Madame Coulomb from Poona as though it were proof she had in fact written from there the letter which Madame Coulomb had produced for the *Christian College Magazine*. Madame Blavatsky pointed out that exhibition of an envelope was not proof of the text of the letter it was alleged to have contained. She asked him to show her the letter she was alleged to have written, or any of 'her' alleged letters, but this he refused, though he had some of them, which he had obtained from Madame Coulomb, in his pocket. She said she had posted a letter to Madame Coulomb from Poona, but to quite different effect, and the purported letter was fabrication. In a written commentary on the letters which she gave him, she said:[9]

All depends on knowing who is 'Christofolo' – a little ridiculous figure in rags, about three inches high, she wrote to say it had accidently been destroyed . . . 'Christofolo' was a name by which she called an absurd little figure, or image of hers. She gave nicknames to everything.

Madame Blavatsky remembered that Madame Coulomb had written to her that Christofolo had melted in the sun, and that she returned some joking answer, but not in the terms alleged,[10] 'That I should write such *bosh* is impossible, not *in my style* at all'.

Olcott heard that at an Anglo-Indian dinner in Madras, Hodgson had expressed the opinion that Madame Blavatsky was 'a Russian spy'.[11] He called on him, taking with him Oakley, and said later he thought they had succeeded in convincing him the charge was 'puerile and unfounded'. (If Hodgson was serious, why had he not made his statement in a police station instead of at a dinner-party?)

Following a sudden appearance of the Master Morya, Madame Blavatsky made a recovery, as she had done at Philadelphia, and by 10 February she was out of bed and on her feet again.

She was, however, still subject to palpitations of the heart, and Dr Mary Scharlieb wrote a statement that:[12]

Madame Blavatsky is quite unfit for the constant excitement and worry to which she is exposed in Madras. The condition of her heart renders perfect quiet and a suitable climate essential. I therefore recommend that she should at once proceed to Europe, and remain in a temperate climate – in some quiet spot.

Mary Scharlieb
M.B. and S.L. London

The Council had therefore no option but to accept Madame Blavatsky's resignation of her post as Corresponding Secretary. It resolved that, to mark its respect for her, 'the vacancy caused by her retirement will not be filled'. Her passage was booked at once.

During these last days, General Morgan received a letter from Madame Coulomb's solicitor, threatening him with proceedings unless he withdrew a description of her as 'a forger'. He stood firm, determined to justify his words, which would have brought about the exhibition of the letters in Court. Unfortunately, Madame Coulomb did not proceed.

Madame Blavatsky sailed on 31 March, accompanied by Dr Hartmann, Babaji Krishnaswami Iyengar (whom Koot Hoomi had instructed to take as his mystic name that of a more senior chela, Dharbagiri Nath, but who was more often known as Babaji or 'the little man') and Miss Mary Flynn. Madame Blavatsky was unable to mount the gangway and had to be hoisted aboard in a hospital chair.

Just after she had gone, Olcott, brooding over one of the libels in Madame Coulomb's pamphlet, which was that Madame Blavatsky had had illegitimate children in Cairo, thought to send for the Tamil woman who had nursed H.P.B. through her illness in February.[13]

> The *ayah* affirmed and declared her willingness to go into court and testify that her late mistress had never been a mother. She even went so far as to say that whatever marriage she had contracted must have been a merely nominal one. Adult readers will understand my meaning.

Meanwhile, Hodgson was still sniffing around in India. He had seen Hume and he had been to Bombay, where he had routed out Hurrychund Chintamon. It will be remembered that Madame Blavatsky had, soon after their arrival in India, very publicly accused Chintamon of misappropriating to his own pocket a donation they had made to the Arya Samaj. Hodgson came back and, gloating, told Olcott[14] that Hurrychund Chintamon had shown him a letter written by Madame Blavatsky from New York saying she could make Olcott believe anything she liked by just looking at him. This hurt him more than anything else in his whole life, and for twenty-four hours he was 'almost ready to go down to the beach and drown myself in the sea'. At last it came to him that whatever H.P.B., in her human caprice, might have written, all that mattered was that he should continue in his duty to the great Masters whom they both served. It came 'to me like the flash of a great light, and there was peace'.

Of course. Perhaps in that moment he had passed the initiation in which it is said one has to stand alone. But he should have realised that if she had written anything of the sort it was meant as a joke – letters do not smile – and that anyway, he did not have the letter before him and the account he had received of it might have been belied by the text.

CHAPTER 61

Beneath Vesuvius

Madame Blavatsky and her party landed at Naples on 12 April 1885. There is a saying, 'See Naples and die!' but it is the Bay of Naples that affords a panorama of breath-taking beauty: its focal point is Vesuvius, the crater turning in the evening light from bronze to bloom of grape, violet and at last indigo, a thin plume of smoke arising (when I was there, in my teens with my mother) against a primrose sky. The city of Naples, however, is slummy and dirty. The thing to do is to find a place outside it. Madame Blavatsky probably chose Torre del Greco, on the volcano's flank, because of its being (when I was there) the railway station from which one could walk the few yards down to the ruins of Pompeii.

Yet the hotel, with tiled floors to give coolness in summer, was cold, and she wrote to Olcott asking him to send her rug so that she might have it beneath her feet at her writing-table.

He was sending her a pension of £20 a month from the funds of the Theosophical Society, which, in terms of today's purchasing power, would have been upwards of £5,000 a year, though she had to pay for attendance out of it. Touching donations from Indians of two northern branches helped her. She was unhappy, however, and she blamed Olcott for having gone to the Society for Psychical Research, excited its interest and brought all this misery upon her. This he felt to be unfair.

In the April issue of the *Christian College Magazine*, Patterson announced his possession of a letter written by Madame Blavatsky in 1880 to Madame Coulomb before she had come from Ceylon, saying that since she had left her husband she had lived with Metrovitch; to him and others she had borne three children. As if, Madame Blavatsky wrote to Sinnett, had this been true she would have written to tell Madame Coulomb![1] But Patterson has destroyed a point he had made in his October issue, in favour of the Coulomb documents, which was that their number did not grow. The forger, such as Titus Oates or Dangerfield, 'goes on producing as the hour may demand'.[2] So, now, Madame Coulomb. This new letter cannot have been amongst those shown to Gribble as constituting the whole collection or Gribble would have detailed it.

In a letter to Mohini dated from the Hotel del Vesuvio, 17 May, Madame Blavatsky blamed Sinnett's books for:[3]

> thrusting occultism and its mysteries into the teeth of a prejudiced unprepared public . . . Had phenomena and the *Masters* been sacredly preserved among and only for Theosophists, all this could not have happened. But it is my own fault as much as his. In my zeal and devotion to the Cause I have permitted publicity and as Subba Row truly says 'committed *the crime* of divulging things most sacred and holy that had never been known to the profane before' and now comes my Karma.

In a letter to Mrs and Miss Arundale of 16 June she explains further:[4]

> Such as Subba Row – uncompromising *initiated* Brahmins, will never reveal even that which they are permitted to. They hate too much the Europeans for it . . . [He said] 'You have been guilty of the most terrible of crimes. You have given out secrets of Occultism – the most sacred and the most hidden. Rather *that you should be sacrificed* than that which was never meant for European minds. It was time to throw doubt into their minds. Otherwise they should have pumped *out of you all that you know*'. And he is acting on that principle.

Here we have one crux of the disaster. Long before, Olcott had noticed that the Brahmins, accustomed from immemorial ages to keeping their secrets to themselves, had eyed with a mixture of jealousy and disapproval the exhibition of phenomena and exposition of secrets presented by Madame Blavatsky. They surely had the feeling that such disclosure was impropriety and indiscretion amounting nearly to deep sin, bound to bring retribution. The

Masters Morya and Koot Hoomi, with their greater authority, had persuaded their Chohan to permit a portion of the secret teaching previously withheld to be made accessible to the profane. This they had done in their compassion for that profanity, for the sake of the chance of thereby helping towards the light at least a few of those who would otherwise remain in darkness. These Brahmins who joined the Society, their scruples overruled, had gone along with it so long as things were going well; but, once disaster seemed impending, they had at once reverted to type, to their initial feelings that such disclosure could only damage the mysteries. They thought the only way to mend the hole in the veil was to bluff and say there was nothing sacred here, nothing for Hodgson to stay for; he should go away. Thus they became the worst enemies of H.P.B. personally, and also of what the Masters had intended. In a later letter to Mrs Sinnett, Madame Blavatsky explains:[5]

> Mahatma K.H. holds him [Babaji], Damodar and Subba Row for two thirds of Mr Hodgson's *mayas* . . . It is *they*, who, irritated and insulted at his appearance at Adyar, regarding his [Hodgson's] cross-examination and talk about the *Masters* – degrading to themselves and blasphemous with regard to Masters; instead of being frank with H. and telling him openly that there were many things they could not tell him – went to work to augment his perplexity, allowed him to suggest things without contradicting them, and threw him out of the saddle altogether. You see, Hodgson counted without his host; he had no idea of the character of the true Hindu – especially of a chela – of his ferocious veneration for things sacred, of his reserve and exclusiveness in *religious* matters; and they (our Hindus) whom even *I* had never heard pronounce or mention one of the Masters *by name* – were goaded into fury in hearing Hodgson make so cheap of those names – speaking laughingly of 'K.H.' and 'M' – etc. with the Oakleys.

It will have been noticed that neither Mohini, in the interview he gave to the Committee of the Society, nor any of the Indians in any of the statements printed from Theosophical sources, ever uses the names 'Morya' or 'Koot Hoomi'. They use phrases such as 'Colonel Olcott's Master' for the former, and 'Mr Sinnett's correspondent' for the latter. This plainly seemed to them the proper form of reference, combining absence of equivocation with propriety in abstinence from the naming of Holy Ones. Madame Blavatsky and Olcott may have used the names when talking privately, but even today Theosophists do not like uttering the names of the Masters needlessly. They refer to them by their initials, or if they do name them do so in lowered voices so as not to cause them annoyance. When Hodgson walked in, an Australian, bright and brash, breezily pronouncing out loud the names, 'Morya' and 'Koot Hoomi', which chelas had never in their lives uttered, it must have given them a shock, like that occasioned by blasphemy. For them, Hodgson was a profane man. They would have seen it as their duty to induce him to withdraw. It does not seem that Olcott had warned them to expect him. If Madame Blavatsky and Colonel Olcott had been there when he arrived, to make them a little speech and tell them he was a person to be welcomed, everything might have been different. He had had the unfortunate idea of just walking in, so as to surprise them, and it was fatal to his reception by the chelas. Coming unexpectedly, asking questions, he would have cut the figure of a robber. Nobody exposes the best that he has to such a man. A miser does not say, 'Look, I have gold!' He says, 'I am a poor man, with nothing worth stealing. What you see glinting is only brass'. From Hodgson's questions, he seemed to be trying to steal their most sacred secrets. The defence was obviously to pretend they had no sacred secrets, only profane ones. Anybody with knowledge of the Indian mind can see they would try to mislead Hodgson by pretending to him all was sham so that he would lose interest, and cease to profane the precincts with his presence.

This may illuminate the latter story of Damodar. Unable to endure the Europeans left at Adyar after Olcott's return to Burma, he determined to find his Master Koot Hoomi and set out for Tibet. When Olcott returned to Adyar, he met the chief of the coolies who had accompanied Damodar from Darjeeling into Sikkim, by whom he had sent back certain things, including his diary, up to the date he was last seen. From this it appeared he had received assurance that somebody would come from Tibet to fetch him and that a meeting-point had been arranged. On 23 April 1885, after giving his diary to the chief of the returning coolies, he was seen climbing a

steep path alone. Malicious people tormented Olcott by telling him his clothes and bon⟨
been found only a little further along it. Olcott did not doubt that Damodar's clothes had been
found. The light garments he had worn in India would have afforded too little protection against
the Tibetan climate, and when he changed them for the warm Tibetan clothes brought to him,
he probably just dropped the ones he had come in at the roadside as a symbol that his old life
had been left behind.

Over a year later, Olcott received at Adyar, on 7 June 1886, a letter sent to him from a Mr
Tookaram Tatya, dated 5 June and posted in Bombay. On a blank page he found precipitated a
letter concerning Damodar:[6]

> The poor boy has had his *fall*. Before he could stand in the presence of the 'Masters' he
> had to undergo the severest trials that a neophyte ever passed through, to atone for the
> many questionable doings in which he had over-zealously taken part, bringing disgrace
> upon the sacred science and its adepts. The mental and physical suffering was too much
> for his weak frame, which has been quite prostrated, but he will recover in course of time.
> This ought to be a warning to you all. You have believed 'not wisely but too well'. To
> unlock the gates of the mystery you must not only lead a life of the strictest probity, but
> learn to discriminate truth from falsehood. You have talked a great deal about karma but
> have hardly realized the true significance of that doctrine. The time is come when you
> must lay the foundation of that strict conduct – in the individual as in the collective body –
> which, ever wakeful, guards against conscious as well as unconscious deception.
>
> K.H.

Damodar had reached his Master, the Master he had longed to meet face to face since first he
had seen him in a dream as a child, but not exactly to be told 'Well done!' for his part in the
Hodgson affair.

CHAPTER 62

Würzburg

In her last letter to Sinnett from Torre del Greco, Madame Blavatsky says she is leaving for a place in Germany called Würzburg,[1] 'It is near Heidelberg and Nuremberg, and all the centres one of the Masters lived in, and it is He who advised my Master to send me there'. The reference is perhaps to the Hungarian Master who, as the Comte de Saint-Germain, lived from 1774 to 1775 in Schwabach and Anspach – though one of the other Adepts is said to have lived in Nuremberg in the fifth century. Madame Blavatsky was concerned for Koot Hoomi.

On arrival she wrote to Sinnett:[2]

> 6, Ludwig Strasse,
> Würzburg
> 19th August, 1885

> . . . If you have never given a thought to what may be His suffering in the *human* intervals of His Mahatmaship – then you have something yet to learn. 'You were warned' says His Chohan – and He answers – 'I was'. Still He says He is glad he is yet no Mejnoor, no dried up plant, and that had He to suffer over and over again – He would still do the same for He knows that real good for humanity has come out of all this suffering, and that books such as *Esoteric Buddhism* and *Karma* would not have been written for years to come had He not communicated with you, and had not orders been given to me to do what I have done – stupidly sometimes as I may have carried them out.

She says that Madame Coulomb,[3] 'began building her plan of treachery in 1880 from the first day she landed in Bombay with her husband, both shoeless and penniless . . . She offered to sell *my secrets* to the Rev. Bowen of the *Bombay Guardian* in July 1880 . . .'. She also says that she remembered the Buddha's injunction to feed even a starving serpent, and tried not to hate her.

Madame Blavatsky is indignant against Hodgson and Sidgwick,[4] 'What right have they to accept the Coulomb letters as *genuine* when I have never been allowed to look at one? Hodgson came daily to dine and eat and drink at Adyar; he had them in his pocket . . .'. Ill, she had been unable to leave her room; he had come up several times to see her, but not to give her a chance.[4]

> Of course, without seeing the *letters*, I cannot help you to any clue to the mystery. I know how it was done . . . Alexis Coulomb's handwriting is naturally like mine. We all know how Damodar was once deceived by an order *in my handwriting* to go upstairs and seek for me in the bedroom in Bombay when I was in Allahabad. It was a trick of M. Coulomb, who thought it good fun to deceive him, 'a chela' . . . Unfortunately that bit of a note was not preserved . . . I have seen Coulomb copying one of such scraps of mine, at his table, in a scene shown to me by Master in the astral light . . .

Actually, Madame Blavatsky's hand is not difficult to copy. I made some experiments, incorporating left-hand gap and so on – and next morning wondered, for a moment, why there were scraps in Madame Blavatsky's writing lying about.

In a letter mentioning Hodgson, Koot Hoomi writes to Sinnett,[5] 'You must have understood by this time, my friend, that the centenial [*sic*] attempt made by us every century to open the eyes of this blind world – has nearly failed'. The words 'every century' have been crossed out, so 'centennial' is clearly meant. He refers to the dissensions that have riven the Society. At Adyar, the Indians chelas now hate the Europeans, and Hartmann and Lane-Fox hate Damodar, now removed to Tibet. Whilst this renders the Society vulnerable, yet a trial of this sort was inevitable. In ancient Egypt, the candidate for initiation was subjected to testing ordeals, which western Freemasonry did its best to reproduce by mechanical means. All these were to bi. the latent weaknesses within a controlled framework:[6]

> The aspirant is now assailed entirely on the psychological side of his nature. His course of testing – in Europe and India – is that of Raj-yog and its result is . . . to develop every germ good and bad in him in his temperament. The rule is inflexible, and not one escapes whether he but writes us a letter, or in the privacy of his own heart's thought formulates a strong desire for occult communication and knowledge . . . as the water develops the heat of caustic lime so does the teaching bring into fierce action every unsuspected potentiality latent in him.

Might I offer the Master a couple of gardener's images? Hot-house cultivation brings plants on faster, but develops any fungi they may have on them. Fertiliser brings on the plants you want, but also the weeds you don't. In a sense, the latter are easier to seize and pull out when they have become large enough to see, which may have been what Jesus meant when he spoke of the tares in the wheat. This applies not only in the sense of a few members of a specially brought on group developing badly, but within the community of each individual's thoughts and feelings; along with spiritual aspiration may come pride, intolerance, rivalry and the rest. Therefore some get swamped. Hence the danger of premature candidatures. This needs to be remembered even in the case of the wretched Coulombs.

In Europe, both Mohini and Babaji were giving trouble. Mohini had been walking in a wood near Paris with a Miss Leonard when she bared her bosom to him. This he told to Babaji, who told Solovioff, who told Madame de Morsier; she may have been the one who told Madame Blavatsky. The latter 'cold with horror',[7] Mohini being a chela vowed to celibacy, wrote a letter referring to Miss Leonard as a Messalina and a Potiphar. She next received a letter from Miss Leonard's solicitor, threatening action for libel, but addressing the envelope to 'Mme. Metrovitch otherwise Mme. Blavatsky',[8] which itself would give cause for such action. All calmed down when the solicitor, without denying his client's gesture, offered to show Madame Blavatsky letters from Mohini to her[9] which would make clear that it had not been unprovoked but solicited by him, and far from disgusting had delighted him.[10] Deeming therefore that his chela's conduct was a matter only for the Master Koot Hoomi, Madame Blavatsky sent the solicitor a letter of apology to his client for having called her a 'Messalina' and a 'Potiphar'. (She realised Miss Leonard was like the rest of them wrestling with the Dweller.)

Far worse, Olcott seemed to have doubted her. This emerges from a letter she wrote to Sinnett,[11] '. . . *poor, poor Olcott*, I can never cease loving him, one who was my devoted friend and defender for ten years, my *chum* . . .'. If he had had his hour of losing faith, it would explain why he dragged his feet when she wanted him to initiate an action for libel against the Coulombs. Truly, the 'hour of trial' had come, not only for the Society and its minor members, but for the 'chums'.

On the last day of 1885, somebody brought her the Hodgson Report.

CHAPTER 63

The Hodgson Report

Hodgson believed the Coulomb letters to be genuine. From that first mistake followed all the others. Nobody who believed Madame Blavatsky had written those horrible letters could believe her in anything, and seriously to investigate anything claimed by her would be a waste of time. Ours is wasted by detailed analysis of the Hodgson Report (as they call it in the Society for Psychical Reearch today, emphasising that responsibility for it rests upon him and those others whose names appear as of the Committee that adopted it, and not upon the Society, which has no corporate view).

Briefly, Hodgson decided to believe the Coulombs in everything. He believed the Mahatmas to be Monsieur Coulomb, wearing over his head and shoulders the dummy head and shoulders cut out and painted by his wife. Apparently it had no eye-holes, for Coulomb explained that by looking straight downwards he could see from inside it sufficiently well to walk. Did it not occur to Hodgson that painted, unblinking eyes, with eyeballs that never moved, could never be taken for those of a real person? Olcott had seen Morya very close, when he came to the house in Bombay in 1880. Morya's height, given by Olcott as 6 ft 6 in. or 6 ft 7 in., would make him difficult to impersonate. If Coulomb had been this height, Hodgson would have told us to clinch the case. Did it not occur to Hodgson that for a person to talk through a dummy head there must be a slit for the mouth, otherwise the sound would be coming from the wrong placè, a mouth, moreover, that must be seen to move with the articulation of speech? Did it not occur to Hodgson that voices are distinctive, and that Olcott must at once have recognised Coulomb's? Could Coulomb ride a horse? Morya's horse was seen by several as he rode up on it, dismounted and left it tethered outside.

Likewise with the meetings with Koot Hoomi; at Amritsar, for instance, would the Sikhs guarding the shrine have accepted amongst their number Monsieur Coulomb with a dummy head and shoulders over his own? At the second of the meetings in Lahore, when both Brown and Damodar were with him, there was considerable conversation. Olcott comments on the special sweetness of Koot Hoomi's voice.

On only one point does Hodgson differ from the Coulombs. They proclaimed all the persons who saw or received letters from any of the Masters were dupes of Madame Blavatsky, including Damodar and excluding only Pillai. Hodgson makes Damodar and Pillai confederates. He did not like Damodar, perhaps because Olcott had said Damodar could travel in the astral, perhaps because Damodar had refused to let him into Madame Blavatsky's rooms in her absence and indeed because Damodar had encouraged him to imagine the phenomena fake, perhaps for a combination of all these reasons. The reason why Casava Pillai had to be made a confederate is that he spoke Tamil, and somebody speaking Tamil was needed to have spoken to Ramaswamier in that language when impersonating Morya to him in Sikkim.[1] Hodgson does not ask whether Pillai could ride a horse; a person who has not ridden before cannot just mount one and ride. Morya approached at the gallop in wild country and it was his horsemanship that caused Ramaswarmier to take him for one of the Raja's officers. Now it happens that Pillai did on one occasion don the yellow robe and cap of the Gelukpa. This was on instructions from Koot Hoomi, in two letters,[2] undated but received in 1882 while Madame Blavatsky was in Bombay, at some time between her visit to Nellore (mentioned) and her removal to Adyar at the end of the year. One of the letters (the first?) fell to him in the compartment of a train in which he was travelling from Allahabad to Mogul Sarai, a railway junction near Benares. The purpose of this dressing up was, however, that thus clad he should accompany another chela to see Sinnett at his home. Now, an element of play-acting has here to be admitted since it should not have been necessary for Pillai to appear in this attire; but I would guess that Sinnett had become childishly importunate in his expressions of desire to see some outward and visible sign that it was really someone in Tibet from whom he received the letters. Koot Hoomi probably did not wish to break some Tibetan chela's training just to send him on what should have been an unnecessary errand, and chose instead to send a walking cap and gown prop in the person of Pillai, who wanted an occasion to redeem an indiscretion at Nellore in showing everyone the first letter he received. If on his return from the Sinnetts' he was so indiscreet as to boast of having worn the yellow hat and robe, it could have given the Coulombs the idea of transporting the episode to Sikkim, to 'meet' Ramaswamier's testimony. Moreover, such a second indiscretion would explain why Pillai figures amongst those who, having been given some encouragement at the beginning, were dropped.

But what is it Hodgson conceives? That Madame Blavatsky, when ill, set out upon a long and exhausting journey from Bombay to Sikkim, to meet no one, on the offchance that despite her feints she would be followed by someone who would, in a wild place, encounter Pillai, all dressed up, and be addressed by him in Tamil? Suppose the hoped-for persistent follower had been one whose native tongue was Hindi, Gujerati, Marathi or Telugu? In any case, we know that Ramaswamier brought Olcott Morya's answer to a question that had not gone through Madame Blavatsky.

Naturally, there is a great deal in the Hodgson Report about the shrine. By going on and on about it, the impression is created that its authenticity or otherwise is of cardinal importance. Even today, one meets people who imagine the allegation it had a false back puts in question the authenticity of *The Mahatma Letters*. The questions are unrelated. What people understand by *The Mahatma Letters* is the volume of letters from Morya and Koot Hoomi to Sinnett, published in Barker's edition under that title, the manuscript mass of which is filed at the British Museum as The Mahatma Papers. These are the letters that contain the teachings. There are 129 of them, occupying 456 pages of print. They reached him at his home in Allahabad, in Simla, in London or wherever he was staying. Only one, occupying about two pages, came through the shrine, and it contains nothing of importance.

Those interested in the shrine will find a detailed analysis of its construction in *The Hall of Magic Mirrors* by Victor Endersby, an engineer who shows the impediments there would have been to its operation in the manner described. Adlai Waterman (Walter Carrithers) in his monograph *Obituary: The 'Hodgson Report'*, challenges the good faith of Hodgson with regard to his plan of the premises. In particular, Mr Carrithers notes (on his p.39) that Hodgson's p.326 bears a citation of Mrs Morgan's statement that Madame Blavatsky had a sideboard made on which the servants could set dishes, pushed by them through the hatch in the north wall of her room, so as not to disturb her by coming in to lay the table. Madame Coulomb (on her p.71) inadvertently described this sideboard as 'a corner buffet', that is, triangular, so that it would fit into the north-west corner, its north side beneath the hatch. However, Hodgson, in his plan, has moved the sideboard to almost the middle of the west wall, so as to be opposite the shrine in the occult room and appear to illustrate his assertion (p.221) that its purpose was to hide the hole through from her room to the back of the shrine. In this position it would not have been accessible from the hatch, and why make a triangular or corner-sideboard except to fit into a corner?

But anyway, what communications came through the shrine? Ten short notes to Olcott, mostly from Illarion; one or two from Morya, occupying eight pages in the large print and smaller page size of *Letters from the Masters of Wisdom* (second series); the last three notes from Morya to Ramaswamier, occupying just over two nearly empty pages in the same; possibly one or two (but certainly a minority) of the notes from Koot Hoomi to Mohini Chatterjee; and the few lines relative to the saucer found there by General Morgan in Madame Blavatsky's absence and Madame Coulomb's presence.

As one would expect, Hodgson tries to prove that the Mahatma Letters were written by Madame Blavatsky. One opens out two plates of what appear to be facsimiles of passages in Madame Blavatsky's hand and Koot Hoomi's hand (from samples submitted by Sinnett) and also lines of isolated letters abstracted from the two hands, intended to demonstrate their similarity. They are not facsimiles. They are in Hodgson's words (see p.284) 'copied from tracings of my own made from the original documents, and hence many of them exhibit a tremulous appearance which is not characteristic of the original MS'. Mrs Sidgwick admits the point and its disadvantages (p.379), yet avers 'Still, they are quite sufficiently accurate to help the reader understand the discussion'. No: their being copies of tracings made by Hodgson makes them worthless. As photolithography was available at that date, one can think of no reason for using this method, save that Hodgson wished to strengthen and exaggerate the similarities in order to make his points more 'plainly'.

The similarity between Madame Blavatsky's and Koot Hoomi's hands to which Hodgson attaches the most importance is that in both can sometimes be found a small 'a' with a gap in the left-hand side. 'It is so peculiar that were it found but rarely in both sets of writings, or commonly in one and rarely in the other, it would still be a tolerably definite indication of identity of handiwork . . .' But it is not all that peculiar. Scattered through Eric Singer's several books on graphology, there appear amongst his samples in very different hands, mostly chosen to illustrate some quite different point, small 'a's in which the gap occurs on the left. Dr Vernon Harrison, a consultant graphologist specialising in detection of forgery, assures us that he has on his files a number of specimens with this left-hand gap, notably in President Eisenhower's hand.

Coming to faults in English,[3] Hodgson notes Madame Blavatsky and Koot Hoomi both write 'your's' for 'yours' and 'thiefs' for 'thieves'; but trouble with the apostrophe and failure to recognise an irregular plural are both common to foreigners. I am surprised to find in his Koot Hoomi column 'fulfill, dispel' against Blavatsky's 'expell'. One does not even need to be a foreigner to double a letter where it should be single, or the reverse. More significant is 'defense', in both hands, which is French for 'defence', but if that is the worst Hodgson can do on spelling, it is not much.

Coming to phrases, Hodgson offers 'I give you an advice' (Koot Hoomi) against 'to give as impartial an evidence' (Blavatsky). Hodgson probably thinks both are French. The French do indeed say '*un témoignage*', which is what Blavatsky means by 'an evidence', and '*un conseil*', literally 'an advice'; but so do the Germans: '*einen Rat folgen*' is (literally translated) 'to take an advice'. The mistake is therefore one which must come naturally to German-speaking people as well as to those who speak French. Hodgson gives 'the best she knew how' (Koot Hoomi) against 'the best I knew how' (Blavatsky). Now it is true that the French say 'the best' where we would say, 'as well as', but so do the Germans. He gives 'along hundred of side-furrows' (Koot Hoomi) against 'with hundred others' (Blavatsky); but English seems to be peculiar in wanting either 'a hundred' or else 'hundreds of'. There are several examples of wrong prepositions and mistakes in the sequence of tenses of verbs, but what foreigners do not make them? There is one real classic, 'one who understands tolerably well English' (Koot Hoomi) against 'you speak very well English' (Blavatsky). If there is a mistake I have had to correct more often than any in the English of foreigners, it is this one, the placing of the adverb between the verb and its direct object. In *Living English Structure*, W. Stannard Allen,[4] the book out of which I used to teach idiomatic structures to foreign students recommended to me for private coaching by the Phonetics Department of University College, London, the following is stated in the chapter on adverb order (on p.11); 'Students especially those speaking Latin and Slavonic languages are very fond of separating verb and object with an adverb, "I speak well English" '. Certainly French has '*Il parle bien l'Anglais*' and in a great crowd of other languages the structure is the same (though curiously in Russian the adverb comes first – '*On xorosho govereet po-Ruski*' – 'He very well speaks Russian'). But many Asians also place the adverb between the verb and its object. I have had a good deal to do with Indians, corresponded with them, taught them and helped to mark examination papers for Cambridge Higher Certificate sent in from schools in Asia. There are examples of the structure in the writings of the Indians quoted in Theosophic literature and in the SPR Report; for instance, on p.109 of the 1884 Report, in the testimony of Prince Harisinghji Rupsinghji, 'I visited again the shrine', instead of, 'I visited the shrine again', or 'I again visited the Shrine', or even, 'Again I visited the Shrine'. This sequence ought to be impossible in German, which has the verb at the end of the sentence; yet we find in Hartmann's pamphlet, p.45, 'Damodar re-opened in an instant the Shrine', a whole adverbial phrase that should have gone either at the beginning or the end, and Hartmann was an American-born German.

It is not by showing this structure common to Koot Hoomi and Blavatsky that one will prove them to be one person; by that reasoning Prince Harisinghji Rupsinghji and Dr Hartmann should both be Madame Blavatsky in disguise. Hodgson was not an expert in linguistics. His contention is that Koot Hoomi's mistakes are French, whereas his peculiarities ought to be German rather than French[5] (presumably because he spoke with Professor Fechner, who lectured at Leipzig); but as we have seen above, several of the mistakes are of a kind that can equally well be made by Germans, not to speak of orientals. There is, however, just one of Hodgson's pairs of parallels that is perhaps significant, 'So more the pity for him' (Koot Hoomi), 'So more the pity for those' (Blavatsky).

It is a pity Hodgson does not identify the letters of Madame Blavatsky from which he picks his samples, to permit us to check them.

As to the handwriting samples sent to F.G. Netherclift for his opinion, Netherclift is now known to have made mistakes in other cases, and handwriting experts are today no longer as sure as they were of their ability to distinguish hands. The K.H. handwriting I shall consider later, but with regard to the papers sent to Netherclift[6] as the 'incriminating' letters of Madame Blavatsky, how do we know they were the pages bearing the supposed 'incriminating' passages composed by the Coulombs? He may have been sent a few of the innocent pages genuinely by Madame Blavatsky. He may have been comparing Blavatsky with Blavatsky and, of course, said they were the same, unaware that the passages supposed to be 'incriminating' were not amongst those shown him. After all, he will not have understood what the whole controversy was about. Suspicion that the selection of the papers submitted to Netherclift was not made honestly deepens when one sees that one of the documents submitted to him for comparison with Madame Blavatsky's 'acknowledged hand' was the envelope addressed by her to Madame Coulomb. Whatever was the point of submitting the envelope? There was no 'incriminating passage' on the envelope. As Madame Blavatsky herself pointed out to Hodgson, exhibition of an empty envelope does not constitute proof of what it is alleged once to have contained. He had not taken the point, but had submitted it to Netherclift as constituting one of the 'incriminating' documents, which was futile and deliberately dishonest. The other documents mentioned are a letter beginning '*Ma Chère Madame Coulomb*', text unspecified, and one beginning, '*Ma belle chère amie*'.

Several of Madame Blavatsky's letters begin '*Ma chère Madame Coulomb*' (My dear Madame Coulomb). There is no saying which one this is, and it may have been a genuine one in which nothing forged was inserted. Netherclift, however, lists one of those submitted to him as beginning, '*Ma belle, chère amie*' (My beautiful dear friend). None of the letters printed in Madame Coulomb's pamphlet or the Hodgson Report begin thus. Madame Coulomb was not beautiful, according at any rate to Hartmann's description. Can this be a letter Madame Blavatsky had written to somebody else, which Madame Coulomb sequestered instead of posting? Hartmann says she was given to picking up correspondence not addressed to her. The only thing I can find in the printed letters at all resembling it (Coulomb, p.63), occurs not at the beginning but near the end of a letter, when, apparently answering a question, Madame Blavatsky tells Madame Coulomb she can use the carriage to go to church . . . 'even to the Archbishop . . . *Enfin, cela vous regarde, ma belle amie, cela vous regarde*' (Well, it's your affair, my beautiful friend, it's your affair). Here it is mildly mocking. I cannot see anything damaging in the passage even if Madame Blavatsky did write it. She was frank about not liking 'Churchianity' and it may be genuine.

One item in Netherclift's list, 'The Mahatma has heard' may be a three-line scrap (Coulomb, p.66), in which the Mahatma is made to say some request will be granted on condition of patronage. Against this, Madame Blavatsky has written 'A lie', but there could have been other letters containing this phrase.

Netherclift appears not to have been shown any of the 'incriminating' passages in ungrammatical and bastard Italian–French. Not only were these the essential passages which should have been shown to him – and to Sims of the British Museum, from whom a second opinion was sought – but samples of the Coulombs' hands should have been submitted to them for comparison. The question should have been: 'These are the passages in dispute, this is Madame Blavatsky's hand, these are Monsieur and Madame Coulomb's hands; which of the three hands do the disputed passages most resemble?' The experts were given no chance.

It is important that both Netherclift and Sims first thought the Mahatma Letters were *not* by Madame Blavatsky. It was only after Hodgson had called on them and, very improperly, pointed out to them similarities they had failed to notice that (he says) they changed their opinions to accord with his.[7] In other words, Hodgson interfered with these witnesses. Likewise, he interfered with Hume. Hume wrote him a letter saying that, although all connection between himself and Madame Blavatsky had long ceased, he did not believe that a woman as clever as she was would have been so stupid as to write to Madame Coulomb the purported letters, which would put her in her power. He thought that some parts only might be genuine. Hodgson tells us that he afterwards laid before Hume evidence that caused Hume to change his opinion. But he does not present a statement of Hume in which this change of opinion is expressed. We have it only as 'hearsay' from Hodgson that Hume was brought to bring his opinion into line.[8] In a law court, such tampering would not be tolerated.

A note is contributed by Mrs Eleanor Sidgwick concerning the two phenomena which took place in the absence of Madame Blavatsky, in trains. Regarding the train from Paris to Calais, in which Olcott and Mohini testified they had a carriage to themselves all the way, she suggests either Madame Blavatsky or Babula, since they were in Paris at that time, must have got into the carriage before Olcott and Mohini did, and tucked the letter up somewhere so that the motion of the train when it started would dislodge it and make it fall down to Olcott as if miraculously.[9] This ignores Olcott's statement that nobody entered the carriage even for a moment except the porter who put in their luggage, and begs the question how Madame Blavatsky could know in which carriage they would sit.

As to the train between Dresden and Leipzig, Mrs Sidgwick notes it as suspicious that Olcott and Hübbe-Schleiden were not alone in the carriage. One of the other passengers could have been a confederate.[8]

It is very easy just to suppose in this way. As Kingsland says, 'might have', 'may have' and 'could have' appear throughout the Report.[10]

When Hodgson went to see Madame Coulomb at St Tome, she told him that with regard to Mohini's account being in Madame Blavatsky's sitting-room with her and Damodar when they had seen the Master Koot Hoomi on the terrace, it was she, Madame Coulomb, who had on this occasion impersonated the Mahatma. She had changed into a long muslin robe, in the bathroom (later Damodar's room), put the dummy head and shoulders on over her own and, carrying a bunch of roses, passed through a cupboard with a secret double back into the occult room. From it there was a door to the terrace. There, she crouched low and crept along until she was before the window of the sitting-room, where she raised herself up and was seen. She produced the roses as if miraculously from the folds of her muslin robe and threw them to those in the sitting-room. Mohini had said that the Mahatma looked so real they had asked him to prove he was there only in his astral body by vanishing miraculously, moving away from a tree, lest it be thought to have been utilised, to the end of the terrace, from which there was no way down. Koot Hoomi walked to the end of the terrace and vanished. How she managed to vanish must have posed a problem for Madame Coulomb, but Hodgson does not require her to answer it. He has her proceed east and 'pass through the new room' (which, however, had not been built at the time in question, although he misleadingly shows it on his plan) and then says there were any number of ways by which she might have got down from the terrace, a drop of 15 or 20 ft according to Mohini's estimation. She could have climbed from it into a tree (despite Mohini's statement that there was no tree nearby), she could have descended a ladder or she could simply have leaped or dropped. 'Indeed, I have myself often, as a lad, performed a greater "drop" feat than would be required for leaving the terrace without the help even of a ladder'.[11] That is as may be, but Madame Coulomb was not a lad. We do not know her age, but Hartmann's description is of an elderly woman, and handicapped by wearing a dummy head without eye-holes – unless the phantom of the projected new room gave her cover behind which to take it off. So cumbered, it would have been hard enough even to get over the balustrade without having to negotiate a ladder, spring into and descend a tree, leap or hang drop. But what is really outrageous is that Hodgson does not require her to commit herself as to how she got down, but leaves her with all her options open.

How could Professor and Mrs Sidgwick have accepted such slovenly investigation? Surely, it was obvious from this one story that Madame Coulomb would make up *anything*.

There is a further point, disguised from them by Hodgson's presentation. Madame Coulomb claimed to have destroyed the dummy head 'in a fit of disgust' long before the headquarters was moved to Adyar. How, then, was she able to use it at Adyar. How, indeed, had her husband managed to disguise himself in it in order to pretend to the Ross Scotts and others to be the Mahatma Morya in December 1881, seeing that the reference to its destruction ended a purported letter of Madame Blavatsky saying she would not be back before 25 October? And how had Pillai been able to disguise himself in it to ride about in Sikkim to astonish Ramaswamier in the autumn of the following year? Hodgson gets her out of her difficulty; he noted, 'she afterwards made another'.[12] This is not, however, stated by Madame Coulomb either in the articles in the *Christian College Magazine* or in her pamphlet. Probably she had never noticed that the opening paragraphs of Madame Blavatsky's letter from Simla to which she and her husband supplied the forged ending about 'Christofolo' date it prior to 25 October 1881. Hodgson, however, had noticed the difficulty. He covered up for her, omitting from his quotation the sentences that date it so awkwardly early, yet – just in case Sidgwick or anybody else should have the *Christian College Magazine* or the pamphlet to hand and notice the devastating contradiction within Madame Coulomb's testimony – added on his own initiative, 'she afterwards made another'. He left them to suppose she must have said it somewhere within the pamphlet if they could only find the place, and gave himself the option, in case they pressed him, of saying she told him by word of mouth. I must agree with Mr Carrithers, who I see noted this point in his monograph, that it destroys Hodgson's integrity. He was not the honest investigator deceived by the Coulombs' craft; he was the crafty counsel for the prosecution veiling from the jury a fatal flaw in the testimony of the chief witness he had called. Hodgson was a Doctor of Laws.

At Adyar, Hodgson had been shown a saucer which he had been assured (by whom?) was the one that had been in the shrine. When he saw Madame Coulomb at St Tome, however, she showed him one like it but broken and stated that her husband had, during the moments General Morgan supposed him to be fetching glue, opened the back of the shrine, removed these pieces and substituted one that was intact. She had, she said, bought both the saucers from a shop in Madras for 2 rupees 8 annas each. Hodgson enquired at the shop and was told they had sold two porcelain pin-trays, for cash, at 2 rupees 8 annas the pair, in July and that Madame Coulomb was in the shop on that day.[13] How was this known? Did she buy something else for which she paid by cheque or which she had debited to an account? Hodgson does not tell us. He does not tell us whether the shop sold, or did not sell, any pin-trays at a date subsequent to the phenomenon, or whether they formed a unique pair or formed part of a mass-produced range. The anna was a sixteenth part of a rupee, and the rupee, the Bank of England tells me, stood in 1883 at 1s. 7½d. Decimalised, that is 9p. Multiplying by 15 to bring it to its purchasing power in the early 1980s, that gives us a price of £3.37. Whether this was for the pair or each one, it is not the price of an antique or rare piece such as Madame Blavatsky would be likely to place in the shrine, or such as the shop would buy from a wholesaler as a single pair. There would not be a worthwhile profit on an article priced so low unless it was dealt with in numbers, in which case one would suppose sales of it to be frequent over a period. More significant, Hodgson failed to invite Major-General Morgan to identify as one of the pin-trays the saucer or small tray he had seen in the shrine. Nobody even tells us what colour it was, or whether it was plain or patterned, modern or antique.

Madame Coulomb showed Hodgson some undergarments belonging to Madame Blavatsky, which she must have stolen. These had a metallic stain, resembling iron-mould, and she told him it was made by a musical-box she carried under her dress to produce the sound of a bell, as in the trick, 'Is your watch a repeater?'[14]

Madame Blavatsky, when Hodgson came to accuse her of this, said the stain was made by a bunch of keys she carried beneath her dress. Naturally, her word was discounted by Hodgson. Madame Coulomb had told him that on occasions the musical-box was carried by Babula, who would play it from the roof or another room or outside the house.

I obtained from the Westminster Archives a photostat of a document showing that Mrs Arundale was the owner of the whole house, 77 Elgin Crescent, and I went to see it. Including the basement and attic, there are five storeys. The basement would be the kitchen, the attic the servants' bedrooms and the second floor the bedrooms of the Arundales and their guests. The dining-room would normally be on the ground floor and the sitting-room on the first. Now, like many houses in Kensington, it has a pillared porch. On to this, somebody on the first floor could, indeed, step out, though the windows are not french ones. Theoretically, there would be nothing to prevent somebody from pushing up the lower part of one of the small windows above the porch, climbing out on to it and standing on it to play some musical instrument. But he would be very visible from the street; and as the massive porch is a notable feature of the house, would none of those persons interested in the sound, Myers, Gurney, Thurstan, Barrett, Ionides, not to speak of Mrs and Miss Arundale, have thought to look out through the big front windows of the sitting-room to see if there was someone standing on the porch producing it? The psychical researchers had all thought the sound came from within the room, from somewhere in the air above the table. It was midmorning, so the curtains would be open.

What is particularly bad is that the Final Report makes no mention that Myers, Gurney and Thurstan had testified to the genuineness of the bell phenomena, and that their testimonies had been cancelled from the proofs of the 1884 Report, the whole bell phenomena being deemed of too little importance to enter into. It became of sufficient importance only when Madame Coulomb alleged it was fake, so the defence was cancelled and the prosecution substituted. Specially relevant in the cancelled passages was Myers' point that the sound was not like that produced in the trick 'Is your watch a repeater?' To cancel this assertion of Myers and yet insert Madame Coulomb's assertion that it was as in 'Is your watch a repeater?' was iniquitous. How could Sidgwick have preferred the testimony of a woman such as Madame Coulomb to that of trusted members of his own Committee?

Evidence was of sufficient interest to merit inclusion only when it was against Madame Blavatsky. What kind of a court is this – for, make no mistake, this is not an investigation but a prosecution – in which the prosecutor sits on the bench with the judge, witnesses are coached in what they have to say, and witnesses for the defence are suppressed by decree?

It is a curious weakness of the Report as a whole that it does not consider what the Mahatma Letters say. This, to my mind, is as though, on receiving a letter from some foreign country, one should spend all one's time arguing as to whether it had come by air mail or surface instead of opening and reading it. Their contents are surely relevant to their authorship. Can one really imagine that the author of profoundly penetrating and thoughtful teachings, such as those given in the notes to Hume and in the letters to Sinnett capable of descending to the silly little fake magical tricks with which Hodgson imagines Madame Blavatsky constantly to occupy her time? It makes no kind of sense.

But one must not omit Hodgson's conclusion. He is faced with the question why Madame Blavatsky should have spent her days 'in the production of a varied and long-continued series of fraudulent phenomena'.[15] He could not attribute the foundation of the Theosophical Society to her desire to make money, since its officers told him it was largely dependent on gifts of money from her. Therefore, he decided she was a Russian spy. Why? Madame Coulomb had shown him a piece of writing in Madame Blavatsky's hand, referring to 'the approaching act of the Eastern drama' and saying it will require 'more careful preparation than did the last war'. The facsimile he reproduces shows the paragraph to start in the middle of a sentence, and to end with the words, 'their country and their Czar',[16] enclosed in quotation marks. The quotation marks re-open before the next paragraph, which begins beneath it. The whole fragment is, therefore, extracted from the words of somebody else.

Madame Blavatsky told Hodgson the passage was from a Russian work she had translated for Mr Sinnett, for *The Pioneer*.[17] Sinnett later confirmed this, writing that the passage was from Colonel Grodekoff's *Travels in Central Asia*, which he had commissioned her to translate from the Russian for serialisation in *The Pioneer*.[18] The serial ran for several weeks. The passage in question was not one of those printed, but he had had to commission her to translate the whole book as without seeing the whole of it in English he could not pick out the parts suitable for printing. Hodgson nevertheless reproduced it in the Report as his 'evidence' against her.

He says he told her one day that according to the newspapers there were Russian military movements on the Afghan border. She showed 'excitement', and exclaimed that 'it would be the death-blow of the Society if they got into India.[19] To Hodgson's convoluted mind, this was proof that he had surprised her into disguising from him that what she wanted was the contrary of what she said. He has no other 'evidence'.

Does it not occur to Hodgson that all the manipulations with which he credits her would leave her no time for spying? Perhaps he has not studied espionage. Spies of the highest class insert themselves into the services of the country on which they are spying; those in the lowest in taverns and brothels frequented by soldiers and sailors. In the one case as in the other, the spy has to fit into the surroundings and not stand out.

Madame Blavatsky had no access to papers or persons to spy on. There is just one way in which a cultural society may be sinister; that is by serving as a recruiting ground. People may be drawn to it to study the art of philosophy of a foreign country; then tendentious ideas are put to them, and if they respond it is suggested to them they might like to do some work for it. A most suspicious thing is if it is not appealing for funds. A society genuinely concerned only with philosophy, poetry or the like has difficulty in paying its way. If all its literature is most beautifully printed upon the best quality paper and its premises are expensive, then, if the subscription fees multiplied by the number of the members are not sufficient to pay these costs, and it is not appealing for funds, there is hidden money behind it. Is this shown in the annual balance sheet? The source may be some harmless, wealthy person – or a foreign power. In the latter case, indicative clues are likely to be found even in the public lectures and literature on the bookstall. If the Theosophical Society was serving as a cover for Russian interests, there should have been literature tending to show how much better treated the Czar's Asian subjects were than those of the British Crown, suggestions for Indo-Russian cultural exchanges, implication of deep cultural affinity between India and Russia and sponsored visits to Russia. If British intelligence had the least suspicion of the Society, it would have had one or two men join to find out about it. The Society showed no symptoms of unexplained income, and never promoted interest in Russia. (In the twentieth century, Annie Besant would work for Indian independence, but she was not on the scene yet, and her attitude in many ways departed from Madame Blavatsky's.)

Again, if I put myself into the skin of a British intelligence officer of that time who was wondering if it was for any Russian purpose Madame Blavatsky had come to India, the thing to check up on would have been her contacts. Did she direct her steps to persons known or suspected of Russian agency? Here, it is curious to note that the only person amongst those with whom she came in contact who is known to have expressed himself open to solicitation from Russia, Hume, received from Koot Hoomi a rebuke for priding himself on not being a patriot. Had Madame Blavatsky and the teachers from whom she took her orders been working in the Russian interest, they would have seized on Hume, whereas they dropped him – dropped the man who would become known as the Father of the Indian National Congress (he became its first General Secretary in 1884).

Koot Hoomi's warning to Sinnett that Russia was massing troops on Tibet's Chinese border was meant for transmission to the British government; and only two days after, Madame Blavatsky had written to Sinnett (on 2 November 1880) that her letters *From Caves and Jungles of Hindostan* to the Moscow *Gazette* were so little 'a secret that in my last letter to the Russian papers from Simla it was from some of the officials themselves that I got the needed information'. Now, if this means anything at all, it means the British had, on that occasion, used her for what is known in the jargon of the intelligence services as 'disinformation' – probably only of the simple, bluffing kind, that all along India's northern borders there were British troops massed in inconceivable density. She acted as a British agent, not professionally (her spirit would have revolted against it) or continually, but she did at that moment. Her temperamental sympathies were with the Indians, and she did not love the British, whom she felt to be stiff in their manners and unintuitive; but politically, she accepted the edict of Shigatsè that they had to remain, to keep out worse, worse being her own former compatriots, the Russians. That the threat from Russia was sensed as real is shown in a cartoon by Tenniel, in *Punch*, March 1885, showing a bear glowering down from the mountains (of Tibet?) upon the plains of India, and a lion saying to him 'No, you don't'.

Not long after this we shall find Madame Blavatsky writing to Sinnett,[20] 'Master says that the hour for the retirement of you English has not struck nor will it – *till next century* and that "late enough to see even Dennie an old, old, man" as K.H. said some time ago'. Dennie was the Sinnetts' son. We first heard of him in a letter from Madame Blavatsky to Sinnett in 1880,[21] 'Mr Sinnett is advised by M to make it a special duty to prevent his little son being made to eat meat – not even fowl'. Dennie was born in May, 1877. He would, therefore, have been 70 when the British in fact withdrew from India in 1947, which makes the Masters' prophecy work out close to time.

Anyway, as Madame Blavatsky understood it from this, nineteenth century risings could only end in useless bloodbaths, and must not be encouraged. Hodgson had hold of the wrong end of the stick.

But what is one to make of Sidgwick? That is a puzzle. A classical scholar, he was Knightbridge Professor of Moral Philosophy at Cambridge. His *Method of Ethics* is respected. Broad's *Five Types of Ethical Theory*[22] gives him more space than Spinoza, Butler, Hume and Kant. The unsophisticated may be forgiven for failing to see through specious logic, but he of all people should have seen that Hodgson's list of parallel misspellings, grammatical errors and so on in Blavatsky and Koot Hoomi, whilst it might interest and suggest, could prove nothing. As it is formulated in one of Aristotle's rules relating to the syllogism, 'From two particular propositions, nothing follows'.[23] He failed to put his finger on any of the 'undistributed middles' in the logic of the argument. Let us think about the sort of people those who formed the Committee were as a group. Most were Cambridge people, closely connected. Myers and Gurney had both been Sidgwick's pupils. That probably explains why they behaved in a manner so supine, allowing their own testimonies to be cancelled on his direction; the habit of deference was ingrained in them. A Committee on which figure a man, his wife and two of his pupils can hardly be said to consist of independent persons. A jury so constituted would never be tolerated. Had their backgrounds been more miscellaneous, there would have been a better chance that at least one would stand out against the others and say 'I take a different view'. They all belonged to what C.P. Snow called 'the small world', curiously insulated from the world outside its own familiar walls. But why did they found a Society for Psychical Research if they were hostile to anything psychic? They were not absolutely hostile, but belonged to that immediate post-Darwinian generation that, having had its Christian faith shattered, asked if it might not be possible scientifically to gather evidence of man's psychic and perhaps after all immortal nature. They ought, then, to have been precisely the sort of people it was Madame Blavatsky's life work to try to help. But their tiny probes around the fringes of the vast psychic unknown were very timid. They interested themselves in ghosts and telepathy. But telepathy almost everyone experiences, and ghosts are very British. Many of the stately homes of Scotland and England boast hauntings by them, and they come on to the stage in *Macbeth*, *Hamlet* and *Julius Caesar*. Being so much a part of our heritage, it would have been natural to start by wondering if there could be something in them. No native English tradition, however, prepared them for the things Madame Blavatsky did, or said that her Mahatmas could do. Projections on the astral plane, precipitation of letters and the passage of solid objects through solid objects were too advanced for them. Their minds boggled. Perhaps, also, the very idea of there existing, in Tibet, a hierarchy of beings with minds superior to their own and powers undreamed of by the world, was not comforting but disturbing. It sounded to them like a fanciful construction. It *had* to be untrue, and had to be dismissed, almost hysterically spewed out.

In her history of *The Society for Psychical Research*, Renée Haynes writes:[24]

> Caution can all too easily harden into suspicion . . . a lethal mixture of superiority and self-righteousness which can turn what should be an impartial enquiry into a ferocious inquisition . . . any subsequent report of such an enquiry tends to be a Case for the Prosecution.

CHAPTER 64

The Mahatma Letters:
the manuscripts

The great body of the Mahatma Letters, that is, all those addressed to Sinnett, are in the British Museum. The first time I went to see them I took with me my friend, Mr Timothy d'Arch Smith. As a bibliographer, he was curious to see the paper and ink or pencil, and I could trust his expert eye not to miss anything about these. The papers upon which they were written were revealed as very miscellaneous, of all sizes, colours and characters. Some are on very thin paper, perhaps not made for writing on at all, but others are on good quality notepaper, bearing, as he drew to my attention and as I perceived for myself on holding it up to the light, the chain lines that occur in the manufacture of laid paper and the manufacturer's watermark. In other words, it could have been bought anywhere.

The ink is very strange. I had expected to find Morya's writings in red, Koot Hoomi's in blue. Nothing had prepared me for the bewildering variety of tints, shading one into another or superimposed. Particularly eye-catching is XII, which starts in red, changing on ff.118–20 through violet into blue or black. Sometimes the ink appears to have floated out from the stroke made, vaguely to surround it, as though the author had been writing in the rain or the recipient had kept it in a cupboard under a roof that leaked. It ends, 'P.S. My writing is good but the paper rather thin for penmanship. Cannot write English with a brush though; would be worse'. Morya was aware, then, that it did not look well, although he was doing his best. The paper was plainly absorbing his ink and drawing it out from his strokes after the manner of blotting paper. A brush is used to write Chinese and also Tibetan. I have a Tibetan prayer-wheel, given to my parents in 1913 by the then Prime Minister of Tibet, Kusho Horkang Dzaza; the inscription on the scrolls inside seem to have been done with a brush, moreover on very thin, almost transparent, paper, always referred to by my mother as Chinese rice-paper, which has had the same effect of sucking the ink.

Odd in a contrasting way is III B. This is the phenomenon of the 'pillow dak', the note found in Mrs Sinnett's cushion. In contrast to Morya's, it is on a good quality modern notepaper, and looks as if it was written quickly and with ease, but the ink, which starts black, shows signs of turning to red at the end. This is particularly noticeable in the signature, but appears also just above, in the cross-bar of a 't'.

The simplest explanation would be that Morya and Koot Hoomi shared the use of one desk, fitted with two ink-wells – as some used to be – one for red ink and one for black or blue, but they had between them only one pen, which, whichever ink it was dipped into, retained traces of the other. Yet in the stroke of one of Koot Hoomi's 't's in III B, the red and the black strokes seem to be separate. There is not a blend of inks, as in Morya (XII), but a writing twice, in black and in red. A lot of the letters show this overwriting, sometimes with lead pencil, sometimes with blue crayon.

The letters which are wholly in blue crayon, as are some of Koot Hoomi's, show little lines of white through the blue, as though the paper had been laid, whilst being written upon, on something such as wood or a cloth-bound book, the grain of which had come through.

In the letters written in ink, whether Koot Hoomi's or Morya's, one sees the thick and thin of a pen, and the thickening at points where it rests and returns, as in the curl of a 'c'. These are, of course, absent in the crayon, whether blue or red. But some of Morya's letters seem to start in red ink and end in red crayon.

They are very odd. They are like nothing one has ever seen before.

I wrote to the Keeper of Manuscripts, and asked if experts in the Department could, with modern procedures, say anything about the letters in the course of which the writing changed colour, asking them to be so good as to direct their attention specially to III B (Koot Hoomi's of the pillow dak) and XII (Morya). The reply I received was from Dr C.J. Wright, who had looked at them with the Conservation Officer:

> . . . we examined the signature at the bottom of III B with a microscope and came to the conclusion that the signature was written in black ink first then over-written in red ink at a time when the black ink may still have been damp. In the tail of the final 'g' the two colours are quite distinct. Letter XII we examined under a Video Spectral Comparator. Viewed under a blue-green light, through a red filter, it is quite clear that two inks are being used. On f.118, beginning with 'which possessed', the purple ink luminesces, appearing white on a television screen, while the red ink used on the first half of the folio absorbs light and appears black. It is possible that there may have been two ink-wells in use, for in some words traces of red ink clearly still adhered to the pen.

Hodgson, when he came across a place where pencil could be seen as well as ink, took it to mean that Madame Blavatsky had first written the whole letter in pencil, in a style of writing differentiated from her natural hand, and then inked it over. But no forger in the world could be so stupid as to write the forged text first in pencil and then ink it over. Surely an intending forger would have the wit to practise making the letters in the required style until they were able to create and connect them freely. Even more certainly, no forger would write first in black and then go over 'inconspicuously' in red, to make the feigned hand look more convincing. Whatever is being done, it is not tampering that tries to be inconspicuous. The writer, it seems to me, is going over his own work, trying to increase legibility. Perhaps I think of this because I so often take hurried pencil notes (as in the Manuscripts Department where pens are not allowed) and afterwards ink them over for preservation from rubbing, at the same time forming the letters more clearly. In some of the cases, I fancy the ink has been gone over in pencil so as to defeat the tendency of the unsuitable paper to draw the ink out from the strokes. My overall impression is that the writers have had difficulty with their materials, and that the constant going-over represents an attempt to surmount them.

III B, the letter that was found in the pillow, is watermarked 'L-J D L & C'. Some of Madame Blavatsky's letters (in the following files) are on paper made by the same manufacturer; for instance 45288, f.43. It is a good thing Hodgson did not notice this, or he would have used it as another nail to drive into her.

As for the handwriting, the hands of Koot Hoomi and Morya appear distinct from each other and from Madame Blavatsky's. At least, I was never in any doubt which I was looking at, though I thought I ought to ask the opinion of the Museum's expert. On this head, Dr Wright wrote:

> I fear that usually there is no hard and fast way of establishing the similarities and divergencies between one example of handwriting and another. Expert opinions tend to be only as good as the experts themselves, and the most one can hope for is a balance of probabilities. The press, as in the case of the Hitler diaries at the time of writing, tends to exaggerate the ease of the process and the certainty of the result . . .
>
> I would agree that the hands of the two Mahatmas and of Madame Blavatsky appear quite distinct, but it seems to me that there are marked similarities in some letter forms between her own hand and that ascribed to K.H. For instance the capital Ts of 'This' and 'The' in III B are very like the capital Ts in Madame Blavatsky's letters (Add.MS.45288, ff.43, 49, 50).

He thought some of their capital Ms alike, some of their capital As, and both occasionally formed a small 'a' so that the space came on the left, instead of at the top right, as in most people's writing.

Quite the most singular feature of Koot Hoomi's writing, however, is that he invariably places a horizontal line over the small 'm'. Though he explains to Sinnett that this is to prevent confusion with 'un' and similar forms, it inevitably gives it the look of Russian 't'; which consists of three vertical strokes joined at the top with a horizontal (like cricket stumps). The Russian character for the sound of our 'sh' is the same, but the other way up. When written by hand, both of these letters are formed like our 'm', but with a stroke above or below it, added afterwards, to show whether it is a 't' or a 'sh'. This roofing of the 'm' does not occur in Morya's letters. (Neither does it occur in those of Serapis – tall, narrow and pointed – or Illarion – more flowing and open, to judge from the facsimiles reproduced by Jinarajadasa; the Serapis and Illarion letters, to Olcott, are at Adyar.) It does not occur in Madame Blavatsky's own writing ever, as it would be bound to do if the idea of using a roofing stroke to distinguish letters was one into which she unconsciously lapsed even when writing English. It is special to Koot Hoomi, and appeared even in his 1870 letter to Madame Fadeyef. Again, if the idea came from Russian, there should have been a corresponding under-stroke to distinguish the 'u' or 'w', but there never is.

In his letter to Sinnett, Koot Hoomi had referred to 'my old-fashioned habit of little lines over the 'm's . . . out of tune and time with modern calligraphy'. One does not find these little lines in English writing, however old-fashioned, or in French. I again consulted Dr Wright. He said that in mediaeval Latin these little superscript lines used to be used, but above vowels, to show that 'a following "m" or "n" had been left out, for economy of space, not to distinguish letters'.

Then I thought of German, and wrote to Mrs Gabriele Reinsch of the Goethe Institute, to ask if little horizontal lines above the line were used to distinguish 'n' and 'u'. She replied, 'It was the custom in German handwriting to differentiate between "u" and "n" by making horizontal strokes above the "u" and quite a number of people still do so today'.

So there we have Koot Hoomi's use of little horizontal marks above the line to distinguish letters. Turning up my photocopies of letters of Frederick the Great, Prince Carl of Hesse-Cassel and other German contemporaries of the Comte de Saint-Germain, I saw that they always used these little marks above 'u', except where there was an umlaut.

But Mrs Reinsch added that there had been another German usage, now entirely discontinued, of using these little horizontal lines above 'm' and 'n' to show that the letter is meant to be doubled (presumably for economy of space). She sent me an example of c.1660. It seems that Koot Hoomi has confused two German uses, to put a superscript over the 'u' to distinguish it, and to put one over the 'm' for a different purpose; doubtless this is a legacy of his days in Leipzig. Hodgson wanted his style of writing, if he authentically existed, to have German 'peculiarities'. It has; and they were not recognised by Hodgson.

As to the rest, Koot Hoomi crosses his 't', often with an extraordinarily long bar. Madame Blavatsky also uses a somewhat long bar, but with pressure that is weak and wobbly, whereas his is firm. Because of his superscript lines and long 't' bars, Koot Hoomi's letters do present a somewhat spectacular series of above-the-line horizontals, what is below being rather full and nearer to upright than Madame Blavatsky's lean and forward-sloping hand. There are some similarities in the formation of letters: particularly in the occasional small 'a', in which the curve over the upper part is made not from the left but from the right, so that the space comes on the left. Nevertheless, the overall look of Koot Hoomi's writing does to some extent put me in mind of Devanagari, in which the letters are upright and rather full, many of them having horizontals at the top, so that the impression can almost be given of a line along the top from which things are hanging. Devanagari is the alphabet of Sanskrit and Hindi, and also of Tibetan – a Mongolian language written in Devanagari.

The note found in the pillow, III B, though it has the little lines over the 'm's as always and long bars to the 't's, does not have overall the typical look of Koot Hoomi's hand. Oddly, it has somewhat the look of Sinnett's, except for the signature, which is in a different, heavier hand than the rest. I am not suggesting Sinnett forged it, but this brings me to the occult side of these productions.

The 1884 Report refers, on p.20, to precipitation as being 'on previously blank paper', an impression gathered from Olcott and others, so one cannot blame Hodgson for following suit. It is what most Theosophists seem to believe. But yet, except in the cases of the drawings Madame Blavatsky caused to appear on previously blank paper and the Mahatmic messages that appeared in the blank spaces left in letters from other people, apparently imposed during transit, this description does not fit the primary data. Neither Sinnett nor Olcott exposed blank paper and waited for writing to appear on it. With the bulk of the Mahatma Letters, it was the whole letter that precipitated, paper and all, often complete with envelope, sometimes of silk, sometimes of paper printed with Chinese characters. In Lahore, Olcott felt Koot Hoomi's letter form itself within his hand. In London, Leadbeater saw a letter from Koot Hoomi form itself within Madame Blavatsky's hand. In Mohini's testimony to the SPR of 3 December 1884 he describes how, in Bombay in 1882, when he was in a room with Damodar and two others, Damodar, who had been writing at a table, called out to the others to attract their attention, and they saw a letter in the process of formation:[1]

> . . . it seemed to grow. First there was only a small bit, which expanded until an envelope was fully formed. It was addressed to one of us in the familiar writing of a Mahatma. The addressee took it up and found there were really two letters, but so closely pressed together as to be easily mistaken for one. In fact he was not sure that the second letter, which was to me, did not form itself in his hand. It is to be stated that Madame Blavatsky was not in the room at the time of this occurrence.

To Damodar and Mohini, the letters would presumably have been from Koot Hoomi. Where did the matter from which they were formed come from? We have Olcott's testimony that in New York he once saw a white mist emanate from Madame Blavatsky's body and form itself briefly into Morya (his head and shoulders only, not his full person, as when the Master entered his room on another occasion). In that particular instance, it would appear to have been from Madame Blavatsky's body that the matter was drawn out to make a temporary vehicle of the Master. I would suggest that in the case of precipitated letters, the material for the paper was drawn either from paper in the possession of the Masters or their chelas, or from paper in the possession of Madame Blavatsky or of the recipient. Then, at what moment and how was the writing imposed on it? It will be remembered that in one of his early letters, Koot Hoomi said that one of his chelas, Disinherited, had given him a stock of paper that he happened to have, but that he would have to use it sparingly as there were no stationers' shops in Tibet. Does that mean that he wrote on this paper and then the whole thing was disintegrated into minute particles, which re-assembled themselves at the place to which they were precipitated? This explanation might seem the best to fit some of the cases, particularly that of letter XII, from Morya, on the thin paper. He had obviously written that by hand, having great difficulty because of the tendency of the paper to absorb the ink. The precipitation would show all the signs of the writer's trouble with his materials, as it would be his product that would be precipitated.

On the other hand, III B was sent by Koot Hoomi from a Kashmir valley, where presumably he had no paper. He might have used his trip to Amritsar to buy paper, but even if he did, it was probably packed on to his horse and he had perhaps not thought to buy ink and a pen, having these in Tibet. Now, one remembers that in the Kiddle incident the trouble came through Koot Hoomi's precipitating while on horseback to a chela, who in his turn precipitated the letter (with mistakes) to Sinnett. One remembers also that Koot Hoomi reproached Sinnett for not showing him the proofs of *The Occult World*, as there were certain things he would never have allowed to go into print, one of them being the signature 'Koot Hoomi Lal Singh'. The 'Lal Singh' had been added by Djwal Khool, creating a sort of pseudonym he thought fitting to Koot Hoomi, but which Koot Hoomi would never have allowed. Since it had appeared on some of the letters, it had not mattered as long as they remained private, and he had forgotten about it; but he would have insisted on its removal had he seen the proofs. Now, the letter found in the pillow is signed 'Koot Hoomi Lal Singh', and therefore by Djwal Khool, and that heavy hand, which is not the hand of the main body of the letter, is Djwal Khool's hand. So, following the explanation given in the case of the Kiddle incident, Djwal Khool had to read, in some form we can only imagine, the text that Koot Hoomi was precipitating to him mentally; then, from this kind of trace on the atmosphere, he had to precipitate a text in physical ink on physical paper. Is he the person with one pen and two ink-wells? In that case, could he have precipitated XII as well, having on that occasion only thin paper to write on or, as Morya says 'my writing is good . . .', did they both have a desk with two ink-wells but only one pen? Where was Djwal Khool? One imagines him being in some intermediate place, but perhaps he was at the Masters' home in Shigatzè. When he precipitated III B, in any case, he was passing on a letter which came upon no paper and had to arrive upon paper. The paper used was some that was in

Sinnett's house; either Sinnett's or Madame Blavatsky's, as she was staying with him. Why is the writing so like Sinnett's? Perhaps because Koot Hoomi had in his mind's eye the letters he had received from Sinnett in that small, neat, running hand, and that, complete with its mark of penmanship, reproduced itself in the trace received by Djwal Khool and furthered by him into the cushion. Koot Hoomi cannot have signed it at all, since the whole of the signature, not only the 'Lal Singh', is in Djwal Khool's hand.

It is important to realise that there was, on the majority of occasions, this person in the middle through whom mistakes could occur. Madame Blavatsky was furious when she saw 'carbonic acid',[2] which was what the Master had 'dictated', so to speak, come out in the final precipitation to Hume as 'carbolic acid', through the mistake of the chela in the middle. This was not always Djwal Khool. Madame Blavatsky could precipitate, and therefore she sometimes fulfilled this role. Olcott understood this; he asked Morya how he could know which of the letters he received from him were really written by him, with his own hand, and which were written by Madame Blavatsky, for the Master, in the Master's hand, signed for him and precipitated for him. Probably the usual intermediary (or occult secretary) for Koot Hoomi was Djwal Khool, and the usual one for Morya was Madame Blavatsky. Why, then, is Koot Hoomi's writing more like hers than Morya's is? I do not know.

Djwal Khool, Madame Blavatsky explained to Sinnett, spoke English even better than Koot Hoomi did. On the other hand, she had seen other chelas precipitating who hardly knew English at all, taking the English out of her head. This, presumably, was because she was present and therefore the easiest source, and it doubtless seemed to them not to matter much if the English they found in her head was imperfect, stamped with her style, so long as it was comprehensible to the recipient. One remembers also Koot Hoomi's letter to Hume in which he referred to the two-way transference between the Master and the pupil. The Master taught the pupil, obviously, but any kind of special knowledge – of a science or of a language – possessed by the pupil was an addition to the Master's resources. Morya knew almost no English, but took his English from the head of either Olcott or Madame Blavatsky, as convenient. All these instances make it very understandable that there should be innocent traces of her style in the Mahatmic writings. Writing to two German Theosophists at this moment, January 1886, she said she did on some occasions send letters as from Morya, signing them for him after sending them in his writing, although not on his instructions, and taking on herself to send what she sincerely thought he would have wished; sometimes she included mistakes. Yet is this more than may be sometimes done by an ordinary secretary, who, knowing her employer to be busy, thinks to spare him by answering a letter for him, putting into it what she knows to be his usual views and signing it *per pro*?

To revert to paper, there is a curious point that escaped Hodgson. In the first of the Simla phenomena, it was a leaf of pink paper which she tore from a pad and confided to the air and which was found in a tree with a message on it. This must have been in Koot Hoomi's mind when, in III A, he quipped, 'I have no pink paper'. Yet, his long XXIII, which answered Sinnett's scientific question and prophesied the twentieth-century development of radio astronomy, is written entirely upon pink paper. Now, unless she had given him her pad when they met at Amritsar, he must, from Tibet, have used the material of her pad to make (by a reduplication phenomenon) sheets on which to precipitate his writing, or the chela in the middle must have done so. It is our ignorance of the methods involved, which are often very complex, which bedevils our attempts to understand exactly how this or that happened.

In one letter[2] she refers to precipitation as 'photographic reproduction from one's head', but earlier she referred to different methods, both requiring the letter to be precipitated to lie open before the chela (whose discretion must therefore be trusted). In the easier method, every line had to be passed over the forehead, the breath had to be held and the letter kept in place until a bell notified that it had been read and noted. (Did the recipient then receive a physical counterpart or something that endured in the astral light only so long as the precipitator was holding text to forehead?) A more exigent method was to burn the letter to be transmitted, in 'virgin flame',[3] flame not caused by striking a match or anything with brimstone, as that would reduce it to an ash too heavy to travel. The flame must be made by rubbing with a transparent, resinous ball, a 'firestone' that no naked hand must touch. 'I cannot do that', she confided to

Sinnett, but where the chela had the ability the ash made the journey. Does this mean that it reconstituted itself on arrival? In that case, the recipient's paper would not be involved.

A third method of precipitation seems to be described in an early letter (of August 1882), where she says that should Masters' letters be examined under a microscope, the [4]

> microscope will often show him several layers of various stuffs – black lead, and powder and ink etc., for I have often seen M sit with a book of most elaborate Chinese characters that he wanted to copy, and a blank book before him and he would put a pinch of black lead dust that was before him and then rub it in slightly on the page; and then over it precipitate ink; and then, if the image of the characters was all right and correct in his mind the characters copied would be all right, and if he happened to be interrupted then there would be a blunder and the work would be spoiled.

This glimpse of Morya at work seems to explain best the mixed mediums that can be discerned in his letters in the British Museum, while human factors may explain the variations in the handwriting. Some of the Morya letters run diagonally across the page, in a hand that looked different from the more usual one in which they run horizontally.

Madame Blavatsky does not help us with regard to these vagaries, but, in a letter written to Sinnett on 6 January 1886[5], just after reading the Hodgson Report, she says she had felt ready to die and had called upon the Masters; she could not see them so long as she was awake, but when she slept saw them both, and relived scenes which explained how their style and hers had developed similarities:[6]

> I was again (a scene of years back) in Mah. K.H.'s house. I was sitting in a corner on a mat and he was walking about the room in his riding dress and Master was talking to someone behind the door. '*I remind can't*,' I pronounced in answer to a question of His about a dead aunt. He smiled and said, 'Funny English you use'. Then I felt ashamed . . . and began thinking (in my dream or vision, which was the exact reproduction of what had taken place word for word 16 years ago), 'Now I am here, *speaking nothing but English*, in verbal phonetic language I can perhaps learn to speak better with Him'. (To make it clear with Master I often used English, which whether bad or good was the same for Him as he does not speak it but understands every word I say out of my head, and I am made to understand Him – *how* I could never tell or explain if I were killed *but I do* . . .) Then . . . three months after . . . I was standing before Mah. K.H.'s near the old building taken down he was looking at, and as Master was not at home, I took to him a few sentences I was studying in Senzar in his sister's room and asked him to tell me if I translated them correctly – and gave him a slip of paper with these sentences written in English. He took and read them and correcting the interpretation read them over and said, 'Now your English is becoming better – *try to pick it out of my head, even the little I know of it*'. And he put his hand on my forehead in the region of memory and squeezed his fingers on it (and I felt even the same trifling pain in it, as then, and the cold shiver I had experienced) and since that day He did so with my head daily, for about two months. Again the scene changes and I am going away with Master who is sending me off, back to Europe. I am bidding good-bye to his sister and her child and all the chelas. I listen to what the Masters tell me. And then come the parting words of Mah. K.H. laughing at me as he always did and saying, 'Well, if you have not learned much of the sacred Sciences and practical Occultism . . . you have learned, at any rate, a little English. You speak it now *only a little worse* than I do!' and he laughed.

The scene is invaluable, not only for what it tells us of how she learned her peculiar English, from Koot Hoomi, but for the picture it gives us, the sole picture we have, of her life with Morya and Koot Hoomi while living at the latter's house in 1870.

There is a helpful detail she does not mention, but which I found in an unexpected place, Mr Peter Fleming's account of the Younghusband expedition to Lhasa (1903–4), which encamped for a while in January at Phari Jong – entering which Koot Hoomi had looked round to see the goat eating the letter brought to him from C.C. Massey. Fleming prints a good photograph of Phari (or Pari) Jong, a massively square fort with heavily buttressed corners, rising from a desolate plain, and refers to,[6] 'the letters home (mostly in pencil; ink froze) from Phari'.

Does this explain why so many of Morya's and Koot Hoomi's letters are written in crayon, and why even those letters written in ink are sometimes overwritten in crayon or pencil? Could it even explain the frequent unsatisfactory quality of the impression made in ink? Suppose that to thaw it, the writer had on his table a candle or a spirit stove? I look at the silver kettle on tripod over wick and container for spirit, given to my parents in Calcutta as a wedding present and used by them as long as they were in India to make their tea when camping out. Supposing Morya and Koot Hoomi placed their ink-well, or the ink still in the manufacturer's bottle, in something like that – or, removing the kettle part of it, held the ink in its container over the flame with tongs? It would then liquify, but would it do so in a satisfactory fashion? Even as the pen left it to begin writing on the paper, would it begin to freeze again, resulting in places where the impression was so slight as to need overwriting with crayon or pencil? Could little crystals of ice remain and become transferred to the paper, afterwards melting? Is the runniness of the ink, the appearance of its floating out so often from the stroke of the pen, caused perhaps not by the blotting-paper-like absorbency of the paper but tardily thawing crystals of frozen ink?

The Masters' houses in the ravine, where it was possible to grow vegetables, will not have been as cold as this, but both Morya and Koot Hoomi travelled about a good deal within Tibet, and some of their letters may have been sent – or transmitted by chelas – from places as cold as Phari Jong.

CHAPTER 65

Note on the Hare brothers' book

The hostile book, *Who Wrote the Mahatma Letters?*,[1] by the brothers Harold Edward and William Loftus Hare, has been dealt with by Beatrice Hastings,[2] and I will add only a few further points. Their arguments based upon Madame Blavatsky's 'immaculate French' (note that) and its supposed intrusion into the Koot Hoomi letters, I have largely answered in answering Hodgson, but the Hares stoop even to the collection and comparison of split infinitives, as 'to either follow' (Blavatsky) against 'to there assume' (Koot Hoomi). Have not the Hares heard English people splitting their infinitives? One of their examples of her French influence backfires – in the citation from Koot Hoomi, 'little time to explore back letters'.[3] It is not in French but in German that the word 'back' – '*zurück*' – is commonly used in compounds; i.e. '*zurückbeziehung*' (back reference). German influence was what Hodgson thought Koot Hoomi's style ought to show but did not.

The Hares present an extraordinary theory. If in middle age you write slowly and carefully, what emerges is your hand as it was when you were younger. Russian writing is large and round. Koot Hoomi's writing is large and round; therefore it is Madame Blavatsky's younger hand emerging as it was before European and American influence taught her to write 'smaller, sharper, narrower'.[4]

I am always in international correspondence. Moreover, during the war, I was an Examiner for the Postal Censorship Department of the Ministry of Information, reading letters from all over the world. It was our business to pick out from the enormous mass of innocent letters entering or leaving this country any that might be from enemy spies and should be tested for possible presence of a concealed message in invisible ink, cipher or other means. For this work we received a training which included instruction about tell-tale characteristics to look for. As to handwriting, there are one or two elementary points, such as that Germans (and most other continentals) cross their sevens, yet I can only say that if there existed an infallible means of detecting the nationality of a writer from the writing, we should have been glad to know of it.

Russians do not always write 'large and round', even in their own language. I have before me a book, *Rooskië Þocherki* (*Russian Handwriting*),[5] which exhibits facsimiles of fifty-five hands. They are of all types, some small, some angular. As for Madame Blavatsky's younger hand, we have in her Ramsgate notebook her hand on her twentieth birthday. It is small, sharp and angular. I cannot imagine what the Hares mean by Morya's using the Russian small 'r'.[6] The Russian small 'r' is our small 'p', which Morya's certainly is not. In the examples indicated, he makes a high and vigorous left loop, making of it a more important character than in many of our hands.

The Hares' great theme is that the Mahatma Letters show no trace of oriental culture, only of French. Yet their own French is not faultless, and they do not always recognise the oriental. They cite a comment upon a passage of Eliphas Levi made by Koot Hoomi, 'We never bury our dead. They are burnt or left above the earth'.[7] The Hares assert this translates French, '*sur terre*'; but the French for 'above the earth' would be '*au dessus de la terre*'; '*sur terre*' means 'on earth'.[8] Now, Koot Hoomi is agreeing with Levi about the unhealthiness of burying corpses so that they disintegrate only slowly. He certainly did not mean it was healthier to leave them lying on top of the earth, to rot in and pollute the air, which would be far worse. What he has in mind, surely, is that while Hindus cremate, Parsees and Tibetans practise 'sky burial'. The deceased is carried up on to the flat roof of the house (or other convenient ground), where the priest, with a deft knife, dismembers the body and offers it to the vultures. It sounds gruesome but is said to be very clean. Koot Hoomi's preference for it surely does show oriental culture, but the Hares did not recognise the allusion.

Recognising the absurdity of Hodgson's trying to make Madame Blavatsky out a Russian spy, the Hares diagnose her motive for what they consider pretence as mere anti-Christianity; 'Not one religion came under her lash save Christianity'.[9] Hinduism comes under the Mahatmas'; both the exclusive and uncharitable caste system of the Brahmins and the degraded and cruel rites of the popular religion are attacked. Indeed, Morya's choice of mystic name suggests Brahminism as the prior target, but one would not expect the Hare brothers to appreciate that.

They pose, throughout, as devastating know-alls; yet it is often their own ignorance that comes through. Opposing her explanation that she learned her English largely from Koot Hoomi, they list Egypt amongst the countries in which they allege she could not have got along without it.[10] They must have thought Egypt was part of the British Empire already. In fact, it was still under Turkish suzerainty, ruled by Abbas I as Viceroy for the Sultan, and the only strong west European influence was still French. In any case, there is a gulf between the command of language needed to book a ticket or a room and to discuss concepts of profundity.

They mock Djwal Khool's picture of the ravine in Tibet, saying it shows no glimpse 'of distant snow capped mountains'[11] such as are shown in *The Epic of Everest*. They must imagine Tibet to consist entirely of Himalayan scenery. The peak of Everest is in Nepal, and Shigatsè is on the flat tableland of Tibet. For the same reason their 'point' that Djwal Khool could not have been 'paddling' in a stream that should have been a rushing torrent fails. It was not the Sun Kosi he was fording with a pole. Then, they say Morya's house looks like 'an English seaside tea-garden or grotto . . . Something like a cross surmounts the gable'.[11] I have yet to see an English tea-garden with Nepalese arches, roof and lattices, and Tibetan features. What surmounts the roof is the prayer-flag pole without which no Tibetan house is complete, and what is fluttering from it (not crossing it) is plainly a prayer-flag, with the characteristic divided points. The Hares did not recognise a prayer-flag because they did not know what a prayer-flag was.

CHAPTER 66

Countess Wachtmeister

Constance Wachtmeister, daughter of the Marquis de Bourbel and Constance, née Buckley, was the widow of the Swedish Count Karl Wachtmeister. In the autumn of 1885 she left Stockholm for what was intended to be a holiday with friends in Italy. As she was packing, she heard a voice say, 'Take that book'. It was a book on the Qabala and Tarot. Puzzled, she put it in her suitcase. On the way, she made a stop with the Gebhards, at Elberfeld. Frau Gebhard mentioned that Madame Blavatsky was at Würzburg, on her own. Countess Wachtmeister wrote to Madame Blavatsky asking if she could be of any assistance. She received a somewhat putting-off letter, which was almost immediately followed by a telegram begging her to come at once. Having sent Miss Flynn away, Madame Blavatsky had only a maid, Louise, and really did need further assistance. She had first put the Countess off, she explained, because her rooms at Würzburg included only one bedroom and she thought the Countess would not wish to share it. Her Master, however, had told her she should not have put her off, and that was why she had sent the telegram. She had bought a screen that could be put down the middle of the bedroom. 'Master says you have a book for me, of which I am much in need'.[1] The Countess Wachtmeister knew whose voice she had heard in Sweden.

Madame Blavatsky now kept hours different from those of her New York days. She woke at 6 a.m., and after a cup of coffee brought by Louise would work at *The Secret Doctrine* until 9 a.m., when breakfast was served. After breakfast she would continue working until 1 p.m., when Louise would ring a bell to announce that the main meal of the day was ready. At this, Madame Blavatsky might appear or might not, and Louise would consult Countess Wachtmeister as to what to do with the dinner, which would spoil if it had continually to be put back and heated up again. After perhaps some hours, Madame Blavatsky would emerge, wanting something to eat. The dinner would be by this time uneatable and to prepare another would take too long, so they would send out to a hotel for a take-away dish. (Why did they not think of giving her poached eggs on toast with some vegetable, which could have been done in a couple of minutes?)

After 7 p.m. and supper, she would work no more, but play patience. Laying out the cards soothed her and she did not care to talk about Theosophy. (This may be analogous to Krishnamurti's reputed reluctance to talk about profound things over meals. One must have some relaxation.) At 9 p.m. she would take go to bed.

During the whole of the months in Würzburg, the Countess only knew her to go out three times. She had enough trouble to hobble between couch, writing-table and dining-table.

Countess Wachtmeister made fair copies of *The Secret Doctrine* as it progressed; one of these was sent to Olcott for his editorial work on it, in consultation, where it concerned Hindu scriptures, with Subba Row. Madame Blavatsky also asked Countess Wachtmeister to check quotations she had made from works she had seen only in the astral light. She explained that she would create a vacuum in front of her in which pages would appear as in a mirror; this meant she had to read the print back to front, which was rather a strain. Sometimes it was difficult to find where physical copies of the books were housed. The Countess resorted to a friend in Oxford, who would go to the Bodleian to find the sources of the quotations submitted, sometimes with their page numbers given the wrong way round. One quotation was eventually traced to a manuscript in the Vatican, and the friend in Rome whom Countess Wachtmeister prevailed upon to search for the quotation found that Madame Blavatsky had got only two words wrong, which curiously were blurred in the original.[2]

Madame Blavatsky was not now performing phenomena, for it was by doing that she had wrecked her health. Nevertheless, phenomena occurred. After Madame Blavatsky retired to her couch, she would read her Russian newspapers for a while before sleeping. Although the screen cut off her light from the Countess' half of the room, the light from the lamp, reflected on the ceiling, disturbed her. One night, she could tell from the regular sound of Madame Blavatsky's breathing that she had dropped off to sleep, leaving the lamp still burning. The Countess tiptoed round the screen and turned it out. Almost at once, it was alight again. How had the wick, having been turned down, turned itself up again and re-lit itself? The Countess turned it down for the second time and again it started up. For the third time she went round the screen and turned down the lamp, and this time she stayed to watch what happened. A brown hand materialised itself and turned it up again. The Countess called out to Madame Blavatsky to wake her. She woke, gasping, 'My heart! Countess, you have nearly killed me. I was with Master. Why did you call me back?'[3]

Hartmann, who was now helping to organise the Theosophical Society in Germany, wrote asking for an instruction from the Master. Madame Blavatsky told the Countess to tuck Hartmann's letter into the frame containing the portrait of the Master. If he wished to answer it, he would take it. The Countess did as she was bid, then began to read a book. When she looked up from it about half an hour later, the letter had vanished.[4]

A few days afterwards, the postman came with some letters, one of which was from Hartmann. It was bulky and the Countess was surprised that stamps to a higher value had not been required. When she opened it, she found the letter from Hartmann which she had tucked into the Master's portrait, plus a fresh letter from Hartmann, with writing in the margins that was not in Hartmann's hand, answering his questions.

Countess Wachtmeister asked Madame Blavatsky why she did not use her powers to alleviate her own circumstances. Madame Blavatsky said it was an absolute condition of the teaching she received that none of the powers she developed should ever be used by her for herself.[5]

CHAPTER 67

Solovioff

In an undated letter, Madame Blavatsky tells Sinnett she hears that Myers has written to ask Solovioff whether,[1] 'he still maintains he saw Master at Elberfeld, Miss Glinka *ditto* . . . Solovioff answers *he does* . . .'. She also says she does not see why Sinnett and his wife should delay their intended visit to her on account of her aunt's being with her at her lodgings, 'Rugmer's Hotel is nearby . . . The Solovioffs are there. They remain with me for a month longer'.

Therefore, Sinnett tells us, when he and his wife arrived in the autumn of 1885, they stayed at the hotel, along with 'the Solovioffs'.[2] Sinnett puts the inverted commas because it was later learned they were not man and wife. The woman presented by Solovioff as his wife was his wife's sister.[3]

I cannot think Ms Meade is correct in identifying as Justine Glinka the wife's sister who stayed at Würzburg with Solovioff as his wife. In none of the source material can I find any statement that Justine Glinka was Solovioff's sister-in-law. Moreover, Madame Blavatsky had met Justine Glinka, both in Paris and in Elberfeld, and it seems obvious from her above quoted letter that to her, Miss Glinka and the supposed Mrs Solovioff were two different people.

Madame Blavatsky was upset because cohabitation with a sister-in-law was 'a crime in Russia'; to make it worse, her Aunt Nadyezhda, who seemed to have been the one who had, after her return to Russia, discovered how they had been imposed upon, informed her that Solovioff had first seduced the girl when she was under age.[4] The Czar, if he heard of this, would certainly dismiss Solovioff from his post as a Page of Honour.

It appeared that there had been an angry scene back in Russia.[5] Madame Fadeyef had written not only to Madame Blavatsky but to Madame Zhelikhovsky, and Vera had taken her letter to Solovioff and indignantly bearded him with it. This was a most ill-judged move, for it provoked him into retaliating by threatening to expose Madame Blavatsky for immorality and charlatanism, and for being a Russian spy. This last particularly nettled Madame Blavatsky, as during the time he had been in Würzburg, Solovioff had made her a proposition which she had felt wise to notify Sinnett about orally, while he was there too. She probably gauged the situation rightly when she wrote to him now:[6]

> Solovioff is either crazy or acts so because having compromised himself with his *offer of espionage* to me he is now afraid I should speak and compromise him at St. Petersburg . . .
>
> Solovioff will not forgive me for rejecting his propositions.[7]

A spy who has exposed himself as such, by trying to make a recruit and failing, makes himself useless to the service that employs him, since the one he tried to recruit knows what he is and his security is gone. Also, it is possible that, at least in polite fiction, a Page of Honour should not have been engaged in the dirty game of espionage. Solovioff had so compromised himself with Madame Blavatsky as to give her the power to destroy him. His reaction was to try to destroy her first.

What was, however, vexatious was that,[8] 'Solovioff threatens me moreover that Mr Blavatsky is *not dead* but is "a charming centenarian" who had found fit to conceal himself for years on his brother's property – hence the false news of his death'. She was concerned because, if true, this meant that her marriage to Betanelly, though dissolved, had been bigamous. She wrote:[9]

> May be what Solovioff tells me of old Blavatsky . . . is a wicked fib of his, and perhaps it is not. I never had an official notification of his death, only what I learned from my Aunt at New York and again here. 'His country seat was ruined', he 'himself had left years ago' and news had come 'he was dead'.

Russia has no central registry of births, deaths and marriages. They are recorded only at the town hall of the district in which they took place. If the district is unknown, it is impossible to know which local records to have searched. There was, therefore, no way in which Madame Blavatsky could have checked. Her delusion as to his age may have deceived her as to natural probability. He would, in 1885, if still alive, have been 78, but in 1875 only 57. The date of his death has still not been discovered.

Solovioff had blundered doubly, exposing himself to her both in incestuous cohabitation with his sister-in-law and in espionage. He had given her the means to destroy him. To discredit and destroy her was therefore his first business. He circulated copies of what he alleged to be a letter she had written to him,[10] 'my *soi-disant* [so called] CONFESSION (!) of immorality, having invented the Mahatmas, forged letters etc.'.

Vera had demanded to see the alleged original letter of her sister, or at least a copy certified by a public notary as being a true copy, but this was refused; Madame Blavatsky's nephew, Rotislav Nikolayevich Yarmontoff, a son of Vera by her first marriage who was now in the Dragoons, was pursuing the matter for the honour of the family.

This letter, which has never been seen, is presumably the 'original' of the so-called 'Confession' letter published by Solovioff in the *Russky Vestnik* after her death, which became, in the English translation commissioned by the Society for Psychical Research, the infamous book *A Modern Priestess of Isis*. Sidgwick wrote a preface for it.

In it, Solovioff claims it was Madame Blavatsky who offered him her services as a spy for Russia. Naturally, he says nothing about having brought his sister-in-law to stay at Würzburg as his wife, but represents himself as having arrived and stayed solo. He details endless conversations he says took place between himself and Madame Blavatsky, in which he makes her make compromising utterances; he also says that he saw fall from the folds of her dress a little bell, and caught sight, in her rooms, of a stock of envelopes with Chinese writing such as the K.H. letters arrived in. Why the last should have been considered compromising, I fail to see. They are very ordinary commercial envelopes, and it would have been natural enough for Koot Hoomi to have bought them during one of his trips to China. But they are made to sound something that might be supposed to be occult. It must be apparent even to the least sophisticated reader that Solovioff may be making these conversations and incidents up as he goes along.

As for the appended letters, purported to be from Madame Blavatsky, they are curious. There is a much quoted one she is alleged to have written to A.N. Aksakoff, a Spiritualist, on 14 November 1874, from 23 Irving Place, New York. In this she is made to refer to a letter received by Andrew Jackson Davis impugning her morals, and to say that it was true. She is made to wail about having suffered for her 'past'; to escape from that and from those who knew her youth, she has fled to America, and she begs Aksakoff:[11]

> Do not deprive me of the good opinion of Andrew J. Davis. Do not reveal to him that which if he knew it and were convinced, would force me to escape to the ends of the earth. I have only one refuge left in the world, and that is the respect of the spiritualists of America, who despise nothing so much as 'free love'.

Nothing we know of Madame Blavatsky supports her having written this letter. She always vigorously maintained her morality, and her only known references to Andrew Jackson Davis hardly suggest he was a person whose opinion would specially matter to her. At the time she is alleged to have written this, she had just returned from Vermont and her first meetings with Colonel Olcott, and all her thoughts would have been about him. Moreover, a woman so desperately anxious to conceal an indiscreet 'past' would surely have tried to appear conventional. Her proceeding to share an apartment in New York with Olcott surely shows indifference to appearance.

She is made to write that she, 'was a "materialist" till I was nearly thirty'. We know that she was never a materialist. She is made to say Daniel Home converted her to Spiritualism, but we know from her own pen that she never met Daniel Home.[12] 'Whilst I have seen the medium Home, I was not acquainted with him'.

In a further letter she is said to have sent from Hartford on 13 December 1874, she is made to refer to a letter which, addressed to New York, was delivered supernaturally in Philadelphia.

Solovioff may have seen some of her old addresses on genuine letters to Aksakoff, but on 13 December 1874, she had not yet been to Philadelphia. The allusion is obviously to the letters addressed to Olcott at his office in New York, which were delivered to him in Philadelphia without having been re-addressed from his office; but that did not happen until February 1875. The letter is a forgery.

Interesting, also, is the so-called 'Confession' letter, to Solovioff:[13]

> I will even take to lies, to the greatest of lies, which for that reason is the likeliest of all to be believed. I will say and publish it in the *Times* and in all the papers that the "master" and Mahatma K.H. are only the product of my own imagination: that I invented them.

Apart from the fact that it is not a confession, since it says it would be the biggest of all lies, it has an antecedent. Earlier, she had written to Sinnett:[14]

> I know one thing, that if it came to the *worst* and Master's truthfulness and notions of honour were to be impeached – then I would go to a *desperate expedient*. I would proclaim publicly that *I alone* was a liar, a forger, all that Hodgson wants me to appear that I had indeed INVENTED the Masters and thus would by that 'myth' of Master K.H. and M. screen the real K.H. and M. from opprobrium.

The only saving grace in the Hodgson Report, as she saw it, was that in it the Masters themselves had not been vilified; their existence had merely been denied. Had their existence been admitted but their motives impugned, she would have denied their existence to save their honour. As she wrote, 'BY MASTER'S BLESSING OR CURSE'.

Solovioff may have heard her speak in this vein and woven remembered phrases into his concoction. That it is his concoction one can be sure from its comparison of herself with profligate women of history who had 'given, even *sold* themselves to the entire male sex'. Madame Blavatsky always rebutted with indignation any imputation of sexual laxity.

None of these letters has ever been seen. They exist only on the printed page and have no coporeal bodies. The letters of Madame Blavatsky and papers relating to her fall into two main groups; those in the possession of Olcott at his death, which are at Adyar, and those in the possession of Sinnett at his death, which are in the British Museum. The 'letters' printed by Solovioff are nowhere.

CHAPTER 68

The medical certificate

It happened that while at Würzburg Madame Blavatsky had to consult a Dr Oppenheimer about a trouble with her bladder, which necessitated an intimate examination. After it, she wrote to Sinnett:[1]

Private

I enclose the medical certificate of Prof. Oppenheimer who made 'a minute and exact examination' since my illness finds itself complicated now by some congenital crookedness of the *uterus* . . . which crookedness kills at once the missionaries and their hopes of proving me the mother of three or more children. He had written a long and complicated statement of the reason *why* I could never have not only children, but anything in the shape of an extra since *unless an operation is now made* – they can't get at that blessed uterus to cure it. I thanked and *declined*. Better *die* than have an operation made. But knowing this shall probably have to be read in my defence – I did not permit him to go into physiological particulars and asked him simply to certify the fact that I *never had* any child or children, nor *could I have them*.

. . .

Yours dishonoured in my old age
H.P. Blavatsky

When she says 'dishonoured', she means by the intimacy of the examination to which she had submitted, though the doctor's finding armed her against defamation.

The certificate reads:[2]

The undersigned testifies, as requested, that Madame Blavatsky of Bombay – New York Corresponding Secretary of the Theosophical Society – is at present under the medical treatment of the undersigned. She suffers from *anteflexio uteri*, most probably from the day of her birth; because, as proven by a minute examination, she has never borne a child, nor has she had any gynaecological illness.

[signed] Dr Leon Oppenheimer

The signature of Dr Leon Oppenheimer
is hereby officially attested,
Würzburg, 3rd December, 1885.
The Royal Medical Officer of the District
[signed] Dr Max Roeder

We the undersigned, hereby certify that the above is a correct translation of the German original letter.
Würzburg, November 4th, 1885
[signed] Hübbe Schleiden
Franz Gebhard

Madame Blavatsky added a postscript to her letter to Sinnett:

. . . The Dr [Oppenheimer] says that *Gynaecological* 'illness' means 'woman's functions' and shows *intactness* (as Mme Noury of Stead's trial has it) Hübbe Schleiden explaining to me blushingly that 'it is a *delicate* and *scientific* way of putting it, and *very clear*'.

The Stead referred to is William Thomas Stead, the English reformer. To prove the ease with which young girls, even virgins, were sold, sometimes by their mothers, straight into prostitution, he bought one himself for £5, so provoking the trial which rocked Victorian England.

Countess Wachtmeister, excited, wrote to Sinnett,[3] 'The doctor has given me to understand that Madame is still a *virgin*'.

Both the certificate and the interpretation placed on it have, however, been attacked by Madame Blavatsky's enemies, particularly Ms Meade. She avers that in those days a prudish woman would not have submitted to a gynaecological examination by a male physician, that at the age of 54 the womb would have so shrunk that it would be impossible to tell whether or not a child had been born from it and that *anteflexio uteri* would not prevent childbirth.[4]

To me it is inconceivable that a professional man, with his reputation to maintain, would certify that he had examined a patient if he had not. Dr Leon Oppenheimer was a specialist in gynaecology, and a friend of mine who is a medical practitioner, Dr Margaret Little, assured me, 'The cervix after childbirth never returns to its nulliparous state. The gynaecologist would be able to say whether or not Mme Blavatsky had had a child'. It is true that an anteverted or forward-tilting uterus, common enough, does not prevent childbearing. The proof that Madame Blavatsky had not borne a child would be in the nulliparous state.

Uterine displacements tend, however, to cause bladder trouble, particularly cystitis. In this connection Dr Little consulted on my behalf *Novak's Textbook of Gynecology*, H.W. and G.S. Jones, 10th ed. (William & Witney, Baltimore and London, 1981) and *History of Urology*, L.J.T. Murray (Charles Thomas, Springfield, Illinois, 1972). Presumably it was because Madame Blavatsky complained of cystitis that the doctor looked to see if there was any abnormality. Dr Little commented:

> The virginity question is a bit tricky, as one feels that, if true, it would certainly have impeded the gynaecologist somewhat and normally any examination would be under anaesthetic . . . If not, I would be inclined to doubt the intact hymen. There is, of course, a lot of mythology about intact hymens. Normal anatomy varies very much: God only knows how many women in the past were accused of indiscretions they had never committed.

I wrote to Adyar, asking if they could let me have a photocopy or the German text of the certificate as Countess Wachtmeister queried whether the word 'illness' correctly translated the German. They sent me a photostat of a certified copy of the German, and the word was '*Krankheit*', which was indeed correctly translated as 'illness'. Dr Little, however, suggested it could be a euphemism for venereal disease, which would mean that Madame Blavatsky's not having had it was relevant to what she wanted proven, that she had not lived a loose life. The certified copy also showed the name as Oppenheimer, as given by Madame Blavatsky in her letters, not Oppenheim, as given by Olcott, when printing the English translation in his *Old Diary Leaves*.

I sent Dr Little photostats of the further texts reproduced by Mary Neff, from the archives at Adyar. Somebody must have thought the certificate insufficiently precise, for a second one was produced,[5] 'I hereby certify that Mme. Blavatsky has never been pregnant with child and so consequently can never have had a child. Oppenheimer'. With this, in the Archives, is the fourth page of a letter by Madame Blavatsky. As the earlier part of the letter is missing, the person it was written to cannot be identified, but it was probably Olcott. The surviving page reads:[6]

> Here's your stupid new certificate with your dreams of *virgo intacta* in a woman who had all her guts out, womb and all, by a fall from horseback. And yet the doctor looked, examined *three* times, and says what the Professor Bodkin and Pirgoff said at Pskoff in 1862. I could never have had a connection with any man without an inflammation, because I am lacking something and the place is filled up with some crooked cucumber.

Madame Blavatsky was a little muddled in writing that her womb had come out in her horse-riding accident. She still had it, or it could not have been observed to be anteverted. What she is trying to tell Olcott is that she has to disappoint him, in that the doctor cannot certify her *virgo intacta* as her hymen has disappeared, she supposes when she fell from horseback in Mingrelia.

Nevertheless, there is a condition which would impede intercourse. This seems to be Countess Wachtmeister's understanding of it, from an attached letter by her:[7]

10th February [1886]

Dear Friend and Brother,

Here is the certificate you desire to have . . .

. . . The Doctor told me that, though no doctor can positively certify whether a woman has lived with her husband or not, on account of the virginity being lost by a fall or hard exercise, to the best of his belief Mme. Blavatsky had not lived with a man . . . The Doctor also said that in his experience he had examined girls of 10 to 12 years of age, knowing them to be pure and virtuous children, yet their virginity was gone owing to a fall . . .

C. Wachtmeister

By 'virginity', hymen is meant here.

There is at Adyar, amongst Olcott's papers, a further fragment by Madame Blavatsky, again with the first page missing, beginning on p.2:[8]

he brought his instruments, looking-glass or mirror to look *inside* and other horrors. When he did he asked in astonishment, 'Were you ever married?' 'Yes', I said, 'but never had any children' – not wanting to go into physiological particulars. 'No, surely', he answered, 'how could you, since for all I can see, *you must never have had any connection with your husband*'. I said this to Mr Sinnett, and Mme. Tidesco who had assisted at the operation corroborated . . .

He says, I have from birth the uterus crooked or hooked inside out, and that I could not, not only *never have children* but that it is now the cause of my suffering with my bladder . . . and that if I had ever tried to be *immoral* with anyone . . . I would have had each time an inflammation and great suffering . . . I sent the certificate to Sinnett for he says he *needs it*. It is a great shame, but a great triumph likewise.

After reading this, Dr Little wrote:

light finally dawned. Enclosed some little drawings sideways section, which I think may answer your problem. Presumably either the uterus or the cervix was so distorted as actually partially to occlude the lumen of the vagina, which would account for the worthy professor's astonishment. One wonders, doesn't one, about the history of the marriage. Presumably intercourse was so painful that they abandoned it at the first attempt. She must have had a LOT of trouble from urinary infection and I think in her place I would certainly have had the operation made, even in those days. Her mind must truly have been upon higher things. Poor woman.

If the uterus was bent like a hooked cucumber, that may explain Madame Blavatsky's later reference to,[9] 'the doctor's certificate that I never bore a weazel, not only a child'. In this picturesque phrase may be a reference to its reduced capacity as a container. There would not be room for a baby to grow in it.

If intercourse with her husband was abandoned after one attempt, it would explain both the 'physiological particulars' into which she did not wish to enter and Nikifor's failure to obtain an annulment.

I asked Dr Little what kind of physical symptoms Madame Blavatsky, assuming she was suffering from inflammation and infection of the bladder, or cystitis, would feel that would cause her to consult a doctor. Dr Little replied she would have pain during and, even more, after urination and constant calls to urinate, with, however, little water passing; hence repeated calls to try again and more pain.

I wondered if this could have any bearing on what some people represented as Madame Blavatsky's uneven and crotchety temper. To explain that one has a cold, a headache or toothache is socially acceptable; to explain such a urinary malaise would be impossible, especially in Victorian society. There would be the irritation of its being impossible to explain the problem, added to that of the trouble itself.

Then something else occurred to me. Could such an infection of the bladder extend to the kidneys and so cause the dropsy and the overweight? Dr Little replied that it could. But as I gathered that dropsy could also result from a weak heart, was there any way to decide between the causes in this case? Dr Little said that if the heart is the cause, the first symptom noticed is cyanosis (skin turning blue), puffiness only appears much later. Nobody ever commented on Madame Blavatsky's skin colour, so probably it was normal; it was the puffiness that was noticed by others, even back in New York days. The unkind and ignorant have attributed her overweight to gluttony. It would have made no difference had she starved herself. Naturally, the overweight caused by the dropsy would have added to the burden of the heart. Removal of the uterus would have been the only cure. Such a malformation of it might perhaps have been caused by an interruption in the supply of blood to her when she was a foetus.

CHAPTER 69

Ostend

The question was where Madame Blavatsky would go next. Olcott wrote from Adyar on 16 January 1886:[1]

> Dear Chum,
>   . . . Begin putting away in a stocking, shillings, francs or thalers, towards paying your expenses here in case the coast becomes clear between this and Oct. and you are ordered to come. I shall do the same.

She felt, however, somewhat 'off' Adyar since its failure to support her. Countess Wachtmeister wanted to take her back to Sweden with her, but she did not want to go there. Eventually it was decided that she should join Vera and her children at Ostend, breaking the journey at Elberfeld. On 16 May, she was helped on to the train by Countess Wachtmeister and Miss Kislingbury – whom she had not seen since New York days, but who had just read the Hodgson Report and been so outraged she had come to support her. At the Gebhards Madame Blavatsky slipped on a parquet floor, further injuring her leg. This protracted her stay, and Vera and her daughter of the same name came to join her at the Gebhards'.

The younger Vera tells us that one morning when she came down to breakfast, her Aunt Helena asked her what a 'pie' was. Vera Vladimirovna was beginning to explain that a pie was an English dish when Madame Blavatsky retorted that it was a term used in mathematics and she was asking her because she was supposed to have done mathematics at school. The girl went to look at the page of the manuscript over which her aunt was brooding, and read '$\pi = 31\cdot4159$'. Then she understood that 'pi' not 'pie' was meant, and said that the decimal point should be shifted one point to the left: '$\pi = 3\cdot14159$'. She asked her aunt how she could write about things she did not understand. Madame Blavatsky said she often had to do that. This numerical thing had been in a passage dictated by her Master before she went to bed the previous night, and she had woken up sure she had taken it down wrong.[2] (In *The Secret Doctrine* there is a passage concerning the use made by ancient Egyptian architects of the ratio to the circumference of a circle.)

Towards the end of July or beginning of August, the three moved to Ostend, where at 17 rue de l'Ouest, Madame Blavatsky took a spacious suite of rooms with a piano. She still had her maid, Louise, but Countess Wachtmeister returned and wheeled her along the Esplanade in the bath chair to which she was now confined.

On 23 August, Madame Blavatsky wrote to Sinnett,[3] 'Lane-Fox wants to come and see me and (please keep it confidential) Mrs ANNA KINGSFORD!! Wants to come and see me and asks me now at least to place her in communication with the Masters!!!!!!' Mrs Kingsford and her colleague, Edward Maitland went first to a hotel nearby, but they were not comfortable there and Madame Blavatsky invited them to stay in her rooms. Countess Wachtmeister, who sat up with them every night, says they usually started by arguing a philosophical question from different points of view but ended by agreeing.

In the winter Madame Blavatsky was very ill, and after a night in which she seemed about to pass away she told Countess Wachtmeister her Master had given her a choice: she was free to die now, or she could sacrifice the release and go to England to found a school.[4] Just after that, the Keightleys asked her to go to London.

CHAPTER 70

London

On 1 May 1887, H.P.B. was helped aboard a ship, and on arrival in London she was driven to the suburb of Upper Norwood, to Mabel Collins' cottage, Maycot. This was close to the dominating towers of the Crystal Palace, and rather small. Visitors to Madame Blavatsky sat on her bed and on her desk.

The Keightleys studied the pile of manuscript, now three feet high. They thought *The Secret Doctrine* was the greatest philosophical work of the century, but that it needed rearrangement and editing, which they undertook. They also prevailed upon her to add commentaries in explanation of matters they found obscure[2] – not to be confused with the ancient *Commentaries*, to which the text alludes.

A Blavatsky Lodge was formed, with G.B. Finch as its President, and as she could not continue to edit *The Theosophist* so far from Adyar, a new magazine was started, with her to edit it – called *Lucifer*, meaning 'Light-bearer'. The poet W.B. Yeats came – he assured John Eglinton that the Theosophical Society 'had done more for Irish literature than Trinity College in three centuries'.[3]

When Countess Wachtmeister returned in September 1887, Madame Blavatsky and she moved to the Keightleys' house, 17 Lansdowne Road, Holland Park. This does not, as authors unfamiliar with London have imagined, mean it overlooked a park. Nevertheless, it was in a nice street with some trees, had a small front garden and larger garden at the back, and was within easy reach of Kensington Gardens.

It was here that William Kingsland first met her. In his book, he makes the point it was by her philosophy and personality alone that he was impressed, as she was no longer performing phenomena. She was too weak and had come to see the futility of it. She returned his call, and played Schubert's 'Erlkönig on his piano.[4]

An important new pupil was Alice Leighton Cleather. Her husband, Colonel W.B.G. Cleather, Retired, did not join the Society but conceived a respect for Madame Blavatsky, who would roll him cigarettes and wrote him a diploma of honorary membership.[5]

Yeats brought Maud Gonne. Oscar Wilde's wife, Constance, became a member. Ernest Rhys, editor of the Everyman Classics, came, and Dr Carter Blake, with whom she discussed geology.

W.T. Stead, editor of *The Review of Reviews*, came, and afterwards admitted she almost convinced him 'of this life being a mere probation'.

'Saladin' (Stewart Ross), Editor of *The Agnostic Journal*, came; he would later write, 'She was almost the only mortal I have ever met who was *not* an impostor . . . she did not possess even a single rag of the cloak of hypocrisy'.[6]

Don José Xifré, friend of King Alfonso XII and Queen Isabella II of Spain, wrote, 'I felt that the glance of H.P.B. had penetrated and destroyed the personality that I had been up to that moment . . . mental tranquillity and moral equilibrium were attained on making her acquaintance'.[7] He was organising the translation of all her works into Spanish.

All this activity was very close to Sinnett's house, 7 Ladbroke Gardens, and both Mrs Cleather and Kingsland believed it was from jealousy he now turned against her – because people who had flocked to him flocked to her.[8]

There was pressure on her to place herself at the head of an almost independent European Section. Judge wrote to warn Olcott that in America there was a Dr Elliott Coues claiming to have received letters from the Masters and scheming to take over the whole Society. Further, Judge suggested to Madame Blavatsky that to satisfy the European and American members who wanted something more to do on their own, she should create an Esoteric School.

Olcott was worried by these developments, fearing to see the Society splintered, and he sailed for England aboard the *Shannon*. On 22 August, the day before the ship entered Brindisi, a letter fell to him in Koot Hoomi's writing. It was a long one, the gist of which was that he should be the one responsible for the administration of external affairs, but that in occult matters he should give way to Madame Blavatsky:[9]

> Since 1885 I have not written, nor caused to be written save through her agency, direct or remote, a letter or line to anybody in Europe or America, nor communicated orally with or thro' any third party . . . She is *our direct agent.*

Olcott found Madame Blavatsky surrounded by the final proofs of *The Secret Doctrine.* He was introduced to the new people about her, including her doctor, Dr Z. Mennell, who told him the microscope revealed 'enormous crystals of uric acid in her blood'.[10] Dr Margaret Little thinks this must be a euphemism. They would have been in her urine if she had them. Dr Mennell informed Olcott that to return to the heat of India would kill her. Olcott had just bought a property, Gulistan, at Ootacamund, which he had thought they might share in their old age. He stayed for two months, during which the most beautiful of all the photographs of them together was taken, in the garden.

He chartered a British Section of the Theosophical Society, and on 9 October issued an order in Council forming an Esoteric Section under the sole direction of Madame Blavatsky.

Volume 1 of *The Secret Doctrine* appeared in October 1888, Volume 2 at the end of the year.

CHAPTER 71

The Secret Doctrine: prefatory remarks

The Secret Doctrine is thought of as extraordinarily difficult to understand. For this reason, many people feel that it would be beyond them, at the outset of their Theosophical reading, and so they start by reading the books by Annie Besant and Leadbeater, thinking by beginning with something simpler to prepare themselves for the great work. This is a mistake. Their works are not on the same plane. They simplify at the cost of leaving out what is deepest, and, by shifting the emphasis to what is more easily seizable, radically distort the picture, introducing notions that are their own, not Blavatsky's. They use the word 'astral' with a meaning different from hers, and after reading them one finds oneself having to unlearn when one begins to read *The Secret Doctrine*. There is – as with Krishnamurti's writing – no way to prepare oneself to read the book. One just has to start reading it. Yet some counsel may be given.

I should like to pass on a hint that was given me when, almost forty years ago, I began reading it for the first time, 'If you do not understand, do not go back, go on'. This is because it is not like a book on geometry, where, if one has not understood one theorem one will not understand the next, which builds upon what was earlier established. In *The Secret Doctrine* one is introduced to ways of thinking that are strange, but if what is connoted by a particular term or intended to be conveyed by some poetic image eludes one at the first encounter, one may later be able to glean it. This is because the work is very loosely organised, and the exposition is often repetitious. This may be a structural fault, but it affords one a number of second chances. Indeed, Madame Blavatsky's habit of going over the same ground a number of times in the endeavour to make it clear does sometimes achieve its purpose, for in re-stating she may use different words, employ some fresh simile, and suddenly what was incomprehensible before is clear.

She is like an ear cocked to the sounds of outer space, and, as if she did not always see what was close, she shows little ability to organise literary material. Things are sometimes brought in before one has got to them in the story, yet most of the allusions do have their key, if one can find it in the jungle. It is said that the Masters thought it well to leave it this way, since the need to search must force the reader to do his own work, asking himself whether this implied a hint of that, so provoking him to explosions of the intuition. The truth then becomes really possessed by him for himself, as it would not be if he merely found it totally set out.

People who keep going back to the beginning of a paragraph to find out why they are not understanding the end of it rarely progress beyond a few pages. This is a pity, because it is said that to read the whole book straight through from the first page to the last – there are 2,135 without the index – is to pass through an initiation. One may not, even after one has reached the end, feel confident of being able to give an account of what one has read. Yet one's attitude has changed, one's mind has widened, one's perspectives opened out, one has been exposed to . . ., has glimpsed . . ., seized . . . One is not the same person that one was when one began.

CHAPTER 72

The Secret Doctrine:
source and plan

The Secret Doctrine is based upon the *Stanzas from the Book of Dzyan*. Typically, we have to reach Volume 5 (Adyar edition), p.389, to be told what this is. 'The BOOK OF DZYAN – from the Sanskrit word "Dhyan" (mystic meditation) is the first volume of the Commentaries upon the seven secret folios of *Kiu-te*'. (It will be recalled that Koot Hoomi said the second syllable should be pronounced 'tee' or 'ti'). There are thirty-five volumes of exoteric or relatively public volumes of *Kiu-te*, copies of which are to be found in every Gelukpa monastery, but they ought to be called the 'Popularised version of the SECRET DOCTRINE, full of myths, blinds and errors'. The fourteen volumes of commentaries, however, are not commentaries upon this – except for a few recently added ones pointing out the errors – but commentaries upon 'one small archaic folio, THE BOOK OF THE SECRET WISDOM OF THE WORLD', kept 'secret and apart' at Shigatsè. (If it was within the Monastery of Trashi Lhünpo or in the Museum in the Ravine, I should think it has now been removed to some even more remote and safer place.) It is upon cylinders, in the sacred language unknown to philologists, Senzar, of which the Sanskrit known to philologists is the inferior descendant.

Actually, she gives us both stanzas, in poetic prose and in commentaries, in prose which is only slightly less poetic; and despite the way she expresses it above, I think the stanzas are from the 'small archaic folio' and the commentaries from the fourteen volumes of commentaries on it which are on cylinders.

The Secret Doctrine comprises two main parts, *Cosmogenesis* (birth of the universe) and *Anthropogenesis* (birth of man or humankind). In the original edition, there were just two thick volumes, under these names. In the Adyar edition, which is what many people will have nowadays, there are six volumes, the original 1 having become 1 and 2; the original 2 having become 3 and 4; 5 being material written for the original edition but for some reason dropped from it, partly collected by Mrs Besant (therefore one sees that the original readers would never have discovered what the *Stanzas from the Book of Dzyan* were). It also includes the EST instructions. 6 is the index.

After an introduction and *Proem*, Volume 1, *Cosmogenesis*, begins with seven *Stanzas from the Book of Dzyan*, each with numbered verses. The rest of the book consists of the commentaries upon the stanzas – the commentaries from the cylinders – followed, in each case, by her (or her Masters') explanation of what the commentaries mean. Although always referred to the stanza and verse, these can be discursive, and it is as well to keep one's finger in the stanzas (the bar on going back does not refer to the stanzas), so as to keep in mind where one is in the whole.

Volume 1 having dealt with the birth of the universe, down to the formation of the solar system, one expects the story to go straight on from there, but it is (vexatiously, it seems to me) broken by a whole volume of chapters on occult symbolism, not uninteresting in themselves, but unrelated to the story and to each other.

It is not until Volume 3 that we return to the *Stanzas from the Dzyan* and pick up the story again, to learn how the human races developed. This is much easier than Volume 1, because while most of us find it very difficult to imagine what it was like before the manifested universe came into being – that state of things which was no thing yet not nothing – all of us understand what people are, even if we are told the earliest ones were very different from us. The most difficult part is at the beginning.

Volume 4 consists of rather disparate essays, organised into two parts, 'The Archaic Symbolism of the World Religions' and 'Science and the Secret Doctrine Contrasted'.

Volume 5 is a mixed bag, containing at the beginning some lives of particular occultists, which the Keightleys had persuaded her to drop from the original edition; followed by a lot of snippets of matter probably dropped from the original edition as too occult and better suited to the Esoteric School; the explanation of what the *Stanzas from the Book of Dzyan* are, dropped perhaps because to suggest their location seemed indiscreet; and an all-important chapter on the Buddha, dropped perhaps because of the contention it might arouse.

CHAPTER 73

The Secret Doctrine, I, Cosmogenesis

The *Proem* refers to a circle with nothing in it, followed by the same circle with a dot in the middle, followed by the same with the dot become a horizontal line across the middle, then by the same with the horizontal line crossed by a vertical one, and lastly by the cross without the circle round it. These five diagrams tell the whole story of the birth of the universe, of ourselves and our adventures or misadventures so far as we have come, but in a form too encapsulated to be understood by the uninitiated. They figure upon successive palm leaves of inconceivable antiquity, by some unknown process rendered indestructible by water, air or fire.

Perhaps this gives us the needed clue to what is meant when it is said that the *Stanzas of the Book of Dzyan* is a 'small archaic folio', for a folio, of any sort, sounds rather modern. The bound book is modern. It may, however, be that the *stanzas*, like the preceding diagrams, are upon palm leaves, the whole succession of them being in some manner sewn together.

From the *Proem* we pass to the *Stanzas from the Book of Dzyan*. It is not explained who translated them into English, but it was probably Koot Hoomi. He has used English as much as he can, but here and there he has used a Sanskrit word to translate the Senzar or even a homely Tibetan word, the text that follows endeavouring to explain the meaning of these words for which no English equivalent was found.

The stanzas are printed in bold type, and I will give the first of them entire:

Stanza 1

1 The Eternal Parent, wrapped in her Ever-Invisible Robes, had slumbered once again for Seven Eternities.

2 Time was not, for it lay asleep in the Infinite Bosom of Duration.

3 Universal Mind was not, for there were no Ah-hi to contain it.

4 The Seven Ways to Bliss were not. The Great Causes of Misery were not, for there was no one to produce and get ensnared by them.

5 Darkness alone filled the Boundless All, for Father, Mother and Son were once more one, and the Son had not yet awakened for the new Wheel and his Pilgrimage thereon.

6 The Seven Sublime Lords and the Seven Truths had ceased to be, and the Universe, the Son of Necessity, was immersed in Paranishpanna, to be outbreathed by that which is, and yet is not. Naught was.

7 The Causes of Existence had been done away with; the Visible that was, and the Invisible that is, rested in Eternal Non-Being – the One Being.

8 Alone, the One Form of Existence stretched boundless, infinite, causeless, in Dreamless Sleep; and Life pulsated unconscious in Universal Space, through that All-Presence, which is sensed by the Opened Eye of Dangma.

9 But where was Dangma when the Alaya of the Universe was in Paramârtha, and the Great Wheel was Anupâdaka?

It will be evident that we are in the Nirvana of the preceding universe, that is, the Pralaya of the one before ours. The words 'Seven Eternities' are used with the meaning of seven seemingly infinite periods of time, seven very long aeons. In this first Stanza is the assurance that Nirvana is but a rest, not an end. All the causes and all the beings in it were gathered up into it, gathered into the All that is One, and they are still there. What is this state, that seems to be called, of persons, psychologically, Nirvana, and of worlds and universes, Pralaya? It was explained in Koot Hoomi's early letter to Hume, which ought to have been given again here, for nowhere else is it explained so comprehensively. It is the state wherein the interaction between the positive and negative polarities known as electricity has lessened until it has become nil. The poles are in one. If I may dare to introduce an image of my own, which has come to me as I write, the angle between them has reduced from 180 to zero. At the lowest and heaviest point in the wheel of manifestation, Manvantara, it was 180, the widest possible distance apart, opposition. The interaction between them was therefore the most violent time and most dramas occurred then. Now we are at conjunction, the conjunction reached after the circuit of the previous wheel was completed. But in that conjunction it appears that there are stages, since we are arrived in the seventh of them. Therefore, it must be that, as in human sleep, even though there seems to be naught but the breathing, something is happening, something is being gone through, after falling into the deepest part of it, preparing us to waken for the new day.

In the universal Pralaya, this state has entered its seventh and last aeon. In this first stanza, the sleep still seems to be complete. The second stanza describes a state so little different from it the author fears the reader will not tell any difference, yet there is a difference:

Stanza 2

1 . . . Where were the Builders, the Luminous Sons of the Manvantaric Dawn? . . . In the Unknown Darkness . . .

2 . . . Where was Silence? Where were the ears to sense it? No, there was neither Silence nor Sound; naught save the Ceaseless Eternal Breath, which knows itself not.

3 The Hour had not yet struck; the Ray had not yet flashed into the Germ; the Matripadma had not yet swollen.

4 Her Heart had not yet opened for the One Ray to enter; thence to fall, as Three into Four, into the Lap of Maya.

5 The Seven were not yet born from the Web of Light. Darkness alone as Father–Mother, Svabhavat; and Svabhavat was in Darkness.

6 These Two are the Germ, and the Germ is One. The Universe was still concealed in the Divine Thought and the Divine Bosom.

Some of the dots are in the original, but I have slightly shortened the stanza. One sees that what is negated is beginning to be thought of. The Builders are being looked for. They should be awakening any moment now. The Sons of Light must soon be seen, the Seven. The wheel may be still Anupadaka (parentless), yet the Ray is being excitedly expected to fall into it, as the three-fold that will inform the four-fold structure of matter. That is, the electrical polarities are expected to begin to start working again, permitting the Sons of Light or Dhyan Chohans, the highest kind of gods – the highest fruits of the previous universe and previous universes – to re-embody themselves.

In the third stanza, the excitement becomes ever more intense, the joyous expectation of almost unbearable keenness:

Stanza 3

1 . . . The last vibration of the Seventh Eternity thrills through Infinitude. The Mother swells, expanding from within without, like the Bud of the Lotus.

The Matripadma, mentioned in the stanza before, was the mother-Lotus, which is now swelling out from within.

2 The Vibration sweeps along . . .

and all the things happen that were prefigured in the preceding stanza.

3 Darkness radiates Light, and Light drops one solitary Ray into the Waters, into the Mother-Deep. The Ray shoots through the Virgin Egg, the Ray causes the Eternal Egg to thrill, and drop the non-eternal Germ, which condenses into the World-Egg.

This is the arrival of the One in discrete masses of swirling gaseous matter, though

5 The Root remains, the Light remains, the Curds remain, and still Oeaohoo is One.

After this it begins to get more difficult, because there are a lot of terms to be explained and the activities of the gods become more complex. What needs to be understood is simply that they are all doing something, according to their various predispositions and abilities. They are moulding the curds of chaos into swirling nebulae, to become systems of stars. If they did not act, if all had to start from the beginning as though they were not, one can imagine that it would take too long, would not get done in the space-time of the universe now being formed. Each universe evolves beyond those that preceded it, thanks to the activities of those who, before the close of the last one, had attained, in their varying degrees, to such a stage of evolution as to be able to help in forming the new one. There is everything to give a shape to, so as, as far as possible, to lessen the violence and raggedness of chaos. Yet they cannot smooth it entirely. There are adventures and misadventures.

Our sun was not in the beginning the centre of a system of his own. He was the biggest amongst several who found themselves swirling about in proximity. Mars and Mercury had been stars in their own right, though only very small ones, in the previous universe, and coming too near this slightly larger one had the misfortune to be captured. This was not agreeable to them, and is the cause of some 'ancient rancour' felt by them, yet, being gods, they have accepted their accidental subservience with philosophy, and help loyally in the new system of which they find themselves part.

It seems to become apparent rather than be explained that some of the gods gather around themselves the fiery matter of chaos so as to become stars or systems of stars. Madame Blavatsky never uses the word 'galaxy', because in her time it had not been understood by science that the Milky Way comprised a vast spiral-shaped system of stars of which our sun was a humble member, so the term was not used; but when she talks about our system of stars, that is what she means. Far greater than our Solar Logos must be a logos of our galaxy.

10 Father-Mother spin a Web, whose upper end is fastened to Spirit, the Light of the One Darkness, and the lower one to its shadowy end, Matter; and this Web is the Universe, spun out of the Two Substances made in One, which is Svabhavat.

11 It expands when the Breath of Fire touches it; it contracts when the Breath of the Mother touches it.

12 Then, Svabhavat sends Fohat to harden the Atoms. Each is a part of the Web. Reflecting the 'Self-Existent Lord', like a mirror, each becomes in turn a World.

Stanza 4

1 . . . Listen, ye Sons of Earth . . .

This is the first we have heard of the Earth, and it is not altogether clear whether we have got to it yet or where we get to it. We have certainly reached it by Stanza 6, verse 7, wherein it is 'thy Small Wheel'. The last two stanzas tell of the doings of particular gods in regard to our Earth and its first inhabitants, but this seems rather to trespass on the terrain of *Anthropogenesis*, and I shall find it more convenient to treat their doings there.

In this more than rapid survey, I have used my own language rather than search for phrases in Madame Blavatsky's text, using perhaps some images of my own. This is because I have had to compress into a very few pages what has taken the 339 pages of her *Cosmogenesis*, which I could hardly do if I had to make actual quotations from a work conceived upon a huge scale. The explanation of every term or phrase involves her in detailed and sometimes contentious expositions – for instance, it is explained (p.119ff.) that the exact meaning of the terms 'Alaya' and 'Paramartha' is at issue between differing schools of Buddhists who conceive their meaning differently, and rather than attempt to follow and sort out the convolutions of the argument it seems better to let the intuition have its chance to play. There is the danger of losing the wood for the trees.

I have tried to find and recreate the shape of the wood. May I be forgiven.

CHAPTER 74

The Secret Doctrine,
II, Anthropogenesis

Between the stanzas ending *Cosmogenesis* and those beginning *Anthropogenesis*, a considerable number devoted to the three early Rounds have been left out. That is because the Masters despaired of rendering them intelligible, and thought best to proceed straight to what concerns us more closely, our own globe as it begins to acquire physical form, and our own appearance upon it. It is possible that the long intervening section concerning symbolism, apparently so ill-placed, was strategically inserted to give us the sense of time's having passed and prepare us for taking up, with discontinuity, in the middle of something.

Stanza 1

1 The Lha which turns the Fourth is Servant to the Lha(s) of the Seven, they who revolve, driving their Chariots around their Lord, the One Eye [of our World]. His Breath gave Life to the Seven. It gave Life to the First.

2 Said the Earth: 'Lord of the Shining Face, my House is empty . . . Send thy Sons to people this Wheel. Thou hast sent thy Seven Sons to the Lord of Wisdom. Seven times doth he see Thee nearer to himself, seven times more doth he feel Thee. Thou hast forbidden thy Servants, the small Rings, to catch thy Light and Heat, thy great Bounty to intercept on its passage. Send now to thy Servant the same.'

3 Said the Lord of the Shining Face: 'I shall send thee a Fire when thy work is commenced. Raise thy voice to other Lokas: apply to thy Father, the Lord of the Lotus and his Sons . . . Thy people shall be under the rule of the Fathers. Thy Men shall be mortals. The Men of the Lord of Wisdom, not the Sons of Soma, are immortal. Cease thy complaints. Thy Seven Skins are yet on them . . . Thou art not ready. Thy Men are not ready.'

4 After great throes she cast off her old Three and put on her new Seven Skins, and stood in her first one.

Some of this, if one has begun to become accustomed to a certain kind of idiom, is clear at a glance. 'Lha' is Tibetan for 'god'. It is probably Koot Hoomi who, in translating from the Senzar, has slipped into what to him is a homely term, forgetting he did not introduce it earlier. Although we are in the Fourth Round, the fourth, here, probably means the Earth, as the fourth physical globe counting out from the sun. Indeed, we shall find Madame Blavatsky takes it so. The Lord of Wisdom will be Mercury (in Sanskrit, Buddha is both wisdom and the planet Mercury). It is nearer to the sun than Earth is; we might think it too hot, but the Earth is complaining of being less advantageously placed. Its informing spirit – for the Earth is a being's body – is asking for help, and not at once receiving it.

Stanza 2

5 The Wheel turned for thirty crores more. It constructed Rupas; soft Stones that hardened, hard Plants that softened. Visible from Invisible, Insects and small lives . . . After thirty crores she turned round. She lay on her back; on her side . . . She would call no Sons of Heaven, she would ask no Sons of Wisdom. She created from her own Bosom. She evolved Water-men, terrible and bad.

6 The Water-Men, terrible and bad, she herself created from the remains of others. From the dross and slime of her First, Second and Third she formed them. The Dhyani

came and looked . . . the Dhyani from the bright Father-Mother, from the White Regions they came, from the Abodes of the Immortal Mortals.

7 Displeased they were. 'Our Flesh is not there. No fit Rupas for our Brothers of the Fifth. No Dwellings for the Lives. Pure Waters not turbid, they must drink. Let us dry them.'

8 The Flames came. The Fires with the Sparks; the Night-Fires and the Day-Fires. They dried out the turbid dark Waters. With their heat they quenched them. The Lhas of the High, the Lamayin of Below came. They slew the Forms which were two and four-faced. They fought the Goat-Men, and the Dog-Headed Men, and the Men with fishes' bodies.

9 Mother-Water, the Great Sea wept. She arose, she disappeared into the Moon, which had lifted her, which had given her birth.

10 When they were destroyed, Mother Earth remained bare. She asked to be dried.

Note that in *Anthropogenesis* the numbering of the verses is continuous through the stanzas, of which there are twelve. In *Cosmogenesis* it is not.

The Earth, not at first receiving sufficient help, tried to create from what she had, but managed only to produce monsters. The situation attracted the attention of a higher kind of gods. There is a deep mystery about who these were. Gods are of different kinds. Not all want to become Regents of stars or planets. The Flames, who were intelligence itself, seem to be of a different order. The Fires of the Night are the higher, belonging in some more direct way to the Darkness (or non-manifested Light) that preceded the manifested Light.

The moon or Soma, is in *The Secret Doctrine*, the fourth or D globe of the chain preceding our chain of globes. At the time when it was published, this was totally at variance with astronomical theory, that the moon broke off from the Earth. Since the manned landings on the moon, however, it has been realised the moon is very old, certainly not younger than the Earth. *The Secret Doctrine* says she is the Earth's mother. The more advanced among humanity did not evolve during the previous Rounds of the Earth. They came straight across from the moon, Globe D to Globe D. The waters rising towards the moon; Blavatsky refers to the moon's action on the tides.

Stanza 3

11 The Lord of the Lords came . . .

12 The great Chohans called the Lords of the Moon, of the airy bodies: 'Bring forth Men, Men of your nature. Give them their forms within. She will build coverings without. Males–Females will they be . . .'

The Lords of the Moon who are summoned are beings who completed their human evolution on the moon, so they serve as gods on this planet. They have to 'bring forth', not in the sense of generate, but provide forms for those who evolved on the earlier globes of this planet and need their first experience in human bodies. The Earth can provide the matter for their physical bodies; it is the subtle lining within the physical that the Lords of the Moon are being asked to create.

This they do by oozing them forth from their own bodies. The First Root Race of this globe was still aethereal, without colour. The bodies of its individuals were the merest films, insensitive to temperature, not subject to death, sexless, multiplying their kind by oozing them from their own bodies; as they themselves had been oozed by the Lunar Pitris (fathers) upon seven parts of the first continent to rise from the waters, which will be the last to remain, the only one that, having once risen, never disappears, whence it is called the Imperishable Land. Where is it?

She says it is ever watched by the Pole Star.[1] This suggests the North Pole. The difficulty is that there is at the North Pole only water. Further, she gives to the Second Root Race the Hyperborean continent, stretching south west (strictly, all directions from the North Pole are due south) to cover Arctic Asia and Europe.

So what is left? She told us in the first volume that Mount Meru, the 'abode of the gods . . .'[2] is the North Pole'.[3] In the *Vishnu Purana* and others, Meru is a mountain, but one of her themes is that the Puranas are not about India but about the early Root Races and their continents. 'Meru' means different things at different levels. In the uterus, it is the amnion, and in relation to our globe it is the matrix,[4] which sounds a suitable place for the first humans to be born from. In *Isis Unveiled* she said the name of America had nothing to do with Amerigo Vespucci (whoever heard of a land being named after the Christian name of an explorer?), but everything to do with Meru.[5] In *The Secret Doctrine* she tells us Meru represents the seventh principle, Atma, or spirituality, and is the seat of Brahma and the true Olympus. The significance of America lies in its being the prolongation of the Imperishable Land or Meru throughout the two hemispheres[6] (so presumably the distributor of its influence to all latitudes). Yet in Volume I she referred to 'Mount Meru, which is the North Pole'. Why does she think the North Pole is in North America? According to a modern geological work, *Earth's Shifting Crust*, by Charles H. Hapgood,[7] which carries a preface by Albert Einstein, it once was, though not always in the same part of it. So which part is Meru, the Imperishable Land? Whether according to the geological theory just alluded to or to its rival, the continental drift theory, whatever else comes and goes, Greenland is always there, always the same shape. Certainly it has proved imperishable. Its rock is pre-Cambrian, that is to say the oldest known. I think the Imperishable Land is Greenland. There may or may not be on it some particular peak that is Meru. The interior is blank on the map (untroubled by profane eyes). Yet Meru does not have to be a spectacular mountain, for Madame Blavatsky says that to clairvoyant sight a great cone, like that shown rising from the Buddha's head, representing the radiation of his spirituality, can be seen rising from it, whilst at its antipodes can be seen a vast concave depression or pit, from which pours forth all foulness. The poles are the head and vent of the body; Shamballa, not yet risen from the waters, its heart. (She does not exactly say, but I think there is an implication that while Meru is the seat of the gods, or Lunar Pitris, and perhaps of others who have an origin other than ours, and therefore though they do their duty by ours cannot really feel with us; Shamballa is the dwelling of those very high ones who, having evolved from our own humanity, though they may by now have passed the Pitris, can feel with us. It rose only after humanity had become endowed with mind.)

With the help of a second influx of rather higher gods from the moon, the Second Root Race was developed. It was not markedly different from the First, which had merged and disappeared into it. It was still sexless, and reproduction was by budding.[8]

The first two Root Races had been Borean, but the land of the Third Root Race occupied the Indian and Pacific Oceans. Ceylon (Sri Lanka), Madagascar, Australasia and Easter Island are remains of it. For it, she borrows the name of Lemuria, with acknowledgements to Mr P.L. Sclater, who opined on zoological grounds that Madagascar, Ceylon and Sumatra must have been one.

The Third Root Race was dark in hue, still huge, still only semi-solid, and hermaphrodite. Reproduction was by exudation of drops of sweat,[9] which became eggs with hard shells, within which the young matured and from which they hatched. What was still lacking was anything in the way of mind.

Stanza 4

17 The Breath needed a Form; the Fathers gave it. The Breath needed a Gross Body; the Earth gave it. The Breath needed the Spirit of Life; the Solar Lhas breathed it into its Form. The Breath needed a Mirror of its Body: 'We gave it our own!' – said the Dhyanis. The Breath needed a Vehicle of Desire: 'It has it!' – said the Drainer of Waters. But Breath needs a Mind, to embrace the Universe; 'We cannot give that!' – said the Fathers. 'I never had it!' – said the Spirit of the Earth. 'The Form would be consumed were I to give it mine!' – said the Great Fire. Man remained an empty senseless Bhuta.

We come, now, to the most dramatic event in the whole history of our globe. It had become obvious that progress here was slow, and our plight attracted an intervention. 'The Sons of Wisdom, the Sons of Night . . . the Lords of the Flame . . .'; they are called by so many names.

The Night of which they were Sons seems to be that of the darkness (which is not Darkness) that precedes the Day of Manifestation, and I have heard it suggested that it means they were conscious even during Pralaya. They were triangles, not cubes; i.e. their principle was that of intelligence. They were the essence of intelligence. They did not come from the moon. They did not come from any part of our planetary chain. Where did they come from? Madame Blavatsky is notably reticent about saying it outright, yet it transpires through significant passages. She quotes the commentary on the cylinders:[10]

> *Light comes through Shukra [Venus], who receives a triple supply, and gives one-third of it to the Earth. Therefore the two are called 'Twin-sisters' but the Spirit of the Earth is subservient to the 'Lord' of Shukra.*

> *. . . Every sin committed upon Earth is felt by Ushanas-Shukra. The Guru of the Daityas is the Guardian Spirit of the Earth and Men. Every change of Shukra is felt on, and reflected by, the Earth . . .*
> *Every world has its parent Star and sister Planet. Thus Earth is the adopted child and younger brother of Venus . . .*

Although the inhabitants of Earth *are of their own kind*, this sympathy between the two globes brought some of the Sons of Mind (Manasa) to come here.

Stanza 7

25 How did the Manasa, the Sons of Wisdom, act? They rejected the Self-born. They are not ready. They spurned the Sweat-born. They are not quite ready. They would not enter the first Egg-born.

26 When the Sweat-born produced the Egg-born, the twofold, the mighty and powerful with bones, the Lords of Wisdom said, 'Now we shall create.'

27 The Third Race became the Vahan of the Lord of Wisdom.

'Vahan' means 'vehicle'.

One remarks a certain progression in the races, not only with regard to increasing bodily substantiality but also to modes of reproduction. The First Race was 'sexless'; the Second was 'a-sexual' (this may sound the same, but they are contrasted so there must be some difference). The Third was 'Androgyne or Hermaphrodite'. This seems to imply the possession of male and female organs (which the earlier races had not), though both contained within each individual, who used them internally in order to reproduce. Even within the mould so achieved, there were changes. A fluid was evolved to harden the shells of the eggs (which the drops of sweat had become), so that the human foetus was able to gestate for several years within the eggs (which were now enormous), and it hatched as a sizeable child, able to look after itself.

Madame Blavatsky thinks it helpful to compare the modes of reproduction in the early human Root Races with those noted in primitive physical organisms: that of the First has correspondence with the division by fission of the amoeba; that of the Second with the budding seen in some kinds of plants (I would instance cacti) and in sea-anemones; that of the early Third with the throwing off of spores by mosses and mushrooms; that of the early-middle Third, just before the period at which we are arriving, to the hermaphroditism of the majority of plants and some primitive animals such as worms and snails, in which male and female organs appear in the same individual.[9]

What she wishes us to see is that there is 'no permanence in any particular mode of reproducing life'.[11]

A detail she does not mention until later, but which it seems appropriate to bring in here, is that the androgynous Third, being a unitary being, had only a single eye, in the middle of the head, so that it could see backwards as well as forwards. I think she must mean in the crown of the head, so that it was able to swivel. This would make it face upwards to the sky, I would suggest like a daisy (day's-eye). The example she gives is a lizard which has three eyes,[12] one in a depression in the crown of its head – significantly, the lizard is found in New Zealand, a remnant of the Lemurian continent.

This was the race into which the gods from Venus had come, at sacrificial diminution of their own lustre, to incarnate, so as to stimulate in it the development of mind.

Unfortunately, the next development was not as intended:

Stanza 8

29 Animals with bones, dragons of the deep, and flying Sarpas were added to the creeping things. They that creep on the ground got wings. They of the long necks in the water became the progenitors of the fowls of the air.

30 During the Third, the boneless animals grew and changed; they became animals with bones; their Chayas became solid.

31 The animals separated the first. They began to breed. The two-fold man separated also. He said, 'Let us as they; let us unite and make creatures.' They did . . .

By 'separated' is meant divided into two sexes, as at present. Madame Blavatsky shows that Darwin, in his *Origin of Species* came very close to divining that all aminals had been androgynous before they became bisexual. He noted:

one sex bears rudiments of various accessory parts appertaining to the reproductive system, which properly belong to the opposite sex . . . some remote progenitor of the whole vertebrate kingdom appears to have been hermaphrodite or androgynous . . . In the mammalian class the male possess rudiments of a uterus with the adjacent passages in the vesiculae prostaticae: they bear also rudiments of mammae, and some male marsupials have traces of a marsupial sac . . . Are we then to suppose some extremely ancient mammal continued androgynous, after it had acquired the chief distinction of its class . . .?

How, she asks,[13] having come so near to divining the secret doctrine of the stanzas, did he shy away from where his logic was leading him? Was it some illogical revulsion from the idea that made him answer his own question? 'It seems improbable'. Why improbable? The only reason given by Darwin is that hermaphroditism is not found in amphibians. One has to go down to fishes to find it in the vertebrate kingdom. From the point of view of *The Secret Doctrine*, that is irrelevant so far as concerns human development, since we did not come from the lower vertebrates of this planet. We have been animals, certainly, but much, very much longer ago. For the more developed amongst humanity, that was on the moon. On this globe, humans were before the animals.

That the animals should separate into sexes was perhaps inevitable, since, as we began to approach nearer to the mid-point of the Round, the angle of polarity between the electrical positive and negative was widening. What was not expected was that humans should do the same.

Was it the fault of the Sons of Wisdom from Venus? Perhaps it was. They had come to endow humans with mind, but such an endowment may have been unbalancing.

Blavatsky does not deal with their possible responsibility for this unwanted development, but she does make the point that it was:[14]

no part of the evolutionary law that the Fifth Principle (Manas) should receive its complete development before the Fifth Round. All such prematurely developed intellects . . . in our Race are *abnormal*; they are those whom we have called the 'Fifth Rounders'.

It will be remembered that Koot Hoomi had said all great philosophers, artists, scientists and statesmen are Fifth Rounders. We would not have them but for the gods from Venus. They brought the gift of development to the level expected only of the Fifth Round (at any rate to those able to receive it) while we are only in the Fourth Round. It is, she says, the incitement to the acquisition of knowledge which provoked the fall into sexual generation, prior to which there was no death, which is the real meaning of that story about Adam and Eve and the serpent in the book of Genesis; that, once one has the key, is truer than Darwin, for it derives from the wisdom-doctrine of the stanzas via Babylon, but, at so many removes as to have become further distorted than in the Puranas, which already show distortion. The serpent, in esoteric traditions, is the symbol of knowledge. She says nothing of the symbolism of the apple. It is everywhere sacred to Venus, but why? May I suggest that it is because if one cuts an apple through its equator, one sees in each half a perfect five-pointed star? The pentagram is inscribed by the seed-cases. The apple is signed. I also wonder why the serpent is knowledge. Could it be because it coils and its coils form the spiral of life, built upon the Golden Ratio of 1:618034, displayed in the whorls of a sunflower seed-head, a snail's shell and discernible in the human figure? A cobra's head, poised above its coils, could be said to dominate the cycles. It was grotesque to personify the Sons of Mind as the Devil; yet the gods from Venus were 'Rebel Angels' in that they brought us forward faster than was in the plan for this system of worlds. In that sense, the lunar gods were obeying and the Venusian gods were rebellious, yet the 'war in Heaven' is a misleading phrase. There was a difference of view as to how fast we could be brought on safely. To draw a parallel, the Chohan never really believed the Theosophical Society would succeed, as in his view humanity was not ready for the revelation, yet, since the Masters Morya and Koot Hoomi wished to try he did not prohibit their initiative, but even lent some support to it, hoping against the voice of his own experience to be proved wrong. The Sons of Venus were not cast down; they fell, in the sense that natural karma entailed their incarnating in the divided bodies, or at least it was so in the case of some of them. Some, it seems, the 'virgin ascetics' or Kumaras, though they have since that time been here, have never yet been born of man and woman.

The Secret Doctrine is wholly on the side of the Flames or Sons of Mind who came to us from Venus; had they not taught us to 'skip' an intermediate stage?[15]

> the cyclic pilgrimage of this Round would have had to be performed through all the planes of existence half unconsciously, if not entirely so, as in the case of animals. It is owing to the rebellion of intellectual life against the morbid inactivity of pure spirit that we are what we are – self-conscious, thinking men, with the capabilities and attributes of Gods in us, for good as much as for evil.

There was, however, one heavy casualty:

> 32 Those which had no Spark took huge she-animals unto then. They begat upon them dumb races. Dumb they were themselves. But their tongues untied. The tongues of their progeny remained still. Monsters they bred. A race of crooked red-haired monsters going on all fours. A dumb race to keep the shame untold.

Today, intercourse between different species produces no progeny, and even the progeny of horse and donkey is sterile. It is said the Third Race had bones, but they were probably still only soft, supporting bodies still only semi-solid. The union with the she-animals was fertile, and those who had entered into it found themselves doomed to incarnation in their misshapen progeny. They became the ancestors of the anthropoids. She agrees with de Quatrefages that the apes descend from man, not man from the apes.[16] She refers not to the gay little monkeys that swing by their tails, which we are left to presume natural animals, but to the tailless ape, genus pithecoid. Its history can be told from its development from foetus and new-born infant. There is always a recapitulation of the earlier forms through which it has passed before the final form is reached. In the human, the forehead improves as it grows. In the ape, it is the other way round. She cites Gratiolet for the observation that the forehead is at one moment of a certain height, then recedes, the skull flattening and the facial bones and jaw projecting. This recapitulation of the history of the ape shows it to have been better than it is. These French scientists are nearer to the occult doctrine than is Darwin.

Here I would interpose that the modern medium of television gave us recently on the BBC a picture of an orang-outang mother and child, in which it was astoundingly obvious that the head of the baby was better than that of the mother; it was almost human, betraying, as Madame Blavatsky would say, the human past of the race. Moved by this, I looked up 'orang-outang' in Maunder's *Treasury of Natural History* (1870), one of the books from my grandfather's library, and read, 'In early youth, it is remarkable for its rotundity of cranium and height of forehead;

but these outward marks of superior mental power disappear as the animal advances in age'. All apes look unhappy. Madame Blavatsky says they will regain their human form, but it will not be until the beginning of the next round.

Even for the humans who abstained from bestiality, the division into sexes brought further changes. They could no longer see out of their eye. Skin grew over it, and hair over the skin. Then bone crept up and formed a harder layer, beneath which the eye was buried. Unable to see, the eye shrank down and receded into the middle of the head – the atrophied seat of the soul, the pineal gland. She salutes Descartes, and for a description of the gland draws upon Quain,[17] but observed that anatomists can only examine pineals that are dead. They can never see one that is functioning. To replace it, two new eyes worked their way to the surface, no longer at the top of the head but in the front, near the top. With the two new eyes came the development of complete symmetrical design, two of everything, practically all the way down. We have become used to it now, and take it for the norm, but it is the result of our fall into bisexual generation. (When she implies that prior to the fall there was only one of everything, does that mean Lemurian humanity had to hop, like kangaroos? They have two legs, yet use them as one, and the kangaroo is a Lemurian animal.)

She deals with organic changes, not with psychology. It may, however, be imagined that the experiencing of these changes, particularly the losing of the original, only eye, gave to the individuals the sense that something was going wrong, and that it was a punishment for having divided like animals into sexes, so occasioning that sense of shame and guilt that has caused humans to clothe themselves.

What she does say is that with the division into sexes there took place another division. There were those who still felt themselves to be their immortal and divine selves, held fast to spirit, and within the altered frame, tried to live according to the good law, and those who lost the sense of their divinity, adhered only to matter and became destructive. 'The struggle between the two began from the very day they tasted of the fruit of the Tree of Wisdom'.[18]

To put it in a biblical way, in Lemuria Adam and Eve were still in Eden. Where it is said, (Genesis I: 27), 'male and female created he them', that means in one. It was when they ate the fruit that they found themselves separated into male and female sexes and Eden was lost. The cross within the circle had become simply the cross.

Stanza 10

38 Thus, two by two, on the Seven Zones, the Third Race gave birth to the Fourth; the Sura became A-sura.

The last phrase means that the gods from Venus who had incarnated in the human race lost some of the power, though not the nature, of gods, in as much as they became subject to the limitations of the bodies. For them, this must have caused suffering, but from the point of view of the humans, 'This was the Golden Age when the gods walked the earth and mixed freely with mortals.'[19]

39 The First, on every Zone, was moon-coloured; the Second yellow like gold; the Third red; the Fourth brown, which became black with sin . . .

This related to the first four sub-races of the Fourth Root or Atlantean Race.

, 40 Then the Third and Fourth became tall with pride. 'We are the Kings; we are the gods.'

The gods from Venus still reigned, as divine kings, but the many humans who had become materialistic, insensate with pride, raised themselves up against them.

41 They took wives fair to look upon. Wives from the mindless, the narrow-headed. They bred monsters, wicked demons, male and female . . . with little minds.

So, a part of the Atlanteans repeated the sin of the mindless, mating with the progeny of the Lemurians' mating with beasts. They were the more deeply responsible for their sin, in that, their own mentality being by now keenly developed, the gap between themselves and the beasts was wider. Incarnating in their progeny, they became the pithecoids we know. We are told nothing of Atlantean women, only of this renewed bestiality of the men.

Here I should like to interpose a thought, which is not in Madame Blavatsky, but which comes to me as I write. In the fourth sub-race of the Fourth Root Race, of the Fourth Round of the Fourth Globe of our chain, the nadir of the whole cycle was reached, and – to pick up my earlier geometrical symbolism – the angle between the positive and negative, male and female, electrical poles, had increased all the way from 0 to 180. The difference between the sexes was, therefore, at its widest, the opposition between them at its most violent. The masculine sought the feminine at its earthiest, its furthest remove from spirit. Hence, she-animals were preferred by them to women. They sought the complement not at their own level but at a rung beneath it, so dragging themselves further down. Bestiality is probably very rare today, but seems to have been with these early races the primary sin. Except for pride, it is the only one mentioned in the stanzas. Recurring again and again, plainly it was very grave, and for two reasons. One is that association is important in occultism. To associate with a higher being, to whose level one aspires to raise oneself, is most beneficial. To guide, teach and train one junior in understanding also brings its reward; but to descend to the inferior's level of vibration can only pollute one. Moreover, from a god's-eye point of view, the human population being still small, what was hoped of those privileged to incarnate was that they would generate more bodies – but wholesome bodies – in which the souls still awaiting their turn could incarnate. The polluted forms, being too vile to offer those in the queue, were fit habitations only for those who had generated them, who became the pithecoids we know, gorilla, chimpanzee, orang-outang . . . and the queue could not shorten as fast as it should. Phallic worship developed:

> 42 They built temples for the human body. Male and female they worshipped. Then the Third Eye acted no more.

(It had been disappearing over a long period.)

Stanza 11

> 43 They built huge cities. Of rare earths and metals they built. Out of the fires vomited, out of the white stone of the mountains and of the black stone, they cut their own images, in their own size and likeness, and worshipped them.

There was extraordinary mental development, though applied only to material things. Discovering a law of nature yet to be rediscovered, they built carriages that transported them through the air. Descriptions of Rama, travelling in his air-boat, show that the *Ramayana*, though composed late (by this time-scale) carries over to us a reminiscence of an Atlantean story.

She has one chapter, 'The coming race', anachronistically placed in the previous volume, which becomes relevant here. She refers to the work of a Mr J.R. Keely, who defined electricity as 'a certain form of atomic vibration', and to his estimation of the number of vibrations per second, or 'molecular, inter-molecular, atomic . . . inter-atomic . . .' the number increasing as the table progresses. Beneath the table, she says that Mr Keely was not allowed (by the Masters of Wisdom) to push his researches beyond the limit he did, because:[21]

> that which he had unconsciously discovered is the terrible sidereal Force known to, and named by the Atlanteans MASH-MAC . . . it is the *Vril* of Bulwer-Lytton's *Coming Race*, and of the Coming Races of our mankind. The name *Vril* may be a fiction; the Force itself is a fact . . .
>
> It is this vibratory Force which, when aimed at an army from an *Agniratha* (fire-chariot) fixed on a flying vessel or balloon . . . would reduce to ashes 100,000 men and elements as easily as it would a dead rat.

In Bulwer-Lytton's novel, *The Coming Race*, his imagined people possessed a universal power which provided the illumination for their streets and within their homes, and the motor of air-borne vessels and all other forms of transport. It could heal, but it could also kill, on such a scale that, were it used, the entire human race would be wiped out. This made warfare unthinkable, and so had ushered in an age of universal peace.

We do, she says, need the force, because, as she quotes Keely:[22]

> The coalmines of the world cannot long afford the increasing drain made upon them. Steam has reached the utmost limits of power and does not fulfil the requirements of the age. It knows that its days are numbered. Electricity holds back with bated breath, dependent upon the approach of her sister colleague . . .

This refers to the coming force. On the other hand, says Madame Blavatsky, we could not at the present time be allowed to rediscover it, or we would misuse it as a weapon of war. Europe could be reduced in a few days to primitive chaos and 'no man left to tell the tale'.[23]

I sent photostats of the pages about this to my friend Dr Margaret Little, whose husband John is a physicist (formerly at the University of Strathclyde), asking if he would be good enough to read them and say if it appeared to him that the line of research Keely was prevented from following further could have led to nuclear fission. Dr Margaret Little replied, saying her husband thought that, on the information about Keely's ideas given here, they would have led to television rather than to the bomb. On the other hand, he was impressed by the passage about the need for another power, and the whole was most oddly apocalyptic. Could it be that the 'wires' had got crossed somehow, and that Madame Blavatsky had got the right idea, a true perception, even if the nature of the steps towards it were as given by Keely incorrectly conceived?

If, with their spiritual degeneration, the Atlanteans had nuclear power, was it with this they bombed the land till it let the waters in that covered them, rather than that they were destroyed by the gods as a punishment for their sin? Madame Blavatsky says it was not exactly either. The tilt of the axis of the Earth was not always the twenty-three and a fraction degrees that it is now. It has been both more and less. There are limits between which it oscillates. When it reaches one of the limits and changes direction, there is a cataclysm. The dates when they must come are known to the Masters of Wisdom, who were given the calculations, it seems, by Narada and Asuramaya.

Who are these two? Asuramaya, we are told, was the great astronomer of the Atlantean civilisation, but he based his calculations on data given him by Narada. Narada is the most mysterious figure in *The Secret Doctrine*. He seems to have been one of the gods who came from Venus, was perhaps the chief of them, but peculiar things are said of him. He:[24]

> is the sole confidant and the executor of the universal decrees of Karma and Adi-Buddha; a kind of active and ever-incarnating Logos, who leads and guides human affairs from the beginning to the end of the Kalpa . . .
> What Narada is cannot be explained in print; but it may be remarked that if there is in the Hindu pantheon a Deity which resembles Jehova in tempting by 'suggestion' of thoughts . . . it is Narada . . . to serve universal progress and evolution.

He visits the infernal region, Patala, the South Pole, and is perhaps the pupil of:

> the Serpent who bears the Seven Patalas and the entire world like a diadem upon his heads, and who is the great teacher of Astronomy.
> . . . Narada is said, as soon as he dies in one body, to be reborn in another.

This surely might be said for the Masters of Wisdom or at least some of them, but it is obviously said of Narada in some special sense. Since the gods from Venus are all self-sacrificing, if he visits the infernal regions perhaps it is to try to redeem what would otherwise be lost souls. The lunar gods set an example but do not go fishing for those who fail to follow it. A high standard is expected of those who become pupils of the Masters, and if they sink too badly they are dropped, at any rate until they try to do better. Narada perhaps occupies himself with the wicked, to attempt to redeem them. It is also he who marks the terms of cycles.

That may be significant with regard to cataclysms. Yet it should not be thought there was only one. There were several, with vast aeons of time between them. There was a long period during which the holy had grouped on an Atlantic island, the White Island, in the Puranas *Ruta*. Colonel Wilford wanted to make this Britain, but, she says, it was close to the Tropic of Cancer, between 22° and 24° N.[26] Tenerife, she suggests, is a vestige of it, and the Cap Verdes– actually they lie south of the latitudinal belt she gives, and I wonder if she does not mean the Canaries.

Yet it may have spread a bit, for she also says that for the people there, Mount Atlas was the representative of Meru, the mountain where the gods dwelt. For an age, the people defending the good law here were at perpetual war with the besieging forces of darkness. Did the darkness seem to be gaining? She quotes a passage from the series of commentaries parallel to the one she usually followed:

> *The Kings of Light have departed in wrath. The sins of men have become so black that Earth quivers in her great agony . . . The azure seats remain empty. Who of the brown, who of the red, or yet of the black races can sit in the seats of the blessed, the seats of knowledge and mercy?*

This seems to imply the gods had withdrawn, at least from visibility. 'For in the age when the Gods forsook the Earth . . . the ecliptic had become parallel with the meridian'.[27] What follows by way of astronomical explanation I find difficult to comprehend, and it seems to me there is confusion in a semi-scientific book which she has gone to in search of terms. After years of mulling over it attempting diagrammatic representation and setting up solid models and moving them around, I know what I *think* she means, and will be so hardy as to re-express it, in terms which at least mean something to me, and therefore, may to others. There was a time when the Earth was lying on its side, so that twice a year the poles of its axis of rotation were pointing straight at, and straight away from the sun, and if one were standing at the one now called the North Pole, at noon on midsummer's day one would have the sun, in its conjunction with the Bull's Eye (Aldeboran) amongst the Rain Stars (Hyades) – through which the Solsticial Colure then ran – directly above one's head, with Aquarius and Leo at the opposing termini of one's horizon; while if one stood at its antipodes, one would see the whole of the other half of the zodiac arching over the middle of the midnight sky, the great red star of the Scorpion (Antares) glaring down from directly above one's upturned face. Thus it was at the moment of the cataclysm, in which the lands that filled what is now the Atlantic went beneath the waves, to the accompaniment of a great deluge of rain, which completed the devastation.

The gods did not cause the cataclysm, but only they knew where and when it was coming, even to the minute, and its imminence provided an occasion to scan humanity and make a judgement as to which individuals were worth saving. To them, messengers were sent to advise them in which direction they should remove. Thus, the evil of Atlantis perished.

46 All Holy saved, the Unholy destroyed. With them most of the huge animals, produced from the sweat of the Earth.

Stanza 12

47 Few men remained. Some yellow, some brown and black, and some red remained. The Moon-coloured were gone forever.

It is implied rather than explained that one of the places to which the saved were guided was Egypt. At any rate, Egypt was a colony settled by the gods from Venus, who formed the Divine Dynasties and gave the people wheat. She draws to attention that though the other grains have 'been traced to primogenital forms in certain species of wild grasses' (what countryman does not know wild oats and wild barley?) 'wheat has hitherto defied the efforts of botanists to trace it to its source'.[28]

Another part of the saved were taken to Shamballa, an island newly risen in a sea that is now the Gobi Desert. From these the Fifth Root Race, the Indo-European, was developed.

48 The Fifth produced from the Holy stock remained; it was ruled over by the first Divine Kings.

49 . . . [The serpents] who re-descended, who made peace with the Fifth, who taught and instructed it.

So the stanzas end, on this note of reconciliation and hope – not that we are out of trouble yet, but the wise ones have come back to us.

CHAPTER 75

The Secret Doctrine: the Kali Yuga, Krishna, Buddha and Maitreya

The stanzas ended with Vaivasvata Manu's leading out from the doomed lands of Atlantis those from amongst whom the Fifth Root Race would be formed. Madame Blavatsky does not say much about the Fifth, that to which we of the Indo-Germanic or brown and white belong. With their ancestors' timely extraction from the old Atlantic continent, the worst was passed. The Cape Horn of human history had been rounded. We had passed the midnight of the Earth's incarnation, not that there would not still be black patches. The worst weather sometimes follows the winter solstice, and the coldest and darkest part of the night seems to be after midnight. But yet, the sun of the day or year is rising.

Humanity as a whole has passed the mid-point of its Kali Yuga (Black Age), yet each Root Race has its Kali Yuga, and that of the fifth began at 2 hrs 27 min. 30 sec. on 16 February 3102 BC.[1] (The reader should not be frightened by two juxtaposed tables, in the first of which the Kali Yuga is given as having commenced 4,989 years before 1887, the year in which she was writing, and the second of which gives the duration of the Kali Yuga as 432,000 years.[2] The second table was taken from an article which had been contributed to *The Theosophist* of November 1885 by Rao Bahadur P. Screenivas Row. She lifted it, with acknowledgements, but apparently without re-reading, at any rate without noticing that the Kali Yuga here referred to, and accorded this long duration, was that of the whole course of humanity on this planet, and that its appendage to the table above created the impression we had most of it still to go, which would be depressing.)

Krishna died, killed by an arrow, on 16 February 3102 BC, and it is on the day of his death that our Kali Yuga commenced.[3] (Should not those of our astrologers who want the zodiac pegged to a fixed starting point, instead of the Vernal Point, which regresses through the constellations with the precession of the Equinoxes, consider as their alternative starting-point the degree of the eclipse at the beginning of the Kali Yuga, as given above?)[4]

But who was Krishna, that his death should mark a cycle? Because *Anthropogenesis* is mainly the story of the human races in the mass, not much is said about those who became the great teachers. We may perhaps glimpse that each Root Race has its own Manu, Vaivasvata being the one for the fifth, and that the Manu, who incarnates to project the physical type, has as his particular care the evolution of the physical forms, and is the ruler. Each sub-race also has its own Manu.

The Buddhas, on the other hand, are concerned less with regulating the external behaviour of the people than with the education of consciences and spiritual understanding. He whom we know as the Buddha, whose name was Gautama, Prince Siddhartha, heir to the throne of Kapilavastu on the Ganges, which he renounced to pursue his meditations, is the Buddha of the Fifth Root Race, called the Fourth Buddha because, as she had explained in a letter from Würzburg to Sinnett,[5] for the First Root Race the equivalent office was performed by a Dhyan Chohan, none from our humanity yet being ready, so that the Buddha for the Second Root Race was the First Buddha, and so on. The letter ends with a table;[6] it is not very clear, yet it conveys the idea that one who is destined to be a Buddha makes a previous public incarnation as Bodhisattva. This is a term used by Buddhists in various ways. Dr Suzuki, in his *Mahayana Buddhism*, uses it for anyone who has renounced Nirvana to stay and help mankind, and Madame Blavatsky sometimes uses it so, but here she is using it as a title for the incarnation of a Buddha-to-be in which his career is (in my phrase) a full dress-rehearsal for what it will be in the one in which he assumes Buddhahood. So is the significance of Krishna that he was Maitreya's Bodhisattva incarnation? In his person, then, people would have been getting a fore-glimpse of what the Buddha to the Sixth Root Race would be like, even before the Buddha for our own Fifth Root Race had come.

It is the special distinction of Gautama Buddha (born c.563 or 560 BC) that he is the first, and indeed still the only human (except for Tsongka-pa, who however, is himself), to have achieved the status of a Dhyan Chohan, able to rove interstellar space in full consciousness, whilst still continuing at will in his physical body on earth.[7] Does this imply that he can bring his attention to more than one thing at a time? For Masters of Wisdom less than he, omniscience is still serial; they may be able to know what is going on in any part of the globe if they bring their attention to it, but can like ordinary people only bring their attention to one thing at a time.

In the fifth volume of *The Secret Doctrine*, the chapter, 'The mystery of Buddha' begins, 'Now the mystery of Buddha lies in this . . .'[8] What it lies in, apparently, is that, like all those great ones who have, of their compassion, tried to teach humanity how to do better, he gave out too much. (Herein, it may be noticed, he falls into line with Narada, disobedient to the Solar Logos, our humble Masters of Wisdom, not disobedient but very nearly forcing the hand of their Chohan.) Though his attainment and divulgation brought about the illumination of many who received his teaching, its suddenness did upset some adherents of traditional Brahmanism, and for this there was (contrary tradition notwithstanding) a karma. To deal with this, he came back about fifty years after his death in the person of 'Shankara, the great Vedantic teacher of India'.[9] (This, one may observe, is in line with what seems to be a principle, elsewhere evident, that if one has offended against a particular people, one's karma is to be reborn into that people.) What follows is difficult to understand, but I think what she means is that this was not a reincarnation in the usual sense but an especially close overshadowing of another individual, so that he might be said to be acting in and through him, or the two as one. (When Madame Blavatsky wrote to Sinnett excitedly from Würzburg that she had just been informed Shankara had made himself the real head of the Theosophical Society, she certainly thought of him not as an incarnation of the Buddha but as a distinct individuality.)

After that time, he overshadowed one or two people.

In a further chapter, 'Tsong-Kha-Pa – Lohans in China', she repeats what she had earlier written in *The Theosophist*, that Tsongka-pa was 'an incarnation of Amita Buddha Himself'.[10] The capital H is significant here, and I think her simple meaning is that Tsongka-pa was not another person overshadowed by the Buddha, but the Buddha, fully reincarnated. Moreover, this is in line with Koot Hoomi's references to him in the Mahatma Letters. He exhibited in his physical person, she goes on to say, characteristics which distinguish a Buddha.

His most apparent impact was upon Tibet and China (she mentions Chinese monasteries, near Tien-t'ai and at Yinigching in Chusan where his teaching used to be conserved, though the conserving Lohans have since had to find a more remote retreat).

Nevertheless, she thinks of his incarnation as Tsongkapa as especially significant as being the one in which he directed his initiated teachers to make a special effort to enlighten the Pelings (westerners) 'each century, at a certain specified point of the cycle'[11] (which we know from Koot Hoomi to be the last quarter of each century).

Other teachers – the evolved thinkers amongst us – have already attained in the Fourth Round to Fifth Round consciousness, but his consciousness is already that of the Sixth Round. He will overshadow a 'chosen individual . . . every decimillenium',[12] but will not reincarnate again on this globe; he will do, when we are all on the next planet.[13]

CHAPTER 76

Attacks on *The Secret Doctrine*

That Max Müller would jeer was forseeable. In her *From the Caves and Jungles of Hindostan*, Madame Blavatsky had reproved him as a stay-at-home scholar of texts who had never set foot in India, for 'rolling in the mud' L. Jacolliot, the French missionary, who had spent twenty years in the country. Müller will not have read that, for it had not yet been translated from Russian, but just because he was what she said, he attacked her because hers was not the orientalism of the texts he knew. In the *Nineteenth Century* magazine of May 1893, he wrote that her teaching was:

> simply a medley of well-known though generally misunderstood Brahmanic or Buddhistic doctrines . . . everything is muddled or misunderstood. If I were asked what Madame Blavatsky's Esoteric Buddhism really is, I should say it was Buddhism misunderstood.

She would say it was Buddhism corrected. What Müller has not understood is that she never attempted to present the Buddhism of the texts, or the Vedanta of the texts either. Theosophy is not an introduction to Buddhism or Vedanta. Most of the Buddhists and Vedantin texts were by this time in English translation, to which those interested could proceed direct. *The Secret Doctrine* is an independent teaching which cites ancient oriental works only to show where glimpses of it transpire through them or point out where they have departed from it, on the authority of her Masters.

The Spiritualist, Coleman, ever seeking to destroy her, devoted five issues of the *Religio-Philosophical Journal* (Chicago) – 10, 17, 24, 31 August and 24 September 1889 – to an assault on it. Seeking to catch her in contradiction, he asserts that in *Isis Unveiled*, II, p.367, she said the human being had six principles, which in *The Secret Doctrine* had become seven. If, however, one looks up the reference in *Isis Unveiled*, one finds she does not give this from herself. She finds in the Egyptian texts the names of five, or perhaps six, principles.

Worse, concerning the nature of elemental spirits, he says that in *Isis Unveiled*, I, xxix, these never evolve into humans, whereas in *The Secret Doctrine*, I, p.277, they were disembodied or future humans. The first obviously is correct, and the second she could never have said. Looking up the page in *The Secret Doctrine*, I find nothing about spirits of the elements (gnomes, undines, sylphs and salamanders) on it. The passage concerns the numerical basis of the Jewish Kabbalah, and she cites an authority on Jewish esotericism for the information that:

> Elohim is a 'general abstraction' which we call in mathematics 'a constant co-efficient' or a 'general function' entering into all construction, not particular; that is, by the general ratio 1 to 31415 . . . Jehova, in the abstract sense of a 'one living God' is a single number . . . the Zohar, as witnessed by the Book of Numbers . . . gave out . . . the same doctrine as we do; that is, it makes man emanate not from one Celestial MAN but from a Septenary Group of Celestial Men, or Angels . . .

Her reference is not to the 'little people', inferior to humans, which belong to a line of evolution different from ours and who will therefore not evolve into us; but to beings infinitely superior to humans, those who had become gods on the lunar chain and, as related above, oozed out from themselves, upon seven zones of the first continent, forms in which the primitive humans of the First Root Race might incarnate. Coleman claimed to be an authority on Pali texts. His incomprehension of Jewish ones was abysmal.

CHAPTER 77

Annie Besant

Annie Besant called herself a materialist. Her materialism was her revolt against the conventional Christianity in which she had been brought up. Unhappily married to a clergyman, she had walked out, teamed up with Charles Bradlaugh, become a Socialist and fought for the Trade Unions. Together they had published *The Gospel of Atheism*. At war with all the world for these and other causes, she had yet begun to feel there was something missing in her life. Seated one evening in deep thought, she heard a voice, later to become to her the holiest on earth, tell her the light was near.[1]

A fortnight later, early in March 1889, W.T. Stead, editor of *The Review of Reviews*, asked her to review *The Secret Doctrine*. Hitherto, she had been scornful of what she had heard of Theosophy; but she took the heavy volumes home and began to read, read on and on, and knew that she was a materialist no longer.

She wrote to Madame Blavatsky, asking if she might call and see her, and received a reply, dated 15 March, assuring her she would be welcome. She asked her closest colleague, Herbert Burrows, to come with her; they took the train to Notting Hill and on a soft spring evening walked to 17 Lansdowne Road. They were shown in, and Madame Blavatsky turned round from the table at which she was working, to say, 'My dear Mrs Besant, I have so long wished to see you'.[2] She talked of this and that, nothing occult, but as they rose to go, she said, 'Oh my dear Mrs Besant, if you would only come among us!'[3]

Desire to do so fought with fierce rebellion within Mrs Besant. She saw the look that would come into Bradlaugh's eyes if she told him she had become a Theosophist. To join would mean being rejected as an apostate by so many who had sustained her in her many campaigns, even in the law courts.

She went back to 17 Lansdowne Road, again taking Burrows, to ask about the procedure for joining. Madame Blavatsky asked them if they had read the Report issued by the Society for Psychical Research. On their saying they had not, she lent them a copy and told them to read it before they decided. They read it; they saw that everything turned on the Coulombs, and they rejected it. Annie Besant went to the office of the Theosophical Society, at 7 Duke Street, Adelphi, and signed an application for membership. Then she went again to 17 Lansdowne Road, knelt down before Madame Blavatsky, and said, 'Will you accept me as a pupil and give me the honour of proclaiming you as my teacher before the world?'

Tears sprang into Madame Blavatsky's eyes. She put her hand on Annie Besant's head, and said, 'You are a noble woman. May Master bless you'.[4]

Yet even after telling Bradlaugh, there was one further pain. One of the causes for which they had fought was woman's right to contraception. They had published a pamphlet entitled, *Fruits of Philosophy: or, the Private Companion of Young Married Couples*, by Charles Knowlton. This caused them to be prosecuted for issuing an obscene publication. They had come up for trial before the Lord Chief Justice of England, Lord Cockburn, and were each sentenced to six months' imprisonment.

As a result of further legal moves, they neither of them served this; Annie Besant wrote *The Law of Population*, and they recommenced selling *Fruits of Philosophy*. This time, Annie Besant found herself deprived of the custody of her daughter.

If Madame Blavatsky had not understood what *Fruits of Philosophy* was about, she must have been made aware by Anna Kingsford's complaint and the espousal of that complaint by Koot Hoomi. Koot Hoomi had condemned it in terms of such strength as had not been used even by the Lord Chief Justice.

Madame Blavatsky had to explain to Mrs Besant that the Masters were not on her side in respect of her crusade for contraception, and she asked her to discontinue it. Mrs Besant had had in mind poor working women who could bear no addition to their families. Madame

Blavatsky said she would not judge a poor woman who availed herself of the means offered, but those means did nothing to reduce the root of the problem, which was that:

> the abnormal development of the sexual instinct in man – in whom it is far greater and more continuous than in any brute – is due to the mingling with it of the intellectual element, all sexual thoughts, desires and imaginations having created thought-forms, which have been wrought into the human race, giving rise to a continual demand, far beyond nature . . .

whereas sexual passion could be,[5] 'trained and purified into a human emotion, which may be used as one of the levers in human progress, one of the factors in human growth'. It was therefore for men and women,[6] 'to hold this instinct in complete control, to transmute it from passion into tender and self-denying affection'.

It may be retorted that if Madame Blavatsky was sexually inexperienced she knew nothing about it. But the fullness and care of her reply suggests she had been instructed as to what she should say. When the Chohan had long ago warned of the tide of 'degrading brutal materialism' which would lead the 'ignorant masses' into 'unrestrainedly indulging their animal propensities', he probably had *The Fruits of Philosophy* in mind, as one of the prime instruments of it. From the moment, therefore, that Annie Besant showed signs of moving towards the Theosophists, there would have been at Shigatsè an alert readiness to make a conversion in an important field, and it is likely that Madame Blavatsky would have been counselled as to how to put things to her.

Beyond the reasons given, there were others, which she would later give to the Esoteric School. Whether or not she gave any indication of these further reasons as early as this, Annie Besant had to go back to her poor women and tell them she had been wrong.

It was the hardest thing she ever had to do.

CHAPTER 78

Prevision of the great world wars

The German Emperor, Kaiser Frederick III, had recently died after a reign of only three months. Strangely, Madame Blavatsky looked into his dreams, just prior to his accession. The article she wrote on what she saw, entitled 'Karmic visions',[1] starts with a flash-back to the year 496. Clovis (466–511), King of the Franks and founder of the Merovingian dynasty of France, is seated within a linen tent, on a raised seat covered with skins. He has only just been baptised a Christian at Rheims, but now he is at war with the Alemanni, a Germanic tribe, and the prisoners are being brought up for him to decide their fates. One is an elderly woman, a seeress of the old Norse religion. she rebukes him for his needless ferocity, and tells him that for his punishment he will be reborn into this people he has vanquished, to find that supreme power, just when it seems his, escapes him. Incensed, he jumps up on to his impromptu throne and, crouching on it like a beast, drives a spear through her throat, impaling her to the ground with it and killing her to stop her voice.

The scene shifts to San Remo, on the Italian Riviera. It is March 1888, and he sits looking over the sea. He feels the peace and beauty of the scene, but yet his spirit is strangely laden. He cannot remember what weighs upon it, but the song of a lark soaring prompts to him the thought that *its* voice will be heard again tomorrow. 'Shall ever mine?' (Was the seeress a bard?)

He falls into a hideous dream, of:

> fallen millions . . . in stagnant ditches . . . in pools of blood under a sky black with smoke . . . A population clad in iron armour. Two score millions of men dead to all spiritual aspiration . . . A legion of war-puppets in their collectivity . . . as though a heartless, proud Fiend had clutched with iron hand the minds of a whole country. By what wicked enchantment has he brought the people back to those primeval days . . . ? The whole world is bathed in breathless expectation. Not a wife, not a mother but is haunted in her dreams by the black and ominous storm-cloud that overhangs the whole of Europe . . . Oh woe and horror! . . . I read the fatal destiny upon the brow of Europe's youth . . .

The Franco–Russian War had excited him, but even that has become repulsive to him and he wants only to keep his country out of bloodshed. He wakes, to be told his father, Kaiser Wilhelm IV, is dead. The Kaiser, now, is himself, and he has to return at once.

In the train, he falls into a troubled dream. Re-living a medley of past lives, some of them female, he remembers himself as maiden, mother and aged woman; he meets the Norns of Past, Present and Future. Past tells him that in the last life but one he wielded a blood-stained hand. Future shows him a parliament wherein meet members (he one of them) representing all the nations of the world. War has become unthinkable. He is about to feel most relieved, when a shadow falls between and he is made to understand this civilized scene belongs to the far future, after most of the present world has destroyed itself by 'vril'. The train stops, and he wakes to find himself received by 'endless lines of troops . . .'. Within three months, he died of cancer of the throat.

This was his soul's memory of the injury he had inflicted upon the seeress, imprinted on his physical form. But his sense of a burdened soul seems to have inactivated him. I wonder . . . if he had found the energy to assert himself so that two world wars did not take place, would not the cancer in his throat have receded?

CHAPTER 79

Who had Blavatsky been?

Madame Blavatsky's study of Clovis and Kaiser Frederick III gives us something we need, a chance to see the way an individual's karma works from life to life. It also raises a question: if she could now read the past incarnations of another, did she know her own? If so, she never said.

Leadbeater, in a peculiarly muddled paragraph in which he first confuses Joseph with Francis Rákóczy, goes on to say that he became the Comte de Saint-Germain, and 'at the time of the French Revolution worked much with Madame Blavatsky, who was at that period in incarnation as Père Joseph'.[1] But Père Joseph was not in incarnation at the period of the Revolution. I think Leadbeater confuses him with Joseph Balsamo (he seems to have Josephs on the brain), better known as Cagliostro, who was in incarnation then.

Cagliostro was born on 2 June 1743 at Palermo, and he perished miserably, a prisoner of the Inquisition, at San Remo on 26 August 1795. If there is a point on which Madame Blavatsky is unbalanced it is the Catholic Church. It has its sins, but her attacks upon it are emotional and her scalding pages on the Inquisition take up a disproportional amount of space in *Isis Unveiled*. This bitterness would be more than explained if she had ended her last existence in one of its gloomier cells – for heresy consisting of participation in Freemasonry. Cagliostro was, like Blavatsky, a magician. Further, he was a healer; he had learned a doctrine in Egypt and perhaps from Saint-Germain. Also, his portrait shows a face extraordinarily like Madame Blavatsky's.

As for Père Joseph, he was born on 4 November 1577, probably at Tremblay, near Paris, and died on 18 December 1638. He was a Capuchin monk, and hours of his daily life were given to contemplation and prayer; he was also a fair poet. What he is better known for is that he allowed himself to be drawn into politics and imagined he could combine with the religious life office as Foreign Minister under Cardinal Richelieu – behind whom he has been seen as the 'grey eminence' – First Minister to Louis XIII. In this capacity, he was head of the French Secret Service, a crafty and feared spy-master with agents all over Europe. Madame Blavatsky was certainly not a spy; but is it possible that Hodgson, convinced without reason, beyond all reason, that she was one, was unconsciously reading the psychic emanations of Père Joseph? He became one of the most hated men in Europe. This was because he deliberately prolonged the Thirty Years War, by which so much of Germany was devastated and which produced famine and atrocities. Aldous Huxley has written an absorbingly interesting book about him, *Grey Eminence*. His motive emerges as the reduction of the power of the house of Hapsburg which, with its Vienna–Madrid axis, aimed at the hegemony of Europe, and its replacement as the primary power by the French Bourbon monarchy, which he thought to be God's will. Now, certain of the most distinguished Theosophists, Francis Bacon, Francis Rákóczy, the Comte de Saint-Germain and, later, Garibaldi with, it would seem, the Venetian Master behind him, regarded the Hapsburg hegemony as a bad thing, so that in this sense one can say Père Joseph was in good company. Only, his means consisted in playing one power off against another, with duplicity in that he would, in conversation with different Princes, urge them to policies that must be their ruin, setting them to disastrous war with one another; the end result being that of weakening the Hapsburg Emperor and strengthening the French monarchy. What Huxley sees as ironical is that he succeeded so well that the subsequent French King, Louis XIV, became so grandiose and aggressive that he united Europe against him (as it had united formerly against the Hapsburgs), while exhausting the resources of his country and especially the poor, whose condition became worse and worse. He therefore bred, eventually, the need for the French Revolution. But here there is a further twist, which Huxley could hardly be expected to see.

It is sometimes said that it was Cagliostro who launched the French Revolution. He had been arrested in connection with the affair of the diamond necklace. At the great trial his innocence was seen and he was discharged from the case, which continued against others. But whilst awaiting it, he had spent unpleasant months in the Bastille and seen the plight of the long-term prisoners, some of whom had never had trial. In London afterwards, he replied to a question about whether he would ever return to France with a letter for publication, saying he would do so only if the Bastille had first been turned into a public garden. This was received as an incitation to pull it down. The storming of the Bastille was the first blow struck in the Revolution, and its date, 14 July, is still kept as France's national day. Was it occultly appropriate: it was Cagliostro who undid the work of Père Joseph? One must correct one's past errors.

Would the Masters have picked for a sensitive mission a being with the karma of Père Joseph? To achieve something major, one must have someone who is Someone, a being with extraordinary capacities, already proven. Perhaps, also, the course of Père Joseph was but an aberration from his usual one.

Olcott tells us that while Madame Blavatsky and he were both still at West 34th Street, New York, they fell talking one evening about Paracelsus. Suddenly her manner and voice changed. She put her hand into his and asked, 'Will you have Theophrastus as a friend, Henry?'[2] The real name of Paracelsus was Phillipus Aureolus Theophrastus Bombast von Hohenheim. He was born on either 10 or 14 November 1493, at Einsiedeln, near Zürich, and died on 24 September 1541. Educated at the University of Basel, he was a chemist, alchemist and physician, but was out of accord with the medical theory of his day. His researches brought him to the anticipation of the homeopathic principle not established until 400 years later. One of his sayings was that imagination tends to be truer than science; another was that we understand nature as we are nature, so understand God as we are God. He travelled widely, visiting Egypt and also Russia, where he was at one point taken prisoner by the Tartars. Could this link with Madame Blavatsky's familiarity with Tartars? Could Aldous Huxley's puzzled reproach to Père Joseph, 'His place was with the antidote-makers, not with the brewers of the poisons'[3] harp, unconsciously upon the life-long search of Paracelsus for the antidotes to diseases?

One might also think about a hint given by Morya. Olcott asked him about her ungovernable temper and was told to look into the history of the Dolgorouky family, from whom she descended by her maternal grandmother. There was a Jakob Dolgorouky, sent by Peter the Great on various embassies, captured and held prisoner for eleven years in Sweden (remember Madame Blavatsky's refusal to go to Sweden); but after his escape, in 1712, he became Peter the Great's first senator.[4] His fame rests chiefly upon his having torn up a decree signed by Peter the Great, saying that since it was unjust it must have been without reflection that the Czar signed it. This assertion he repeated when Peter entered the Senate. Peter said, 'Let the decree be suspended. I will consider further . . .'. He went out, and no more was heard of the decree. Also, when Peter locked himself into his room, refusing food or water after his son's death, it was Dolgorouky who reasoned with him through the door, and finally threatened to break it down, unless the Czar opened. Peter opened it. Do the dates fit? 1639–1720 – that fits nicely between Père Joseph and Cagliostro.

The above are all men; but Madame Blavatsky always seemed awkwardly at home in her feminine body.

CHAPTER 80

The Voice of the Silence

In July 1889, Madame Blavatsky was so far recovered as to go for a holiday with an American Theosophist, Mrs Ida Chandler, to the Forêt de Fontainebleau. The atmosphere of the oaks and firs so revived her vitality that she was able to rise from her bath chair and view the château on her legs. They were joined by Annie Besant and Herbert Burrows, who had been in Paris to attend a labour conference from 15 to 20 July, and came on to Fontainebleau to find Madame Blavatsky writing *The Voice of the Silence*.

It was, she explained, from the *Book of Golden Precepts*, verses in the same series as the *Stanzas of Dzyan*. The earliest were pre-Buddhistic, and the original, which included some verses added later, was 'engraved upon thin oblong squares', and there were copies on disks or plates. Usually they were kept upon the altar of the temple attached to any school of Mahayana Buddhism. Knowledge of them was obligatory in that school from which the Society had received its teachings (Shigatsè). Although they could be transcribed into Tibetan, the original was inscribed in ideographs, which anyone who had learned them could read straight off into his own language, Tibetan, Chinese, Japanese or even English. Thirty-nine of them she remembered by heart (it will be remembered that Koot Hoomi mentioned her having learned Senzar stanzas by heart) and it was some of these she was now putting into the best English she could.

The Voice of the Silence[1] is about the renunciation of Nirvana. It is divided into three fragments. 'The voice of the silence', 'The two paths' and 'The seven portals'. The precepts in Part I are good for the attainment of Nirvana:

4 The Mind is the great Slayer of the Real.
5 Let the Disciple slay the Slayer.

(This does not mean the disciple has to become stupid; but the analytic mind, unless it is first quieted, stifles the intuition.)

21 Give up thy life, if thou wouldst live.

(This has its parallel in Jesus' words, 'He who saveth his life shall lose it'.)

75 . . . Look not behind.

(Attempts have been made to personalise to Madame Blavatsky this injunction not to look back into the past. It has nothing to do with her. All religious disciplines have proscribed looking backwards – witness the fate of Lot's wife and the story of Orpheus and Eurydice. Krishnamurti dislikes psychoanalysis because it is only in the present one can act and the analysis is concerned with the past; while one is analysing the past one is missing the challenges of the present.)

75 Do not believe that lust can ever be killed out if gratified and satiated.

(This is what the Chohan prophesied as the error that would become widespread in the twentieth century.)

98 Now rest beneath the Boddhi tree . . . thou art the Master of SAMADHI . . .

Yes, the disciple has now attained the ability to become a Nirvanee, but Part II begins:

101 And now, O Teacher of Compassion, point thou the way to other men.
103 The Paths are two . . .
123 If thou art told that to become an Arhan thou hast to cease to love all beings – tell them they lie.
126 If thou art taught that sin is born of action and bliss of inaction, tell them that they err.

127 The Dharma of the 'Eye' is the embodiment of the external and the non-existing.

128 The Dharma of the 'Heart' is the embodiment of Bodhi, the Permanent and Everlasting.

135 . . . Inaction in a deed of mercy becomes an action in a deadly sin.

142 The Shangna robe, 'tis true, can purchase light eternal . . . but O Lanoo, it also kills – compassion.

143 . . . this is the *open* PATH, the way to selfish bliss, shunned by the Bodhisattvas of the 'Secret Heart', the Buddhas of Compassion.

145 To don the Nirmanakaya's humble robe is to forgo eternal bliss for self, to help on man's evolution. To reach Nirvana's bliss but to renounce it, is the supreme and final step – the highest on Renunciation's Path.

179 The PATH is one, Disciple, yet, in the end, twofold . . . At one end, bliss immediate, and at the other – bliss deferred. Both are of merit – the reward: the choice is thine.

180 The One becomes the two, the *Open* and the *Secret* . . .

182 Thus, the forest Path is LIBERATION.

183 But Path the Second is – RENUNCIATION . . .

187 The 'Secret Way' leads to Paranirvanic bliss – but at the close of Kalpas without number . . .

188 But it is said. 'The last shall be the greatest' . . .

It becomes very evident it is hoped the Path the reader will choose is the second. Shigatsè is for making Bodhisattvas.

CHAPTER 81

Coleman's Attack: Theravada versus Mahayana points of view

As might be expected, Coleman included in his attack an implication that *The Voice of the Silence* was spurious:[1]

> *The Voice of the Silence*, published in 1889, purports to be a translation by Helena P. Blavatsky from a Thibetan work . . . In this work are intermingled Sanskrit, Pali, Thibetan, Chinese and Singhalese terms – a manifest absurdity in a Thibetan work . . . this allegedly ancient Thibetan work . . .

But it is not a Tibetan work, either purportedly or allegedly. If he had read her foreword, he would have seen she said it was a Senzar work, though kept in the temple at Shigatsè.[2] She never learned Tibetan, but did learn some Senzar. If she hesitated in her translation, Koot Hoomi would probably supply a word from whichever oriental language he thought would be most meaningful to western readers. Neither is the practice of drawing upon more than one language discreditable. L. Adams Beck, in his preface to his *Life of the Buddha*, says,[3] 'I have employed Pali or Sanskrit words and names alternatively as I thought they would be more familiar or easier to remember'.

One must remember that Coleman was a Pali scholar, and that Pali is the language of the text on which is based the Theravada Buddhism of Ceylon and Siam, which avers that the Buddha never gave any secret or esoteric teaching. The Mahayana Buddhism of China, Tibet, Korea and Japan, based upon Sanskrit, Tibetan and Chinese texts, holds that he did, but those who wrote dowm some of his teachings in Pali suppressed it.[4] There is a radical doctrinal difference. Theravada Buddhism denies the survival of individual identity, which it holds to be absorbed in the One; hence, it does not believe even in the Buddha's continued existence. According to its devotees, he was absorbed into Nirvana, having left us his example of how to do it. Mahayana Buddhism, on the other hand, holds entry into Nirvana a lesser thing than renunciation of Nirvana so as to remain with humanity, voluntarily, in order to help it. Tucci refers to 'the individualist tendency dominant throughout Mahayana Buddhism'.[5]

E.A. Burtt, introducing Mahayana, says of the Bodhisattva:[6]

> on attaining enlightenment he does not leave the world behind and enter Nirvana by himself; he remains in the world, appearing like an ordinary person, but devoting his compassionate skill to the aid of others.

Dr Daisetz Teitaro Suzuki, who seems to be the foremost Japanese Mahayana scholar, writes:[7]

> Mahayana does not ask its followers to escape the metempsychosis of birth and death for the sake of entering into the lethargic tranquility of Nirvana; for metempsychosis is in itself no evil, and Nirvana in its coma is not productive of any good. And as long as there are souls groaning in pain, the Bodhisattva cannot rest in Nirvana; there is no rest for his unselfish heart . . . until he leads all to the eternal bliss of Buddhahood.

Theravada was the first form of Buddhism known in the West, and the allegation that what Madame Blavatsky was giving out was not Buddhism at all is explained very largely by the fact that she had gone to the teachers of the Mahayana form, not yet familiar. Evans-Wentz, in his *Tibetan Book of the Dead*, is treating of a work, the *Bardo Thodol*, that ante-dates Tsongkapa, yet went to Madame Blavatsky's *The Secret Doctrine* for an esoteric interpretation of it, and observes that his guru:[8]

The late Lama Kazi Dawa-Samdup was of opinion that, despite the adverse criticism directed against H.P. Blavatsky's works, there is adequate internal evidence in them of their author's intimate acquaintance with the higher *Lamaistic* teachings, into which she claimed to have been initiated.

Dr Suzuki, reviewing *The Voice of the Silence*, wrote in his journal, *Eastern Buddhist:*[9]

The Voice of the Silence is the true Mahayana doctrine. Undoubtedly Madame Blavatsky had in some way been initiated into the deeper side of Mahayana teaching, and then gave out what she deemed wise to the western world as theosophy. It is true that some things were added and some subtracted from the pure Mahayana doctrine according to the extent of her knowledge and her judgement.

We shall find *The Voice of the Silence* vouched for by a yet higher authority.

CHAPTER 82

Olcott's last visit

After a quick visit to Paris to view the new Eiffel Tower, Madame Blavatsky returned through Granville and Jersey, in 'an old washtub called a steamer'. To enter the tiny Channel Island ports the ships have to be small, and in the choppy seas, around the rocks, pitch about like nutshells. She recovered from her sea-sickness in St Helier, then in St Aubin.

She was back in London to welcome Olcott when he arrived at Lansdowne Road on 4 September 1889. They sat up until 2 a.m., New York style. He had just returned from Japan. The Japanese had told him only he could reunite all the divergent schools of Buddhists and had asked him to be head of the Buddhist religion in Japan. He had asked whether, in order to take up this post, he might resign the Presidency of the Theosophical Society to Madame Blavatsky, but Morya would not allow this.

She had another desk pulled up to hers, so that they could work side by side. She was correcting proofs of *A Key to Theosophy*.

He had to leave on a tour of Wales and Ireland. In Dublin, he stayed with Mr Fred Dick and his Scottish born wife, Annie Piper, née Laing, my great-aunt.[1] The most mystical of the Dublin Group, 'A.E.' (George Russell) encapsulated the message of *The Secret Doctrine* as, 'The destiny of every man . . . is to become a star'.[2]

Returning to England, Olcott lectured in Birmingham and Leek in Staffordshire, then rejoined H.P.B. He was with her when a London paper reprinted from an American one Dr Elliott Coues' allegation that Madame Blavatsky had been expelled from the Theosophical Society. She replied pointing out that it was Coues who had been expelled.

Olcott had to leave again, to lecture in Edinburgh, Bradford and Newcastle. Then he returned to London to see Madame Blavatsky for the last time, before sailing for Colombo on 26 December. She had made him the sole representative of the Esoteric School in Asian countries, with discretionary authority, and wrote to him,[3] 'I love you more than anyone on earth save Master, my friendship and brotherly affection for you are eternal . . .'.

CHAPTER 83

The Esoteric School

It was Judge who had urged Madame Blavatsky to form an Esoteric School, and it was he who drew up the rules – very likely with a Master behind him, as he maintained, yet they have not been treated as particularly sacrosanct, having been changed at some later time or times. The essential idea was to pick out from the many who might have joined the Theosophical Society from more or less idle curiosity, without much sense of commitment, those of pledged seriousness, to whom it might be possible to communicate a little more than in her books.

It is doubtless to Judge, also, that we owe it that she put her Instructions on paper. How else could he receive them in America and circulate or read them to those he was forming into the American section of the Esoteric School? Olcott, when he came in with the idea, naturally had, also, to receive the Instructions, to read or circulate to those he formed into its eastern section. In her first Instruction, she warned her pupils that:[1]

> As soon as anyone pledges himself as a 'Probationer' certain occult effects ensue. Of these, the first is the *throwing outward* of everything latent in the nature of the man: his faults, habits, qualities, or subdued desires, whether good or bad . . . if a man is vain or a sensualist, or ambitious . . . all those vices are sure to break out, even if he has hitherto successfully concealed and repressed them. They will come to the front irrepressibly, and he will have to fight a hundred times harder than before . . .
>
> THIS IS AN IMMUTABLE LAW IN THE DOMAIN OF THE OCCULT
>
> Its action is the more marked the more earnest and sincere the desire of the candidate, and the more deeply he has felt the reality and importance of his pledge.

There is in each one of us a Mr Hyde who when he is brought out becomes the Dweller on the Threshold; he is not, as in Bulwer-Lytton's novel[2] a devil external to oneself, but, as in Stevenson's,[3] the Mr Hyde within us, lurking, perhaps unsuspected, until the day of his final eradication in one's total purification.

She warned her mixed class she would have to refer to all parts of the body without exception, and those who could not face this had better leave. She had to start with the uterus, of which she issued three diagrams in section, showing an embryo within it.[4] The embryo and other contents and parts of the uterus corresponded with cosmic principles, the seven orifices in the face and other parts of the body. Thus, (1) the embryo to the mathematical point, the sun, Atma and the auric envelope, Hiryanagarbha or Augoeides, blue and the mouth (because since the Fall, the third eye is no more and the creative power has fallen to its present position); (2) the amniotic fluid of Akasa, Mercury, Buddhi, yellow and the right eye; (3) the amnion to ether, Venus, indigo, the left eye . . . She also presents tables showing the correspondences of the spectrum with the musical scale,[5] in solfeggio, wherein it will be seen that the planetary correspondences do not follow the order of the globes in the solar system. She says this is because the spectrum is illusory, for just as there are colour-blind people who cannot distinguish between red and green, so we are all (except Adepts) colour-blind in that we can distinguish only three primary colours and have to mix those to make substitutes for the others, such as red and yellow to make orange, a substitute for the light red too fine for us to see (does she mean what we call the ultra-violet?). Also, sun and moon stand for two planets we cannot see (not Uranus and Neptune). Her tables in strip form had best be thought of as bent round so that the red, do, and violet, si (ti) meet, and the middle can be seen to be the green fa. The middle F on the piano is the average of all the sounds of nature on this planet and therefore the note of this planet. Here I wish she had said a word about pitch. That of all pianos is not the same. The piano-tuner creates an appropriate series of intervals starting from the middle C he feels to be natural to the piano. If most of those on which she had played sounded to her about right, they had what is now called orchestral pitch; those bought new today have new philharmonic pitch, which is practically a semi-tone higher. Madame Blavatsky is postulating an absolute middle C, or rather, middle F, from which the appropriate intervals should be created. How does one know what this is? She says that it can be heard in the moaning of the wind or rustling in the leaves; through the risings and falls of the tune can be heard the returns to the true fa. This is the green (or average of all the greens) of the Earth's vegetation. It is because we share with the animals red blood, ruled by Mars, that our start is made from the blood-red do of middle C. (Is this why *The British Grenadiers* is in C Major?) G, sol (so) and blue seems to go to Jupiter. (This fits *God Save the King* in G.) Mi, that is E, she tells us, corresponds to yellow and Buddhi, which is why the *Aum* is good chanted on this note". That leaves us to fill in, orange and the Sun for re or D – musicians think of D as a "bright" key – la or A for indigo and Manas, and ti or B for violet and the moon.

She begins to speak of Kundalini. When it touches the pineal it will awaken the third eye. Even now, this sometimes opens in deep sleep. In deep sleep our consciousness is in the auric egg, wherein is registered in the Akasa the memory of all our previous existences. In deep sleep we know all our previous incarnations and have an idea of those to come. It is because we cannot yet bring the physical brain to vibrate at this level that we cannot remember when we wake.[6]

> . . . the Pineal Gland, at the upper pole of the human body, corresponds with the Uterus (in the female and its analogue in the male) at the lower pole; the peduncles of the Pineal Gland corresponding with the Fallopian Tubes of the Uterus.

She speaks of the spinal cord. In it are the three 'vital airs' of Kundalini: Sushumna, the central one, and the female Ida and male Pingala starting on either side of it. The spinal cord connects the generative organs and the brain, and because of the role of these airs, purity of life is important. The sympathetic cords also play a role, and :[7]

> At the end of the next Round, Humanity will become once more hermaphrodite, male-female, and then there will be two Spinal Cords in the human body. In the Seventh Race, the two will merge into the one. The sexually creative power of man is not natural, or rather was not at the beginning. It was an abnormal diversion from the course of human and divine nature, and all tends to make away with it. Man in the end of the Sixth and Seventh Races will not have sexual organs . . . with the evolution of the Races the Sympathetic Cords will develop into a true Spinal Cord, the two Cords growing together and so forming one. We are returning up the arc, with self-consciousness added. The Sixth Race will correspond to the 'Pudding Bags', the First Root Race, but will have the perfection of form with the highest intelligence and spirituality.

Which Round does she mean? Whatever the time-scale, sex is on its way out (perhaps not immediately, but in the long run). Now perhaps we understand why the Masters live celibate.

How will these changes come about?[8]

> . . . till the end of the Third Root Race (when androgynous man separated into male and female) the ten orifices existed in the hermaphrodite, first potentially then functionally . . . Woman being left with the full or perfect number 10 . . . was deemed higher and more spiritual . . .

It is intimated that the essential modification or re-creation will be made from the feminine body. Does this mean that on the ascending arc the more advanced souls will opt for feminine births?

There are implications here which she does not explore. We have, since her time, seen a tendency for the sexes to become more alike; but whereas women, in their endeavour to improve their position, started by copying men, it looks, upon this exposition, as if it is for men to take women as their model – not in the pathetic sense of transvestism, but in adding to their masculine qualities those virtues that have always been thought specially to characterise women: care to preserve and cherish, gentleness, refinement, modesty, chastity. In the far future:[9]

When ether fills the air, there will be born children without fathers. In Virginia there is an apple of a special kind. It does not blossom, but bears fruit from a kind of berry without any seeds. This will gradually extend to animals and then to men. Women will bear children without impregnation . . . in the Seventh Round, Buddhas will be born without sin.

It looks as though we have to eat again of the apple in order to prove the Virgin Birth, not as a symbol but a prophecy.

CHAPTER 84

Avenue Road

The lease of 17 Lansdowne Road lapsed in July 1890, and Mrs Besant placed in trust for the Theosophical Society her own house, 19 Avenue Road, St John's Wood.

On the last day before they moved there, Countess Wachtmeister, thinking to give Madame Blavatsky a little pleasure, took her for a drive in Hyde Park, 'in the fashionable hour'. Mrs Alice Leighton Cleather and Mrs Cooper-Oakley (she hyphenated her maiden name to her husband's) were in the drawing-room when they returned, and Mrs Leighton Cleather says that Madame Blavatsky was in a passion, crying, 'Not a Soul among them – not one!'[1] It is to be hoped this is not to be taken literally. People parading in their finery can look vapid.

Mrs Cleather confessed to a sinking of the heart with regard to the move. Asking herself what caused this, she realised it was because it was to Mrs Besant's house.[2] She feared she would become too managing and too dominating an influence.

Avenue Road runs down towards the north-west corner of Regent's Park. Today, the huge houses on it are mainly residences of ambassadors and their suites. Rolls-Royces tend to be parked in front of them, and it is said the faults on the St John's Wood telephone exchange result from all their 'scramblers'. No.19 included a hall, which would become the Convention Hall.

Madame Blavatsky was installed on the ground floor, in the front room to the left of the front door, from which she could look out across the bushes which screened the drive from the road. There was also a big garden at the back.

Soon after they moved in, somebody took a photograph of the interior of the hall. When it was developed, there was seen on it about 12 ft from the ground the head of a man, with a distinguished oval face, moustache and small black beard. Mrs Cleather asked Madame Blavatsky about this. Madame Blavatsky said it was the Master Illarion, who had immediately after the event told her what had happened. He had looked in and, unexpectedly, been caught by the camera.[3] (Presumably he must have densified his astral body more than he intended, or the camera's eye was more sensitive than the photographer's.) I asked the General Secretary of the English Section of the Theosophical Society what had happened to this – the only photograph of an Adept – but it appeared not to be in the possession of the Society. It may have been Mrs Cleather's property.

Madame Blavatsky now picked from the membership of the Esoteric School a limited inner group. For its meetings she had a special small room constructed, leading out of hers, and no one save the members was allowed into it. Mrs Cleather tells us there were twelve members: six women, Mrs Besant, Countess Wachtmeister, Mrs Cooper-Oakley, Miss Laura Cooper (later married to George Mead) and Miss Emily Kislingbury; and six men, George Mead, Archibald Keightley (Bertram was in America), Walter Old, Claude Wright, Herbert Coryn and Edward T. Sturdy. They were always arranged symmetrically, in a semi-circle facing Madame Blavatsky, the six women to her left and the six men on her right. They all had their appointed places and their own chairs.[4]

The arrangement suggests a meditation group. For a lecture or discussion it matters little who sits where, but for meditation, if both sexes are to be present, it is considered to make a better magnetism if they are opposed symmetrically. They probably sat partly in silence, endeavouring to raise their consciousness to that of the Masters, to receive their blessing and their silent instruction.

On 15 August, Madame Blavatsky had her first glimpse of London's slummy East End, when she was driven to 193 Bow Road to open the Club for Working Women.[5] It was to be managed by Mrs Besant and Miss Cooper.

Meanwhile, Madame Blavatsky's health flagged. Her pupils would wheel her into Regent's Park, to be refreshed by the rolling grassy stretches, and it was in the Zoological Gardens that she nearly fell out of her bath chair when leaning forward to save a child that had run in front of the wheels.

In the new year, however, it was felt that she must have a change of air, and they took her down to Brighton, where they visited her in relays, to wheel her along the front, to see the sea, unusually flat for that blustery place. One wonders what she, who had known the genuine Orient, made of the Dome and the Pavilion.

Even if Brighton had braced her, she was not really well again after her return to London.

Her last days were agitated by litigation. On 20 July 1889, the *New York Sun* had printed an article by Coues, alleging that an old friend of her family, Prince Wittgenstein, had been her lover, and that from 1857 to 1858 she had lived in Paris as one of the *demi-monde*. The missionaries in India sent him the Coulomb forgeries to support his attack on her, and that is how they have disappeared – without ever having been seen since.

The curious allusion to the period 1857–8 is evocative of Meyendorff's affair with Nathalie Blavatsky. It may well have been during that period that the child which Madame Blavatsky was persuaded to adopt was begotten.

Madame Blavatsky sued for libel, Judge filing the suit for her in America. In the following year, the newspaper's attorney admitted in pre-trial hearings that the allegations could not be proven, and on 26 September 1892, they printed a statement of regret that they had been 'misled' into printing Dr Coues's article, which contained allegations 'without solid foundation'. By way of amends, they printed on another page an article by Judge, describing her personality, qualities and virtues. But by the time this noble vindication appeared, Madame Blavatsky was no longer able to read it.

In April 1891, an influenza epidemic hit England, and almost everyone in 19 Avenue Road went down with it, the worst affected being Madame Blavatsky. Annie Besant had left for America, bearing H.P.B.'s last letter to the American Convention. Countess Wachtmeister, busy all day, had to sleep at nights, and Mrs Cooper-Oakley was forbidden by Dr Mennell to nurse Madame Blavatsky as she was too ill herself. Thus, it was mainly Miss Laura Cooper, who lived in from 21 April, who sat up with her, in addition to a professional nurse. On 26 April, Madame Blavatsky's temperature reached 105° and she slept for most of the day. After that the fever decreased, but on 30 April she developed a quinsy in her throat which gave her trouble in swallowing and breathing. Poultices brought some relief, but the difficulty in swallowing or speaking remained. On 6 and 7 May she rose for a little and walked about in the sitting-room. At 5 p.m. on 7 May, Dr Mennell, finding her sitting up and playing patience, congratulated her on her courage. She replied, 'I do my best, Doctor'. Her voice was scarcely above a whisper, but she rolled a cigarette – the last she ever rolled – and handed it to him. In the night she was restless, but at 4.00 a.m. on 8 May, she seemed easier. At 7 a.m. Mrs Cooper-Oakley came in to relieve her sister so that she might sleep for a few hours, but at 11.30 a.m. she was woken by Claude Wright, who told her H.P.B. had taken a turn for the worse. Mrs Cooper-Oakley had gone, but Old was now there. Madame Blavatsky was now sitting up in her big armchair. For a long time, Old and Wright knelt in front of her, each holding one of her hands, while Laura Cooper sat beside her, putting an arm round her to support her head. The hands of the clock reached 2.25 p.m. When she passed away, it was so quietly that they did not know the exact moment when it happened.[6]

Olcott was in Australia when he felt suddenly that H.P.B. was telling him she was dying. The next day, 9 May, he wrote in his diary, 'Had an uneasy foreboding of H.P.B.'s death'.[7] On 10 May he wrote, 'This morning I feel that H.P.B. is dead. The third warning'. On 11 May, a cablegram arrived, 'H.P.B. dead'.

He cancelled his tour and sailed home immediately. The cremation had taken place at Woking on 11 May, the address read by Mead, so he went to Avenue Road, where he found Mrs Besant. They went into Madame Blavatsky's room and stood in silence for a while.

CHAPTER 85

The Panchèn Lama's endorsement

In 1925, the Panchèn Lama was in Pekin. That is the Ninth or Sixth Panchèn Lama, Lobsang Tub-ten Cho-gyi Nyima, as he writes his name, pronounced Lopsang Tubten Chökyi Nyima. Before describing how he came to endorse Madame Blavatsky's writing, we should try to learn something about him and how he came to be in Pekin. This means going back to the background of the Younghusband expedition. At the beginning of this century, the British had become worried because of what they had heard of a Siberian Mongol, Agnan Dorjief, who had established himself in Lhasa, where he had acquired extraordinary influence over the Thirteenth Dalai Lama, whom he was persuading that Shamballa was St Petersburg. Letters written him by Curzon, as Viceroy, were returned unopened.

On 1 January 1898, the British Ambassador at St Petersburg had recorded an interview with Count Witte, 'then the most powerful politician in Russia'[1] (he was Madame Blavatsky's first cousin). Count Witte disturbed him by producing from his desk a map of China, placing his hand here and there on it and saying Russia would probably absorb all this territory; then, putting his finger on Lanchow (which is near Koko Nor and Kumbum), he said that the Trans-Siberian Railway (over the construction of which he had presided) would in time run a branch to that town. All this worrying intelligence convinced Lord Curzon it would be best for the British to be in Tibet first, and in 1903 he sent Younghusband, fired with the same view, upon what was first called a punitive expedition, to reclaim financial reparation for some trouble we had been caused. The Dalai Lama fled before his advance. The Ninth (or Sixth) Panchèn sent a lama from Trashi Lhünpo to call on Younghusband at his camp at Khampa Jong, convey His Holiness' compliments, and suggest that what the British had come about might be better discussed if they would first withdraw to within their own territory. Younghusband went on to Lhasa. In Lhasa, he found the Dalai Lama had fled. He was told he had gone in company with Dorjief, and it was believed they had gone to Mongolia – where, in fact, the Dalai Lama was addressing himself to the Russian Resident at Urga. Younghusband compared this behaviour unfavourably with that of the Panchèn, who had addressed an embassy to him. He conceived the idea that the Chinese could declare the Dalai Lama's rule ended and invite the Panchèn to come to Lhasa in his place. The Chinese were only too prompt to oblige, but it does not seem that the Panchèn moved from Trashi Lhünpo, and it was with Ti Timpoche, Grand Lama of Ganden, in whose hands the Dalai Lama had left his seal, that on 6 September 1904, in the Potala, Younghusband signed the Treaty of Lhasa.

In 1905, the Panchèn accepted an invitation to India, and was received by the Prince of Wales and the new Viceroy, Lord Minto. In the following summer, 1906, Sir Charles Bell visited him at Trashi Lhünpo – it was after all to the Panchèns that the eighteenth-century British missions of Bogle and Turner had been addressed – and found him a charming man, but unwilling to assume a political role.

The Dalai Lama was now back in Lhasa, but in 1910 the Chinese invaded Tibet, and this time he fled to India. That is how it came about that on 13 January 1913, my parents received at Fort William, Calcutta, the Dalai Lama's Prime Minister, Kusho Horkang Dzanza, who had come to be shown over a British fort and be instructed in how it was organised.

By this time the Dalai Lama was back in Tibet, the Panchèn, who had been induced to hold the reins during his absence, having hastened to meet him and hand over.

The Dalai Lama had by then conceived a resentment against the Panchèn Lama, and showed it in depressing Trashi Lhünpo, bearing down upon it with punitive taxes and calling on it to contribute to the reconstitution of the army. In 1922 the Panchèn appealed against this to the British. The British reply was that it could not interfere in a non-British internal matter.[2] This drove him, in desperation, straight into the arms of the Chinese.[3]

Whether or not it is true as alleged by the Dalai Lama's historian that the Panchèn had opened secret negotiations with the Chinese from Trashi Lhünpo, he came, obviously, to fear that a *coup* was about to be mounted against him, and, with a small party, fled in the night.[4] Behind him he left a reproachful letter, saying he would return when he had found a mediator.[5] The Lhasan government, when it learned of his flight, sent out a party to arrest him, but when it reached Sining, it learned he had already passed into China.

McGovern must have seen him only shortly before he left. Arriving at Shigatsè in disguise, early in 1923, he glimpsed him in a palanquin as he was carried in procession through the streets, and had the impression of 'a man with a very gentle and refined expression, with a look almost of shyness'.[6] He arrived in Pekin in February 1925.

Mrs Leighton Cleather, since Madame Blavatsky's death, and Colonel Cleather's, had been living in India. Hearing that the Panchèn was now in an accessible place, she, her son Gordon and Basil Crump, left for Pekin, where they arrived in December 1925, and asked for an audience. They were warmly received, and he requested them to have *The Voice of the Silence* reissued, exactly as Madame Blavatsky had written it. Since her death, Adyar editions had incorporated what were meant to be amendments, but they did not meet with his approval. He would permit the correction only of what were obviously printers' errors. It was, he said, 'the only true exposition in English of the doctrine of the *Mahayana* and its noble ideal of self-sacrifice for humanity'.[7]

In all these conversations, it was Gordon Cleather, who had learnt Tibetan in India and in Ladakh, who acted as interpreter.[8]

The Panchèn gave them his photograph to be reproduced with the reissue (showing him looking much as in McGovern's snap), and wrote out with his own hand four lines in Tibetan, for use as a frontispiece:

All beings desire liberation from misery.
Seek, therefore, the causes of misery and expunge them.
By entering on the path, liberation from misery is obtained.
Exhort, then, all beings to enter the path.

Mrs Cleather and Crump noticed that, in addition to the three Tibetan scripts used for different purposes, there was another script in which His Holiness sometimes wrote. It was neither Sanskrit nor Chinese, and they supposed it to be Senzar.[9] A Chinese translation of the four lines, and a note in Chinese, was contributed to the Pekin edition of 1927, by Wang Wing Ching, one of the Panchèn's aides. As His Holiness was destined never to leave Pekin, he probably saw it emerge from the press.

In their editorial foreword, Mrs Cleather and Crump quote a letter from Madame Blavatsky to a German Theosophist, saying that in the Himalayas there was 'a nucleus of adepts of various nationalities, and the Tashi Lama knows them and they act together . . . My Master [M] and K.H. and several others I know personally, are there coming and going',[10] and they add 'Madame Blavatsky knew the predecessor of the present Tashi [Panchèn] Lama very well'.[11]

The endorsement of this by the Panchèn is his endorsement of everything.

CHAPTER 86

The significance of Blavatsky

If we believe that Madame Blavatsky did know what she was talking about, that she was in receipt, from her teachers at Shigatsè, of a body of doctrine which, if it cannot wholly be demonstrated, has at least, with passage into the twentieth century, acquired positive checks, we are assured of our immortal souls. We are assured of them within a context more precise, and better able to answer for itself under enquiry, than is offered by Christianity. If one consults *The Oxford Dictionary of the Christian Church* under the headings 'Immortality', 'Heaven' and 'resurrection of the dead', the promise of what is going to happen to us is surprisingly sketchy and uncertain. It seems we must lie in our graves, doing nothing, until the Second Coming at the end of the world. Then, if we pass the Judgement, we shall find ourselves once more clothed in our bodies, as they are now, either by collection of all the particles that disaggregated at death, or else, as St Paul thought, by endowment with new ones, in which we shall enter into the dwelling-place of God and His angels and remain for ever, enjoying the Beatific Vision. The mechanics of this are awkward, and the division between the saved and the damned too simple, allowing nothing for all the shades of grey that divide sin from virtue, and no time for the correction of our faults and the deepening of our understanding. One feels that one is faced with a presentation simplistic rather than simple. There has to be something that has not been understood by the clergy. One feels that the doctrine of Purgatory was brought in to deal with the crudity. Even that was denied by St Augustine, who held that the fate of each man was decided immediately on his death. Enlightened modern churchmen no longer believe in hell – save as the psychological state of refusing to know God.[1] But they are, in their enlightenment, improving upon the received dogma.

Despite the unacceptability of so much of the doctrine, despite, also the revulsion felt by some for the adoration of the bloodstained figure on the cross that tends to sado-masochistic morbidity, many prefer Christianity to Buddhism because it promises one the immortality of one's own soul and reunion with one's loved ones in recognised form. Christina Rossetti looks forward to the day when we shall all rise from our tombs and find one another again:[2]

> Each with his own not with another's grace,
>   Each with his own not with another's heart,
>   Each with his own not with another's face

This is precisely what Buddhism, as popularly understood, seems to deny. Indeed, the editorial of the Buddhist Society's periodical *The Middle Way* for May 1984 avers 'Buddhism even snatches away from us our fond belief that we ourselves have some kind of fixed identity; no, we are told, you have no lasting soul or essence'.[3] In that case, I am not a Buddhist, but though the article following quotes the Fifth Dalai Lama (Ngawam Lopsang) for what is perhaps the same view, it certainly was not Madame Blavatsky's. She knew the Eighth Panchèn, Jè Pèdèn Chökyi Trakpa Tènpé Wangchuk very well, and his understanding of the teaching was endorsed by his successor, Lopsang Tubten Chökyi Nyima. Perhaps the Dalai and the Panchèn Lamas teach different things. It is not impossible. (After all, the Catholic and Anglican Churches have a different understanding of what the bread and wine become.)

Now it seems to me that the Theravada Buddhists and all mystics who want to deny individual immortality insist upon a total monism from the feeling that so long as there is an 'I', that 'I' must be in competition with 'You', striving in a selfish way to put 'You' down. Now obviously, if I think I can obtain my happiness at the cost of your unhappiness, I am in ignorance, but surely it is only a very undeveloped mentality that thinks in that way. As St Paul said, we are all 'members of one another'.[4] This poetic way of putting it perhaps strikes the balance, for it affirms both the unity and the plurality within the unity that allows for love. If all are one, there can be no love, but only oneness. Whether or not he thought of this, the Sufi mystic, Inayat

Khan, wrote, 'The joy of communion is even greater than the joy of at-one-ment, for all the joy of life lies in the thought of "I" and "you".[5]

Madame Blavatsky, while putting it to her pupils in the Blavatsky Lodge that we would never be able to understand and feel for one another if we were separate and not of one essence, yet reveals herself not so far from Christina Rossetti when, in *The Secret Doctrine*, she affirms,[6] 'Withal, the Monad of every living being . . . is an individual Dhyan Choham distinct from others'. She loved Sir Edwin Arnold's *Light of Asia* and asked that lines from it be read on anniversaries of her death; yet whilst she accepted the image of the dewdrop's slipping back into the shining sea, she held that it came out again, recognisably the same dewdrop, at the next rebirth of the universe:[7]

> For however limitless, from a human standpoint, the paranirvanic state, yet it has a limit in Eternity. Once reached, the same Monad will re-emerge therefrom, as a still higher being, on a far higher plane, to recommence its cycle of perfected activity.

And again, as a quotation from the Senzar shlokas at Shigatsè,[8] 'The Thread of Radiance which is imperishable and dissolves only in Nirvana re-emerges from it in its integrity on the day when the Great Law calls all living things back into action'.

The significance of Blavatsky is that, thanks to her, we do not have to choose between a faith and a philosophy. If, as her enemies allege, what she teaches is not Buddhism, it is an improvement on it. She has given us our immortality within the grandest design we have been privileged to glimpse.

The 'Bolt' or
Dondoukoff-Korsakoff letters

There is one collection of letters I have not drawn upon. That is the sixteen purporting to have been written by Madame Blavatsky to Prince Dondoukoff-Korsakoff, Governor-General of Odessa, which made their appearance on the scene rather late. It was in 1926 that Annie Besant received a letter from a Mrs Elsa Lorsi-Stephani, a member in Vienna, saying that a journalist, Mr Pierre Bolt, had sixteen letters from H.P.B. to sell. They had been brought to Vienna by a Russian diplomat and were the property of a Russian lady, presumably the heiress of Prince Dondoukoff-Korsakoff, who was very poor and wished to make some money from their sale. Enclosed were photostats of four pages from the letters, and also of the back and front of an envelope said to have contained one of them. Mrs Besant refused the letters, not because she doubted their authenticity but because the price asked was too high.

The letters were next heard of in 1932, when Mr Bolt offered them to Dr Gottfried de Purucker, then General Secretary of the Point-Loma Theosophical Society in America. He declined them for the same reason, but in case the Society should ever be able to afford the price, asked for photostats. These never arrived.

They were heard of again in 1939 in Lisbon, where Mr Bolt had been befriended by a Madame Jeanne S. Lefèvre of the Theosophical Society in Portugal. To her he explained that his real name was not Pierre Bolt, which was his pseudonym as a journalist, but Leo Ladislav Séméré, and that he had been born Hungarian. The letters, he told Madame Lefèvre, had been sold to him by an Austrian soldier who had gone to Russia to help the Bolsheviks and found them in one of the great houses which they sacked. He would leave them in his will to the Theosophical Society in either Portugal or England but did not wish them to go to Adyar.

He then left for France, taking the letters; there he was overtaken by the German occupation, and also by illness. At the persuasion of Madame Lefèvre, he sent the leters to Mademoiselle Cécile Bayer of the Theosophical Society of France. They were still in her possession when he died, in 1942, at Grasse, under the name of Joseph Louis Barrault. When Mr Jinarajadasa came from Adyar on a visit to Paris in 1947, Mlle Bayer simply handed them to him.

My experience, both as an author and as a founding director of Fuller d'Arch Smith Ltd, dealers in rare books and manuscripts, would have been to distrust these letters because of their unsatisfactory provenance – two different stories have been given. However, the letters were published in *H.P.B. Speaks*, Vol.II, ed. Jinarajadasa (Adyar, 1951) and I began reading the text without first having read the introduction. As I read the text, I found myself disliking, then distrusting and finally rejecting, before I looked to see the provenance, to determine if there was anything wrong with it.

The letters are dated from August 1881 to June 1884. In the first, introducing herself as one whom he knew well in their youth, she begs Prince Dordoukoff-Korsakoff to send on for her a letter to her uncle, General Rotislav A. Fadeyef, her two aunts (his sisters) both being in Carlsbad so that she has no means to learn his address. (Would Vera not have been able to give it to her, or would the aunts not have been accessible even in Carlsbad?) In the next, she thanks him for his reply and for asking her about her life. It is upon this hook that the rest hangs. Phrases that begin to cause disquiet concern the adoration in which she is held in India: 'The poor fools will deify my ashes in the manner of those of Gautama Buddha and Krishna . . . the Buddhists look upon me as a deity fallen from the clouds . . . I quickly learned Sanskrit and Pali [but she never claimed to know either] . . . Colonel Olcott although President is my pupil and has to obey me [well, yes, in the sense that the Masters had told her to teach him, and he obeyed them, whose instructions he could only get through her – but would she have put it thus boastingly?] . . . I can go to Lhasa in Tibet *when I like* [she never speaks of going to Lhasa and was not interested in Lhasa, only in Shigatsè] . . . My address? "H.P. Blavatsky", no more . . . they look on me as a saint, poor fools! . . . an incarnation of Sakyamuni Taghagata, of a Buddha' [blasphemy].

Side by side with this exultant vein runs an apparently despairing one, 'God (O Lord! if only one could be certain He exists!) [She did not believe in a personal God, but had no uncertainty as to the existence of the gods, whilst the ineffable One was a matter of fact to her] . . . between the Blavatsky of 1845–65 and the Blavatsky of the years 1865–82 there is an unbridgeable gulf'. De Zirkoff takes this to mean that the coma in which she lay for so long after the fall from her horse in the Caucasus, was an occult one, marking some stage in her development; but when one sees it in context, there is no reference to the coma or the accident, and the change is not for the better. The purported letter continues, 'Between the first and the last there is the Christ and all the celestial Angels and the Holy Virgin, and after the last there is the Buddha and Nirvana, with the bitter and cold conception of the sad and ridiculous fiasco of man's creation'. There are several references to having lost at this time the only being she ever loved, buried in Kiev, and I think what is meant is that the death of the child, Yuri, destroyed her warm Christian faith and that she took up Buddhism as second best, which is but a mockery. 'Do you know, I was a hundred times happier in the days when I was hungry and lived in a garret? . . . I at least believed in something, at least in a *Russian* God, and now that I live comparatively in luxury and am worshipped by heathens as well as by English fools, I have ceased to believe in *anything*'. In that spirit, she would never have converted anybody. It is inconceivable that she could ever have referred to her adored Indians as 'heathens'. What of her known total devotion to the Masters? Morya is brought in, but as a mysterious, almost romantic figure, without indication that he gave a teaching of substance. He first appeared to her on Waterloo Bridge when she was about to commit suicide, and there is no mention of Hyde Park or Ramsgate.

A letter dated from 'Sikkim-Ghum, October 1st' is referred by Jinarajadasa to 1882, yet does not quite fit what we know. She is writing, she says, from the Monastery of Ghum (in British India, not Sikkim, notes Jinarajadasa). 'It was too late to go to Shigatsè . . . but I decided to go to the Lama Monastery [unreal-sounding name this, too much like the Monk Monastery – and it was not for her to decide where she would go; she was told] . . . The frontier is a fast-flowing stream with a swinging bamboo bridge – on the other side . . . the Lama Monastery'. Ramaswarmier said the frontier with Sikkim was a river over which a boatman told him he had taken her in a boat on 5 October, but that she had already returned. If the frontier with Tibet is meant, she was not on this occasion allowed to cross it. Two Englishmen who were waiting were refused permission to cross the string bridge, but she was allowed over, and spent three days in a house at the foot of the Lama Monastery . . . 'I only saw Koot Hoomi for 3 hours' [no mention of Morya]. Why did they let her pass? 'It is because I am an incarnation of the Buddha'. It is inconceivable to me that Madame Blavatsky could ever have written this blasphemy. Anyway, it was not in a monastery in Tibet but in a hut in Sikkim that she met Morya and Koot Hoomi at this time, and her mood was very different.

If she did have occasional moments of overweening self-exaltation, that is what the Greeks called *hubris*, the pride that provokes the gods, and it could have been that which drew upon her the karma of the Coulomb forgeries and all the trouble with the Society for Psychical Research. Yet there is enough doubt as to the origin and authenticity of these letters for me to be unwilling to accept that solution and weave it into the text – or to include on this basis a strange assertion that she married Blavatsky because she had found in alchemical books that had belonged to her great-grandfather, Prince Dolgourouky, that a Red Virgin had to be married to a Stone or Hierophant, for which she mistook him. There is no warrant for supposing Prince Dolgourouky possessed an alchemical library. In alchemy, everything means something else. The sun means sulphur, because it is yellow; the Green Dragon means copper, because when copper is exposed to the open air it turns greenish; and the Red Virgin means mercury, because Mercury rules the astrological sign of Virgo and mercury's sulphate, cinnabar, is stone of reddish or flamingo colour. Alchemy is all about the marriage of mercury to sulphur to produce the Stone – by which, however, the alchemists do not mean mercury sulphate or cinnabar but Gold, by which they do not mean gold, either, but something mystical.

I do not believe that Madame Blavatsky, even in her teens, would have been so silly – especially as she is made to say that before she was 15 she had read all the books and 'soon neither Paracelsus, Khunrath nor C. Agrippa would have had anything to teach me'. I do not believe, either in the rest of the letter, which relates how, having failed to find the stone in Blavatsky, she sought it everywhere she went, which meant retaining her own virginity whilst making 'physiological researches' entailing 'a cold depravity' – this seems to lean on the forged 'confession' letters to Aksakoff and Solovioff – until Morya appeared to her on Waterloo Bridge and promised her both the Virgin and the Stone.

She is made to say that, returning to Europe from the East in 1871, she 'was wrecked near the Cape'. It is idle to say, as Jinarajadasa does in his note, she must have meant a cape in Greece. 'The Cape', in respect of a passage to or from India in those days, could only mean the Cape of Good Hope, and why, after the Suez Canal had been opened, would she be there? She herself, in her biographical information to Sinnett, says she went back through the Suez Canal, where people were still recalling how the Empress Eugénie came to open it.

If, as I contend, the letters are forged, who forged them? They are partly in French and partly in Russian, and therefore probably by a Russian. Several of them are on the stationery of the Theosophical Society, some on that of its Corresponding Secretary. It is as dangerous to leave stacks of blank, headed stationery about as books of blank cheques. The picker-up could have been Solovioff. As the letters invented by him which appear in the back of his book are in print only, one may doubt whether he had talent as a forger of handwriting, but he may have retained Theosophical stationery in case he should one day think of a use for it and the forgery may have been done on it by somebody else.

I do not regard the envelope, which bears Indian and Russian postmarks, as forged. But as H.P.B. remarked in another context, exhibition of an envelope is no proof of what it is alleged to have contained. She probably wrote a letter to the Prince for which something more saleable has been substituted. Incidentally, if the hand on the envelope is hers, then the address 'Yevo Ciyatel'stvoo Knyasyoo . . .' (To His Highness Prince . . .) shows that she did not place a horizontal stroke over the m-shaped character which is the Russian 't' – another nail in the coffin of the Hodgson Report.

It is my impression that Theosophists are too little alert to the prevalence of literary forgery. When a person's name has acquired sensation value, there is always the likelihood of forged writings being produced to deceive dealers and bedevil biographies. There was the notorious *Don Leon*, in the metre and rhyme scheme of Byron's *Don Juan*, but obscene. Forged letters have been produced as from Byron, Oscar Wilde, Aubrey Beardsley and Charles Dickens. More recently there have been the forged Hitler diaries. These passed the scrutiny of the handwriting experts; and it was only when Lord Dacre (Hugh Trevor Roper) realised the provenance was not as he first thought he had been told that a more intensive scrutiny of the content disclosed such disaccord with historical facts that forgery became obvious.

In this case, there are two provenances, given at different times by the same person. If the heiress of Prince Dondoukoff-Korsakoff had them, why do we not know her name? And why did she give the letters to 'Bolt' to sell instead of to a reputable dealer or auctioneer. Why did she not deal on her own behalf and so save the commission? Perhaps it was because 'Bolt' knew he could not answer these questions that he changed the story. But then, it would have to be a very unusual Austrian soldier who went to Russia to help the Bolsheviks and brought back this booty. If neither story is true, it is probable that the real provenance is disreputable.

It surprises me that those at Adyar should not have seen the tenor of the letters was anti-Theosophical and could only offer ammunition to the enemies of Madame Blavatsky. This brings me to another question, which, until I showed this chapter to Mr Timothy d'Arch Smith, puzzled me: if the letters were fabricated to sell to the Theosophical Society, why were they not tailored to suit it?

Mr d'Arch Smith, who does all the buying and selling for Fuller d'Arch Smith Ltd, agreed with all I had written about the dealing, but added the suggestion they had been offered to Theosophists because dealers had refused to buy for the sum asked, or to buy them at all. Indeed, I have always understood from him that if someone comes offering to sell letters, there are questions to be asked. Is the attempting vendor their legal owner? If not, can he show formal authorisation to act as the agent for the owner? This is important: one does not want to find oneself being sued by someone who claims ownership or, even worse, facing criminal proceedings for receiving stolen property. Moreover, the question, 'How do you come to have them?', which may have to be pressed rather searchingly, has the strongest possible bearing on the next one, which one asks oneself, 'Are they genuine?'.

It could well be because 'Bolt' found dealers too suspicious that he at last thought to offer the letters to Theosophists.

Spelling and Pronunciation
of Tibetan names

The spelling of Tibetan names causes much confusion. This is because transliteration from the Sanskrit yields dismaying clusters of consonants, difficult to remember because they are impossible to pronounce and which in fact are not pronounced by Tibetans, so that the reader struggles with them needlessly. On the other hand, the imitated pronunciations offered by writers untrained in problems of phonetic transcription are often inconsistent and misleading. In one book, first published in German, they seem to be given for the German ear but are left unchanged in the English translation. Spellings are different in almost every book one opens, so that one can be unsure whether the subject of reference is the same. I have used the transcription for English readers devised for me by Dr Philip Denwood, Lecturer in Tibetan at the School of Oriental and African Studies of the University of London, but here set against them are the transliterations found in some books.

Phonetic spelling	*Transliteration from Sanskrit*
Chögi Nyima	Chos-kyi-nyi-ma
Drèpung	'Bras-spungs
Gandèn	Galdan
Gédun Druppa	dGe-'dun-grub-pa
Gèlukpa	dG e lugs pa
Gyètsap Darma Rinchèn	rGyal-tshab Dar-ma-rin-chen
Jamyang Chojè	'Jam-dbyangs-chos-rje
Jè Pèdèn Chökyi Trakpa	rJe-dpal-Idan ch'os-kyi grags-pa Bstan-pahi
Tènpé Wangchuk	dban p'yug
Khèdrup Jè	mKhas-grub rje
Kèsang Tsetèn	Bzkai-bzabg Tshe-brten
Lopsang Chögyèn	Blo-bzang-chos-rgyan
Lobsang Tubtèn Chökyi Nyima	Blobzang Tub-ten Cho'gyi Nyma
Ngawam Lopsang	Ngag-dbang-blo-bzang
Panchèn Rimpochè	Pan chen Rin po che
Phakpa	'phags-pa
Sönam Gyatso	bSod-nams-rgya-mtsho
Shigatsè	gZis kha rtse
Trashi Lhünpo	m bKra-shis-lhun-po
Tsang Yang Gyatso	Tshangs dbangs rgya mtsho
Tsongkapa	Tsong kha pa
Ü	Dbus
Wénsapa	dBen-sa-pa
Yapsè sum	Yab-sras gSum
Yongtan Gyatso	Yon tan rgya mtsho

In the above phonetic transcription, è and é are as in French, ö and ü as in German and lh as the voiceless ll in Welsh Llan . . . (which is merely l without vibration of the vocal chords).

ch is as in English 'church'; j is as in English 'jam'; ng is as in English 'song', even when initial; ph is never f; th is never as English th; u is as the short oo in English 'look'

All syllables are stressed equally and are best pronounced level (because Tibetan is a tone language and rises or falls in pitch can alter the meanings of words).

Italian forms of words

The following list shows the Italian forms of words found in the French of the letters purporting to be from Madame Blavatsky to Madame Coulomb.

Italian and Coulomb	*French*	*English*
affare	affaire	affair
altra	autre	other
amor	amour	love
bene	bien	well
camera	chambre	room
c'e	il y a	there is
certo	certain	certain
del	du	of the
di	de	of
Dio	Dieu	God
e	et	and
fatte	faites	make
il	le	the
moneta	argent	money
padre	père	father
roba	robe	dress
si	se	reflexive pronoun
saluto	salue	salute
San	Saint	Saint
sopra	au dessus de or sur	above or on
testa	tête	head
tardi	tard	late
tropo	trop	too
trova	trouve	finds
vi	vous	you
vostra	vôtre	your

Additional oddities

Jiuseppe (cross between Italian Giuseppe and French Joseph)

à revoir

Abbreviations used in Notes and Bibliography

Collected Writings	*H.P. Blavatsky: Collected Writings*, ed. Boris de Zirkoff (Wheaton, USA, & Adyar, 1966–85), fourteen volumes
Incidents	*Incidents in the Life of Madame Blavatsky*, A.P. Sinnett (Redway, 1886)
Isis Unveiled	*Isis Unveiled, a Master-Key to the Mysteries of Ancient and Modern Theology* (Bouton, New York, 1877), two volumes; (Theosophical University Press, Pasadena, 1960), two volumes. Page references are to the latter.
Letters	*The Letters of H.P. Blavatsky to A.P. Sinnett*, ed. A.T. Barker (Fisher Unwin, 1925)
Mahatma Letters	*The Mahatma Letters, to A.P. Sinnett from the Mahatmas M & K.H.*,transcribed, compiled, and with an introduction by A.T. Barker (Rider, 1923)
ODL	*Old Diary Leaves*, Henry Steel Olcott (New York, 1895–1910), first four volumes
Private and Confidential Report	*Private and Confidential First Report of the Committee of the Society for Psychical Research Appointed to Investigate the Evidence for Marvellous Phenomena Offered by Certain Members of the Theosophical Society* (privately printed), (1884)
Proceedings	*Proceedings of the Society for Psychical Research*
Report of Observations	*Report of Observations Made During a Nine Months' Stay at the Headquarters of the Theosophical Society at Adyar (Madras), India*, F. Hartmann (Scottish Press, Madras, 1884)
The Secret Doctrine	*The Secret Doctrine, the Synthesis of Science, Religion and Philosophy* (TPC, 1888), two volumes; (Adyar, 1938), six volumes. Page references are to the latter.
TPC	Theosophical Publishing Company
TPH	Theosophical Publishing House
TPS	Theosophical Publishing Society

Notes

CHAPTER 1

[1] All astrologers agree in putting Cancer on the Ascendant, the difference of opinion being only as to the degree. In any case, one will have with that Ascendant: Sun Leo 18; Moon Libra 9°; Mercury Virgo 9°; Venus Libra 9°; Mars Virgo 2° 50′; Jupiter Aquarius 17° 15′; Saturn Virgo 3° 12′; Uranus Aquarius 12° 16′; Neptune Capricorn 20° 50′; Pluto Aries 11° 30′; Moon's North Node Virgo 2° 50′ (Equinoctial Zodiac). I will not work it more finely for the faster moving bodies, the degree of the Ascendant being speculative.

[2] *Kak Ya Bila Malen'koi* (*When I was Little*), Vera Petrovna Zhelikhovskaya (St Petersburg, 1894), p.245.

[3] *Incidents*, pp.13–14.

[4] *Mémoires d'une Petite Fille Russe* (*Memoirs of a Little Russian Girl*), Vera Zhelihovskaya (Paris, 1896), pp.10–11. This book is basically a French translation of *Kak Ya Bila Malen'koi*, but with the matter somewhat reshuffled – chapters differently divided up and re-titled – and a different set of illustrations. Helena's name, which figures in Russian as Elena (pronounced Yelyona), here appears as Lolia (Lolya in *Kak Ya Bila Malen'koi*). Both books are written for children.

[5] Ibid., p.252.

[6] Ibid., p.190.

[7] Ibid., p.195.

[8] Ibid., pp.200, 250.

[9] *Incidents*, p.29.

[10] Ibid., pp.37–8; *Letters*, p.150.

[11] *ODL*, I, p.458.

[12] *Moyo Otrochestvo* (*My Adolescence*), Vera Petrovna Zhelikhovskaya (St Petersburg, 3rd ed., undated), (sequel to *Kak Ya Bila Malen'koi*), p.165.

[13] Ibid., p.167.

[14] Ibid., p.168.

CHAPTER 2

[1] *Collected Writings*, VI, pp.293–4.

[2] Ibid., I, pp.338–51.

[3] Library of the Society for Psychical Research, unpublished letter to Hurrychund Chintamon, 4 May 1878.

[4] *Incidents*, p.40ff.

CHAPTER 3

[1] *Collected Writings*, I, pp.117–86.

[2] *Letters*, pp.143–4.

[3] British Museum, Additional MSS.45287, LX; *Letters*, pp.143–4.

[4] 'Madame Blavatsky, a Theosophical occult apology', in Frank Leslie's *Popular Monthly*, February 1892.

CHAPTER 4

[1] *The Masters and the Path*, C.W. Leadbeater (Adyar, 1925), p.45.

[2] British Museum, Additional MSS.45287, LXI; *Letters*, p.150.

[3] *H.P.B. Speaks*, ed. C. Jinarajadasa (Adyar, 1950), I, p.221.

[4] *British India's Relations with the Kingdom of Nepal, 1857–1947*, Asad Hussain (Allen & Unwin, 1970), p.53.

[5] Op. cit, loc. sit.

[6] *Reminiscences of H.P. Blavatsky*, Countess Wachtmeister (TPH, 1893), pp.56–7.

[7] *Thirty Views and Scenery of Ramsgate*, anon. (undated, but obviously mid-nineteenth century).

[8] *The Grotto*, Howard Bridgewater (Margate, 1955), p.16; see also *The Shell Temple*, Conan and Nellie I. Shaw (Margate, 1945) and *Archaic Britain*, Harold Bayley (Chapman & Hall, 1919).

[9] *Isis Unveiled*, II, p.401.

CHAPTER 5

[1] *Isis Unveiled*, I, pp.595–8.

[2] *Collected Writings*, I, pp.lxi–lxii.

[3] *From the Caves and Jungles of Hindostan*, XXI; 'Sir John Login and Juleep Singh', Lady Login, *London Illustrated News*, 24 June 1885.

[4] *Letters*, p.151.

CHAPTER 6

[1] *Incidents*, p.48.

[2] *The Theosophist*, April 1891, and *ODL*, I, p.265.

[3] *Trespassers on the Roof of the World*, Peter Hopkirk (Murray, 1982), p.47.

[4] *The Theosophist*, ibid., and *ODL*, ibid.

[5] *To Lhasa in Disguise*, Wm Montgomery McGovern (Butterworth, 1924), p.35.

[6] *The Theosophist*, ibid.

[7] *Madame Blavatsky*, Marion Meade (New York, 1980), p.70.

[8] *Priestess of the Occult*, Gertrude Marvin Williams (New York, 1946), p.28.

[9] *Madame Blavatsky and her Theosophy*, Arthur Lillie (1882), pp.12–13.

[10] Hopkirk, ibid., pp.83–91.
[11] *Collected Writings*, I, p.xlii.
[12] *Seven Years in Tibet*, Heinrich Harrer (Hart-Davis, 1953), p.39.
[13] *Isis Unveiled*, II, p.627.
[14] *Francis Younghusband*, George Seaver (Murray, 1952), p.61.
[15] *Isis Unveiled*, II, p.628.
[16] *Travels in Tartary, Tibet and China*, E.R. Huc (1852), II, pp.148–9.
[17] *Isis Unveiled*, ibid.
[18] British Museum, Additional MSS.45287, X; *Incidents*, p.55.
[19] *Isis Unveiled*, II, p.621.

CHAPTER 7
[1] *Incidents*, p.56. This and the following passages are all from Vera's narrative.
[2] Ibid., pp.60–3.
[3] Ibid., p.62.
[4] Ibid., pp.67–70.
[5] Ibid., pp.70–4.
[6] Ibid., pp.91–8.
[7] Ibid., p.83.
[8] Ibid., pp.105–6.
[9] Ibid., pp.106–8.
[10] Ibid., p.111.
[11] *Collected Writings*, VI, pp.291–2.
[12] Ibid., III, pp.211–8.
[13] Ibid., I, pp.9–10.
[14] Ibid., I, p.xlvi.
[15] *Personal Memoirs of H.P. Blavatsky*, Mary K. Neff (Rider, 1937), pp.187–8.
[16] *ODL*, II, p.135.
[17] *Letters*, p.143.
[18] *Incidents*, p.56.
[19] Ibid., pp.112–6; *Collected Writings*, I, pp.xlv–xlvi.

CHAPTER 8
[1] *H.P.B. Speaks*, ed. C. Jinarajadasa (Adyar, 1950), I, p.51.
[2] *Collected Writings*, I, pp.12–17.

CHAPTER 9
[1] British Museum, Additional MSS.45287, LXXVII; *Letters*, p.189.
[2] Ibid., LX; *Letters*, pp.143-4.

CHAPTER 10
[1] The following details are from *Garibaldi*, Jasper Ridley (Constable, 1974).
[2] *Collected Writings*, I, 55n.
[3] *ODL*, I, p.9.
[4] British Museum, Additional MSS.45287, LX (*Incidents*, p.144).

CHAPTER 11
[1] British Museum, Additional MSS.45287, LV; *Letters*, p.152.

[2] Ibid.
[3] Ibid.
[4] On this point I consulted Mrs Shirley Warner, directress of the Rectory Riding School, Wymington, Rushden, with whom I had taken a refresher course of riding lessons. I recollected that she had competed in a long distance event. She said that was over a 41-mile course. Everybody completed it in about the expected time of six hours, at the expected average trotting speed of seven miles an hour, usual in long distance as it is less tiring to the horse than when the pace is varied. It was recognised as a strain on a horse, and the horse had to be examined by a vet before the start and at the half-way halt – and that was in gentle Northamptonshire country, using roads and paths. In terrible country, she doubted if they would make more than half that rate. Again, it was a question not only of how much the horse could do but of how much the rider could endure.

CHAPTER 12
[1] *To Lhasa in Disguise*, William Montgomery McGovern (Thornton Butterworth, 1924), p.176.
[2] *The Vishnu Purana*, trans. H.H. Wilson (1848–70), III, pp.60–1.
[3] McGovern, ibid., pp.338–9.
[4] *Trespassers on the Roof of the World*, Peter Hopkirk (Murray, 1982), p.46.
[5] British Museum, Additional MSS.45286, XVI; *Mahatma Letters*, pp.478–9.
[6] *My Land and My People*, The Dalai Lama (Weidenfeld, 1962), p.18; McGovern, *passim*.
[7] *Tibet*, Thubten Jigme Norbu and Colin M. Turnbull (Chatto, 1969), pp.206–7.
[8] *The Tibetan Book of the Dead*, Evans-Wentz (Oxford, 1927), p.170n.
[9] McGovern, ibid., p.161.
[10] *Narratives of the Mission of George Bogle to Tibet and of the Journey of Thomas Manning to Lhasa*, Clements R. Markham (Trubner, 1876), p.100.
[11] *The Secret Doctrine*, V, p.391.
[12] *Journey to Lhasa and Central Tibet*, Sarat Chandra Das, (Murray, 1902), p.199.
[13] *Initiations and Initiates in Tibet*, Alexandra David-Neel (Rider, 1932), p.20n.; *The Religions of Tibet*, Giuseppe Tucci (Routledge, 1980), p.160.
[14] Das, ibid., p.57n.
[15] Das, ibid., p.12.
[16] *Personal Memoirs of H.P. Blavatsky*, Mary K. Neff (Rider, 1937), p.143, quoting letter to Hartmann of 1886.
[17] *H.P. Blavatsky and the Masters of Wisdom*, Annie Besant (TPH, 1907), p.9, quoting an attempted table of dates in Madame Blavatsky's life, found by Mrs Besant at Adyar, in a hand unknown to her: '1866 . . . to the

Kumlun [*sic*] mountains and Lake Palti and Tibet'. Boris de Zirkoff will be correct in transposing this to 1868 (*Collected Writings*, I, p.xlviii), but as Mr Walter Carrithers has pointed out in his paper *Behind the Mask* (privately circulated), incorrect in taking the list of places visited to indicate a route. The Kwen or Kuen Lun Mountains and Lake Palti (Yamdok or Yandro Tso) are both in Tibet but on opposite sides of Shigatsè. The unknown note-jotter was muddled, and perhaps confused Kuen Lun with Kum Bum.

18 *India and Tibet*, Francis Younghusband (Murray, 1910), p.233.

19 *The Canadian Theosophist*, vol.VIII, June 1927, report of an illustrated talk given on 15 Maÿto the Toronto Theosophical Society. Major Cross, who was in Toronto with his wife, Dr Cross, and daughter, intended returning to Tibet.

20 *Letters from the Masters of Wisdom*, Letter XXXVIII, p.90; also *Second Series*, facsimile facing pp.4–5. Together with the Master's letter, at Adyar, is a letter from Nadyezhda Fadeyef to Olcott, explaining the phenomenal manner of its delivery.

CHAPTER 13

1 British Museum, Additional MSS.45287, LXI; *Letters*, p.153.
2 Ibid., Additional MSS.45288, XCV; *Letters*, p.215.
3 Ibid., Additional MSS.45287, LXI; *Letters*, p.153.
4 *ODL*, I, pp.432–3.
5 *Isis Unveiled*, I, p.413.
6 *Collected Writings*, I, p.11n.
7 British Museum, Additional MSS.45287, LXXVIII; *Letters*, p.189.
8 Ibid., *Letters*, pp.189–90.
9 *Personal Memoirs of Madame Blavatsky*, Mary K. Neff (Rider, 1937), p.43; *Collected Writings*, I, p.xlix.
10 British Museum, Additional MSS.45287, LXI; *Letters*, p.154.
11 Ibid., *Letters*, pp.153–4.
12 *ODL*, I, p.28.

CHAPTER 14

1 *ODL*, I, pp.28–9.
2 Ibid., p.20.
3 Ibid., pp.21–2.
4 Ibid., pp.440–1.

CHAPTER 15

1 *ODL*, I, p.1.
2 The Supreme Court, Hall of Records, New York County, Index GA 719–0–1.
3 *ODL*, I, p.3.
4 Ibid., p.4.

CHAPTER 16

1 *ODL*, I, p.1.
2 Ibid., p.4.
3 Ibid., p.6.
4 Ibid.
5 Ibid., p.9.
6 *Incidents*, pp.137–8.

CHAPTER 17

1 *Isis Unveiled*, I, pp.xxix, 319 and *passim*.
2 *ODL*, I, p.19.
3 The Supreme Court, Hall of Records, New York County, Index GA 719–0–1.
4 *Priestess of the Occult*, Gertrude Marvin Williams (New York, 1946).
5 *Madame Blavatsky*, John Symonds (Odhams, 1959), p.73.

CHAPTER 18

1 *Some Unpublished Letters of Helena Petrovna Blavatsky*, ed. Eugene Hollis Corson (Rider, 1929), pp.122–6.
2 *ODL*, I, pp.13–14.
3 Ibid.,pp.127–8.
4 *ODL*, I, pp.35–37.

CHAPTER 19

1 *ODL*, I, pp.56–7.
2 *Collected Writings*, I, pp.83–4.

CHAPTER 20

1 *ODL*, I, pp.79–80.
2 *Collected Writings*, I, pp.89–90.
3 Ibid., p.86; *ODL*, I, pp.73–5.
4 *Letters from the Masters of Wisdom, Second Series*, pp.11–13.
5 *Collected Writings*, I, p.90.
6 *Letters from the Masters of Wisdom, Second Series*, p.18.
7 Ibid., p.36.
8 Ibid., p.17.
9 Ibid., p.20.

CHAPTER 21

1 *Letters from the Masters of Wisdom, Second Series*, pp.30–2.
2 Ibid., pp.41–2.

CHAPTER 23

1 *ODL*, I, p.205.
2 Ibid., p.208.
3 Ibid., p.207.
4 Ibid.
5 Ibid., pp.208–9.
6 Ibid., p.245.
7 Ibid., p.345.
8 Ibid., pp.210–1.
9 Ibid., pp.238–9.
10 Ibid., p.247.
11 Ibid., pp.275–6.
12 Ibid., pp.267–8.
13 Ibid., p.244.

[14] Ibid., p.267.
[15] Ibid., p.458.
[16] Ibid., pp.424–6.
[17] Ibid., pp.412–3.
[18] Ibid., pp.216–7n.

CHAPTER 24
[1] *Isis Unveiled*, I, p.14.
[2] Ibid., p.15.
[3] Ibid., p.387.
[4] Ibid., pp.330–1.
[5] Ibid., p.421.
[6] Ibid., II, pp.10, 41, 50, 95 and *passim*.
[7] Ibid., pp.508, 510.
[8] Ibid., pp.116–7, 281.

CHAPTER 25
[1] *Personal Memoirs of Madame Blavatsky*, Mary K. Neff (Rider, 1927), p.170.
[2] *People from the Other World*, Henry Steel Olcott (Hartford, Connecticut, 1875), p.356.
[3] Ibid., p.293.
[4] *Napoleon III*, Albert Guérard (Harvard, 1943), pp.6–7.
[5] *Incidents in my Life*, D.D. Home (Longmans, 1863), p.124; *D.D. Home, his Life and Mission*, Madame Home (Kegan Paul, 1931), pp.59–60; see also *The Shadow and the Light, a Defence of Daniel Dunglas Home*, Elizabeth Jenkins (Hamish Hamilton, 1982), for the whole of the Napoleon and 'foot' affair, as well as movements.
[6] Home, ibid., p.113; Mme Dunglas Home, ibid., p.65.
[7] Home, ibid., p.115; Mme Dunglas Home, ibid., p.53.
[8] *The Mysterious Madame, A Life of Madame Blavatsky*, 'Ephesian' (C.E. Bechhofer Roberts) (Lane, Bodley Head, 1930), p.34.
[9] *Collected Writings*, I, pp.203–4.
[10] *Memoirs of Count Witte*, translated by Abraham Yarmonsky (Heinemann, 1931), pp.6–7.
[11] *With Bayonets to Lhasa*, Peter Fleming (Harte-Davis, 1961), p.29.
[12] Frank Leslie's *Popular Monthly*, XXXVIII, February 1982.

CHAPTER 26
[1] *H.P.B. Speaks*, ed. C. Jinarajadasa (Adyar, 1950), I, p.222.
[2] *ODL*, I, pp.429–31.
[3] Ibid., pp.436–7.

CHAPTER 27
[1] Library of the Society for Psychical Research. What is possessed is not the original letters, the loan of which Professor Sidgwick requested in a letter to Chintamon of 4 November 1891 – after Madame Blavatsky's death. The writing is not hers, and occasionally summarises instead of copying passages. At least least two hands appear. Neither of them looks oriental, and I would think that the making of the extracts was by members of the SPR staff. The main hand (Mrs Sidgwicks?) is very difficult to read. The letters have never been published. This is probably because the SPR were disappointed that they were not as incriminating as had been hoped, while the Theosophists very likely have not known of their existence.
[2] *H.P.B. Speaks*, I, p.190.

CHAPTER 28
[1] *ODL*, I, p.51.
[2] Ibid., p.473.
[3] Ibid., p.307.
[4] *Hammer on the Mountain*, Howard Murphet (TPH, Wheaton, 1972), pp.84–6.
[5] *ODL*, I, p.475.
[6] Ibid., p.361.
[7] *Collected Writings*, I, pp.414–5.
[8] Ibid., p.420.
[9] Ibid., p.429.
[10] Ibid., p.431.
[11] Ibid., p.433.

CHAPTER 29
[1] *ODL*, II, pp.5–6.
[2] Ibid., p.10.
[3] Ibid., p.20.

CHAPTER 30
[1] *ODL*, II, pp.42–3.
[2] Ibid., p.45.
[3] *Private and Confidential Report*, pp.48–9 (transcript of informal conversation with Olcott).
[4] *ODL*, I, p.280.

CHAPTER 31
[1] *ODL*, II, pp.48–9.
[2] Ibid., pp.49–50.
[3] Ibid., pp.51–8.
[4] Ibid., p.60.
[5] Ibid., p.66.
[6] Ibid., p.69.

CHAPTER 32
[1] *ODL*, II, p.92.
[2] Adyar Archives; see also *ODL*, II, p.97.
[3] *Incidents*, p.171.
[4] Ibid., p.178.
[5] *ODL*, II, p.118.
[6] *Occult World*, pp.39–40.
[7] *ODL*, II, 119–20.
[8] Ibid., p.123.
[9] Ibid., p.133.
[10] Ibid., p.134.

CHAPTER 33
[1] *ODL*, II, pp.136–7.
[2] Ibid., p.147. Olcott writes 28 June, but on 28

June Madame Blavatsky and he were at
Matara in Ceylon. Olcott takes all his dates
from his diary, and the abbreviation 'Jan' can
look much like 'June'.
³ Ibid.
⁴ Ibid., p.200.
⁵ Ibid., p.207.
⁶ Ibid., p.208.
⁷ *Letters from the Masters of Wisdom, Second
Series*, no.29. The letter is not dated, but
Jinarajadasa says it was received on 3
October 1879, for which he gives no reason.
This dating is obviously wrong (though
followed by de Zirkoff in the *Collected Writings*, II, p.83). On 3 October 1879, *The
Theosophist* had only been founded for two
days. The letter is obviously that which Olcott
describes as dropping into his lap whilst Miss
Bates was raging, on 5 August 1880; *ODL*, II,
p.208.

CHAPTER 34
¹ *ODL*, II, p.222.
² Ibid., pp.229–31.
³ Ibid., pp.231–2; *The Occult World*, A.P.
Sinnett (Trubner, 1881, 2nd ed. 1882)
pp.53–5.
⁴ Sinnett, ibid., p.52.
⁵ Sinnett, ibid., p.80.
⁶ Sinnett, ibid., pp.55–6.
⁷ *ODL*, ibid., pp.232–4; Sinnett, ibid., pp.57–
61.
⁸ Ibid., p.237; Sinnett, ibid., pp.62–3.
⁹ Sinnett, ibid., pp.63–4.
¹⁰ *ODL*, ibid., pp.238–40; Sinnett, ibid., pp.67–
70.
¹¹ Sinnett, ibid., pp.67–70.
¹² *ODL*, ibid., p.241.
¹³ Sinnett, ibid., p.74.

CHAPTER 35
¹ British Museum, Additional MSS.45284, I;
Mahatma Letters, p.1
² Ibid., II; *Mahatma Letters*, pp.6–10.
³ Ibid., IIIA; *Mahatma Letters*, p.10.
⁴ Ibid., IIIB; *Mahatma Letters*, pp.10–11.
⁵ Ibid., Additional MSS.42586, IIIC; *Mahatma
Letters*, p.11
⁶ *Occult World*, pp.99–100.
⁷ British Museum, Additional MSS.45284, IV;
Mahatma Letters, pp.11–16.

CHAPTER 36
¹ British Museum, Additional MSS.45284, IV;
Mahatma Letters, p.12.
² Ibid., IX; *Mahatma Letters*, p.44.
³ *The Pelican History of Psychology*, Robert
Thomson (Pelican, 1968), pp.54–6; *Psychology, The Science of Mental Life*, George A.
Miller (Pelican, 1966), pp.108–13.
⁴ *ODL*, II, pp.254–5.

⁵ *Five Years of Theosophy* (selections from *The
Theosophist* (Adyar, 1894, pp.305–6); short
note by R. Ragoonrath Row on the appear-
ance of the names Morya and Kuthumi in the
Puranas, drawing for the former upon the
Matsya Purana (chapter cclxxii), the *Vishnu
Purana* (Wilson, IV, pp.4, 24) and the *Vayu
Purana*, followed by an editorial note by
Madame Blavatsky, drawing upon the Budd-
hist *Mahavamso*. See also *The Secret Doctrine*,
II, p.93 and nn., and IV, p.120 and n.3.
⁶ *The Cambridge Shorter History of India*,
J. Allan, Sir Wolseley Haig, H.H. Dodwell
(Cambridge, 1943), p.32. See also whole
chapter in this work, 'The early Mauryas,
pp.31–41; also, in *A History of India*, J.C.
Powell-Price (Nelson, 1955), the chapter 'The
Mauryas', pp.38–50.

CHAPTER 37
¹ *The Theosophical Movement*, Anon. – i.e.
Robert Crosbie and other members of the
United Lodge of Theosophists (Dutton, New
York, 1925), p.624–5.
² British Museum, Additional MSS.45286,
CXXXIV; *Mahatma Letters*, pp.461–2.
³ Crosbie, ibid., pp.627–8.
⁴ Here lies the origin of an erroneous footnote
by Jinarajadasa to *The Early Teachings of the
Masters*, p.75, that 'the Disinherited' was
Damodar K. Malankvar – which error has
generated passages of scorn from the Hare
brothers in their book *Who Wrote the
Mahatma Letters?* They accuse the Mahatmas,
where they refer to Damodar and the Disinherited as being in correspondence with each
other, as trying to make two persons out of
Damodar. But Damodar and the Disinherited
are two persons. Damodar is a Maratha of
Brahmin caste living in Bombay, disinherited
by his father. The Disinherited (whose real
name we never learn) was disinherited by his
grandfather long before our story opens, and
lives in Tibet, as is evident from his giving to
Koot Hoomi a stock of note-paper he had no
occasion to use, and from his suffering a nasty
accident on a path above a ravine through
setting foot on a magnetised rag set by
Dugpas. Damodar had not at that date been to
Tibet.

CHAPTER 38
¹ *Occult World*, pp.108–11.
² British Museum, Additional MSS.45286,
XCIX; *Mahatma Letters*, p.438.
³ Ibid., Additional MSS.45284, V; *Mahatma
Letters*, p.17.
⁴ Ibid., *Mahatma Letters*, p.21.
⁵ Ibid., Additional MSS.45287, VI; *Letters*, p.8.
⁶ Ibid., Additional MSS.45284, VI; *Mahatma
Letters*, p.22.

7 Ibid., VII; *Mahatma Letters*, p.25.
8 *Letters from the Masters of Wisdom, Second Series*, p.82n.; *Mahatma Letters*, p.36.
9 British Museum, Additional MSS.45284, VIII; *Mahatma Letters*, p.32.
10 Ibid., *Mahatma Letters*, p.37.

CHAPTER 39
1 British Museum, Additional MSS.45285, XXXI; *Mahatma Letters*, pp.240–2.
2 Ibid., XXVI; *Mahatma Letters*, pp.203–44.
3 Ibid., XXVII; *Mahatma Letters*, p.205.
4 Ibid., Additional MSS.45286, CIV; *Mahatma Letters*, p.441.
5 Ibid., Additional MSS.45285, XXIX; *Mahatma Letters*, pp.218–28.
6 *Hints on Esoteric Theosophy*, A.O. Hume (Adyar, 1882), pp.109–10.
7 Ibid., pp.105–6.
8 British Museum, Additional MSS.45288, CLVI; *Letters*, p.305.
9 Ibid.; *Letters*, pp.307–8.
10 *ODL*, II, pp.349–50.
11 Ibid., p.360.

CHAPTER 40
1 *Esoteric Buddhism*, p.19 (4th ed.).
2 British Museum, Additional MSS.45284, XIII; *Mahatma Letters*, p.78.
3 Ibid.; *Mahatma Letters*, p.73.
4 *The Books of Kiu-Te*, David Reigle (Wizard, San Diego 1983), p.68.
5 British Museum, Additional MSS.45284, XIV; *Mahatma Letters*, p.80.
6 Ibid.; *Mahatma Letters*, p.79.
7 Ibid., XII; *Mahatma Letters*, p.68.
8 *Esoteric Buddhism*, 4th ed., p.109.
9 British Museum, Additional MSS.45284, XXIIIB; *Mahatma Letters*, p.157.
10 Ibid.; *Mahatma Letters*, p.177.
11 Ibid.; XII: *Mahatma Letters*, p.67.
12 Ibid.; Additional MSS.45288, CXIX; *Letters*, p.249.
13 Ibid.; Additional MSS.45284, XXIIIB; *Mahatma Letters*, p.164.
14 Ibid.; *Mahatma Letters*, ibid.
15 Ibid.; XV; *Mahatma Letters*, pp.98–9.
16 Ibid.; XIII; *Mahatma Letters*, p.70.
17 Ibid., Additional MSS.45288, Appendix II; *Letters*, pp.379–80.
18 Ibid.; *Letters*, p.377.
19 Ibid.; *Letters*, p.383.
20 *The Tibetan Book of the Dead*, Evans-Wentz (Oxford, 1927), p.28 n.1.
21 *The Religions of Tibet*, Giuseppe Tucci (Routledge, 1980), p.167.
22 British Museum, Additional MSS.45288, Appendix II; *Letters*, p.382.
23 Ibid.; *Letters*, p.284.
24 Ibid., Additional MSS.45284, XXIIIB; *Mahatma Letters*, pp.170–1.

25 Ibid., XXVIIIA; *Mahatma Letters*, p.147.
26 Ibid., XXIIIB (f.284); *Mahatma Letters*, p.175.
27 Ibid., XVIII; *Mahatma Letters*, p.122.
28 Ibid., XXIIIB; *Mahatma Letters*, p.162.
29 *New Scientist*, 15 July 1982, 'Close encounter with a million comets', Victor Clube and Bill Napier; *The Cosmic Serpent*, by the same authors (Faber, 1982) and letter from Dr Clube to the present author, from the Royal Observatory at Edinburgh, of 7 November 1982.
30 British Museum, Additional MSS.45284, XXIIIB; *Mahatma Letters*, p.170.

CHAPTER 41
1 British Museum, Additional MSS.45287, XVIII; *Letters*, p.37.
2 Ibid., Additional MSS.45285, LIV; *Mahatma Letters*, pp.313–4.
3 Ibid., Additional MSS.45287, XIX; *Letters*, p.38.
4 *The Theosophist*, December 1882, pp.67–9.
5 *The Religions of Tibet*, Giuseppe Tucci (Routledge, 1980), pp.133, 136.
6 *The Theosophist*, December 1883.

CHAPTER 42
1 British Museum, Additional MSS.45284, IX; *Mahatma Letters*, p.38.
2 Ibid., XXXII; *Mahatma Letters*, p.243.
3 Ibid., Additional MSS.45285, XXIVB; *Mahatma Letters*, p.180–1.
4 Ibid., LIV; *Mahatma Letters*, pp.320–321.
5 Ibid., Additional MSS.45284, XVI; *Mahatma Letters*, p.116.
6 Ibid., VII; *Mahatma Letters*, p.25.
7 Ibid., VIII; *Mahatma Letters*, p.26.
8 Ibid., Additional MSS.45285, XLIX; *Mahatma Letters*, p.282.
9 *Letters from the Masters of Wisdom, Second Series*, p.96.
10 *The Religions of Tibet*, Giuseppe Tucci (Routledge, 1980), p.325.
11 *The Religions of Tibet*, Helmut Hoffmann (Allen & Unwin, 1961), p.169.
12 *Journey to Lhasa and Central Tibet*, Sarat Chandra Das (Murray, 1902), p.203.
13 Ibid., p.214.
14 Ibid., p.207.
15 *Collected Writings*, X, p.153.

CHAPTER 43
1 *Collected Writings*, IV, p.11; *Secret Doctrine*, V, pp.191–3; see also British Museum, Additional MSS.45284, IX; *Mahatma Letters*, pp.43–4.
2 *An Incarnation of the Snow*, F.W. Bain (Parker, Oxford; & Simkin, Marshall Hamilton, Dent, London, 1908), p.1

3 *Calming the Mind and Discerning the Real*, from the *Lam Rin chen po* of Tsong-kha-pa, translated by Alex Wayman (Columbia, New York, 1978), p.15.

4 The horoscopic positions at his birth were: Sun Sagittarius 7° 10′ 22″; Moon Pisces 29° 35′ 46″; Mercury Sagittarius 13° 33′; Venus Sagittarius 23° 00′; Mars Scorpio 8° 57′; Jupiter Aquarius 25° 11′, Saturn Leo 4° 16′R; Uranus Gemini 8° 02′R; Neptune Pisces 0° 17′R; Pluto Aries 23° 44′R; Node Aquarius 4° 36′ Midheaven Virgo 22, and Ascendant Sagittarius 7° 10′ 22″, assuming the centre of the sun to be upon the horizon. Sunrise at Kumbum would have been about 6.53 a.m. The moon entered Aries at 7.38 a.m., and was semi-sextile Neptune at 8.22 a.m. It was a Tuesday.

5 *Travels in Tartary, Tibet and China*, Evariste-Régis Huc (1852), vol.II, p.47.

6 Wayman, ibid.

7 Huc, ibid.

8 Huc, II, pp.52–4, 57.

9 Huc, II, p.54

10 *Tibet*, Thubten Jigme Norbu (Chatto, 1969), pp.208–210.

11 Huc, II, p.47.

12 Norbu, p.28.

13 Huc, ibid.

14 Wayman, pp.16–17.

15 Wayman, p.23.

16 *The Religions of Tibet*, Helmut Hoffmann (Allen & Unwin, 1961), p.166.

17 Hoffmann, p.167.

18 *The Religions of Tibet*, Giuseppe Tucci (Routledge, 1980), p.37.

19 *The Buddhism of Tibet, or Lamaism*, L. Austine Waddell, (1895), p.59.

20 Wayman, p.25.

21 *Journey to Lhasa and Central Tibet*, Sarat Chandra Das (Murray, 1902), p.180.

22 *The Younghusband Expedition*, Parshotam Mehra (Asia, 1969), p.137.

23 *Tibet, a Political History*, Tsepon W.D. Shakabpa (Yale, 1967), p.91.

24 Hoffmann, p.168.

25 Waddell, p.236.

26 Hoffmann, p.173.

27 Tucci, p.42.

28 Norbu, p.271.

29 *Narratives of the Mission of George Bogle to Tibet and of the Journey of Thomas Manning to Lhasa*, Clements R. Markham (Trubner, 1876), p.lxvii, and *Collected Writings*, IV, p.12.

30 Shakabpa, pp.306–7.

31 *Behind the Mask, Poisoned Popes*, Walter Carrithers (privately circulated, undated).

32 Shakabpa, p.100.

33 Ibid., p.105.

34 Ibid., p.111.

35 *To Lhase in Disguise*, William Montgomery McGovern (Thornton Butterworth, 1924), p.297.

36 Ibid., p.298.

37 Norbu, p.219.

38 Huc, II, p.163.

39 Shakabpa, p.190.

40 Das, p.104.

41 *The Theosophist*, January 1882; *Collected Writings*, VI, p.94.

42 *Lucifer*, September 1884; *Collected Writings*, VI, p.95.

CHAPTER 44

1 *ODL*, II, p.431.

2 *The Religions of Tibet*, Giuseppe Tucci (Routledge, 1980), p.152.

3 *To Lhasa in Disguise*, William Montgomery McGovern (Thornton Butterworth, 1924), p.54.

CHAPTER 45

0 *ODL*, III, p.75.

2 British Museum, Additional MSS.45286, LXXVIII, *Mahatma Letters*, p.381.

3 Ibid., LXXXIII; *Mahatma Letters*, p.395.

4 Ibid., Additional MSS.45285, XLVI; *Mahatma Letters*, p.270.

5 Ibid., XXXII; *Mahatma Letters*, p.243.

6 Ibid., Additional MSS.45288, CCV; *Mahatma Letters*, p.366.

7 Ibid., Additional MSS.45286, LXXVII; *Mahatma Letters*, p.381.

8 Ibid., Additional MSS.45285, LVIII; *Mahatma Letters*, p.337.

9 Ibid., XLIX; *Mahatma Letters*, p.284.

10 Ibid., Additional MSS.45287, VIII; *Letters*, p.12.

11 Ibid., Additional MSS.45286, LXVI; *Mahatma Letters*, p.369.

12 *Letters from the Masters of Wisdom, Second Series*, II, pp.81–3; *ODL*, II, p.441.

13 Published in 'Madame Blavatsky – a tribute', Manly Palmer Hall, in *Theosophia*, May–June 1947.

14 British Museum, Additional MSS.45285, LIX; *Mahatma Letters*, p.338.

15 *Letters from the Masters of Wisdom, Second Series*, II, p.85.

16 British Museum, Additional MSS.45285, LVIII; *Mahatma Letters*, pp.341–7.

17 *Proceedings*, December 1885, p.323. Madame Coulomb's letter, of which the original has unfortunately disappeared, is reproduced in a statement from General Morgan, itself reproduced from his *Reply to a Report of an Examination of the Blavatsky Correspondence by D.J.G. Gribble*. See also General Morgan's earlier article on the phenomenon in *The Theosophist*, December 1883.

18 *ODL*, II, p.464.

19 *ODL*, III, pp.1–2.

20 Ibid., p.17.

21 British Museum, Additional MSS.45287, XXVII; *Letters*, pp.55, 61–2.

[22] *ODL*, III, p.36.

CHAPTER 46
[1] British Museum, Additional MSS.45286, XCIII; *Mahatma Letters*, pp.420–9.

CHAPTER 47
[1] British Museum, Additional MSS.45286, LXXV; *Mahatma Letters*, pp.398–400.
[2] *Letters from the Masters of Wisdom*, Letter XXII, pp.63–4.
[3] British Museum, Additional MSS.45286, CXXIV; *Mahatma Letters*, p.453.
[4] Ibid., Additional MSS.45285, LXVII; *Mahatma Letters*, p.271.
[5] *ODL*, III, p.61.
[6] British Museum, Additional MSS.45287, XXVIII; *Mahatma Letters*, p.63.
[7] Ibid., XXIX; *Letters*, p.66.
[8] Ibid., Additional MSS.45286, LXXXVI; *Mahatma Letters*, p.405.
[9] Ibid.; *Mahatma Letters*, p.403.
[10] Ibid., LXXXVII; *Mahatma Letters*, pp.406–9.
[11] Ibid., Additional MSS.45287, XXXI; *Letters*, p.74.
[12] *Report of Observations*, pp.27–9.
[13] Ibid., p.32.

CHAPTER 48
[1] *Collected Writings*, I, p.475.
[2] British Museum, Additional MSS.45287, XXXVII; Letters, pp.89–90.
[3] Ibid.; *Letters*, p.91.
[4] *Letters from the Masters of Wisdom*, Letter XVIII, pp.49–50.
[5] *ODL*, III, pp.93–5.
[6] *How Theosophy Came to Me*, C.W. Leadbeater (Adyar, 1930).
[7] *ODL*, III, pp.112–38.
[8] *Private and Confidential Report*, pp.35–53.
[9] Ibid., pp.62–4.

CHAPTER 49
[1] *Report of Observations*, pp.24–5.
[2] *ODL*, III, p.74.
[3] *Report of Observations*, p.25.
[4] Ibid., p.33.
[5] *Letters from the Masters of Wisdom, Second Series*, pp.131–2.
[6] *A Short History of the Theosophical Society*, Josephine Ransom (TPH, 1938), p.210.
[7] *Report of Observations*, pp.35–6.
[8] *Proceedings*, p.280.
[9] *Report of Observations*, p.35.
[10] *Adyar Report*, p.86.
[11] *Adyar Report*, p.85.
[12] *Report of Observations*, pp.39–40.
[13] Ibid., p.40.
[14] *Letters from the Masters of Wisdom*, pp.54–5 and ed. note, pp.116–7.

CHAPTER 50
[1] 'H.P.B. at Enghien', William Quan Judge, in *In Memory of H.P. Blavatsky*, by some of her pupils (TPH, 1891), pp.112–6.
[2] British Museum, Additional MSS.45286, LXXXI; *Mahatma Letters*, p.395.
[3] Ibid., XCIB; *Mahatma Letters*, p.418.
[4] Ibid., *Mahatma Letters*, pp.416–7.
[5] Ibid., *Mahatma Letters*, p.418.
[6] Ibid., LIV; *Mahatma Letters*, p.306.
[7] Ibid., LXXXI; *Mahatma Letters*, p.385.
[8] *Proceedings*, December 1885, p.397.
[9] Ibid., p.400.
[10] Ibid., pp.398–9.
[11] British Museum, Additional MSS.45286, XCIB; *Mahatma Letters*, p.419.
[12] Ibid., Additional MSS.45285, XLVII; *Mahatma Letters*, p.172.

CHAPTER 51
[1] *Light*, 12 July 1884; *Incidents*, pp.211–2.
[2] *Incidents*, p.214.

CHAPTER 52
[1] This and the following quotations are from the galley-proofs of the Private and Confidential Report of the Committee of the Society for Psychical Research appointed to investigate the evidence for marvellous phenomena offered by certain members of the Theosophical Society (1884), suppressed in the printed edition of the same as well as in the published Report of 1885. Photostats of them were lent to me by Mr Leslie Price, of the present Library Committee of the Society for Psychical Research, so that I might see the cancelled passages. He tells me, however, that they were first noticed by Mr Walter Carrithers, though they have not been published before.

CHAPTER 53
[1] *My Guest – Madame Blavatsky*, Francesca Arundale (Adyar, 1932) – a posthumous publication – p.38.
[2] Ibid., p.66.
[3] Ibid., p.57.
[4] Ibid., p.80.
[5] Ibid., pp.73–9.
[6] *The Third Mystic, the Self-Revelation of Maria Vela, a Sixteenth-Century Spanish Nun*, Frances Parkinson Keyes (Peter Davies, 1960).
[7] *St Teresa of Avila*, Stephen Clissold (Sheldon, 1979), pp.61–8.
[8] Ibid., p.121.
[9] Ibid., p.115.
[10] Ibid., p.111.
[11] Ibid., p.219.
[12] Ibid., pp.128, 154.

CHAPTER 54
[1] *Private and Confidential Report*, pp.115–6;

Letters from the Masters of Wisdom, Second Series, pp.124–5.
2 *My Guest – Madame Blavatsky*, Francesca Arundale (Adyar, 1932), p.32.
3 Trinity College Library, Cambridge; Ads.MS.c.9725.
4 British Museum, Additional MSS.45285; *Mahatma Letters*, p.323.
5 Ibid., Additional MSS.45286; *Mahatma Letters*, pp.366–70.

CHAPTER 55
1 *Light*, 11 October 1884; *Collected Writings*, VI, pp.288–94.
2 *Madame Blavatsky and her 'Theosophy', A Study*, Arthur Lillie (1895), Chapter XII.
3 Ibid., p.12.

CHAPTER 56
1 *The 'K.H.' Letters to C.W. Leadbeater*, ed. C. Jinarajadasa (Adyar, 1943), pp.6–11, 97.
2 Ibid., p.49.
3 Ibid., pp.50–1.

CHAPTER 57
1 *How Theosophy Came to Me*, C.W. Leadbeater (Adyar, 1930), pp.65–6.
2 Ibid., p.70.
3 Ibid., pp.73–5.
4 Ibid., pp.77–8.
5 Ibid., p.79.
6 Ibid., pp.79–80.
7 Ibid., p.78.
8 *ODL*, III, p.189.

CHAPTER 58
1 *Some Account of my Intercourse with Madame Blavatsky*, Emma Coulomb (Higginbottom, Madras, 1884) – pamphlet reprinting the letters first printed in the September and October issues of the *Christian College Magazine* – p.42.
2 Ibid., pp.67–70.
3 Ibid., p.55.
4 Ibid., p.56.
5 Ibid., pp.56–7.
6 Ibid., pp.15–16.
7 Ibid., pp.42–3.
8 Ibid., p.45.
9 Ibid., p.54.
10 Ibid., pp.59–60.
11 Ibid., p.60.
12 Ibid., p.61.
13 Ibid., p.17.
14 Ibid., p.18.
15 Ibid., p.19.
16 Ibid., p.30.
17 Ibid., p.46.
18 Ibid., p.20.
19 Ibid., p.64.
20 Ibid., p.97.
21 *A Short History of the Theosophical Society*, Josephine Ranson (TPH, 1938), p.153.

CHAPTER 59
1 *A Report of an Examination into the Blavatsky Correspondence published in the Christian College Magazine*, J.D.B. Gribble (Higginbottom, Madras, 1884), p.3.
2 Ibid., pp.3–4, and *passim*.
3 Ibid., p.5, and *passim*.
4 Ibid., pp.4, 11, 12, 13, 15, 16, 18, 19, 20.
5 Ibid., p.18.
6 Ibid., p.24.
7 Ibid., p.13.
8 Ibid., pp.16–17.
9 Ibid., p.28.

CHAPTER 60
1 *ODL*, III, p.189.
2 Ibid., pp.189–90.
3 Ibid., pp.191–2.
4 Ibid., p.207.
5 Ibid., p.208.
6 Ibid., p.219.
7 Ibid., pp.101–2.
8 Paper read to the Society of Psychical Research on 12 April 1983 since published under the title *Madame Blavatsky Unveiled?*, Leslie Price (Theosophical History Centre, 1986).
9 *Proceedings*, December 1885, p.320.
10 Ibid., p.321.
11 *ODL*, III, p.220.
12 Ibid., p.223.
13 Ibid., p.247.
14 Ibid., pp.220–1.

CHAPTER 61
1 British Museum, Additional MSS.45287, XLIV; *Letters*, pp.98–9.
2 *Christian College Magazine*, 'The collapse of Koot Hoomi', October 1884, Vol.II, No.IV, p.19.
3 British Museum, Additional MSS.45287, XLIII; *Letters*, p.97.
4 Ibid., XLII; *Letters*, pp.95–6.
5 Ibid., L; *Letters*, p.122.
6 *Letters from the Masters of Wisdom*, Letter XXIX, pp.75–6.

CHAPTER 62
1 British Museum, Additional MSS.45287, XLV; *Letters to Sinnett*, p.105.
2 Ibid., XLVI; *Letters*, pp.110–1.
3 Ibid., *Letters*, p.110.
4 British Museum, Additional MSS.45287, XLVI; *Letters*, p.114.
5 Ibid., Additional MSS.45286, LXV; *Mahatma Letters*, p.362.
6 Ibid., *Mahatma Letters*, pp.365–6.
7 Ibid., Additional MSS.45287, L, *Letters*, p.123.
8 Ibid., LXXVIII; *Letters*, pp.188–9.
9 Ibid., LXXVIIA; *Letters*, p.188.
10 Ibid., Additional MSS.45288, CLXVIII; *Letters*, p.295.

11 Ibid., Additional MSS.45287, LXVIII; *Letters*, p.119.

CHAPTER 63
1 *Proceedings*, Part IX, December 1885, p.363.
2 *Letters from the Masters of Wisdom, Second Series*, pp.116–9.
3 *Proceedings*, pp.306–7.
4 *Living English Structure, a Practice Book for Foreign Students*, W. Stannard Allen (Longmans Green, 1947), p.11.
5 *Proceedings*, p.305.
6 Ibid., p.281
7 Ibid., pp.381–82.
8 Ibid., p.274.
9 Ibid., p.385.
10 *The Real H.P. Blavatsky*, William Kingsland (Watkins, 1928), p.277.
11 *Proceedings*, p.244.
12 *Proceedings*, p.214.
13 Ibid., pp.218, 321–3.
14 Ibid., p.263.
15 Ibid., p.312.
16 Ibid., p.317.
17 British Museum, Additional MSS.45287, V; *Letters*, pp.6–7.
18 *Incidents*, p.245.
19 *Proceedings*, p.314.
20 British Museum, Additional MSS.45287, LXXXVIII; *Letters*, p.206.
21 Ibid., IV; *Letters*, p.5.
22 *Five Types of Ethical Theory*, C.D. Broad (Cambridge, 1934), pp.143–4.
23 *General Logic*, Ralph M. Eaton (Scribner, 1931), p.99.
24 *The Society for Psychical Research, 1882–1982*, Renée Haynes (Macdonald, 1982), p.22.

CHAPTER 64
1 *Private and Confidential Report*, p.130.
2 British Museum, Additional MSS.45286, CXL; *Mahatma Letters*, p.480.
3 Ibid., CXXXVIII; *Mahatma Letters*, p.471.
4 British Museum, Additional MSS.45287, XVI; *Letters*, p.32.
5 *The Eclectic Theosophist*, No. 68, March–April 1982, pp.6–9.
6 British Museum, Additional MSS.45286, CXL; *Mahatma Letters*, pp.478–9.
7 *With Bayonets to Lhasa*, Peter Fleming (Harte-Davis, 1961), p.121.

CHAPTER 65
1 *Who Wrote the Mahatma Letters?*, Harold Edward and William Loftus Hare (Williams & Norgate, 1933).
2 *The Defence of Madame Blavatsky*, Beatrice Hastings (Worthing, 1937), Section 3 'The Mahatma Letters and Messrs. Hare'.
3 British Museum, Additional MSS.45285, LII; *Mahatma Letters*, p.289.

4 Hare, ibid., p.244.
5 *Rooskië Pocherki* (*Russian Handwriting*), Roman Biske (Jaschke, 1919).
6 Hare, ibid., p.228.
7 British Museum, Additional MSS.45288, Appendix I; *Letters*, p.370.
8 Hare, ibid., p.117.
9 Hare, ibid., p.305.
10 Hare, ibid., p.273.
11 Hare, ibid., p.289.

CHAPTER 66
1 *Reminiscences of H.P. Blavatsky and the Secret Doctrine*, Countess Constance Wachtmeister (TPH, London, 1893), p.20.
2 Ibid., p.36.
3 Ibid., pp.44–5.
4 Ibid., p.50.
5 Ibid., pp.45–6.

CHAPTER 67
1 British Museum, Additional MSS.45287, LXVII; *Letters*, p.117.
2 *The Early Days of Theosophy in Europe*, A.P. Sinnett (TPH, London, 1922), p.83.
3 British Museum, Additional MSS.45287, LXXX; *Letters*, p.192.
4 Ibid., Additional MSS.45288, XCIV; *Letters*, p.215.
5 Ibid., Additional MSS.45287, LXXX; *Letters*, p.192.
6 Ibid., Additional MSS.45288, LXXXVII; *Letters*, p.208.
7 Ibid., Additional MSS.45287, LXXX; *Letters*, p.193.
8 Ibid., LXXVI; *Letters*, p.179.
9 Ibid.; *Letters*, p.180.
10 Ibid., Additional MSS.45288, XCIV; *Letters*, p.214.
11 *A Modern Priestess of Isis*, Vsevolod Sergueyevich Solovioff (Longmans Green, 1895), p.230.
12 *Collected Writings*, VI, p.73.
13 Solovioff, ibid., p.180.
14 British Museum, Additional MSS.45287, LXX; *Letters*, p.171.

CHAPTER 68
1 British Museum, Additional MSS.45287, LXXIV; *Letters*, p.177.
2 *ODL*, III, pp.319–20 (but note that the name should be Oppenheim, not Oppenheimer, as printed); photostat of German text, certified to be a true copy of the original, sent to me from Adyar.
3 British Museum, Additional MSS.45287, LXXIII (annexed to, without separate no.); *Letters*, p.177.
4 *Madame Blavatsky*, Marion Meade (New York, 1980), pp.357–8.
5 *Personal Memoirs of H.P. Blavatsky*, Mary K. Neff (Rider, 1937), p.187.

6 Ibid., pp.187–8.
7 Ibid., pp.188.
8 Ibid., pp.186–7.
9 British Museum, Additional MSS.45287, LXXXIX; *Letters*, p.208.

CHAPTER 69
1 British Museum, Additional MSS.45288, CLXVII; *Letters*, p.327.
2 *Reminiscences of H.P. Blavatsky*, Countess Wachtmeister (TPH, London, 1893), pp.107–8.
3 British Museum, Additional MSS.45288, XCVII; *Letters*, p.218.
4 Wachtmeister, ibid., pp.73–5.

CHAPTER 70
1 *Madame Blavatsky*, Marion Meade (New York), p.389.
2 *Reminiscences of H.P. Blavatsky*, Countess Wachtmeister (TPH, London, 1893), pp.89–95.
3 *Irish Literary Portraits*, John Eglington (Macmillan, 1935), p.44.
4 *The Real H.P. Blavatsky*, William Kingsland (Watkins, 1928), p.38.
5 *In Memory of H.P. Blavatsky*, by some of her pupils (1891), p.193 (from *The Review of Reviews*, June 1891).
6 Ibid., pp.106, 110 (from *The Agnostic Journal*).
7 Ibid., p.187.
8 *H.P. Blavatsky as I Knew Her*, Alice Leighton Cleather (Thacker Spink, Calcutta & Simla, 1922), pp.8–11; and Kingsland, ibid., p.179.
9 *Letters from the Masters of Wisdom*, Letter XVI, pp.52–6.
10 *ODL*, IV, pp.50–1.

CHAPTER 74
1 *The Secret Doctrine*, III, p.20.
2 Ibid., I, p.185.
3 Ibid., I, p.253; V, p.436..
4 Ibid., V, p.422.
5 *Isis Unveiled*, I, p.591.
6 *The Secret Doctrine*, III, p.402.
7 *Earth's Shifting Crust*, Charles H. Hapgood, with the collaboration of James E. Campbell and forewords by Professor Albert Einstein and Kirtley F. Mather, Professor Emeritus of Geology at Yale (Museum Press, 1959).
8 *The Secret Doctrine*, pp.125, 184.
9 Ibid., pp.173–4, 179, 184.
10 Ibid., II, pp.42–5.
11 Ibid., p.125.
12 Ibid., p.298.
13 Ibid., p.127.
14 Ibid., p.175.
15 Ibid., p.111.
16 Ibid., IV, pp.151–2.
17 Ibid., II, p.298.
18 Ibid., III, p.274.

19 Ibid., p.275.
20 Ibid., IV, pp.258–9.
21 Ibid., II, p.286.
22 Ibid., II, p.284.
23 Ibid., II, p.287.
24 Ibid., III, pp.59–60.
25 Ibid., p.277n.
26 Ibid., p.401.
27 Ibid., p.356, and IV, p.354; see also IV, p.406..
28 Ibid., p.372.

CHAPTER 75
1 *The Secret Doctrine*, II, p.387.
2 Ibid., III, p.79.
3 Ibid., I, pp.64–5; IV, p.96.
4 Ibid., II, p.387.
5 British Museum, Additional MSS.45288, CXV; *Letters*, p.242.
6 Ibid., *Letters*, p.243.
7 Ibid., Additional MSS.45284, IX; *Mahatma Letters*, pp.43–4.
8 *The Secret Doctrine*, V, p.363.
9 Ibid., p.364.
10 Ibid., p.393.
11 Ibid., p.396.
12 British Museum, Additional MSS.45284, LVII; *Mahatma Letters*, p.117.
13 Ibid.

CHAPTER 77
1 *An Autobiography*, Annie Besant (Adyar, 1893), 3rd ed., 1939, p.440.
2 Ibid., p.441.
3 Ibid., p.443.
4 Ibid., p.340.
5 Ibid., pp.339–40.
6 Ibid., p.340.

CHAPTER 78
1 'Karmic visions', in *Lucifer*, Vol.II, No.10, June 1888; *Collected Writings*, IX, pp.318–39.

CHAPTER 79
1 *The Hidden Life in Freemasonry*, C.W. Leadbeater (Adyar, 1928), pp.14–15.
2 *ODL*, I, p.240.
3 *Grey Eminence*, Aldous Huxley (Chatto, 1941), p.255.
4 *ODL*, I, p.258; *Peter the Great*, Robert K. Massie (Gollancz, 1981), pp.166–7, 751–2, 805–6.

CHAPTER 80
1 *The Voice of the Silence*, H.P. Blavatsky (TPC, 1889). The verses are not numbered in the original edition, or in the 1927 Pekin edition, or its reprint in Canada of 1984. As, however, the whole is not reprinted here, I have used the verse numbering given in the Adyar Golden Jubilee edition of 1939 so as to

help the reader to locate the quotations. (The page numbering is different in the different editions.)

CHAPTER 81
1. Solovioff, Appendix.
2. *The Voice of the Silence*, (TPC, 1889), pp.107–9.
3. *The Life of the Buddha*, L. Adams Beck (Collins Library of Classics, undated) p.25.
4. *Mahayana Buddhism*, Beatrice Lane Suzuki (Allen & Unwin, 1959), pp.xvi, xix–xx, 2.
5. *The Religions of Tibet*, Giuseppe Tucci (Routledge, 1980), p.44.
6. *The Teachings of the Compassionate Buddha*, E.A. Burtt (Mentor, 1955), p.130.
7. *Outlines of Mahayana Buddhism*, Deisatz Teitaro Suzuki (Luzac, 1907), p.64.
8. *The Tibetan Book of the Dead*, W.Y. Evans-Wentz (OUP, 1922), p.7n.
9. *Eastern Buddhist* (Old Series), V, p.376.

CHAPTER 82
1. Information from her sister, my great-aunt Grace Laing, of Musselburgh; *ODL*, IV, p.201.
2. *Imaginations and Reveries*, 'A.E.', p.41; 'H.P. Blavatsky's influence on Ireland's literary renaissance', W. Emmett Small in *H.P. Blavatsky and the Secret Doctrine*, ed. Virginia Hanson (TPH, USA, 1981).
3. *ODL*, IV, p.25.

CHAPTER 83
1. *Collected Writings*, XII, p.515.
2. *Zanoni*, Edward Bulwer-Lytton (1842). One of the characters presents himself as a candidate for initiation, but from selfish motives, and immediately there appears to him not a majestic Adept but a hideous and devilish figure, who for evermore pursues him wherever he flees.
3. *The Strange Case of Dr. Jekyll and Mr. Hyde*, Robert Louis Stevenson (1886). Dr Jekyll, a scientist, discovers a means of separating the evil from the good in man. A phantom, lustful and murderous, separates itself from him and goes about on its own, committing crimes, while Dr Jekyll remains high-minded. In the unhappy ending, Mr Hyde overwhelms and takes over Dr Jekyll.
4. *Collected Writings*, XII, pp.522–6.
5. Ibid., pp.544, 548, 562.
6. Ibid., p.698.
7. Ibid., p.700.
8. Ibid., pp.532–3.
9. *The Secret Doctrine*, V, pp.562–3.

CHAPTER 84
1. *H.P. Blavatsky as I Knew Her*, Alice Leighton Cleather (Thacker Spink, Calcutta & Simla, 1923), p.19.
2. Ibid., p.21.
3. Ibid., pp.24–5.
4. Ibid., pp.22–3.
5. *An Autobiography*, Annie Besant (TPH, 1893), p.461.
6. 'How she left us', Laura M. Cooper, in *In Memory of Helena Petrovna Blavatsky*, collected contributions (Adyar, 1891), pp.1–8.
7. *ODL*, IV, pp.310–1.

CHAPTER 85
1. *With Bayonets to Lhasa*, Peter Fleming (Hart-Davis, 1961), p.29.
2. Shakabpa, p.220.
3. *Tibet and its History*, Hugh Richardson (Oxford, 1962), p.127.
4. Shakabpa, p.263.
5. Richardson, ibid.
6. McGovern, p.176.
7. *The Voice of the Silence* (TPC, Pekin, 1927), editorial foreword.
8. Christmas Humphreys' papers, Theosophical Library, London.
9. Ibid., p.113.
10. Ibid., p.99.
11. Ibid., editorial foreword.

CHAPTER 86
1. On the Independent Television program, *The Big Question*, in 1983, this was the view expressed by Father Eric Doyle, O. Carm., in answer to a question; the other two members of the panel, the Very Reverend Alan Webster, Dean of St Paul's, and the Reverend Edmund Banyard, representing the free churches, agreed.
2. *The Poetical Works of Christina Georgina Rossetti*, ed. William Michael Rossetti (Macmillan, 1904), p.215, from the poem beginning, 'Bone to his bone, grain to his grain of dust'.
3. *The Middle Way*, Vol.59, No.1, May 1984.
4. *The Bible*, Romans, XII: 5.
5. *The Way of Illumination*, Inayat Khan (Sufi Publishing House, Southampton, 1921), p.92.
6. *The Secret Doctrine*, III, p.308.
7. Ibid., p.309.
8. Ibid., I, p.89.

Bibliography

MANUSCRIPTS AND UNPUBLISHED PAPERS

British Museum (British Library)
Mahatma Papers, Additional MSS.45284, 45285, 45286, 45287, 45288

Society for Psychical Research
Galley-proofs of the 1884 Private and Confidential Report, with the passages cancelled from the text of the printed version
Extracts from letters of Madame Blavatsky to Hurrychund Chintamon and C.C. Massey, in an unknown hand
Copy of Madame Coulomb's pamphlet bearing in the margins handwritten comments by Madame Blavatsky

Adyar
Letters in the handwritings of Monsieur and Madame Coulomb

Trinity College, Cambridge
Journal in the handwriting of Prof. Sidgwick

BOOKS AND ARTICLES

Place of publication is London unless otherwise stated

WORKS OF H.P. BLAVATSKY

Isis Unveiled, a Master-Key to the Mysteries of Ancient and Modern Theology (Bouton, New York, 1877), two volumes; (Theosophical University Press, Pasadena, 1960), two volumes. Quotations are from the latter.
'Mysterious tribes: three months in the Blue Mountains near Madras', in *The Theosophist*, April, May, June, July, August, September, October, November, 1909; January, February, March, 1910; from the Russian of 1883.
From the Caves and Jungles of Hindostan, translated by Mrs Charles Johnston from the Russian of 1880 (TPC, 1892)
The Secret Doctrine, the Synthesis of Science, Religion and Philosophy (TPC, 1888), two volumes; (Adyar, 1938), six volumes. Quotations are from the latter.
The Voice of the Silence (TPC, 1889); (Golden Jubilee Edition, Adyar, 1939); (Pekin edition, 1927)
The Key to Theosophy, being a clear exposition in the form of question and answer, of the Ethics, Science and Philosophy for the study of which the Theosophical Society has been founded (TPH, 1890)
The Theosophical Glossary (TPC, 1892)
H.P. Blavatsky: Collected Writings, ed. Boris de Zirkoff (Wheaton, USA, & Adyar, 1966–85), fourteen volumes
The Letters of H.P. Blavatsky to A.P. Sinnett, ed. A.T. Barker (Fisher Unwin, 1925)
Some Unpublished Letters of Helena Petrovna Blavatsky, ed. Eugene Rollin Corson (Rider, 1929)
H.P.B. Speaks, Letters written by H.P. Blavatsky from 1875 onwards, ed. C. Jinarajadasa (Adyar, 1950), two volumes, but see Appendix I with regard to the second

BOOKS AND ARTICLES ON BLAVATSKY AND HER TEACHING

Reminiscences, studies and biographies: theosophical (roughly chronological order)
Olcott, Henry Steel, *People from the Other World* (USA, 1875)
Olcott, Henry Steel, *Old Diary Leaves* (New York, 1895–1910), first four volumes
Sinnett, Alfred Percival, *The Occult World* (1881)
Sinnett, Alfred Percival, *Esoteric Buddhism* (1883)
Sinnett, Alfred Percival, *Incidents in the Life of Madame Blavatsky* (1886)
Sinnett, Alfred Percival, *The Early Days of Theosophy in Europe* (1922)
Hume, Allan Octavian, ed. *Hints on Esoteric Theosophy* (1882)
Hartmann, Franz, *Report of Observations Made during a Nine Months' Stay at the Headquarters of the Theosophical Society at Adyar (Madras), India* (Scottish Press, Madras, 1884)
Some of her pupils (twenty-seven of them, including Olcott, Judge, Sinnett and Besant), *In Memory of H.P. Blavatsky* (1891)
Wachtmeister, Countess Constance, and others, *Reminiscences of H.P. Blavatsky and The Secret Doctrine* (1893)
Zhelikhovskaya, Vera Petrovna, *Kak Ya Bila Malen'koi* (St Petersburg, 1893)
Zhelikhovskaya, Vera Petrovna, Mémoires d'une Petite Fille Russe (French version of the preceding) (Paris, 1896)
Besant, Annie, *H.P. Blavatsky and the Masters of Wisdom* (TPH, 1907)
Cleather, Alice Leighton, *H.P. Blavatsky, Her Life and Work for Humanity* (Thacker Spink, Calcutta, 1922)
H.P. Blavatsky, A Great Betrayal (Thacker Spink, Calcutta, 1922)
H.P. Blavatsky as I Knew Her, with an addendum by Basil Crump (Thacker Spink, Calcutta, 1923)
Butt, G. Basedon, *Madame Blavatsky* (Rider, 1926)
Kingsland, William, *The Real H.P. Blavatsky, A Study in Theosophy and a Memoir of a Great Soul* (Watkins, 1928)
Leadbeater, C.W., *How Theosophy Came to Me* (Adyar, 1930)
Arundale, Francesca, *My Guest – H.P. Blavatsky* (Adyar, 1932)
Neff, Mary K, *The 'Brothers' of Madame Blavatsky* (Adyar, 1932)
Personal memoirs of H.P. Blavatsky (Rider, 1937)
Bosman, Leonard, and Orchard, Anita, *H.P. Blavatsky, the Light-Bringer* (Dharma Press, 1931)
Hastings, Beatrice, *Defence of Madame Blavatsky* (Worthing, 1937), two volumes
Solovioff's Fraud (John Cooper, Gladesville, Australia, 1984)
Waterman, Adlai E. (pseud. Walter Carrithers), *Obituary, The 'Hodgson Report' on Madame Blavatsky* (Adyar, 1963)
Barborka, Geoffrey A., *H.P. Blavatsky, Tibet and Tulku* (Adyar, 1966)
Endersby, Victor A., *The Hall of Magic Mirrors* (New York, 1969)
Price, Leslie, *Madame Blavatsky Unveiled? A New Discussion of the Most Famous Investigation of the Society for Psychical Research* (Theosophical History Centre, 1986)
Symposium, *H.P. Blavatsky and The Secret Doctrine* (Wheaton, USA, 1971)

Non-theosophical and uncertain
Symonds, John, *Madame Blavatsky, Medium and Magician* (Odhams, 1959)

Hostile
Patterson, George, 'The collapse of Koot Hoomi', in the *Christian College Magazine* (Madras), September and October 1884
Coulomb, Emma, *Some Account of my Intercourse with Madame Blavatsky* (Higginbottom, Madras, 1885)
Gribble, J.D.B., *A Report of an Examination into the Blavatsky Correspondence Published in the Christian College Magazine* (Higginbottom, Madras, 1884)

Solovioff, Vsevolod Sergueyevich, *A Modern Priestess of Isis*, abridged and translated on behalf of the Society for Psychical Research by Walter Leaf (Longmans Green, 1895)

Lillie, Arthur, *Madame Blavatsky and her 'Theosophy'* (1895)

Witte, Count, *Memoirs*, translated by Abraham Yarmonsky (Heineman, 1931)

Roberts, C.E. Beechoffer, 'Ephesian', *The Mysterious Madame* (Lane, 1931)

Hare, Harold Edward and Hare, William Loftus, *Who Wrote the Mahatma Letters?* (Williams & Norgate, 1936)

Williams, Gertrude Marvin, *Priestess of the Occult* (New York, 1946)

Meade, Marion, *Madame Blavatsky* (New York, 1980)

SOCIETY FOR PSYCHICAL RESEARCH

Private and Confidential Report of the Committee of the Society for Psychical Research Appointed to Investigate the Evidence for Marvellous Phenomena Offered by Certain Members of the Theosophical Society (1884)

Report of the Committee appointed to Investigate Phenomena Connected with the Theosophical Society, Proceedings of the Society for Psychical Research (December 1885)

Hall, Trevor, *The Strange Case of Edmund Gurney* (Duckworth, 1963)

Haynes, Renée, *The Society for Psychical Research, 1882–1982, A History* (Macdonald, 1982)

THEOSOPHICAL SOCIETY AND MOVEMENT

The Golden Book of the Theosophical Society, 1875–1925, issued in commemoration of the Jubilee of the Theosophical Society by its General Council, ed. C.J. Jinarajadasa (Adyar, 1925)

Ransom, Josephine, *A Short History of the Theosophical Society* (Adyar, 1938)

Anonymous, *The Theosophical Movement, 1875–1925*. Published anonymously, but will have been by Robert Crosbie and others (New York, Dutton, 1925). This is a publication of the dissident United Lodge of Theosophists. The writers hate Olcott and laud Judge.

LETTERS FROM THE MASTERS

The Mahatma Letters, to A.P. Sinnett from the Mahatmas M & K.H., transcribed, compiled, and with an introduction by A.T. Barker (Rider, 1923). References are to the eighth impression.

Letters from the Masters of Wisdom, 1881–1888, with a foreword by Annie Besant, transcribed and compiled by C. Jinarajadasa (Adyar, 1919)

Letters from the Masters of Wisdom, Second Series, transcribed and compiled by C. Jinarajadasa (Adyar, 1925)

The 'K.H.' Letters to C.W. Leadbeater, with a commentary by C. Jinarajadasa (Adyar, 1941)

Early Teachings of the Masters, 1881–1883, ed. C. Jinarajadasa (Adyar, 1923). This is selections from *The Mahatma Letters*, arranged for convenience.

OTHER THEOSOPHICAL WORKS

Murphet, Howard, *Hammer on the Mountain, a Life of Henry Steel Olcott, 1832–1907* (Wheaton, USA, 1972)

Besant, Annie, *An Autobiography* (Adyar, 1893). References are to the 1939 edition.

Nethercot, Arthur, *The First Five Lives of Annie Besant* (Hart-Davis, 1961)

Nethercot, Arthur, *The Last Four Lives of Annie Besant* (Hart-Davis, 1963)

Collins, Mabel, *The Idyll of the White Lotus* (1884)

Collins, Mabel, *Light on the Path* (TPH, 1911)

Collins, Mabel, *A Cry From Afar* (TPH, 1905)

Collins, Mabel, *The Blossom and the Fruit* (published in *Lucifer* in instalments, 1888)

Head, Joseph, and Cranston, S.L. (pseud. Anita Atkins) (eds), *Reincarnation* (New York, 1961)
Cranston, Sylvia (pseud. Anita Atkins) and Williams, Carey, *Reincarnation, a New Horizon in Science, Religion and Society* (New York, 1984)

TIBET

Tsongkapa
Calming the Mind and Discerning the Real, Buddhist Meditation and the Middle View, from the Lam rim chen mo of Tson-kha-pa, translated by Alex Wayman (Columbia University Press, 1978)

Religion (studies of, by Europeans)
Evans-Wentz, W.Y., *The Tibetan Book of the Dead* (Oxford, 1927)
Hoffmann, Helmut, *The Religions of Tibet* (Allen & Unwin, 1961)
Reigle, David, *The Books of Kiu-Te or The Tibetan Tantras* (San Diego, 1983)
Tucci, Giuseppe, *The Buddhism of Tibet, or Lamaism* (1905)
Waddell, L. Austine, *The Buddhism of Tibet, or Lamaism* (1895)

Dalai Lama and family, memoirs, etc.
His Holiness the Dalai Lama, *My Land and My People*, ed. David Howarth (Weidenfeld, 1962)
Norbu, Thubten Jigme and Turnbull, Colin M., *Tibet* (Chatto, 1969)

Outsiders' travels (roughly chronological order)
Markham, Clements R., *Narratives of the Mission of George Bogle to Tibet and of the Journey of Thomas Manning to Lhasa* (1876)
Huc, Evariste-Régis, *Travels in Tartary, Tibet and China* (1852), two volumes
Das, Sarat Chandra, *Journey to Lhasa and Central Tibet* (Murray, 1902)
David-Neel, Alexandra, *With Mystics and Magicians in Tibet* (Rider, 1921)
David-Neel, Alexandra, *Initiations and Initiates in Tibet* (Rider, 1958)
McGovern, William Montgomery, *To Lhasa in Disguise* (Thornton Butterworth, 1924)
Harrer, Heinrich, *Seven Years in Tibet* (Hart-Davis, 1953)
Harrer, Heinrich, *Return to Tibet* (Weidenfeld, 1984)
Hopkirk, Peter, *Trespassers on the Roof of the World, the Race for Lhasa* (Murray, 1982)

History
Richardson, Hugh, E., *Tibet and its History* (Oxford, 1962)
Shakabpa, Tsepon W.D., *Tibet, a Political History* (Yale, 1967)

BUDDHISM (OTHER THAN TIBETAN)

Beck, L. Adams, *The Life of the Buddha* (Collins, undated)
Burtt, E.A., *The Teachings of the Compassionate Buddha* (Mentor, 1955)
Suzuki, Beatrice Lane, *Mahayana Buddhism* (Allen & Unwin, 1959)
Suzuki, Daizetz Teitaro, *Outline of Mahayana Buddhism* (Luzak, 1907). This and the above represent especially Japanese Mahayana Buddhism. Professor Beatrice Suzuki is the wife of Dr Suzuki.

NEPAL

Britain's Relations with the Kingdom of Nepal, 1857–1947, a Diplomatic History of Nepal, Asad Husain (Allen & Unwin, 1959)
Morris, John, *A Winter in Nepal* (Hart-Davis, 1963)
Kazami, Takehide, *The Himalayas, A Journey to Nepal*, Takehide Kazami (Ward Lock, 1968)

Eskelund, Karl, *The Forgotten Valley, a Journey into Nepal* (Alvin Redland, 1959)

INDIA

Religion

Rig-Veda-Sanhitá, a Collection of Ancient Hindu Hymns, constituting the first Asjtaka, or Book of the Rig-Veda; the oldest authority for the religious and social institutions of the Hindus, translated from the original Sanskrit, Horace Hayman Wilson (W.H. Allen, 1850–88), six volumes

The Vishnu Purana. A System of Hindu Mythology and Tradition, translated from the original Sanskrit, and illustrated by notes derived chiefly from other Puranas, Horace Hayman Wilson, ed. Fitzedward Hall (Trubner, 1867–70), five volumes

Myths of the Hindus and Buddhists, The Sister Nivedita (Margaret E. Noble) of Ramakrishna-Vivekananda and Ananda K. Coomeraswamy, under the supervision of Abanindro Nath Tagore (Harrap, 1913)

The Bhagavad Gita or the Lord's Song, translated by Annie Besant (Adyar, 1904)

Eliade, Mircea, *Yoga* (Routledge, 1958)

Iyengar, B.K.S., *Light on Yoga*, with a foreword by Yehudi Menuhin (Allen & Unwin, 1966)

History

Allan, J., Haig, Sir T. Wolseley, and Dodwall, H.H., *The Cambridge Shorter History of India*, ed. H.H. Dodwell (Cambridge, 1934)

Powell-Price, J.C., *A History of India* (Nelson, 1955)

Prawdin, Michael, *The Builders of the Moghul Empire* (Allen & Unwin, 1933)

Fazl, Abu-L., *The Akbarnama* (biography of Akbar), translated from the Persian by H. Beveridge (Asiatic Society of Bengal, Calcutta, 1912)

Binyon, Lawrence, *Akbar* (Peter Davis, 1932)

Beatson, Alexander, *A View of the Origin and Conduct of the War with Tippoo Sultan . . . and Siege of Seringapatam* (1800)

The Rajputana Gazeteer, I (Office of the Superintendant of Government Printing, Calcutta, 1879)

Edwardes, Michael, *British India 1772–1947, a survey of the nature and effects of alien rule* (Sidgwick & Jackson, 1967)

Cross, Colin, *The Fall of the British Empire* (Hodder & Stoughton, 1968)

EGYPTIAN RELIGION

Ancient

The Book of the Dead: Facsimile of the Papyrus of Ani in the British Museum, Printed by Order of the Trustees (1894)

The Papyrus of Ani, a reproduction in Facsimile edited, with hieroglyphic transcript, translation and introduction by E.A. Wallis Budge . . . (The Medici Society, 1913), two volumes

Budge, E.A. Wallis, *A Hieroglyphic Vocabulary to the Theban Recension of the Book of the Dead . . .* (Kegan Paul, Trench & Trubner, 1911)

Gardiner, Alan H., *Egyptian Grammar, being an Introduction to the Study of Hieroglyphics* (Oxford, Clarendon, 1927)

Hermetic

Mead, G.R.S., *Thrice Greatest Hermes, Studies in Hellenistic Theosophy and Gnosis, being a Translation of the Extant Sermons and Fragments of the Trismegistic Literature, with Prologomena, Commentaries and Notes* (Watkins, 1949), three volumes

GNOSTICISM

Mead, G.R.S., *Pistis Sophia, A Gnostic Miscellany . . .* (Watkins, 1963)

KABBALAH

Mathers, S.L. Macgregor, *The Kabbalah Unveiled, Containing the Following Books of the Zohar, The Book of the Concealed Mystery, The Greater Holy Assembly, The Lesser Holy Assembly* (Routledge, 1957)

ELIPHAS LEVI

The History of Magic, (Rider, 1913)
Transcendental Magic, (Rider, 1896)
Key to the Mysteries, (Rider, 1969)

CHRISTIANITY

Cadoux, Cecil John, *The Historic Mission of Jesus, A Constructive Re-examination of the Escatological Teaching in the Synoptic Gospels* (Lutterworth, 1941)
Morgan, W., *The Religion and Theology of Paul* (Clark, Edinburgh, 1917)
Clissold, Stephen, *St Teresa of Avila* (Sheldon, 1979)
Poems of St John of the Cross, translated by Roy Campbell, preface by M.C. D'Arcy (Harvill, 1951)
Keyes, Frances Parkinson, *The Third Mystic, The Self-Revelation of María Vela, a Sixteenth-Century Spanish Nun* (Peter Davies, 1960)
Huxley, Aldous, *Grey Eminence* (Chatto, 1941)
The Oxford Book of the Christian Church (Oxford, 1958)

PHILOSOPHY

The Works of Plato, translated . . . with analyses and introductions by B. Jowett (New York, undated)
Eaton, Ralph, *General Logic* (Scribner, New York, 1931)
Broad, C.D., *Five Types of Ethical Theory* (studies in Spinoza, Butler, Hume, Kant and Sidgwick) (Kegan Paul, 1934)

BULWER-LYTTON

Last Days of Pompeii (1834)
Zanoni (1842)
The Coming Race (1871)

HOME

Home, D.D., *Incidents in my Life* (Longman, 1863)
Home, Madame Dunglas, *D.D. Home, His Life and Mission* (Kegan Paul, 1931)
Jenkins, Elizabeth, The Shadow and the Light, a Defence of Daniel Dunglas Home (Hamish Hamilton, 1932)

HISTORICAL WORKS

Mowat, R.B. *A History of Great Britain, 1815–1924* (Oxford, 1929)
Smith, G.B., *Outlines of European History, 1789–1922* (Arnold, 1928)
Guérard, Albert, *Napoleon III* (Harvard, 1943)
Kurtz, Harold, *The Empress Eugénie, 1826–1920* (Hamish Hamilton, 1964)
Ridley, Jasper, *Garibaldi* (Constable, 1974)
Eglington, John, *Irish Literary Portraits* (Macmillan, 1935)

Summerfield, Henry, *That Myriad-Minded Man, a Biography of George William Russell, 'A.E.'* (C. Smythe, 1975)
Massie, Robert K., *Peter the Great* (Gollancz, 1981)

GEOLOGICAL AND SCIENTIFIC THEORIES

Donnelly, Ignatius, *Atlantis, the Antediluvian World* (1885)
Hapgood, Charles H., *Earth's Shifting Crust*, with the collaboration of James E. Campbell and forewords by Albert Einstein and Kirkley F. Mather (Museum Press, 1959)
Clube, Victor, and Napier, Bill, 'Close encounters with a thousand comets', in *New Scientist*, 15 July 1982

Index